THE
MARSHALL PLAN
REVISITED

Recent Titles in
Contributions in Economics and Economic History

The Rise of the American Electrochemicals Industry, 1880–1910:
Studies in the American Technological Environment
Martha Moore Trescott

Southern Workers and Their Unions, 1880–1975: Selected Papers,
The Second Southern Labor History Conference, 1978
Merl E. Reed, Leslie S. Hough, and Gary M Fink, editors

The Organization of Arab Petroleum Exporting Countries:
History, Policies, and Prospects
Mary Ann Tétreault

Soviet Economy Today: With Guidelines for the Economic and Social Development of the USSR for 1981–1985 and for the Period Ending in 1990
Novosti Press Agency Publishing House, Moscow

The Era of the Joy Line: A Saga of Steamboating on Long Island Sound
Edwin L. Dunbaugh

The Role of Economic Advisers in Developing Countries
Lauchlin Currie

Perkins/Budd: Railway Statesmen of the Burlington
Richard C. Overton

The European Community and Latin America: A Case Study
in Global Role Expansion
A. Glenn Mower, Jr.

Economics and Policymaking: The Tragic Illusion
Eugene J. Meehan

A Portrait Cast in Steel: Buckeye International and Columbus,
Ohio, 1881–1980
Mansel G. Blackford

The Strategic Petroleum Reserve: Planning, Implementation, and Analysis
David Leo Weimer

United States Oil Policy and Diplomacy: A Twentieth-Century Overview
Edward W. Chester

The Emergence of Giant Enterprise, 1860–1914:
American Commercial Enterprise and Extractive Industries
David O. Whitten

THE MARSHALL PLAN REVISITED

The European Recovery Program in Economic Perspective

IMANUEL WEXLER

CONTRIBUTIONS IN ECONOMICS AND
ECONOMIC HISTORY, NUMBER 55

GREENWOOD PRESS
WESTPORT, CONNECTICUT
LONDON, ENGLAND

Library of Congress Cataloging in Publication Data

Wexler, Imanuel.
  The Marshall Plan revisited.

  (Contributions in economics and economic history,
ISSN 0084-9235 ; no. 55)
  Bibliography: p.
  Includes index.
  1. Economic assistance, American—Europe—History.
2. Europe—Economic conditions—1945–   . I. Title.
II. Series.
HC240.W44   1983   338.91′7304   83-5694
ISBN 0-313-24011-6 (lib. bdg.)

Library of Congress Catalog Card Number: 83-5694
ISBN: 0-313-24011-6
ISSN: 0084-9235

First published in 1983

Greenwood Press
A division of Congressional Information Service, Inc.
88 Post Road West
Westport, Connecticut 06881

Printed in the United States of America

10 9 8 7 6 5 4 3 2 1

Copyright Acknowledgments

  The author and publisher are grateful for permission to
reprint from the following.
  Columbia University Oral History Collection. By permission
of the Trustees of Columbia University in the City of New York,
copyright 1975.
  Herbert H. Lehman Papers, Rare Book and Manuscript Library,
Columbia University.
  Council on Foreign Relations Files, Records of Groups,
Vol. XVIII-A, "Aid to Europe," Digest of Sixteenth Meeting,
April 24, 1950, p. 3. Reprinted by permission of W. Averell
Harriman.

Contents

Tables   vii

Preface   ix

Abbreviations   xiii

  1. Introduction   3

Part I. THE SETTING

  2. Calculations and Formulations   9
  3. Formulation and Promotion   25
  4. Congressional Responses   41

Part II. A STRONG PRODUCTION EFFORT
       AND INTERNAL FINANCIAL STABILITY

  5. Preliminaries: Production Targets and Aid Allocations   57
  6. Increased Production: Expectations, Constraints, and
      Accomplishments   71
  7. The Quest for Internal Financial and Monetary
      Stability   97

Part III. EXPANSION OF FOREIGN TRADE

  8. Europe's Trade and Payments: Basic Problems and
      Early Solutions   121

9. Bilateralism Challenged: The Intra-European
    Payments Agreements   135

10. Toward Multilateralism: Conception and Birth of the
    European Payments Union   155

11. The European Payments Union and Trade
    Liberalization: Problems and Accomplishments   177

Part IV. DEVELOPMENT OF ECONOMIC COOPERATION

12. From Cooperation to Integration: Evolving Concepts
    and Instrumentalities   205

13. European Economic Integration: Methods and Forms   227

14. A Summing Up   249

    Notes   *257*

    Bibliography   *311*

    Index   *319*

Tables

1. CEEC and State: Estimated Deficits of CEEC Countries for 1948 and 1948/51   15

2. Treasury and State: Estimated Deficits of CEEC Countries for 1948 and 1948/51   16

3. PCFA: Estimated Deficits of CEEC Countries for 1948 and 1948/51   17

4. Estimates of Required U.S. Aid for a European Recovery Program   17

5. OEEC Production Targets for 1948/49   60

6. Aid Requests and Aid Recommendations for 1948/49   62

7. Country Allotments and Procurement Authorizations, April 3, 1948, through April 2, 1949   63

8. Aid Requests, Recommendations, and Allotments, 1949/50   67

9. Projected and Actual Increases in Output of Selected Commodities, 1948/49   75

10. Trade of OEEC Countries with Eastern Europe (Including USSR), 1947–52   81

11. Industrial Output per Man-Year, in 1949, for Selected European Countries   90

12. Indices of Industrial Production in Western Europe, 1948/51   94

13. Indices of Total Agricultural Output for Human Consumption in OEEC Countries, 1948/49–1950/51   95

14. Wholesale Price and Cost-of-Living Indices in 1948   98

15. Utilization of Counterparts for Debt Retirement, Cumulative, April 3, 1948–November 30, 1951   108

16. Wholesale Price Indices for Selected ERP Countries   111

17. Wholesale Price Indices for Western Europe, 1948–51   115

18. Cost-of-Living Indices for Western Europe, 1948–51   116

19. ERP Aid and Drawing Rights under the First AIEPC, for the Year July 1948–June 1949   139

20. Drawing Rights Finally Established under 1948/49 AIEPC   141

21. Total Bilateral and Multilateral Drawing Rights Finally Established under Revised AIEPC   150

22. Drawing Rights Established and Utilized, 1949/50   151

23. Terms of Settlement under EPU   175

24. Initial Balances under EPU   179

25. EPU: Original and Revised Quotas   193

26. Western Europe's Gross National Product, 1947–51   251

Preface

Conventional wisdom has long viewed the Marshall Plan as a significant and extraordinarily successful act of philanthropy, motivated by enlightened self-interests and clearly defined national objectives. The Marshall Plan, wrote its official historian, Harry B. Price, in 1955, was "one of the great success stories of all time"; and for the next quarter of a century, both liberals and conservatives have largely taken their cue from him. For the most part, however, historical scholarship has treated the Marshall Plan within the context of post-World War II U.S. foreign policy—most often with reference to the Cold War. Thus, the continuing obsession with the causes and consequences of the Cold War has led, during the 1970s, to scholarly studies that emphasized either the origins of the Marshall Plan or its relations to NATO and various military assistance programs. Other scholars during the same period have focused mainly on the bureaucratic/organizational evolution of the Marshall Plan within the U.S. government. None of these studies attempted the task of penetrating the complexities of the aid program itself and examining the details of its implementation. Nor did they attempt to relate, in a consistent manner, the declared economic goals of the Marshall Plan to its actual economic accomplishments.

The underlying theme of the present study is that, although the Marshall Plan was conceived as and may properly be perceived as an instrument of American foreign policy, it was essentially an economic enterprise. It was an enterprise consisting of a substantial transfer of resources from the United States to a group of West European countries, for the purpose of aiding the latter to undertake specific economic tasks and reach specific economic goals within a prescribed period of time. Accordingly, a retrospective assessment of the Marshall Plan, as an *economic* program, must necessarily take as its point of departure the rationale for, and the specific goals formulated by, its planners. It must then examine and analyze the actual process by which these goals were pursued; and it must, finally, judge the extent to which these goals had been fulfilled by the time the aid program was terminated. Such an assessment is, in fact, the subject matter of the present study.

This revisitation of the Marshall Plan, this examination of its implementation and economic accomplishments, may not yield direct answers to contemporary economic dilemmas confronting both advanced and developing nations. But it may provide clearer perspectives and thereby lessen the occasional temptation either to grasp at simple solutions or to adopt overly drastic measures in the pursuit of national and international economic policies.

Many persons, some knowingly and others not, have contributed to the making of this book. I owe a special debt of gratitude to two good friends at the University of Connecticut: Professor Louis Gerson, who launched me on the idea of undertaking the project; and Professor Thomas Paterson, who offered invaluable advice and guidance, probing criticism, and, above all, unflinching moral support. Several of my colleagues and former colleagues deserve mention for their helpful suggestions and continued encouragement. They are Ramon Knauerhase, William McEachern, Stephen Miller, John Olson, and Ralph Shlomowitz. Special thanks are due to Professor Harold Seidman and to the late John Glynn, both of whom allowed me free access to their private papers and provided me with useful information.

The research for this project was carried over a seven-year period and took me to several libraries and archival collections. By far the largest sources of the archival material examined were the U.S. National Archives (at the Federal Records Center in Suitland, Maryland) and the Harry S. Truman Library in Independence, Missouri. I am greatly indebted to the archivists and staffs of both institutions for their generous help and personal consideration. My research at the HST Library was partly financed by a grant-in-aid from the Harry S. Truman Library Institute, which is gratefully acknowledged here. I am similarly grateful for assistance rendered by the staffs of the George C. Marshall Library; the Oral History Research Office and the Herbert Lehman Papers, both at Columbia University; the Mullen Library, Catholic University of America; the Office of Public Affairs, Agency for International Development; the National Advisory Council on International Financial and Monetary Problems, U.S. Department of Treasury; the AFL-CIO Library; the Library of the Council on Foreign Relations; the British Library of Political and Social Sciences; and the Government Publications Department at the University of Connecticut Library. For help in preparing the manuscript, I am indebted to Mary Lou Nye, whose skill in typing was matched by her devotion to the task.

Last, I should like to express my greatest appreciation to my family—Betty, David, and Sarah—for their support, patience, and understanding during the long years spent by me researching and writing this book. They bore the heaviest burden of the author at work, and it is to them that the finished product is affectionately dedicated.

Abbreviations

AFL	American Federation of Labor
AIEPC	Agreement for Intra-European Payments and Compensations
BIS	Bank for International Settlements
CEEC	Committee of European Economic Cooperation
CIO	Congress of Industrial Organizations
CMP	Committee for the Marshall Plan to Aid European Recovery
ECA	Economic Cooperation Administration
ECA/W	ECA's headquarters in Washington
ECSC	European Coal and Steel Community
EPU	European Payments Union
ERP	European Recovery Program (the Marshall Plan)
ERP/ITUC	International Trade Union Conference on the European Recovery Program
ERP/TUAC	ERP Trade Union Advisory Committee
GATT	General Agreement on Tariffs and Trade
IMF	International Monetary Fund
MDAP	Mutual Defense Assistance Program
MSA	Mutual Security Agency
MSP	Mutual Security Program
NAC	National Advisory Council on International Monetary and Financial Problems
OEEC	Organization for European Economic Cooperation
OSR	Office of the U.S. Special Representative in Europe (in Paris)
PCFA	President's Committee on Foreign Aid (the Harriman Committee)
RFC	Reconstruction Finance Corporation
UNRRA	United Nations Relief and Rehabilitation Administration
WFTU	World Federation of Trade Unions

THE
MARSHALL PLAN
REVISITED

Introduction 1

If the occasion was solemn, it was rendered even more so by the fact that the Secretary of State—himself a solemn and dignified person—was about to deliver an important message to the country and the world. In it, he would paint a bleak picture of Europe's economic conditions and would announce that the United States might be prepared to assist the European nations "in a return to normal economic health" through a program designed to provide "a cure rather than a mere palliative." But the initiative for drawing up such a program, he would go on to state, "must come from Europe," and the program itself "should be a joint one, agreed to by a number, if not all, European nations."[1] The message, whose full significance may have been lost on the assembled audience, has been subsequently credited with the launching of the European Recovery Program (ERP), or the Marshall Plan. Yet even as Secretary George C. Marshall rose to the podium at Harvard University on June 5, 1947, to give the commencement address, the delivery process by which the Marshall Plan was brought into the world had already been under way for some time. It was a process that would culminate nearly ten months later with the enactment of the Economic Cooperation Act of 1948—an act authorizing a four-year aid program for Western Europe.

Historians of the period—some of whom were themselves active participants in its making—have offered us a choice of alternatives in dating the conceptual origins of the Marshall Plan and in identifying those who had initially formulated the basic ideas contained in Marshall's speech. Thus, for example, we are told that well before the end of 1946, some State Department officials had already recognized the seriousness of Europe's economic difficulties and were giving careful consideration to the notion of an integrated European recovery plan.[2]

Around the same time, other officials went so far as to propose that specific commitments should be made by the United States to contribute "substantial economic aid" for the purpose of accelerating European reconstruction and promoting greater economic unity in Europe.[3] The evidence suggests, however, that although the United States did consider ways of meeting the financial needs of several individual European countries, the planning of an assistance program for Europe as a whole remained fairly fragmented.[4]

At exactly what point the decision-making process leading directly to Marshall's speech actually began to take shape cannot even now be clearly determined. According to some, the crucial moment came on February 21, 1947, the day Under-Secretary of State Dean Acheson was officially informed of Great Britain's inability to continue its military and economic aid to Greece.[5] Others have claimed that it was the frustrating experience of the Moscow Foreign Ministers Conference (March 10–April 24, 1947) that prompted Secretary Marshall to instruct the newly established Policy Planning Staff to study the problems of European reconstruction and prepare a plan for action.[6] Still others would date the origins of the proposal, presented by Marshall at Harvard, to the notes on European economic conditions, furiously written by William Clayton (Under-Secretary of State for Economic Affairs) in an airplane on his way home from a meeting in Geneva in mid-May.[7] But if a precise moment or a single individual responsible for initiating this process cannot be identified, the overriding consideration behind the American offer to help Europe can be clearly stated. It was the rapid deterioration of Europe's economies during the severe winter of 1946–1947 and the American perceptions of the consequences of a West European economic collapse.

To say this, however, is to gloss over a complex array of economic *and* political factors that confronted U.S. policy makers during the first half of 1947 and helped influence their eventual response. The deterioration of Soviet-American relations and the threat—real or imagined—of further communist expansion in Europe; Britain's economic and financial difficulties and their political-strategic implications; Germany's economic stagnation and a perceived need to revive her industries and quickly restore her productive capacity; internal economic dislocations and financial instability in most West European countries; the forecasts, early in 1947, of a coming American recession and the concern that Europe's lack of dollars, with which to finance the purchase of American exports, would further aggravate the anticipated decline in domestic demand; the belief that a continuing dollar shortage and balance-of-payments difficulties in Europe could hinder healthy and unrestricted international trade relationships and would thus spell adverse long-term consequences for the American economy; a perceived need for stockpiling strategic materials by this country; the argument that the key to Europe's economic recovery would be increased European production; the thesis that an improvement in Europe's economic health would, in turn, promote long-run political stability and lasting peace on the Continent; and the proposition that Europe's economic, as well as political, strength must lie in European cooperation and eventually unity—all of these, in varying degrees and at different points in time, contributed to the essence of Marshall's message at Harvard and to the formulation of what ultimately emerged as a congressionally authorized European aid program.[8]

It is important to bear these factors in mind, for they serve to underscore the general context within which American policy toward Europe was conceived and evolved. At the same time they offer an insight into the kind of economic problems that the Marshall Plan was created to address. To be sure, a clear definition of the program and its goals was still some way off when Secretary Marshall made his Harvard pronouncement. In fact, in a late June 1947 conversation with the British Ambassador, Marshall himself described his commencement remarks as constituting something between a "hint" and a "suggestion" rather than a plan.[9] Yet the nature of the suggested undertaking could already be discerned: It was to be at once a political and an economic effort—an effort aimed at advancing U.S. foreign policy interests by enabling European countries to pursue specific economic objectives. Indeed, when it finally emerged from Congress, the Economic Cooperation Act called for the achievement, by the countries of Western Europe, of "a healthy economy independent of extraordinary outside assistance" by 1952. To that end, the act stipulated a recovery plan based on four specific endeavors: (1) a strong production effort, (2) expansion of foreign trade, (3) the creation and maintenance of internal financial stability, and (4) the development of (European) economic cooperation.[10]

These, then, were the specific objectives whose fulfillment—with the aid of U.S. financial assistance—was considered necessary to the restoration of a healthy and stable European economy. In setting forth these particular objectives, Congress in effect defined the four main elements of the aid program and thereby established convenient terms of reference by which one may try to judge its ultimate economic accomplishments. And these terms of reference, in turn, provide the conceptual framework underlying the present examination of the Marshall Plan.

Specifically, the central aim of this study is to examine the ways and means by which the four congressionally mandated objectives were pursued and to determine the extent to which each of them was fulfilled by the time the Marshall Plan was officially terminated in late December 1951. Such an examination must necessarily involve a consideration of several sets of questions: What were the views and expectations of American and European policy makers at the outset? What magnitudes of American aid were deemed necessary to meet Europe's immediate and long-term requirements? What terms and conditions were laid down by the U.S. Administration and Congress as the basis for rendering such aid? What commitments were made by the prospective aid recipients? What, if any, targets were set for the fulfillment of the stated objectives? What major economic issues were dealt with by the American aid administrators and the European governments, and what economic and political constraints would dictate their respective actions? What, if any, structural changes occurred in the European economy as a result of the aid program? And, finally, how would changing economic and political realities, during the Marshall Plan period, affect the character and direction of the program?

Chronologically, some of these questions arise, and must be treated, before the others. Thus, Part I of the book focuses on the process by which the European Recovery Program was formulated. It begins with the initial responses to Marshall's speech and takes us—through bureaucratic discussions and decisions, promotional activities, and congressional deliberations—up to the enactment of the Economic Cooperation Act. The purpose here is not to compile an exhaustive legislative history of this act, but rather to sketch the various considerations and influences that led to its final shape and key provisions.

From there the discussion turns—via Parts II, III, and IV—to the main object of the study: the implementation and economic results of the Marshall Plan. Here the approach is largely topical. That is to say, each of the four elements of the aid program is examined individually, in an attempt to highlight its own evolvement from a European-declared commitment—and a congressionally mandated objective—to a functioning component of the recovery plan. Accordingly, each of the four narratives weaves back and forth through time; but they all concentrate on essentially the same time span. One may, in fact, view these narratives as a running account of the *simultaneous* construction of four routes all designed to lead to one selected destination. It will be seen, from this account, that some of the routes were forced into various detours, and that the final destination—a Western Europe independent of extraordinary outside assistance—was not reached within the originally prescribed period of time. But then, the very purpose of the present study is to join the draftsmen, engineers, and road crews—to observe how they coped with their different tasks and how far they have actually travelled.

The Setting

**PART
I**

Calculations and Formulations

2

The formulation of the European Recovery Program (ERP) may be viewed as a process consisting of three, often overlapping, stages. If one takes the Harvard speech as a point of departure, one may identify these stages as follows: (1) the drafting, with the "friendly aid" of U.S. officials, of a proper European response to Marshall's suggestion; (2) the preparation, by the U.S. Administration, of a legislative program to be submitted to Congress and the mobilization of public support for the Marshall Plan; and (3) congressional deliberations and actions. Each of these entailed a series of interrelated tasks and involved the participation of several groups of actors. But underlying the entire process was a basic premise: the unwillingness of U.S. policy makers to endorse another UNRRA-type program, whereby the United States would be called upon to provide other countries with substantial amounts of financial resources to be used largely at the discretion of the recipients. And this premise had its corollary: the Administration's conviction that it would be difficult, if not altogether impossible, to obtain congressional approval for any new aid program, especially one that did not spell out in detail how, and to what ends, U.S. funds would be employed. Hence, the process of translating Marshall's policy statement into an acceptable legislative proposal was essentially an exercise calculated to persuade Congress—and the American public at large—that the proposed program would be so designed as to achieve maximum economic and political benefits for both Western Europe and the United States itself. That exercise began to take tentative shape within less than a month after Marshall's commencement address.

I

It has been correctly pointed out by others that Marshall's speech at Harvard had committed the United States to nothing more than to consider a European plan, to be worked out by the Europeans themselves.[1] And it has also been suggested that the deliberately passive public posture, adopted by the Administration for some time following the speech, was dictated by the desire to avoid premature domestic debates and political confrontations before a concrete plan had actually been developed and presented.[2] Yet while outwardly the Administration—and especially the State Department—sought to play down any American role in the drafting of a European response, existing evidence indicates that such a role was, in fact, being played. Thus, on June 22, barely three weeks after Marshall's speech, William Clayton (in his own subsequent words) was dispatched to London, "authorized to discuss Marshall's proposal with the heads of the principal governments concerned."[3] The decision to send Clayton over had actually been made as early as June 5, and the "governments concerned" were to include those of Britain, France, Italy, and the Benelux countries.[4] On this particular trip, however, Clayton's European discussions were held with only British officials. At their conclusion, an *aide memoire* was drawn by the British participants and, after several modifications, tacitly endorsed by Clayton and U.S. Ambassador to Great Britain Lewis Douglas.[5]

The significance of this document lies in the fact that it was meant to summarize the British understanding—based on their talks with Clayton and Douglas—of the American perception of European recovery and the immediate steps to be taken in response to Marshall's speech. The main items on the agenda, according to this memorandum, were to be (1) a statement, jointly prepared by the countries of Europe, explaining their continuing economic and financial difficulties; (2) statements detailing consumption needs and production capabilities, as well as proposed measures to increase production rates; and (3) "comprehensive schemes" that would specify Europe's overall needs, external aid requirements, jointly agreed-upon economic objectives, and an estimated time period for accomplishing the stated goals. These tasks, the memorandum concluded, should be completed not later than September 1, 1947.[6]

Although both sides agreed that the memorandum must not in any sense be regarded as a commitment, the British sought assurance that it "represented the U.S. Administration's approach to the European economic problem." And Clayton, in reply, "thought [that] this was so."[7] Thus, it may be reasonably argued that Clayton's talks with the British (June 24–26) were indeed intended to provide guidance for what was regarded by U.S. policy makers as a necessary course for the Europeans to follow. And it can also be suggested that, intentionally or not, the same talks laid the groundwork for what would shortly prove to be a far-reaching development, affecting the scope of the aid program as well as future intra-European relationships.

Actually, even before Clayton's arrival in London, British Foreign Secretary Ernest Bevin had already met with his French counterpart, Georges Bidault, in Paris to discuss with him the nature of a European response to the American offer. Their talks took place on June 17 and 18 and resulted in, among other things, a decision to invite the Soviet Union to join Britain and France in taking the initiative of developing a program of European recovery along the lines suggested by Marshall's speech. A joint invitation was thereupon sent to Soviet Foreign Minister V. M. Molotov to participate in a meeting of the three foreign ministers, to be convened for that purpose.[8] The invitation was accepted, and on June 27 the meeting opened in Paris.

What transpired in Paris during the Big Three Conference (June 27–July 2) is a story whose full details lie well beyond the scope and purposes of this study. Nor are we concerned here with the issue of Soviet participation in the Marshall Plan, in general, or the specific reasons for the British-French invitation to the Russians, in particular. What must be noted, however, is that when Clayton and the British held *their* discussion, the tripartite conference was already an anticipated event. Accordingly, the *aide memoire*, drawn up by the British, was intended, at least in part, as a guide for Bevin in the forthcoming meeting. He himself admitted as much when he stated that although "he could not tell what lines would be taken in Paris," he thought "he could use the memorandum with reasonable safety as an approach in the discussions."[9] And it is not *un*reasonable to suggest that, given the nature of the "approach" outlined in the memorandum and the likely Soviet reaction to it, the Paris conference was probably doomed to failure before it even started.

That major differences arose almost immediately between Bevin and Bidault, on the one hand, and Molotov, on the other, is a well-known fact. The Russians had come to Paris primarily to seek more information about American intentions and plans. They therefore proposed that, as a first step, the United States be queried on how much aid it was actually prepared to extend. Bevin, supported by Bidault, strongly objected, and for the moment, Molotov was persuaded to drop this line of inquiry.

Bidault then unveiled a proposal of his own.[10] It called for the establishment of a steering committee consisting of representatives of the three powers and six *ad hoc* committees. The latter would address themselves to existing problems in specific economic sectors (i.e., agriculture, power, transport, iron and steel, raw materials, and foreign trade) and would draw up plans for remedial action. Such plans would be based on detailed economic information and forecasts, to be submitted to the steering committee by each prospective participant in the aid program. A final report would then be prepared by the steering committee and presented to the U. S. government. Molotov responded by opposing Bidault's proposal and attacking any joint attempt to formulate a recovery program as a gross and unprecedented interference in the internal affairs of sovereign states.[11] He proposed instead that each European country, individually, submit estimates of its requirements for American goods and credits. A joint committee would then consider these requests and assign priority to the countries that had suffered German occupation and had contributed to the war effort.[12]

The next day, June 29, Bevin countered by presenting a "single-page" abbreviated version of the French proposal; and two days later, Bidault followed with a second proposal, similar to his first but designed to "reconcile the [apparent] differences of views."[13] Such a reconciliation, however, was not to be achieved, for it had become obvious even earlier that the conference was heading nowhere except toward a breakdown.[14] During the final meeting of the three ministers, on July 2, Molotov, according to Bevin, displayed a "completely uncompromising attitude" toward Bidault's second proposal and accused the British and French governments of persisting in actions that would lead to the division of Europe.[15]

On this note the conference ended, and any remaining questions about Soviet participation in, or interference with, the Marshall Plan were largely removed. Indeed, the only significant accomplishment of which the Russians could boast, in this connection, was their effectiveness in preventing the East European countries under their control from joining the program. And, as a result, the division of Europe into a Western and an Eastern bloc—with all the political and economic connotations carried by these labels—became all but inevitable.

On July 3, 1947, the British and French governments addressed a joint invitation to twenty-two other European countries.[16] The latter were invited to attend a conference in Paris to consider and formulate a European plan for presentation to Secretary Marshall. As is well known, fourteen countries (apart from Britain and France) accepted the invitation, and the conference—consisting of representatives of sixteen nations[17]—opened on July 12. It adjourned four days later, having set up an interim Committee of European Economic Cooperation (CEEC) and charging it with the preparation of a report on the goals and needs of a four-year European recovery program. The first stage had thus begun.

II

In conversations with French officials on the eve of the sixteen-nation conference, Clayton and U.S. Ambassador to France Jefferson Caffery were queried on a number of issues pertaining to the contemplated CEEC efforts. As reported by them to Washington, they had emphasized that any European report submitted to the American government should include the following: (1) an analysis, "understandable to the man-in-the-street in the United States," of the reasons why European recovery has not progressed further in spite of large sums already made available by this country; (2) a sound production program designed progressively to put Europe on its feet within three or four years; and (3) a program sketching in broad lines a type of "European economic federation" designed to eliminate the "small watertight compartments" into which Europe's economy is currently divided.[18] Clayton then departed for Geneva, leaving the Ambassador to keep him and the State Department fully informed of all significant developments during the work of the conference.

It is not entirely clear whether, in offering their advice, especially with regard to the third item, Clayton and Caffery acted under specific instructions from Washington. The evidence indicates that at the time, Secretary Marshall still resisted any suggestions to let U.S. officials become involved in the drafting of the European program, preferring to wait until a European request for American "friendly aid" took a definite form.[19] Nor was there yet a consensus within the Administration itself as to the precise undertakings that should be required of the Europeans.[20] Put differently: There was as yet no agreed-upon basis on which to offer the Europeans meaningful advice on how to proceed with their planned endeavor. On the other hand, the first two items emphasized by Messrs. Clayton and Caffery had already been established (during the June 24–26 London talks) as essential ingredients of a proper European response. And, as will be seen below, several additional "essentials" would soon be presented to the CEEC nations for inclusion in their report.

About one essential undertaking, however, there was no doubt from the very beginning: the necessity to calculate—or, more correctly, estimate—the required amounts of U.S. dollar assistance. Such calculations were to be made by both the CEEC nations, meeting in Paris, and the Administration in Washington. But although they would differ in magnitudes and would, in any event, prove largely speculative, all the prepared estimates turned out to be based on essentially the same criterion—namely, the projected balance-of-payments deficits of the participating countries with the United States and with the rest of the American continent.[21]

It is important to keep this point in mind, for it reflects a much earlier American concern about the potential implications of Europe's balance-of-payments difficulties, a concern that played a major role in the deliberations preceding Marshall's speech. Thus, for example, Paul Nitze (at the time Deputy Director of the State Department's Office of International Trade Policy) later recalled that as early as February or March of 1947, "I wrote a memo to Clayton in which I analyzed the projections we had made by the U.S. Treasury about U.S. surplus; we had [projected] balance-of-payments aggregate surplus of $20 to $25 billion over five years. *There was the probability of a bankrupt world*; thus we had to give priority to an aid program." [22] He might have added, of course, that a bankrupt world could not sustain for long a growing, or even steady, volume of imports from the United States. On this point Ernest Gross was much more explicit when he stated, "It was clear that so long as Europe remained as it was, the U.S. economy would suffer. Our export market was obviously in an exposed and unsatisfactory position." [23]

Nitze's projections implied an expectation that Western Europe's aggregate balance-of-payments deficit with the United States would average between $4 and $5 billion a year over a four-to-five-year period. But Clayton, in his own late-May memorandum to the Secretary of State, estimated that Europe must have, as a grant, some $6 or $7 billion worth of goods per year for at least three years. [24] These figures would put the total amount of required assistance—and by implication the aggregate balance-of-payments deficit of the West European countries—at between $18 and $21 billion over a three-year period. Clayton himself, however, seems to have retreated from his initial position shortly thereafter. In a more detailed statement of estimates, he called for a maximum amount of $16 billion of aid for the period 1948–1951, to be disbursed on a diminishing scale of magnitudes as follows: for 1948, $6.5 billion; for 1949, $5 billion; and for 1950 and 1951, $3 billion and $1.5 billion respectively. [25] He also advised that, during 1948, the bulk of the $6.5 billion should be allocated to the United Kingdom ($2.5 billion), France ($1.3 billion), and West Germany ($1.15 billion); of the remainder, $850 million should be allotted to Italy, and $700 million to the other participating countries. [26]

On the other side of the Atlantic, meanwhile, the Europeans were laboring over their own calculations. Their first round of efforts, however, produced results that Administration officials found unacceptable. Thus, on August 25, 1947, Clayton reported from Paris that "the initial totals of CEEC balance-of-payments deficit with the U.S. for 1948/51 is estimated at $19.9 billion and with the rest of the American Continent, $8.3 billion, making a grand total of $28.2 billion." [27] Clayton added that he told Sir Oliver Franks (the chairman of the CEEC

Executive Committee) that "this figure is out of the question." [28] To this Franks replied that the total could probably be reduced by $5 billion. [29] Yet as late as September 9, 1947, less than two weeks before the CEEC report was actually presented to Secretary Marshall, the Interdepartmental Committee on the Marshall Plan, sitting in Washington, was advised that "the situation to date is briefly that the technicians at the Paris Conference have developed a series of estimated requirements which are *extremely disappointing* to the Department of State." [30] It bears noting, therefore, that by the time the CEEC report was formally presented to the American government on September 22, 1947, its estimates of balance-of-payments deficits had been scaled down, to conform more closely to those of the State Department. The two sets of estimates are summarized in Table 1.

Table 1   CEEC and State: Estimated Deficits of CEEC Countries for 1948 and 1948/51 (in $ billions)

	Deficit for 1948 with		Deficit for 1948/51 with	
Estimated by	U.S.	Total American Continent	U.S.	Total American Continent
CEEC Report	5.64	8.04	15.81	22.44
State Dept. (fiscal)	4.25	6.57	12.90	20.60
State Dept.[a]	5.39	8.28	14.05	22.31

Source: Compiled from figures in Table XI, CEEC General Report, Vol. I; and Staff Papers of the President's Committee on Foreign Aid.

[a] Estimates for 1948 cover the period April 1948–June 1949, and estimates for 1948/51 cover the period April 1948–June 1952.

As can be seen, the State Department had actually prepared two sets of estimates for 1948 and two more for the entire four-year period. The rationale behind this move is easily explained by the position adopted by the State Department when it presented its case to Congress. Ideally, the State Department preferred that Congress authorize, in one stroke, appropriation of funds for the entire four-year program, and that these funds be made available as of April 1948. Failing that, the State Department was prepared to argue—and indeed did argue—that the first round of appropriation should be authorized for a fifteen-month period beginning in April, so as to allow a meaningful time span for the accomplishments of the program to make themselves felt. An added consideration from the Department's viewpoint was the need to put the program into effect as soon as possible, and under the circumstances April constituted an earlier date than July (the beginning of the fiscal year).

Yet while they continued to hope for a fifteen-month authorization, State Department planners had also prepared a set of estimates based on the fiscal calendar. In this exercise they were not alone. Another executive agency—the U.S. Treasury—was also drawing up estimated balance-of-payments deficits, on the basis of the fiscal calendar, for 1948 and 1948–1951. The latter are presented in Table 2, where the corresponding State Department's estimates are reproduced for the sake of easy comparison.

Nor were the efforts of the State and Treasury departments the only contributions to the search for meaningful estimates of balance-of-pay-

Table 2   Treasury and State: Estimated Deficits of CEEC Countries for 1948 and 1948/51 (in $ billions)

	Deficit for 1948 with		Deficit for 1948/51 with	
Estimated by	U.S.	Total American Continent	U.S.	Total American Continent
Treasury (fiscal)	4.65	7.09	13.85	21.97
State Dept. (fiscal)	4.25	6.57	12.90	20.60

Source: Staff Papers of the President's Committee on Foreign Aid.

ments deficits. In fact, the most detailed analysis of the prospective balance-of-payments position of the CEEC countries and the magnitudes of required American assistance was provided by the President's Committee on Foreign Aid (PCFA).[31] Its final report was based on an impressive array of balance-of-payments estimates prepared under various assumptions with respect to import availabilities and import price movements. And although it is not necessary, in the present context, to delve into the committee's calculations, it may be useful to note a sample of its estimates as an illustration. Such a sample is presented in Table 3 and contains estimates drawn up on the assumption that import prices would remain fairly stable throughout the period.[32]

Ultimately, however, it would not be the size of the prospective deficits *per se* that would determine the required amount of American assistance. Rather, it would be the extent to which the deficits could be financed by funds obtained from sources other than the U. S. government. Indeed, the CEEC report itself took care to suggest that "it is clearly desirable that the largest possible contribution for covering the

Table 3   PCFA: Estimated Deficits of CEEC Countries for 1948 and 1948/51 (in $ billions)

Calendar Period	Low availability of imports with		High availability of imports with	
	U.S.	Total American Continent	U.S.	Total American Continent
1948	4.45	6.33	4.92	7.06
1948/51	12.42	15.11	19.06	22.98

Source: The same as for Table 2.

deficits should be made by means of loans by the International Bank" and that "some of this deficit, too, could be covered by private investment or the repatriation of capital."[33] But, having expressed this sentiment, the report then estimated that the actual amount of financing expected from the International Bank would be $920 million in 1948 and slightly over $3 billion for the entire four-year period.[34] Given its own estimates of the prospective deficits, the CEEC concluded that, in practice, the bulk of the required assistance would still have to be provided by the United States.

The same conclusion was obviously reached by the State Department and by the PCFA, although the latter estimated that as much as $5.8 billion would be forthcoming from the International Bank during the entire period.[35] Thus, as seen in Table 4, the process that began with

Table 4   Estimates of Required U.S. Aid for a European Recovery Program (in $ billions)

Estimated by	for 1948	for 1948/51
CEEC	7.12	19.31
State Dept.	6.8[a]	17.98
PCFA	5.75	12.5 to 17.2
Budget Bureau	4.5[b]	--

Source: Compiled from figures in Table XI; CEEC General Report, Vol. I; Report of the PCFA; and miscellaneous documents in John Snyder Papers, Box 11, HST Library.

[a]: For 15 months   [b]: For Fiscal 1949

the projection of balance-of-payments deficits eventually yielded a collection of estimates of required *American* aid—a collection from which the Administration could choose any one or several figures as the basis for its presentation to Congress. And Congress, in turn, could exercise its own prerogative of accepting or rejecting any or all of these estimates when it considered and acted upon the Administration's requests.

III

Estimating the magnitudes of required U.S. assistance was but one task entailed in the preparation of the ERP legislation. Equally important was the need to develop a set of principles on which the character and objectives of the recovery program could be defined. As implied earlier, State Department deliberations preceding Marshall's speech had produced a few key policy concepts but hardly a conclusive and comprehensive recovery plan. An early example of such deliberations is reflected in an office memorandum written by C. Tyler Wood and dated April 7, 1947.[36]

Wood's memorandum was concerned primarily with the structural-operational aspects of a U.S. aid program. Nevertheless, it clearly established the principle that the extension of American aid should be predicated on formal acceptance, by recipient countries, of certain conditions and obligations. Translated into concrete terms, the principles laid out in Wood's memorandum would later mean that (1) the initiation of an aid program would have to be preceded by the conclusion of bilateral agreements between the United States and each recipient country, in which the rights of the United States and the obligations of the recipient would be specified;[37] (2) U.S. funds made available under the program could be spent only with the approval, or at least tacit consent, of the United States; and (3) the United States would have the right to stop or alter the program at any time, for violation of the agreements or for any other reason. In sum, it would have to be a program based on definite commitments undertaken by the recipients, and over which the United States would exercise close supervision. Still, the memorandum stopped short of spelling out specific commitments that might be demanded of prospective aid recipients.

In the aftermath of Marshall's speech, the planning process, which had begun within the State Department, soon extended to encompass other governmental agencies and *ad hoc* groups; but the center of the planning activities remained in State.[38] By late July 1947, as the representatives of the CEEC countries were at work on their report, a consensus appears to have been reached within the Administration on the major—or so-called essential—elements that must govern the recovery plan. And it was to be the main responsibility of the American officials, already assigned to work closely with the CEEC delegates, to ensure that the latter took these essential elements into proper account.

That the assignment would prove to be difficult and frustrating is, in retrospect, quite understandable. The CEEC representatives went to Paris with about as much enthusiasm for the American notion of an integrated recovery program as the Russians had exhibited earlier at the Big Three Conference. It can even be argued that many European governments had concluded—perhaps wishfully—that, with the Soviet Union out of the picture, a substantial amount of American aid was there merely for the asking.[39] Thus, although they may have been willing to pay lip service to the idea of joint and cooperative action in *formulating* a plan, they were hardly prepared to undertake the kind of a searching self-evaluation that, from a U. S. standpoint, the formulation of the plan necessarily implied. Instead, the CEEC regarded its task primarily as one of collating and adding up the goods-and-material requirements of the individual countries, and calculating the dollar amounts needed to finance them. Moreover, given their sense of urgency, the Europeans were determined to accomplish their task with as much dispatch as possible; they even set a tentative deadline—September 15, 1947—by which the report should be completed and presented to the CEEC ministers for formal approval.

U.S. policy makers, however, were just as determined that the CEEC report contain much more than a series of "shopping lists" with price tags attached to them. Accordingly, in early August Paul Nitze met with Messrs. Clayton, Caffery, Douglas, and Robert Murphy, in Paris, to apprise them of the State Department's views on the essential elements of the Marshall Plan—elements to which explicit expression would have to be given in the CEEC report.[40]

What were these "essentials"? The State Department insisted that any European assistance plan should have as its major goal the achievement, within three to four years, of a workable self-sustaining European economy, independent of special outside aid. To this end the participating countries would have to undertake concrete steps to ensure that American aid would be used in the most effective manner. Central to this notion would have to be a commitment to maximum cooperation in measures of self-help and mutual aid among the Europeans themselves. But in addition, several specific obligations would have to be honored. Foremost among these would be the reactivation of the most efficient existing productive facilities, so as to achieve the quickest possible expansion of output. Second, the recipient countries would have to undertake internal financial and monetary measures to stabilize their currencies, maintain proper exchange rates, and restore confidence in their monetary systems. Third, the countries involved would have to pursue measures designed to facilitate the exchange of goods and services among themselves and to foster multilateral intra-European trade. And, finally, they would have to bind themselves—through a multilateral agreement—to a joint organization that would review the progress made by each and all on a continuous basis.

If this package of "essentials" was a hard pill for the CEEC countries to swallow, it was nevertheless a package on whose delivery the State Department insisted. And when it became evident, in late August, that the CEEC representatives either ignored the message or were unable to comprehend its meaning, Under-Secretary of State Robert Lovett recommended to Marshall that George Kennan and Charles Bonesteel be dispatched to Paris, "to carry some *realistic* proposals to be transmitted to the CEEC." [41] In essence, these proposals were merely elaborations of the basic theme outlined above. [42] The main purpose of the Kennan-Bonesteel mission was to reinforce the State Department position and to impress upon the Europeans the seriousness with which it was held. At the same time, the trip would enable Kennan to assess the situation in Paris at close range and report to Washington.

This he did, and it is worth noting, in some detail, his impressions and recommendations. "We cannot," Kennan astutely observed, "look to the people in Paris to accomplish the impossible." [43] Having thus set the tone, he went on to explain: "The ability of the delegates at Paris to draft a recovery program is no stronger than the ability of their respective governments to cooperate, by measures of internal policy and by the acceptance of new international engagements." [44] In other words, Kennan correctly sensed that before the CEEC representatives could produce the kind of report that the United States demanded, a fundamental change in the attitudes of their home governments would have to take place. He also realized that such a change could not come about easily. In light of these realities, he distinguished between two possible courses of action. The State Department could either reject the report, as drawn by the CEEC, altogether or make the report presented in such a way as to avoid any impression of finality. He himself leaned toward the latter choice. "Let [the report]," he advised, "come to us on the understanding that it will be used only as a basis for further discussion; try to whittle it down as much as possible by negotiation; then give it final consideration . . . and decide *unilaterally* what we finally wish to present to Congress." [45]

Although Kennan's appraisal of the prevailing situation was shared by other American officials, their proposed solutions differed from his. Thus, on September 5, 1947, Caffery reported from Paris that "it is evident that CEEC delegations do not feel their terms of reference permit them to prepare reports along lines which meet U.S. conditions." [46] He added that the situation "can be remedied only by new instructions from the 16 govts to their delegations in Paris." [47] But, significantly, "such new instructions will come only, if at all, as a result of vigorous and direct representation by the U.S. Govt to other govts concerned." [48] What Caffery suggested, in effect, was the application of direct diplomatic pressure by the United States, in an effort to persuade the CEEC governments to adopt a new approach and issue new instructions to their delegates at the Paris conference.

Admittedly, this was to be a measure of last resort, designed to postpone the formal adoption of the report by the CEEC and to allow more time for revising the document along lines suggested by the United States. But if the State Department felt at all reluctant to follow Caffery's proposal, the feeling could not have lasted very long. Only two days later Lovett instructed the U.S. ambassadors accredited to the CEEC countries to make formal presentation to the respective foreign ministers and to impress upon them the need for careful consideration, by their governments, of the American list of essentials. [49] And meanwhile, in Paris, the American advisers continued their labor in an effort to persuade the CEEC Executive Committee that "the Report in its present form would, if adopted as final, produce an unfavorable impression in the United States and jeopardize the entire program." [50]

Not until September 11, however, did Secretary Marshall inform his Paris team that "reaction from other govts [to the presentations made by U.S. ambassadors] has in general been favorable and indications are that most representatives at CEEC will support U.S. suggestions." [51] And not until the following day did Caffery, in turn, inform Washington of a breakthrough in the discussions with the CEEC representatives in Paris. As reported by Caffery, a decision had finally been reached by the CEEC representatives to postpone the formal adoption of the report until around September 20–22, and to devote the time remaining until then to revising and improving it. [52] It was further agreed that the report would be issued as an initial, rather than a final, report and that, following its publication, a number of CEEC technical groups would continue their work and would meet with U.S. representatives to discuss possible revisions.

A few days later Caffery again reported that he, Clayton, and Douglas had met informally with the entire CEEC and had gone over final changes in the report. [53] Clayton, he remarked, expressed his satisfaction with the work of the CEEC "but cautioned that Washington might have additional suggestions." [54] In this, of course, Clayton would be proven correct. But for the moment he felt sufficiently satisfied to join Douglas in stating, "In our opinion, [the] initial report contains enough of the essentials of a workable program to permit Congressional committees to commence considerations of interim aid within its framework." [55] Indeed, when viewed in perspective, the published report did contain practically all of the main essentials demanded by the State Department. It pledged the participating countries to (1) a strong production effort, (2) the creation and maintenance of internal financial stability, (3) the development of economic cooperation, especially in the area of intra-European trade, and (4) the establishment of a joint organization to review the progress made under the program. Above all, it gave explicit recognition to the principle of self-help and mutual aid. But at the same time, the report conceded—with the obvious approval of the United States—that "the circumstances in which [it] has been drawn up give it the character of an *initial* report"[56] and that it was thus subject to further revisions.

As it turned out, these "further revisions," when they came, left untouched the essential principles as embodied in the report. Rather, they were primarily aimed at the technical aspects of the CEEC work—that is, the stipulated production and consumption targets, the estimated commodity requirements, and the expected sources of supply and finance. Indeed, following the presentation of the report to the U.S. government, a CEEC delegation headed by Sir Oliver Franks was invited to Washington to review the document with American officials. Although the discussions covered a wide range of matters pertaining to the recovery program, the main emphasis unquestionably was on the extent to which the CEEC estimates could be made to conform with the estimates developed by U.S. governmental agencies and the Harriman Committee.

The nature of this exercise may be gleaned from the fact that, shortly after the discussions began, Franks felt moved to complain about the apparent tendency of the American technical experts to "chip away" at the CEEC requests.[57] He warned that "the cumulative effect of this process . . . would have the result that the amount the [U.S.] Administration might support in Congress might be sufficient to support a *relief programme and not a full programme of recovery.*"[58] But if Administration officials were impressed by this warning, they certainly did not show it. On the contrary, they missed no opportunity to lecture the CEEC delegation on the advisability of exercising restraint in formulating requests for American aid and on the need to plan for a greater use of the CEEC countries' own resources. In fact, U.S. policy makers expressed a few warnings of their own. Thus, during a meeting between the ERP Advisory Steering Committee and the CEEC delegation in early November, Lovett pointedly informed his guests that "from the United States viewpoint, the European recovery program is in a sense a risk both from the economic and political standpoints" and that "U.S. public opinion . . . will require that the European countries take a risk commensurate to that undertaken by the United States."[59] And during the same meeting Averell Harriman intimated that the technical experts on *his* committee "believe that as long as the CEEC countries place abnormal reliance on the United States for fulfillment of food requirements, recurrent crisis will probably develop." [60] The CEEC delegates must have felt the chilly winds blowing across the Potomac more than once during their meetings with American officials in late October and early November of 1947.

* * *

It was to be another month before Lovett could inform Secretary Marshall that "the basic ERP program is complete and the President's message [to Congress] should be in final draft form the end of this week." [61] Lovett was referring, of course, to the ERP draft legislation, as formulated by the Administration. How Congress would act on the proposed legislation still remained to be seen. But it might be noted here that, in formulating the basic ERP program, the Administration in fact followed Kennan's earlier advice: It accepted the CEEC report as a basis for discussion; it whittled it down; and, in the final analysis, it decided unilaterally what it wished to present to Congress.

Formulation and Promotion 3

President Truman's special message on the Marshall Plan was sent to Congress on December 19, 1947.[1] In it, the President enumerated the various considerations that had prompted Marshall's speech at Harvard, described the European responses to it, and outlined the main features of the proposed program.[2] He went on to state that, as developed by the Administration, the program was designed so as to (1) make genuine European recovery possible within a definite period of time, (2) insure that funds and goods supplied by the United States would be used most effectively, (3) minimize the financial cost to the United States, (4) conserve this country's physical resources, and (5) assure a wise and efficient administration of the enterprise.[3] And then, borrowing from both the State Department's and the Harriman Committee's estimates (see Table 4), he requested Congress to authorize the appropriations of $6.8 billion for the first fifteen months of the program (April 1, 1948–June 30, 1949), and a total of $17 billion for the period April 1, 1948–June 30, 1952.[4]

It should be pointed out that the President's message was based substantially on the Administration's draft bill submitted to Congress. And it should also be noted that the major responsibility for drafting this bill had earlier fallen to the State Department. Thus, when Congress began considerations of the proposed legislation, it was primarily, though not exclusively, the State Department that represented and carried the Administration's case. Yet both the Administration's proposal and subsequent congressional reactions to it were in large measure shaped by a variety of domestic pressures and influences that contributed to the final legislative outcome.

I

Although Congress proved to be the final arbiter in the drafting of the ERP legislation, the formulation of the Marshall Plan was, in more than one sense, a joint enterprise. It was an enterprise in which the State Department, as well as Congress, received, considered, and acted upon suggestions and recommendations emanating from various governmental and nongovernmental sources. Underlying this process was the need to secure public support for the Marshall Plan through the cooperation and active involvement of influential citizens and interest groups. Indeed, it may be argued that once the pronouncement at Harvard had been made, the efforts directed at the formulation of the aid program became intermingled with those required for its promotion. And as a result, a great deal of nongovernmental participation contributed to the development of the ERP legislation.

That there was a real and urgent need to "educate" the American public about the Marshall Plan cannot be doubted. In fact, a public opinion survey conducted by the State Department in mid-October 1947 yielded results that must have convinced the Administration that nothing less than an all-out promotional effort would be required to assure the adoption of the aid program. According to the survey, only 46 percent of those polled had heard or read about the Marshall Plan; fewer than 50 percent favored the aid program if it would result in domestic shortages and/or higher prices; and fewer than 25 percent were aware that the program postulated the obligation by Europeans to self-help and mutual aid. And, perhaps most disturbing, almost 60 percent of those polled felt that the Europeans were not working for their own recovery as hard as they should.[5] No less discouraging were the results of several other opinion surveys, taken both before and after the Administration's bill was submitted to Congress.[6] And during the congressional hearings themselves, several witnesses expressed outright opposition to a European aid program, while others expounded solutions that were clearly designed to change the basic character of the Administration's proposal.[7]

In fact, the Administration's early recognition of the need to gain public support for the Marshall Plan had been the main reason for the appointment, on June 22, 1947, of two presidential committees—the Harriman and the Krug committees—and a directive issued to the Council of Economic Advisors. The latter, under the chairmanship of Edwin Nourse, was instructed to study and report on the possible implications of a large aid program for domestic supply availabilities and prices. The committee headed by Secretary of the Interior Julius Krug was assigned the task of analyzing the potential impact of such a program on the natural resources and physical capabilities of the United

States. Finally, the President's Committee on Foreign Aid, chaired by Secretary of Commerce W. Averell Harriman, was to address itself to a wide range of problems and issues inherent in the formulation and implementation of the proposed aid program.

It has been suggested elsewhere that the establishment of the Harriman committee—a group composed of "distinguished citizens" representing major segments of American life—had been urged on the President by Senator Arthur Vandenberg.[8] Others have argued that the idea had been Dean Acheson's.[9] Yet regardless of who could rightly claim this honor, the fact remains: The appointment of the Harriman committee, as well as the charges given to Messrs. Krug and Nourse, was calculated to create favorable publicity for the Marshall Plan. Specifically, it was designed to persuade the American public—and through it, a highly suspicious Congress—that the Administration did not intend to plunge the country into a large-scale foreign aid venture without thoroughly examining its implications.[10]

In retrospect, the Harriman committee turned out to have had much more than a publicity value. Its basic charge—to advise the President on "the limits within which the United States may safely and wisely" extend assistance—was taken by the committee as a license to conduct a full-scale analysis of economic conditions at home and abroad and to interpret the goals and needs of a recovery program in terms of these realities. Its report, which was made public on November 7, 1947, constituted the most comprehensive source of estimated requirements of U.S. aid to Europe, together with recommendations as to how such aid should be used and directed. Moreover, both before and after the completion of its report, the Harriman committee was represented on various policy planning and technical bodies involved in the preparation of the Administration's ERP bill. And it was largely the technical experts of the Harriman committee who carried out the bargaining over estimated needs with the CEEC representatives, following the submission of the CEEC report to the U.S. government. Indeed, the Harriman committee played a central part in the Administration's planning process and appears to have exerted the single most cohesive influence on the legislative proposal submitted to Congress.

II

It is worth reemphasizing that although it was chaired by the then Secretary of Commerce and received support from the Administration, the Harriman committee was *not*, strictly speaking, a government agency. As such, it exemplified the "private," or nongovernmental, component of the joint enterprise referred to earlier. But while it was the most broadly representative among the various private groups directly involved in the formulation of the ERP, it was not the only source of nongovernmental contributions to the planning of the program. Indeed, it may be argued that some of the "essential elements," whose inclusion in the CEEC report the State Department had insisted upon, could be traced to opinions expressed by private organizations in the United States.

Thus, for example, the emphasis on a "strong production effort" may well have had its roots in a warning, sounded by the research department of the National Association of Manufacturers (NAM), that "production is the *key* to the appraisal of the Marshall 'suggestion' " and that "unless the result [of the aid program] will become increased production at home and abroad, *little* if *anything* has been accomplished." [11] Similarly, the fact that, on the same occasion, the NAM raised questions concerning the impact of the program on financial stability and trade barriers in Europe may have provided the basis for two other "essentials": (1) the creation and maintenance of internal financial stability and (2) the progressive elimination of trade barriers by European countries. And by the same token, Harriman's previously noted admonition that the CEEC report placed too heavy a reliance on the United States as a source of supply must have been in part influenced by the proposition, also enunciated by the NAM, that "it would be wrong to imply that the economic and human scars of the Second World War could be healed by the simple process of relying on the productive capacity of one or a few nations. Such an approach is neither realistic nor even plausible." [12]

The NAM was but one of many private organizations and individuals whose views and recommendations were made available—directly or indirectly—to the Administration and Congress. But it should hardly come as a surprise that a basic and fairly similar theme ran through most of these recommendations. Its main message consisted of the proposition that the success of the proposed aid program depended on the speed with which it would be put into operation and on the extent to which the European countries themselves would make efficient use of their own resources, as well as those provided by the United States. With only minor variations, most of the recommendations also called for three specific requirements: (1) substantial expansion of production, (2) establishment of stable and convertible currencies in Europe, and (3) progressive elimination of trade barriers and promotion of European trade. [13]

Quite significantly, private advice giving was not confined to U.S. citizens and groups alone. A case in point was a personal letter from Per Jacobsson, in Geneva, to his friend, Harriman committee member W. Randolph Burgess, dated October 22, 1947. The letter was promptly forwarded by Burgess to Richard M. Bissell, Jr., Executive Secretary of the Harriman committee, with a covering note: "One of the wisest men I know in Europe is Per Jacobsson, . . . and . . . I think you would find it *advantageous* to read the attached letter which I have just received from him." [14]

Jacobsson's six-page letter must indeed have proven to be advantageous reading. For in it he analyzed existing conditions in Europe, as he saw them, and offered several important observations. Chief among them was his emphasis on the principle that American aid—coming in time and in the right quantity—should aim at helping European countries to help themselves. That is to say, "the European countries," in his words, "must be genuinely prepared to carry out *their* part in the work of reconstruction." [15] No less important, however, was his specific concern over the need to establish monetary and financial stability and to readjust exchange rates to more realistic levels. "The real hindrances to [intra-European trade]," he argued, "are now primarily of a monetary character, and will be eliminated only by monetary stability and freedom of exchange transactions." [16] But perhaps most significant was Jacobsson's opinion that the U.S. agency that would be in charge of the Marshall Plan should not "be afraid of attaching *proper conditions* to the granting of aid." [17] He was thus explicitly opposed to the proposition that "the United States should simply provide goods and dollars to be handed freely to the recipient countries . . ." to be used by them". . . without any understanding with the United States." [18]

Jacobsson, of course, was not the only individual who felt that the extension of American aid should be subject to certain principles and conditions. As early as June 1947, former President Herbert Hoover publicly stated, in reference to the Marshall Plan, that "we should *insist* upon certain principles in operations of gifts and loans." [19] And in mid-October 1947, during an "off-the-record" discussion with George Elsey, one of Truman's closest assistants, Harold Stassen suggested that American aid to Western Europe should be conditioned, "with strings attached." [20] What makes Jacobsson's views noteworthy, however, is the fact that they were expressed by a *European* and not, as would have been logically expected, by an American.

Nor was Jacobsson the only non-American observer to express strong views on the need for internal and external financial stability in Europe. Meeting in London during February 1948, the Executive Committee of the International Chamber of Commerce issued a report in which it proposed various measures to ensure that aid extended under the ERP would be used constructively. [21] Its main emphasis was on actions—to be taken by European countries—to control inflation, to establish fiscal and monetary stability, and to adjust exchange rates realistically. [22] And Friedrich Lutz, the Swiss economist, echoed the same sentiments when he wrote: "The ultimate return of the European countries to multilateral trade . . . depends on their own economic policies rather than on the volume of aid they may receive." [23] These policies, he argued, must be aimed at stopping inflation, mopping up excess liquidity, and adjusting exchange rates. [24] It is hardly surprising, in light of such expressions from so many sources, that both the Harriman committee report and the ERP legislation laid so heavy a stress on the need for establishing monetary and financial stability in the ERP countries. [25]

But apart from defining basic purposes and objectives, the preparation of the ERP legislation also required the designation of a suitable organizational apparatus to administer and supervise the aid program. In his message to Congress, the President acknowledged this fact by referring to the "necessity [to establish] effective administrative arrangements adapted to the particular requirements of the program." [26] And, after detailing the various functions that would be involved in the administration of American aid, he recommended "the establishment of a new and separate agency, the Economic Cooperation Administration [ECA], for this purpose." The agency, he went on, "should be headed by an Administrator, appointed by the President and directly responsible to him." [27] What the President did not say, though it was by then a well-appreciated fact, was that the administrative organization of the program had been a hotly debated issue among different agencies of the Executive Branch and would undoubtedly continue to be the subject of discussions between the Administration and Congress.

Important as the organization issue was, the details of the bureaucratic discussions and debates that produced the President's recommendation to Congress need not detain us here. [28] It will suffice to point out that at least one executive agency—the Bureau of the Budget—relentlessly pressed the view that no separate agency was needed and that administration of the aid program should be lodged within the State Department. [29] Most other participants in the debate, including State, favored the creation of a new agency. Among the latter, there were those (e.g., the Treasury Department and the House Select Committee on Foreign Aid) who proposed a corporate form of organization for the new agency, and others (e.g., the Harriman committee) who opted for a noncorporate body. But what *is* noteworthy, in this connection, is that the debate itself extended beyond the executive branch and that private, nongovernmental views on the organization issue were freely offered for the taking and, on at least one occasion, actually solicited.

Thus, for example, proponents of the corporate form of organization included such leading public figures as former Senator Robert LaFollette and Winthrop W. Aldrich of the Chase National Bank. [30] Arguing for a noncorporate body were the National Planning Association

(NPA) and, later, the prestigious Committee for Economic Development (CED).[31] And when the Administration's draft bill—containing the provision for a new agency—was submitted to Congress, Senator Vandenberg turned to the Brookings Institution for an independent opinion on the proper form for the proposed agency. In its reply, the Brookings Institution advised *against* a corporate form of organization and argued in favor of an independent agency with Cabinet status, to be directly responsible to the President.[32]

As far as Vandenberg was concerned, the issue was thus settled. The ECA—and, by implication, administration of the program—should not be subordinated to the authority or control of the State Department. But neither should the ECA possess the character of a corporation, since an independent corporation, according to the Brookings report, might tend to remove the operation of the aid program from under the constitutional authority of the President in the field of foreign policy. The point to be emphasized here, however, is that Vandenberg's conclusion with respect to the organization issue was directly influenced by the views and recommendations of private organizations, and that many of these recommendations were subsequently incorporated into the Economic Cooperation Act. Thus, in the final analysis, the administrative organization of the aid program was as much a product of nongovernmental contributions as were some of its "essential elements."

III

In most cases, however, the promotional activities on behalf of the Marshall Plan did not lead to direct contributions, by private groups and individuals, to its formulation. Even the most active citizen group to lobby for the ERP—the Committee for the Marshall Plan to Aid European Recovery (CMP)—generally preferred "to confine its efforts to the support of the principles of the Plan" rather than to take a position on specific details.[33] Accordingly, the CMP's activities consisted largely of supporting, and mobilizing support for, the ideas of others, rather than of generating substantive ideas of its own. Its role, in short, was that of a promoter rather than a formulator. But so, for that matter, was the role of the majority of the organizations whose support, in promoting the ERP, was sought—and received—by the Administration.

It is difficult to pin down a precise moment during the preparation of its ERP draft bill when the Administration actively began to seek wide public endorsement of the Marshall Plan. But it is reasonable to suggest that the first serious moves in this direction were made during the month of October 1947. The main burden of these efforts was shouldered by the State Department.[34] Their initial thrust was aimed mainly, though not exclusively, at leaders of business and industry, in an obvious attempt to enlist their help.

Thus, in late October a group made up largely of businessmen from all parts of the country was invited to a White House conference, to meet with several high-ranking State Department officials (including Secretary Marshall) as well as Secretary Harriman, Secretary of Agriculture Anderson, and John McCloy, the president of the World Bank. The announced purpose of the one-day conference, chaired by presidential assistant John Steelman, was to enable the group to hear about and discuss current international problems and the need for European economic reconstruction. Although the proceedings of the meeting were "off the record," it is possible to reconstruct the main lines of the argument made by Administration officials, from informal notes taken independently by two of the invited participants.[35] Interestingly enough, Administration representatives did not hesitate to concede that a European aid program might well result in increased inflationary tendencies at home and would probably aggravate existing shortages of certain food items (especially grains) and steel.[36] Nevertheless, they argued, the proposed program was both worthwhile and necessary, since it provided "an effective way to combat Communism and the fear of Communism" and since, "in helping them [West European countries,] we also help ourselves."[37] As if to underscore the real purpose of the meeting, Secretary Marshall pointedly suggested that "it is essential that the plan of action finally adopted should have the support of the American public opinion."[38] The implication could not have been clearer: Those present were being asked to lend their conviction and help in carrying the message to the American people.

No public record exists of any action agreed upon or taken by the participants on that day, October 27, 1947. Yet it is perhaps more than a coincidence that sometime during the evening of the very same day, former Secretary of War Robert Patterson sent night letters to several prominent citizens, inviting them to attend a meeting on October 30, to plan the organization of a citizens' committee to support the Marshall Plan. Of the twelve persons present at that first meeting, five were business executives or industrialists and one was a representative of organized labor.[39] And during the meeting itself it was reported that Winthrop W. Aldrich of the Chase National Bank, as well as former Under-Secretary of State Dean Acheson, had also accepted membership on the Executive Committee of the new organization.[40] Eventually, the CMP Executive Committee would number eighteen members and the CMP National Council, about three hundred fifty. But although the National Council, as well as the many local chapters (committees), was fairly representative of various population groups and organizations, the predominance of business, industry, and organized labor participation in the CMP could not be missed.

A brief account of the structure, composition, and activities of the CMP has been given elsewhere.[41] It provides us with a fairly reasonable, if somewhat simplified, view of just what it was that the CMP set out to accomplish and how it went about pursuing its objectives. Thus, we are told that the CMP Executive Committee registered as a lobbyist; that its main objective was to gain popular and legislative support for the ERP; that it divided its efforts between soliciting private contributions to finance its activities and undertaking a nationwide educational and informational campaign; that it prepared position papers, analyses, and other material for distribution to members of Congress and other interested groups;[42] that it made extensive use of various informational media, organized speakers' bureaus, and sponsored various conferences; that its members appeared as supporting witnesses before congressional committees during the ERP hearings, and its staff prepared testimony for use by other organizations; and that when the ultimate objective—the passage of the legislation—was finally achieved in early April 1948, the CMP staff was disbanded and its operations brought to an end.

Missing from that account, however, is an important element. It was the clear and consistent bias of the CMP in favor of *that* version of the proposed ERP legislation that reflected the views of the State Department and the Harriman committee.[43] Underlying this bias was the special relationship—one might even say, affinity—between the CMP Executive Committee and high-ranking Administration (particularly State Department) officials. And largely because of this relationship, the CMP could at once call upon the State Department for help in its own activities and willingly support the State Department position before Congress and the country at large.

This mutually supporting relationship was reflected, on the one hand, in the public statements and press releases issued by the CMP and, on the other hand, by the frequent appearances of State Department officials as key speakers in CMP-sponsored events. But a more revealing picture of the extent and significance of this interrelationship emerges from the records of the CMP Executive Committee itself. Thus, in early December 1947, even before the Administration draft bill was sent to Congress, the Executive Committee had been informed by Harold Stein, the Director of its Washington office, that "the Secretary of the Senate Foreign Relations Committee had already suggested that we provide a measure of leadership in organizing *favorable* witnesses when the [congressional] hearings begin."[44] A month later, Mr. Stein reported that he "had been working closely with *representatives of the State Department* in lining up witnesses . . ." and that although "the list of these witnesses is still in the process of preparation, [it] will be presented at the next [CMP's] meeting, at which time Mr. Acheson, who worked closely on this, will be present to report on it." [45] Acheson, it further appeared, felt sufficiently free to offer the opinion that "[Robert] Patterson should testify as a representative of the Committee for the Marshall Plan, rather than as a private individual" and that "in order that he might do so, it will be highly desirable for the Committee to discuss certain fundamental questions of policy." [46]

One fundamental question of policy concerned the position to be taken by the CMP on the matter of congressional appropriation for the ERP. Thus, at the January 16 meeting of the Executive Committee, Acheson reported that "the big issue is likely to be the question of the amount voted to cover the fifteen initial months [of the program]." [47] The President, he reminded his colleagues on the committee, "wanted $6.8 billion, but there is talk of only $5 billion in Washington." [48] Although the minutes do not record the discussion that followed, it can safely be assumed that the committee members were quite aware that the President's request for this particular sum was based on State Department calculations. In fact, in its first public statement, issued on December 22, 1947, the CMP had already endorsed the amounts asked for by the President in his message to Congress. [49] Acheson, therefore, may have had little or no difficulty in persuading his colleagues that the CMP should stick to its position. Indeed, the record does show that "it was unanimously agreed that the Committee will stand firm on the $6.8 billion figure." [50] This the committee did. And when, later that month in testimony before the Senate Foreign Relations Committee, former President Hoover challenged the Administration request, the CMP promptly issued a strongly worded press release in which it refuted Hoover's proposals and reiterated its continued support for full appropriation of $6.8 billion. [51]

Yet while it firmly committed itself on the $6.8 billion appropriation issue, the CMP took a more cautious stand on another fundamental question. It refused to be drawn into the debate over the administrative structure of the ERP. Acting, quite likely, on the advice of the State Department, the Executive Committee "decided not to endorse any particular proposal for administration, but to support Senator Vandenberg's efforts to secure impartial advice from the Brookings Institute." [52] Its only positive contribution to the settlement of this particular issue was limited to the rather innocuous statement that "disagreement over administrative machinery should not be allowed to delay passage of [the ERP] legislation." [53]

The continued desire to avoid legislative delays, due to disagreement over the administrative or any other issue, was quite understandable. It, too, was largely a reflection of the State Department concern that differences between the Senate and House versions of the ERP bill, as well as differences of opinion within the Executive Branch, might jeopardize the chances for prompt enactment of the legislation. This concern was clearly expressed by Secretary Marshall himself, in early March 1948, when he stated: "The strategic and crippling situation in Europe makes it imperative that the ERP legislation be enacted without crippling amendments early in April." [54] Marshall added that while "Senator Vandenberg seems to have the Senate situation well in hand," the House situation "is not in good shape. There is danger of delay both in getting a bill out of the House Foreign Affairs Committee and then in getting it to the conference." [55] And although Marshall's remarks were addressed, on this particular occasion, to his Cabinet colleagues in Washington, the echo of his words had already reached the CMP in New York. There, the Executive Committee was informed of Senator Vandenberg's efforts to "get [Congressman] Herter to agree to the Senate version of the bill," but was also told that "the prospects in the House are not certain. . . ." [56] Under the circumstances, all that the CMP could presumably do was to continue to apply the right kind of pressure on the "Republican leadership of the House."

There can be little doubt that during its existence the CMP proved to be a most effective instrument for molding public opinion, at the disposal of the Administration. Its effectiveness has been attributed, by one student of American politics, to its understanding of "the means most effective in influencing Congress on pending legislation." [57] Its strategy, accordingly, "was to stir up 'grass root' sentiment for the Marshall Plan in Congressmen's home districts," [58] and thereby apply pressure on Congress itself. In this endeavor the CMP was quite successful. Yet its success was due largely to its ability to enlist the help of many different interest groups and prominent citizens. In that sense, the CMP constituted a sort of an umbrella organization, which stimulated, coordinated, and complemented the promotional activities of other groups and organizations. But while it was fairly broadly based, the CMP owed most of its strength and influence to the solid endorsement of the Marshall Plan by the leadership of four major interest groups: business, industry, agriculture, and organized labor.

In several respects, however, the contributions of organized labor to the promotion of the ERP differed from those of the other major groups represented on the CMP. These contributions must now be briefly examined.

IV

The involvement of American organized labor in the promotion and, later, administration of the ERP may best be considered within a dual context: the Administration's perceptions of what would be required to "sell" the Marshall Plan to the *people,* as distinct from the governments, of the CEEC nations; and labor's own post-World War II objectives and activities abroad. Briefly stated, American labor's major international objective during the postwar period was to help rebuild strong, free, democratic trade unions in the war-devastated countries.[59] But it should be recalled that there existed at the time two labor federations in the United States—the American Federation of Labor (AFL) and the Congress of Industrial Organizations (CIO). Although both federations were active participants in international labor affairs, their modes of operation took different forms.

The CIO, in 1945, had joined the British Trade Union Congress (TUC) and the Russian All Union Central Council of Trade Unions (AUCCTU) in sponsoring the establishment of the World Federation of Trade Unions (WFTU).[60] It continued its close affiliation with that organization—and was represented on its Executive Bureau and Executive Committee—until May 1949. The AFL, on the other hand, had rejected the WFTU from the start and pursued its international activities on an independent basis.[61] In fact, from the AFL's standpoint, the objective of rebuilding free trade unions abroad necessarily implied the achievement of a corollary one—namely, a universal nonrecognition of Soviet and Communist-dominated trade unions and their isolation from international labor affairs.[62] It was largely for this reason that the AFL had earlier boycotted the WFTU and had chosen instead to maintain direct contacts with various trade unions and trade union centers in foreign countries. And given its attitude, it was only natural that the AFL welcomed the proposed aid program as a means of weakening Communist-led labor movements and an opportunity to sabotage and ultimately break up the WFTU.[63]

From the Administration's standpoint, the cooperation of organized labor was considered indispensable in the efforts to promote the Marshall Plan at home and, especially, abroad. Quite early, U.S. policy makers realized that the success or failure of the program would greatly depend on the attitudes of Europe's labor movements and working classes.[64] They also recognized that a strong endorsement by American labor would serve to counter the effects of a wide-spread propaganda campaign, launched against the Marshall Plan shortly after the break-up of the Big Three Conference, which threatened to alienate large segments of the European labor movement from the American aid program.[65] And organized labor, for its part, understood the nature of its role equally well. As stated by AFL president William Green: "In this connection the AFL has an indispensable service to perform. The wage earners of this country can convince the wage earners of Europe that our government does not seek power over their lives or wants to possess their land. Neither our government nor our employers can carry this all-important message convincingly." [66] And from CIO president Phillip Murray came the following: "We pledge our full and complete support to a [foreign aid] program soundly conceived and soundly executed. . . . The CIO stands ready to assist to the best of its ability in any program of public information." [67]

These were not empty gestures. Both the CIO and AFL were to be actively involved in most facets of the promotional campaign on behalf of the Marshall Plan. And although, by and large, organized labor carried its promotional activities independently, in line with its own interests, it also associated with and contributed to the efforts of other groups. Nowhere was this association more clearly illustrated than in the case of labor's participation in the work of the CMP. Two of labor's most committed internationalists—David Dubinsky and James Carey—served on the CMP Executive Committee, while scores of other labor leaders counted themselves as members of the CMP National Council. But what is particularly illuminating, in this connection, was the willingness of labor, on several occasions, to offer the use of its own resources to the CMP and to report regularly on its own wide-ranging activities. [68] It is hardly surprising, therefore, that Robert Patterson (chairman of the CMP Executive Committee) chose to single out labor in expressing "his appreciation and that of the Committee as a whole for the efforts of organized labor in support of the ERP." [69]

Understandably, a large part of these efforts was expended abroad, in an attempt to enlist the support of European trade unions for the ERP and to neutralize Communist-inspired opposition to it. Yet here, too, the AFL and the CIO had initially adopted different tactics and approaches. Thus, following its 1947 Convention, the AFL announced plans to call a conference of (presumably anti-Communist) labor leaders from the CEEC nations, to consider how labor could promote the economic rehabilitation of Europe under the Marshall Plan. [70] The CIO, at the time, still hoped that mobilization of European labor's support for the ERP could be accomplished within the WFTU. In fact, at the November 1947 meeting of the WFTU Executive Bureau in Paris, James Carey (secretary-treasurer of the CIO) read a statement endorsing the ERP. He then called upon the WFTU to organize, within its framework, a mechanism by which trade union movements from countries affected by the ERP could consult with each other and exchange their experiences in relation to the aid program. [71] Carey's proposal, however, was not formally acted upon. Instead, WFTU secretary-general Louis Saillant, exercising his control over agenda items, deferred discussion of the whole issue of postwar economic reconstruction until the next meeting of the Executive Bureau, scheduled for May 1948.

Not long thereafter, events took a decisive and irreversible turn. [72] In

January 1948, Irving Brown, AFL's representative in Europe, announced that arrangements were being made for a conference of labor organizations, to take place in Brussels in March, to discuss labor's role in assisting European economic reconstruction. This announcement prompted the British TUC to request that a special meeting of the WFTU Executive Bureau be held in mid-February, to consider the WFTU's position on the Marshall Plan. But early in February, returning from a trip to Moscow, the WFTU Secretary-General let it be known that no such meeting could be held before April. Under the circumstances, and after consultations with the trade union centers in the three Benelux countries, the TUC announced on February 18 its own call for a trade union conference, to be held in London on March 8–9. Invitations, jointly issued by four conveners, were addressed to thirty-four labor organizations, including three from the United States—the AFL, the CIO, and the Railway Labor Executives Association (RLEA).[73] And when the first International Trade Union Conference on ERP (ERP/ITUC) opened on March 9, 1948, the representatives of all the invited U.S. organizations were in attendance.

To be sure, the significance of the ERP/ITUC extends beyond its preoccupation with the issue of labor's support for and participation in the Marshall Plan. Indeed, it can be—and has been—argued that the convening of this conference constituted the first crucial step in a process that resulted in an irrevocable split in the ranks of the international labor movement and led, within a year, to the establishment of a new labor organization: the International Confederation of Free Trade Unions (ICFTU). But that particular story lies beyond the scope of the present discussion.[74]

The immediate task facing the conference was the adoption of a joint stand on the Marshall Plan and the relation of free workers' organizations to it. This it did, by issuing a fifteen-point Declaration titled "ERP and the Trade Unions."[75] As may be surmised, this document strongly endorsed the proposed aid program on the grounds that (1) "without American aid [there would be] almost insurmountable difficulties in the way of a reconstruction of the European economic system . . ." and (2) "no unacceptable conditions are attached to the offer of American aid."[76] The Declaration then called on the members of the workers' organizations represented at the conference to "give their whole-hearted support to the necessary measures that each [ERP] country must take to fulfill the requirements of [its] national production program. . . ."[77] And in an obvious acknowledgment of the role played by U.S. labor, the conference placed on record "its high appreciation for the initiative taken by the American Labor Movement, in complete unity of spirit, in the formulation of the European Recovery Programme."[78]

Yet at the same time that it lent its strong support to the ERP, the Declaration left little doubt as to its insistence upon labor's participation in it. Specifically, it urged that "the trade union movement in each participating country shall seek to establish close contact with its government in the administration of their national production programs."[79] More important, the conference unanimously decided to establish a joint organization—the ERP Trade Union Advisory Committee—which would maintain "continuous association with the administrative machinery established by the governments of the participating nations" and would "review the progress achieved in the execution of the Recovery Program."[80] In addition, the ERP/TUAC would be charged with the responsibility of keeping the trade union organizations informed of developments and progress in carrying out the national and overall recovery programs. And finally, it would be empowered to convene another session of the ERP/ITUC should it be deemed desirable.[81] In effect, then, the establishment of the ERP/TUAC amounted to the creation of a permanent machinery, through which labor could continuously assert its self-conceived role in the implementation of the Marshall Plan.

Exactly what that role would entail will be seen in the course of subsequent discussion. For the moment, we briefly return to American labor and the promotion of the Marshall Plan. It was labor's publicly expressed conviction that the revival of free trade unions abroad was essential to the survival of democracy, and that its own most important contribution to world peace and prosperity would be to help achieve such revival.[82] Hence, as noted earlier, the major international objective of both the AFL and the CIO, in the postwar era, was to rebuild strong democratic trade unions in Europe and elsewhere. American labor leaders correctly sensed that an aid program on a scale of the ERP would provide both a structural framework and financial resources that could be utilized in the furtherance of this objective. And, having reached this conclusion, it was only logical that they should lend their vigorous support to the proposed ERP, while at the same time staking out a future claim for labor's participation in the administration of the aid program.

* * *

By the time Congress turned to consider and act on the Administration's ERP bill, the promotional efforts on behalf of the Marshall Plan had already begun to bear fruit. In addition to organized labor, business, and various industrial associations, scores of national and local organizations—including such diverse groups as the American Farm Bureau Federation, Americans for Democratic Action, the National

Grange, the National League of Women Voters, Veterans of Foreign Wars, the Federal Council of Churches, and others—had come out in support of the proposed program. American public opinion, as reflected in a Gallup poll released in early December 1947, had clearly undergone a marked change since early fall: The proportion of those ignorant of, or opposed to, the aid program had declined while the proportion of those in favor had risen significantly.[83] And although domestic opposition to the Marshall Plan continued to be voiced, both before and during the congressional hearings and debate, its effectiveness progressively diminished through the activities of the Committee for the Marshall Plan (CMP) and similarly minded groups. Indeed, in early January 1948, when Congress opened hearings on the proposed legislation, advocates of the Marshall Plan far outnumbered and outshone its opponents.

The second stage in the process of formulating the Marshall Plan was almost over: The Administration had prepared a legislative program, had mobilized public support for it, and had submitted its draft bill to Congress. The third stage was about to begin.

Congressional Responses 4

The strong endorsement of the Marshall Plan by the leadership of labor, business, and other major interest groups virtually assured the legislative enactment of a European aid program. But although passage of legislation was not itself in doubt, the exact nature of its final provisions could not be taken for granted. Indeed, as late as February 1948, three different versions of ERP legislation were still competing with each other. And throughout the course of congressional deliberations, the Administration had to tread a careful path between critics and friends, both within and outside Congress, to salvage most of its original requests intact.

It was to be expected, of course, that Congress might wish to assert its prerogative of either accepting the Administration's proposal or drafting its own ERP legislation. It could also be anticipated that differences would arise between the Senate and the House, although the extent of such differences could not have been assumed in advance. But what obviously could not have been anticipated was that some of those who had actually contributed to the formulation of the Administration bill would turn critics of sort once the bill had been submitted.[1] Nor could it be foreseen to what lengths the groups that helped promote the Marshall Plan would go to assert *their* interests by influencing the legislation pending before Congress. And, for that matter, it could hardly have been known to what extent Congress might accommodate the demands of special interest groups by inserting, in Marshall's words, "crippling amendments" into the Administration bill.

As it turned out, Congress did insert various changes and amendments into the Administration bill. In fact, even before the bill reached the committee-hearings stage, the Administration, responding to Senator Vandenberg's suggestion, had already backed off from its original request for a specific four-year authorization of funds.[2] And by the time the public hearings ended and the Senate Foreign Relations Committee was about to begin its hearings in executive session, the original draft bill submitted to Congress had undergone further revisions, worked out by the committee's staff in collaboration with experts from the State Department.[3] Additional changes—some minor, others significant—were to be introduced in the course of the committee's own deliberations and during the floor debates that followed.[4]

It will be seen below that some of the additions, deletions, and amendments offered by Congress reflected congressional uneasiness over certain aspects of the plan as presented by the Administration, or else a genuine concern about various economic and political implications of the aid program itself. Other congressional responses, however, were directly influenced by the wishes and demands of several domestic interest groups that sought special accommodation under the ERP in return for their public support of the proposed legislation. Such response—and the considerations upon which they were based—resulted in legislative provisions that would later serve to hamper an efficient implementation of the ERP. The most glaring example of these turned out to be the ERP shipping provisions.

I

The struggle over shipping—and the results it finally produced—provides a unique insight into the interaction between Congress, the Administration, and the public during the formulation of the ERP legislation. At issue was the Administration's request for authority to transfer idle U.S. dry cargo merchant vessels to the European nations, under the aid program. Quite early it became evident that the proposal was destined to face an uphill battle. For even within the Executive Branch there arose a sharp conflict over it which, in the opinion of Budget Director James Webb, required the personal intervention of the President.[5] The transfer of U.S. ships, Webb stated, is endorsed by the Department of State, the Department of Commerce, the Army, and the Navy but "is flatly opposed to by the Maritime Commission."[6] Webb, who obviously favored the idea himself, went on to argue that by making U.S. ships available to other countries, the United States would be in a strong position to ask that foreign ship construction programs be reduced, thus conserving steel. Moreover, he pointed out, the carriage of ERP cargo in foreign-operated ships would result in greatly reduced costs to the program, since foreign shipping costs and rates were considerably lower than corresponding American rates.[7] And, as if to emphasize the need for a strong stand on the issue, he concluded: "I am convinced that the authority to dispose of ships cannot be safely left to the Maritime Commission."[8] He proposed instead that under the ERP legislation the authority to sell or charter ships be vested in the President.

The President apparently thought so too. For the draft bill prepared by the Administration contained two separate provisions in which authority to transfer ships was proposed. One of these would have placed in the hands of the ECA Administrator the authority to *charter* "any merchant vessel owned by the United States which the United States Maritime Commission certifies as excess to its current requirements."[9] The second would have empowered him to determine when, and under what conditions, the *sale* of U.S. vessels to participating countries would be in furtherance of the recovery program. Whenever he so determined, "and whenever the President so direct[ed]," the Maritime Commission would be obliged to effect such a sale.[10]

In presenting its case to Congress, the Administration, quite understandably, emphasized the savings-in-cost argument. Thus, very early in his public testimony before the Senate Foreign Relations Committee, Secretary of State Marshall freely conceded that these provisions had been proposed "in order to avoid the tremendous dollar expenditures for freight . . . carried in U.S. vessels."[11] To drive the point home, he informed the Senators that in Europe the price of coal coming from the United States was $24 a ton; of this, "something like $14 is the [cost of] ocean freight," much of which was paid in dollars.[12] The charter of ships, he added, "cuts very considerably the dollar cost of shipment of this material . . . across the Atlantic."[13] Marshall recognized, of course, the implications of these provisions for domestic shipping interests. He admitted that freight revenues, instead of going to American firms, would go, "though in a lesser payment, to the new charter countries that are operating the ships."[14] But to him, the issue boiled down to "whether or not we subsidize, *as an item of cost* of this program, American shipping operated on the American basis with American costs, or whether we proceed . . . to charter on a temporary basis these ships."[15]

Marshall may have impressed the Foreign Relations Committee with his argument, but he most certainly did not impress private shipping interests, who recognized the implications just as clearly as he had. The latter, undoubtedly encouraged by the position of the Maritime Commission, strongly objected to either the sale or the charter of U.S. vessels to ERP nations. Moreover, they insisted on reserving a hefty share of the carriage of ERP supplies for U.S. flag vessels. Their objections and demands, however, might have carried little weight with an economy-minded Congress were it not for the support they received from a strong and influential ally: organized labor. Indeed, after hearing a succession of labor leaders, who passed before them as witnesses, congressional committees were confronted with a tough dilemma. The major theme that was played for them over and over again by representatives of labor concerned the adverse impact of ship transfer on the employment of American seamen.[16] And under the circumstances, the issue was transformed from "subsidies to American firms versus cost savings" to "cost savings versus loss of American jobs."

That the dilemma was real and the choice difficult is clearly illustrated by the deliberations of the Senate Foreign Relations Committee during the hearings in executive session. By that time the Administration had almost given up on one of its original requests—the authority to sell ships.[17] But Ambassador Lewis Douglas, representing the State Department, still sought to save the chartering provision. Reiterating the cost-savings argument, he told the committee that if no ships were chartered, the cost to the United States—even at current freight rates— would be increased by $100 million during the first fifteen months of the ERP. His main concern, he added, was that failure to authorize charter of ships would be taken by American shippers as a license to raise their present rates even higher.[18] One of the principal advantages of the chartering provision, he argued, was that it would give the Administration a club over the shipping interests to prevent them from doing exactly that.[19]

Undoubtedly sympathetic, Senator Vandenberg nevertheless reminded his committee members that they were confronted with the "fundamental challenge that has been raised by all branches of organized labor, which has given us complete support for this legislation, the complaint that this is a blow at the employment of American seamen."[20] To which Ambassador Douglas could only reply by challenging the public testimony of labor representatives and by suggesting that it is "doubtful, actually, that there is any unemployment [of American seamen] at all."[21] But Senator Hatch persisted. "I think it is very important," he said, "that organized labor has come out so strongly in the support of the Marshall Plan. I think they have done a magnificent job. I would not want to endanger that support. . . ."[22] And Senator Barkley expressed a similar concern by wondering aloud "whether, if we went contrary to their [labor's] recommendations in this shipping matter, they would become lukewarm in support of the whole program or not."[23]

It remained for Douglas to switch gears by introducing a new theme into the discussion. If the chartering of vessels was not permitted, he argued, then in all fairness an official amount of steel should be made available to the European countries, so that they may augment their own ship construction programs. "Now, steel," he pointedly added, "is in short supply. Shipping is not. . . ."[24] And to Senator Lodge's lingering concern about the damage, due to foreign competition, that ship transfer would inflict on the American merchant marine, Douglas replied in a surprisingly straightforward manner as follows:

If we are concerned here only with the damage to the American merchant marine, we ought to prohibit the Europeans from reconstructing their merchant marines. Because they can operate ships cheaper than we can and their newly constructed ships will be of higher speed and will be more efficient. So it is only a question of time, it seems to me, if these European countries do recover, when the American merchant marine is going to be confronted with precisely that kind of competition.[25]

Subsequent events, of course, would prove him right.

Although doubts and concerns obviously persisted in the minds of some senators, the committee finally arrived, in Senator Barkley's words, at a "reasonable adjustment" between two extremes. It struck out the "sale" provision but authorized, "with the approval of the President," the chartering, for periods not extending beyond December 31, 1952, of not more than 300 dry cargo merchant vessels owned by the United States and not in operation at the time of the charter.[26] In presenting the committee report to the Senate, Vandenberg justified this provision on the ground that such transfer would permit a saving of some $240 million over the 4 ½-year period of the ERP.[27] He further argued that since the Maritime Commission itself had projected long-range reductions in the size of the active U.S. merchant marine, it made little sense to maintain that fleet at an abnormally high level, for a temporary period, thus "postponing at considerable cost to the United States Government the inevitable readjustment that must be made."[28] And finally, Vandenberg assured the Senate that even the Secretary of Defense himself viewed such charter or transfer as more beneficial than harmful from "an over-all national security standpoint."[29]

None of these arguments, however, could prevail against the pressure that was brought to bear on the Senate (and the House) by organized labor.[30] During floor debate, the Senate eliminated, via the Brewster amendment, Section 11(a)(4) of the committee bill, thus denying transfer of U.S. ships in any form. And, as had been predicted by Vandenberg during the hearings in executive session, an amendment was introduced on the floor, limiting the commodities that could be transported on foreign-flag vessels to 50 percent of *total* ERP procurements. That amendment was subsequently toned down. The act provided that at least 50 percent of the gross tonnage of commodities procured *within* the United States be transported on U.S.-flag vessels, "to the extent that such vessels are available at market rates."[31] But as will be seen later, even in its milder form, this provision would prove a constant irritant to European nations and ECA officials alike and would contribute to unnecessary increases in costs to the program.

II

If the shipping provisions constituted the most glaring accommodation to private American interests, those relating to agriculture came as a close second. Yet in considering the demands of various agricultural interests and translating them into legislative language, Congress was faced with an unusual problem. Surpluses existed, and were expected to persist, with respect to some agricultural commodities. Their producers, supported by Secretary of Agriculture Anderson himself, expected the ERP to help in disposing of their excess supplies.[32] Several other commodities, however, were considered to be scarce relative to domestic needs.[33] And existing and projected deficiencies were not confined to agricultural products. Given the requirements of the American economy, shortages were predicted for petroleum, pig iron, steel scrap, nitrogen, certain kinds of machinery, and other raw materials.

When the Senate Foreign Relations Committee first took up this matter, its members seemed more concerned with the impact of potential scarcities than with the plight of surplus agricultural producers. Indeed, it was this concern that prompted the committee to add a short section, titled "Protection of Domestic Economy," to the Administration bill.[34] In it, the ECA Administrator was instructed to procure commodities in such a way as to "(1) minimize the drain upon the resources of the United States . . . and (2) avoid impairing the fulfillment of vital needs of the people of the United States."[35] He was further advised to procure petroleum and petroleum products, "to the maximum extent practicable," from sources outside the United States.[36] And finally, without once mentioning the word "surplus," the committee bill directed the Administrator, in procuring agricultural commodities, to "provide for the procurement of an amount of each class or type of any such commodity in approximate proportion to the total exportable supply of such class or type of such commodity."[37] The definition of what constituted surplus products was thus presumably left up to him.

But by the time the act itself reached the President's desk for signature, Section 12 of the committee bill had undergone a remarkable change. Although the original intent—protection of the domestic economy—remained ostensibly the same, it had obviously acquired a broader meaning. The concern with actual or potential agricultural surpluses was given much greater prominence than previously, and the Administrator's hands became more tightly tied. Not only was he prohibited from procuring abroad agricultural commodities that were determined by the Secretary of Agriculture to be in surplus domestically, but he was instructed to encourage the purchase of such commodities by the aid-receiving countries.[38] Moreover, the act specified that not less than 25 percent of total wheat shipments under ERP should be in the form of flour processed in the United States.[39] And, as if to add insult to injury, the Foreign Aid Appropriation Act of 1949 imposed a limit on the amount of farm machinery, especially tractors, that could be purchased in the United States with ERP funds. It provided that not more than $75 million worth of such machinery could be exported to the participating countries during the first fifteen months of the program.[40] Thus, while it explicitly acknowledged the interests of U.S. agricultural producers, Congress also appeared bent on undermining the interests of European agriculture. Which was, to say the least, a rather peculiar attitude in view of its own declared objective of promoting industrial *and* agricultural production in the participating countries.

III

It would be wrong to suppose, however, that while ministering to the requirements of special private interests, Congress completely ignored the legislative program submitted by the Administration. And it would be equally wrong to conclude that its preoccupation with the protection of the domestic economy caused it to lose sight of the main purposes and objectives of the ERP—as defined by the so-called essential elements in the CEEC report. It may be recalled that these "essentials" consisted of a set of specific undertakings that were to constitute a joint and effective recovery program based on self-help and mutual aid. Their inclusion in the report implied the obligations of the CEEC countries to observe them. And to ensure that these obligations would be taken seriously, the Administration had insisted on their embodiment both in a multilateral agreement and in a series of bilateral agreements with the United States.

Accordingly, the Administration bill authorized the Secretary of State to conclude, with each country, an agreement signifying its adherence to the purposes of the act.[41] It then went on to stipulate the multilateral pledges and bilateral undertakings that the participating countries would be required to make "as a condition precedent" to receiving aid.[42] In the first place, the participating countries were asked to accept, as legally binding, the obligations that they had assumed in the CEEC report. But in addition to these multilateral pledges—which included the establishment of a joint organization—the bill enumerated no fewer than eight specific commitments to be made directly to the United States. Each country would be required to formally agree

1) To promote industrial and agricultural production in order to become independent of extraordinary outside economic assistance;

2) To take measures to stabilize its currency, establish a valid rate of exchange, and balance its budget;

3) To cooperate with other countries in facilitating and stimulating an increasing exchange of goods and services;

4) To make efficient use of its own resources and those furnished by the United States;

5) To facilitate the sale to the United States of materials for stockpiling purposes;

6) To deposit in a special account the local currency equivalent of U.S. assistance extended in the form of grants;

7) To publish and transmit to the United States quarterly reports of operations under the program;

8) To furnish promptly, upon request of the United States, any information relating to the operations of the program and the use of assistance provided by the United States.

Moreover, the bill empowered the ECA Administrator to terminate the provision of assistance to any participating country whenever he determined that such country was not adhering to the agreement it had concluded.[43]

In drawing up the list of multilateral and bilateral undertakings, the Administration may have been consciously prepared to ignore the sensitivities of potential aid recipients who could surely be expected to regard them as an encroachment on their national sovereignty. It may also have been prepared to encounter and weather a certain amount of criticism from domestic groups that, while endorsing the ERP, would claim that the imposition of such conditions did, in fact, constitute an interference in the internal affairs of participating countries.[44] But if the Administration had hoped to impress Congress with its tough and precise stand on Europe's obligations, it had obviously not reckoned with the sensitivities *and* sensibilities of some senators on the Foreign Relations Committee. To Senator George, in particular, it appeared to be "the most unwise thing to say what these countries shall or shall not do."[45] And Senator Hatch thought it was "wrong [to lay] down hard and fast rules and [tell] those countries You have got to do so and so."[46] Even the usually tough-minded Senator Lodge, referring to the Administration's emphasis on the removal of economic obstacles among the participating countries, conceded that "all we can hope to do anyway . . . is to make them realize that we hope to God they are going to integrate. You can't say, 'You are not going to get a dollar until you get a certain amount of integration.' "[47]

Almost alone Senator Vandenberg continued to press his and the

Administration's case. Since the Europeans themselves had said that they would try to do certain things, he argued, "I don't know why we should not say to them: 'Listen, Bud, this is what you promised to do.' " [48] But Senators George and Hatch stood their grounds, insisting that laying down a rigid condition precedent "is very harsh language," which must be avoided. And after considerable discussion, their views finally prevailed. When the committee reported its bill to the Senate, the reference to "condition precedent" had been eliminated; and the only specific multilateral obligation that was imposed on the participating countries concerned the establishment of a joint and continuous organization. However, the committee bill retained, with some modifications, the eight bilateral undertakings proposed by the Administration and required that they be embodied in formal agreements to be concluded by each country with the United States. [49]

Interestingly, the modifications and additions introduced by the committee reflected, for the most part, the concern over potential shortages of strategic materials in the United States. Thus, whereas the Administration bill merely required each participating country to facilitate the *sale* to the United States of material for stockpiling purposes, the Committee's bill provided for the *transfer* of such material by "sale, exchange, barter, or otherwise. . . ." [50] Moreover, in a newly added section, the Committee authorized the ECA Administrator to "promote, by means of funds available for the purposes of this Act, an increase in the production of materials which are required by the United States as a result of deficiencies or potential deficiencies in the resources within the United States." [51] And Congress itself, while accepting these provisions, went a step farther. It called for the transfer of scarce and strategic materials "for stockpiling or other purposes" [52]; and it added to the eight bilateral obligations a ninth. Under it, participating countries would be required to negotiate (1) a future schedule of minimum availabilities, for purchase by the United States, of materials in which the United States became deficient and (2) an agreed schedule of increased production of such materials, a portion of which would be transferred to the United States, "in consideration of assistance furnished by the Administrator." [53]

A separate but potentially related matter on which Congress felt obliged to express itself concerned the disposition of the special local currency deposits arising out of ERP aid in the form of grants. The working dynamics of these so-called counterpart funds is discussed in some detail in subsequent chapters. For the moment it may be noted that the Administration bill authorized their use "only for such purposes as may be agreed to" between the respective participating countries and the U.S. government. [54] To Congressman Herter the language of this provision seemed at once too vague and too passive. In his bill he stipulated four specific usages to which counterpart funds might be put, and he proposed that they be spelled out in the Senate bill as well.[55]

When questioned by the Senate Foreign Relations Committee about the Administration's views in this matter, Ambassador Douglas replied that although they were not enumerated in the bill itself, "there are six purposes to which it is intended [that] this special account of local currency counterparts can be put by agreement." [56] He cautioned against spelling them out, however, arguing that the disposition of counterparts would, in any event, involve delicate policy decisions and, hence, "to recite . . . the specific purposes to which [they] may be put . . . might get us into a pack of trouble." [57] While accepting Douglas' argument, Senator Vandenberg nevertheless wondered whether the authority to make decisions on the use of counterpart funds should be left exclusively in the hands of the ECA Administrator. He suggested that perhaps the Administrator should be required to consult with the National Advisory Council on International Monetary and Financial Problems (NAC) on this question.[58] And hearing no objections, the committee moved to amend the Administration's language to read: ". . . for such purposes as may be agreed to between such country and the Administrator in consultation with the National Advisory Council on International Monetary and Financial Problems. . . ." [59]

But Congress was not entirely satisfied. In Section 115(b)(6) of the Economic Cooperation Act it required the Administrator to consult not only with the NAC but also with the ECA Public Advisory Board. Moreover, the act specified at least two purposes for which counterpart funds should be used: (1) to promote internal monetary and financial stability in the participating countries and (2) to stimulate productive activity and "the exploration for and development of new sources" of raw materials (Section 115(b)(6)). And when it came to the actual appropriation of funds for the ERP, Congress added yet another constraint. It provided, in the Foreign Aid Appropriation Act of 1949, that not less than 5 percent of each special local currency account "shall be allocated to the use of the United States Government for expenditures for strategic material . . . or for other local currency requirements of the United States. . . ." Congress may or may not have been conscious of it at the time, but by thus amending the Administration's provisions concerning strategic materials and the use of counterpart funds, it potentially intensified the problems the ECA would face in administering the recovery program.

IV

The foregoing account has focused attention on those provisions of the Economic Cooperation Act that would explicitly or implicitly govern the relationship between the United States and the participating countries. These, together with the administrative provisions (i.e., the creation of the ECA; the designation of an Administrator, Deputy Administrator, and Special Representative in Europe; the establishment of special ECA missions abroad; and the creation of a Public Advisory Board), and the specified functions and duties of the Administrator, would help define the operational character of the aid program. There was, however, another important matter on which Congress was requested to act—the authorization and appropriation of funds with which the program could be carried out.

As noted earlier, the Administration had asked Congress to authorize the appropriation of $6.8 billion for the first fifteen-month period, beginning April 1948 and extending to June 30, 1949. But to Senator Vandenberg it seemed necessary that the aid program should come up for review at the "earliest reasonable time" after its inception, when it could be judged "in the light of reality." In fact, he thought it "very important that the time table upon which we operate should produce [such] review as early as possible in 1949," preferably by January 1 of that year.[60] Accordingly, he proposed to his colleagues on the Foreign Relations Committee that instead "of appropriating for 15 months, we appropriate for 12 months," and that instead of $6,800 million, "we use the [comparable] 12 months' figure which . . . is $5,300 million."[61]

Vandenberg's suggestion rested in part on the logical assumption that the lower figure—although it would not, in fact, reduce the actual *rate* of the requested appropriation—could be more easily defended before a cost-conscious Congress. Yet the main thrust of his argument clearly implied a desire to assure proper American (read: congressional) supervision over the program, as well as a concern lest the ERP failed to produce meaningful results from the United States' standpoint. By January 1, Vandenberg told his colleagues, "we shall have available the report of the watchdog congressional committee, which by that time will be infinitely better informed regarding the operations of this enterprise than any Members of Congress are today. By that time," he continued, "you will know to what extent France and Italy are moving forward toward stability. By that time you will know the extent to which the Soviet operation is undertaking the program's sabotage and subversion." And, perhaps more important, he added, "if it is realized and recognized that this program is really coming under its most critical review the first of next year, it will put infinitely greater pressure upon the participating countries to make every possible progress . . . between now and then."[62]

To judge from the discussion that followed, several members of the committee were plainly disturbed at the thought of reducing the amount requested by the Administration. The majority, however, were willing to accept Vandenberg's suggestion, if for no other reason than that it had been made by him.[63] When the vote in the committee was taken, it turned out to be unanimous in favor of the change. And Congress followed suit, limiting the authorization to a "period of twelve months in order that subsequent Congresses may pass on any subsequent authorization."[64] But it remains to be noted that of the $5.3 billion authorized for the twelve-month period, $1 billion was to be obtained by the ECA through borrowing from the U.S. Treasury. In other words, the Economic Cooperation Act authorized *congressional* appropriation of only $4.3 billion for the twelve months beginning in April 1948. And the Foreign Aid Appropriation Act of 1949 subsequently appropriated only $4 billion for a fifteen-month period but authorized actual expenditure within twelve months, on the approval of the President.

If Vandenberg, by calling for an early congressional review of the ERP, sought to protect what he perceived to be the general interests of the United States, other congressional leaders were concerned with a more immediate threat to the welfare and strength of the country. Thus, to Senator Millikin, chairman of the Senate Finance Committee, the funding of the ERP entailed a serious fiscal dilemma that would have to be resolved before Congress settled on actual figures. What specifically worried him was the likelihood that the financial needs of the ERP, together with the anticipated financial requests for other, equally important projects, would impose an "extraordinarily heavy burden" on the budget of one fiscal year—fiscal 1949. He frankly admitted that the problem was potentially all the more aggravated by the prevailing strong sentiment in the Senate for tax reduction. It was apparent to him, he informed the members of the Foreign Relations Committee, "that if we go out full strength on all of these projects we are getting into a very dubious fiscal picture; [and] if we do not, then each project [including the ERP] commences to cannibalize the other."[65]

He came before the committee, Millikin stated, with "a plan that will keep [the ERP] from cannibalizing other legitimate projects and keep other projects from cannibalizing [the ERP]."[66] Specifically, he proposed an amendment under which between $3 and $4 billion would be authorized and appropriated out of the estimated budget surplus of fiscal 1948 and would be placed in a special trust fund, under the management of the Secretary of the Treasury. This amount, which would be considered as spent in 1948, would actually be made available for ERP expenditures during fiscal 1949. The basis for his proposal, Millikin argued, was that "since we have the assurance of a very large surplus in 1948," part of it should be used "to meet the extraordinary financial burden of fiscal 1949."[67] Such a move, he advised, would certainly soften the complaints of those in Congress who might rightly feel that the aid program "is hogging up all of the surplus of the next fiscal year."[68] And to Senator Barkley's direct question as to whether adoption of the proposal would have a mitigating effect on his own attitude toward the ERP bill, Millikin pointedly replied: "If this committee should adopt this amendment, I think that lots of ice in my system would warm and melt." [69]

It remained for Vandenberg to interject that the influential chairman of the Senate Appropriations Commitee, Senator Styles Bridges, felt as deeply as Senator Millikin "about the desirability and necessity of this move," and that favorable action by the Foreign Relations Committee "might melt some of the ice in his veins too." [70] But Vandenberg need not have seriously worried about his colleagues' reaction. For although the committee members duly noted the Treasury's objections to the proposal,[71] and although some of them would have preferred to see the amendment brought from the Senate floor, they clearly recognized the forceful implications of denying Senator Millikin his request. Accordingly, when the matter was put to a vote, the committee unanimously adopted the proposed amendment and included it, as Section 14(f), in its bill. That section provided for the creation, on the books of the U.S. Treasury, of a Foreign Economic Cooperation Trust Fund, and for the immediate transfer into it of $3 billion out of the appropriations authorized by the act. It further instructed that the first expenditures made under the ERP during fiscal 1949 "shall be made with funds requisitioned by the Administrator out of this fund until the fund is exhausted, at which time [it] shall cease to exist." And, as may be surmised, Congress concurred in the committee's wise action and adopted it without change as Section 114(f) of the Economic Cooperation Act.

V

The Senate Foreign Relations Committee had concluded the drafting of its ERP bill on February 17, 1948, and voted unanimously to report it favorably to the Senate. On February 23, the bill (S2202) was introduced by Senator Vandenberg on behalf of himself and Senator Connally. It was read twice, was referred to the Foreign Relations Committee, and was reported back without amendments on February 26. A few days later, floor debate began in the Senate where, on March 13, the bill passed by a vote of 69 to 17. The House took up debate on *its* bill (HR1585) shortly thereafter and passed it on March 31. Differences between the Senate and the House versions were quickly ironed out in conference, and the Foreign Assistance Act of 1948—Title I of which was the Economic Cooperation Act of 1948—was enacted and promptly signed into law (PL472) on April 3, 1948.

In the preceding chapters I have attempted to sketch the main considerations and influences that led to the enactment of this piece of legislation. My intention has not been to compile an exhaustive legislative history of the Economic Cooperation Act, but rather to set the stage for examining the ways in which—and the extent to which—its declared economic objectives were subsequently accomplished. These objectives defined the main economic goals of the aid program, as perceived by the Administration and Congress. But I have also tried to show that underlying the specific objectives, and the goals they represented, was an array of views, considerations and interests that originated outside, as well as inside, the U.S. government.

The ultimate goal of the ERP, as stated earlier, was the establishment in Western Europe of healthy national economies independent of extraordinary outside assistance—a goal whose attainment U.S. policy makers considered to be an essential requisite for the maintenance of stable international economic and political relationships and a continuing expansion of free multilateral world trade. Pursuit of this goal was to consist of four major undertakings, to which sixteen European nations had formally committed themselves in the CEEC report, and which Congress subsequently mandated in the Economic Cooperation Act of 1948. They were:

1) A strong production effort;
2) The creation and maintenance of internal financial stability;
3) The expansion of foreign trade;
4) The development of (European) economic cooperation.

For its part, the United States undertook to help the European nations accomplish these tasks through a substantial transfer of financial resources, to be disbursed and administered by a new agency created especially for this purpose. In carrying out its assigned duties, this agency, the Economic Cooperation Administration (ECA), would have to make choices among alternative uses of resources—choices properly based on the ranking of economic, as well as political, priorities. It would also be faced with the necessity of defending such choices in terms of both existing realities and expected results. And, quite understandably, it would have to persuade both the European governments and, often, U.S. government agencies to accept its considered wisdom and follow its recommended courses of action.

How would the ECA and the European nations go about pursuing their respective tasks? And what would the West European economy be like, in 1952, as a result of their efforts during the three and a half years of the Marshall Plan? These are the questions the present study seeks to answer.

A Strong Production Effort and Internal Financial Stability

PART II

Preliminaries: Production Targets and Aid Allocations

During the hearings on his nomination as ECA Administrator, Paul Hoffman stated: "I conceive of this job primarily as a job in which the Administrator and his staff should keep their eyes on *one goal*, and that is *increased production*." [1] In so viewing his prospective job, Hoffman was merely reiterating a sentiment that had frequently been expressed during the formulation of the ERP and had already suggested a certain ranking of priorities in the implementation of the recovery program. Indeed, even the order in which the four elements of the program had been listed—first in the CEEC report and then in the Economic Cooperation Act—could be taken to indicate the special importance attached by U.S. policy planners to the pursuit of measures and activities that would lead to substantial increases in Europe's productive capacity and output. And this, in turn, appeared to imply that U.S. aid should be so allocated as to enable the ERP nations to carry out their planned production programs to the maximum extent possible. Or, to put it differently: Aid allocations should be largely dictated by the production programs, drawn up by the participating countries, and their specific supply requirements. Hence, before proceeding to examine the *extent* to which industrial and agricultural production would, in fact, increase during the ERP period, it is necessary to consider briefly how the Europeans had conceived of "a strong production effort" and how U.S. aid allocations were actually determined during the early years of the program.

I

Both Congress and the Administration had called upon the prospective European aid recipients to undertake "a strong production effort."

Yet neither the Administration's ERP bill nor the Economic Cooperation Act contained specific quantitative terms by which such an effort might be measured. Congress, in other words, did not stipulate by how much and at what rate Europe's production ought to increase. Nor, for that matter, did it indicate what might constitute a reasonable "expansion of foreign trade," or to what levels should inflationary rates in Europe be brought down.

But if Congress did not go into specifics, the Europeans—under the Administration's advice—had already done so before. In their report, the CEEC nations undertook to aim at certain production targets for several basic commodities, and solemnly promised to use all their efforts to achieve them during a four-year period. Thus, the CEEC report envisaged the restoration, by 1951, of prewar bread grain and other cereal production; large increases, above prewar levels, in sugar and potato outputs; some increases in oil and fats; and as large an expansion in livestock products as would be allowed by available supply of feedstuffs. It also aimed at a one-third increase in coal output above its 1947 level and an increase of about 6 percent above the 1938 level; a 40 percent expansion of electricity output above 1947 and a two-thirds increase in generating capacity compared with prewar; an 80 percent increase in crude steel production above 1947 and a 20 percent increase above the 1938 level; expansion of inland transport facilities, to carry a 25 percent greater load in 1951 than in 1938; and the restoration of prewar merchant fleets of the participating countries by 1951.[2] The participating countries, the report went on to state, "are confident that this huge production programme can be achieved," provided, of course, that overseas supplies are made available "in the right quantities and at the right time."[3]

These ambitious statements, made in the fall of 1947, were designed in large measure to enhance the report's acceptability, first to the Administration and ultimately to Congress. It is doubtful, however, that either the Europeans themselves or the American officials who had worked with them took the achievement of all the targets for granted. Nor did the Administration entertain any illusions about the accuracy of the estimated European balance-of-payments deficits and aid requirements, prepared either by the CEEC or by its own technical experts. The projected production and aid-request figures, submitted to Congress in support of the proposed ERP legislation, were thus based largely on the Administration's perception of what would impress Congress rather than on an honestly felt conviction that the promises made would or could actually be fulfilled on time.[4] And Congress, though undoubtedly aware that a great deal of guesswork had gone into the preparation of the CEEC report, appeared willing to accept its commitments at face value—at least for the time being.

A year later, in the fall of 1948, the Europeans, now members of the Organization for European Economic Cooperation (OEEC), were once again putting the finishing touches on a solemn and, in a sense, more exacting document: *Report to the Economic Cooperation Administration on the First Annual Programme*. In it, they were to present jointly a specific course of action for the year 1948–1949, based on a careful examination and analysis of their individual national recovery programs. Each country's program was to contain plans (read: targets) for production, consumption, imports, and exports of a wide range of commodities. And on the basis of a collective screening of these programs, the OEEC was expected to recommend the division of American aid among its members and to indicate the extent to which their contemplated actions during the coming year would contribute to the recovery progress. Central to such actions, of course, were to be the efforts directed at increased production, as projected by production targets drawn up for the group as a whole. These targets, expressed as percentage increases in outputs above the respective 1947 levels, are shown in the following table. The extent to which they were actually fulfilled is examined in the next chapter.

The circumstances surrounding the preparation of this, the first joint report of the OEEC, will be noted in some detail in Chapter 12. Approved by the OEEC membership after much argument and debate, the First Annual Program was formally transmitted to the ECA on October 16, 1948. But it might be noted that even before the Europeans concluded their negotiations over aid allocations, ECA officials had already begun to formulate their own response, in anticipation of OEEC's submissions. And that response, intentionally or not, was to establish a definite pattern—an alternating sequence of pressures and persuasion, coupled with ongoing reviews and frequent modifications—that would mark ECA policy toward the OEEC throughout most of the ERP period.

The essence of the response had been set forth in an internal ECA memorandum, written by Assistant Administrator Richard Bissell some two weeks before the OEEC presented its report.[5] It was based, interestingly enough, not so much on strict economic arguments as on a tactical conception of what should be the proper relationship between the OEEC and the ECA. This particular conception dictated that the ECA ought to have "a free hand" to accept, reject, or modify any programming proposals submitted to it by the Europeans. Inasmuch as the question at hand concerned the ECA's handling of the OEEC's aid recommendations, the answer, according to Bissell, reduced itself to a simple choice: Either approve the recommendations as they stand or modify them on the basis of some agreed-upon criteria.

To Bissell, the proper choice seemed obvious. The OEEC-screened

Table 5   OEEC Production Targets for 1948/49

Production of	Expected increase	Production of	Expected increase
Bread grains	45%	Copper	16%
Coarse grains	12%	Lead	78%
Beet sugar	26%	Zinc	45%
Oil-cake and meal	45%	Tin	38%
Coal	13.7%	Wood pulp	23%
Coke	32%	Paper	23%
Pig iron	68%	Synthetic textile	33%
Crude steel	50%	Refining capacity	54%
Aluminum	37%	Maritime transport (tonnage)	17%

Source: OEEC, Report to the Economic Co-operation Administration on the First Annual Programme (Paris, October 1948), pp. 21–22.

programs, he argued, must be carefully reviewed before the ECA makes any decision; and the fact that they would be subject to such a review must be made quite clear to all concerned upon their receipt.[6] More important, the ECA should, as a matter of principle, modify the figures submitted by the OEEC. "I believe it is positively undesirable," he opined, "that the ECA approve the OEEC annual figures without change."[7] He did not recommend, he stated, that the ECA deliberately make changes merely for the sake of doing so. But he strongly urged that the agency make "whatever changes [it believes] to be desirable, taking into account the political as well as economic consequences of the changes themselves."[8] As a practical measure, he proposed that the ultimate objective of the ECA review process be to reduce the total amount distributed by the OEEC by "perhaps $50 million, with a fair number of changes, most of them involving only small departures from the [recommended] OEEC figures."[9]

Although they could hardly have been calculated to please the Europeans, or even some of the ECA's own officials, Bissell's recommendations, it must be acknowledged, rested upon a well-reasoned argument. Its point of departure was an astute perception of a basic difference, in both functions and roles, between the OEEC and the ECA. "What goes on in the OEEC," Bissell correctly pointed out, "is not disinterested research and judicial decision but multilateral negotiations." [10] Under the circumstances, he argued, "it will always be necessary to bribe certain countries to secure their agreement"; and, hence, the figures recommended by the OEEC may not necessarily reflect the correct programming needs of its individual members. The ECA, on the other hand, "can observe this process of multilateral negotiations and then, with the knowledge gained in observation, review the results in a disinterested and objective fashion." Such a review, Bissell added, was all the more desirable because it could, and presumably would, correct the errors in the OEEC figures—errors, he felt, that were "perfectly apparent to many of the Europeans themselves." [11]

II

Whatever their merit, Bissell's prescriptions had obviously been accepted, for the evidence indicates that they became standard operating procedures. Thus, when the First Annual Program was formally handed in by the OEEC, it was subjected, in ECA's own words, to "the most careful and exhaustive examination by the Office of the Special Representative in Paris and the ECA staff in Washington." [12] The agency went on to explain that in its "careful review" of the OEEC-recommended program, it "re-examined the judgements implicit in all [the national] figures" that had been submitted to, and scrutinized by, the OEEC. On the basis of this review, the ECA concluded that the specific amounts of aid recommended by the organization were "substantially correct" and that "no major revision in the OEEC aid figures seemed to be called for at the time of their submission." [13]

Perhaps so. Yet the record clearly shows that very soon after their receipt, every single one of OEEC's recommendations was revised by the ECA. (See Table 6.) It shows, moreover, that although most of the revisions were indeed minor, several of them constituted significant departures from the OEEC-recommended figures. And, finally, it shows that all of the revisions, large or small, consisted of *reductions* in the amounts of aid recommended for the respective recipients. The ECA review process thus managed to yield results that exceeded in magnitude even Bissell's own recommendations. The total amount of aid allocated by the OEEC for 1948–1949 was reduced, not by $50 million, as he had proposed earlier, but by nearly $120 million.

Reduced it was, but only, it would appear, on paper. For, as seen in Table 7, the country allotments issued by ECA during the first twelve

Table 6   Aid Requests and Aid Recommendations for 1948/49 (in $ millions)

Country	Country-aid requests	OEEC-aid recommendations	ECA-revised aid figures
Austria	339.3	217.0	215.2
Belgium-Lux	358.2	250.0	247.9
Denmark	149.9	110.0	109.1
France	1,114.9	989.0	980.9
Germany:			
Bizone	446.0	414.0	410.6
French Zone	100.0	100.0	99.2
Greece	211.0	146.0	144.8
Iceland	11.0	11.0	5.2
Ireland	111.0	79.0	78.3
Italy	799.5	601.0	555.5
Netherlands	657.0	496.0	469.6
Norway	104.0	84.0	83.3
Sweden	109.0	47.0	46.6
Trieste	22.0	18.0	17.8
Turkey	85.3	50.0	39.7
U.K.	1,271.0	1,263.0	1,239.0
Commodity reserve	–		13.5
Totals:	5,889.1	4,875.0	4,756.2

Source: Compiled from data in ECA, Recovery Progress and U.S. Aid, pp. 22-56 and p. 65.

months of the recovery program actually totalled $4,953 billion, or almost $80 million more than the aggregate amount initially recommended for distribution by the OEEC. Moreover, during the same period the aid agency approved procurement authorizations totalling $4,891 billion—some $135 million above its own previous estimate of

Table 7   Country Allotments and Procurement Authorizations, April 3, 1948, through April 2, 1949 (in $ millions)

Country	Aid Allotments	Procurement Authorizations
Austria	231.6	231.1
Belgium-Lux	206.7	194.8
Denmark	103.0	103.0
France	1,084.9	1,084.8
Germany:		
Bizone	388.1	384.5
French Zone	94.4	93.5
Greece	177.5	174.9
Iceland	8.3	5.8
Ireland	88.3	87.8
Italy	585.9	582.1
Netherlands	473.9	471.4
Norway	82.8	82.4
Sweden	40.4	39.3
Trieste	13.8	12.3
Turkey	46.0	28.5
U.K.	1,316.0	1,315.6
Commodity reserve	11.4	
Totals:	4,953.0	4,891.7

Source: ECA, Fourth Report to Congress, p. 38 and p. 104.

the total dollar aid required to finance the 1948–1949 annual program. And upon a closer reading of the evidence, the retrospective observer may well be struck by what appears to be an even greater contradiction between the agency's earlier pronouncements and its subsequent actions. Consider, thus, the following statement, made by the ECA not long after it had completed its review of OEEC's aid recommendations.

"It is of great importance to the success of the ERP," the agency stated,

that, once a specified amount of aid had been allotted to a country, the amount should remain fixed for at least a year. . . . The alternative would be to increase a country's allocation of aid during the course of the year if it could demonstrate that it was seriously short of dollar exchange and, likewise, to reduce the amount of aid extended to any country that seemed to have adequate dollar resources. But such a policy would blatantly reward failure and penalize success. The country that failed to live within its means would have a claim on additional aid and the country that managed to accumulate some hard currency reserves would have its aid reduced. There could scarcely be a policy more ingeniously designed to encourage the free and easy spending of dollars and discourage the participating countries from balancing their external accounts.[14]

Well said! Yet a comparison of the third column in Table 6 with the first column in Table 7 suggests that a policy so strongly decried by the ECA, was, in fact, followed. In the case of every single aid recipient, the amount actually allotted during the first twelve months turned out to be different from the amount initially specified by the ECA itself. Nine of the recipients were awarded larger amounts than originally proposed by the agency, while seven received lesser sums. But what is particularly noteworthy, in this connection, is that although it had initially scaled down every one of OEEC-recommended figures, the ECA subsequently reversed itself in the case of five countries. Its first year's allotments to Austria, France, Greece, Ireland, and the United Kingdom were larger than the respective amounts recommended for these countries by the OEEC. In fact, the amount allotted to the United Kingdom during the first year exceeded even the latter's own original request.[15]

The story of the 1948–1949 aid allocations does not, of course, end here. As drawn up by the OEEC, the First Annual Program was to cover the period July 1, 1948–June 30, 1949. Since virtually the entire amount appropriated for the first fifteen months of the ERP had already been obligated during its first twelve months, a supplemental appropriation of $1.150 billion was requested of, and authorized by, Congress to finance programming needs in the second quarter (April–June) of 1949. At the same time, Congress authorized the Reconstruction Finance Corporation (RFC) to advance $1 billion for this purpose, pending the passage of an appropriation bill.[16] And, acting on the strength of these authorizations, the ECA promptly moved to allot this entire sum to the participating countries. Thus, by the end of June 1949— fifteen months after the start of the recovery program—a total of $5.953 billion had been allocated to finance the procurement of goods and services under the ERP, of which some $5.909 billion had been so used.[17] More important still, during the second quarter of 1949, all of the participating countries with the exception of Iceland and Ireland received additional funds which, in nearly every case, resulted in a larger aggregate allotment for the fifteen-month period than the respective amounts initially specified by the ECA.[18]

Can it be concluded, then, that the ECA knowingly rewarded "failure" and deliberately encouraged the "free and easy spending of dollars" by the aid recipients? The evidence simply does not warrant such a sweeping conclusion. What it does suggest, instead, is a fairly obvious fact—namely, that even ECA's own estimates of aid requirements were subject to wide margins of errors, thus necessitating adjustments in aid allocations throughout the course of the year. The reasons for such errors need not be detailed here. Suffice it to say that due to the pressure of time, lack of complete information, and inadequate programming techniques, neither the OEEC nor the ECA was initially in a position to properly appraise and analyze the national programs and aid requests submitted by the participating countries.[19] It may also be said, however, that the very methods employed by the ECA to assess the individual national programs—and to translate them into estimates of anticipated balance-of-payments deficits—were bound to produce, even under the best of circumstances, unreliable aid estimates.[20] But perhaps the most important reason for the deviation of the actual allotments from the original estimates lay in the allocation procedure itself. For while the estimation of the aid requirements had been based on an analysis of the *annual* country programs, the allotments themselves were issued on a *quarterly* basis, following a review of the current status of these programs. As such, the quarterly allotments—though referred to by the aid agency as "installments on the annual allotments for the fiscal year, as recommended by the OEEC and approved by the ECA"[21]—were, in practice, determined by what the ECA perceived to be the financial needs of individual countries during the forthcoming quarter. And as programming and supply requirements changed from quarter to quarter, so obviously did the quarterly financial needs. Thus, it was not only faulty techniques, but also changing economic circumstances that were largely responsible for the observed discrepancies between ECA's declared intentions and its actual aid allocations during 1948–1949.

III

Changing economic circumstances would, of course, continue to affect the programming decisions of European governments and thereby influence ECA aid allotments throughout the ERP period. And so, for that matter, would changing political circumstances, as well as changes in official U.S. perceptions and attitudes. What should be noted here, however, is that essentially the same process of arriving at the 1948–1949 aid allocations was to govern the 1949–1950 allocation round. That is, the OEEC was to receive the national programs and estimated second-year aid requirements, to screen them, and to collectively recommend to the ECA a proper division of aid among its members. And the ECA, for its part, was to conduct its own review of the national submissions and OEEC recommendations and to decide whether to accept or modify the recommended figures.

As seen in Table 8, the total of the individual-country requests for the second year amounted to $4.69 billion. But on the basis of its own preliminary examination of the national programs, the ECA had arrived at a series of national aid estimates totalling only $4.202 billion. Its approach, the agency explained, had consisted of screening the program of each individual country and then "adding the results of [the] individual appraisals together in order to arrive at a total aid figure for the whole group of countries."[22] The OEEC, on the other hand, had limited itself to the screening of "consolidated totals" for all of the participating countries, and thus arrived at an estimated total-aid figure for Western Europe as a whole. In its initial request to ECA, the OEEC had asked for $4.347 billion, without actually recommending how this amount should be distributed among the participating countries.[23] The bitter struggle over the second-year allocations would come later. But it may be pointed out that neither the total amount requested by the OEEC nor the one estimated by the ECA was destined to serve as the basis on which the actual allocations would finally be made. That particular amount was to be determined by the U.S. Congress.

The Administration's request for authority and funds with which to continue the recovery program for another year was submitted to Congress in mid-February 1949. In preparing its case, the ECA had based its financial requests on its own estimates of the second-year aid requirements. Accordingly, it asked Congress to authorize appropriations of $4.28 billion for fiscal 1950 (July 1949–June 1950), of which $80 million were designated as non-program funds.[24] At the same time, it asked for supplemental appropriations of $1.15 billion, to cover the period April–June 1949. These requests, totalling some $5.43 billion, were accompanied by extensive documentation designed to persuade Congress that considerable progress had already been achieved under the ERP, but that continued financial assistance was necessary if the Western European nations were to become self-supporting by 1952. And Congress, after hearings and debate, obliged by authorizing the appropriation of the entire amount requested by the Administration.[25]

Oblige it did, but not for long. The 1949 authorization act, extending

Table 8   Aid Requests, Recommendations, and Allotments, 1949/50 (in $ millions)

Country	Country-aid requests (Dec. 1948)	ECA's tentative aid division (Jan. 1949)	OEEC's final recommendations	Actual allotments
Austria	217.0	197.0	174.1	166.4
Belgium–Lux	250.0	200.0	312.5	221.7
Denmark	110.0	109.0	91.0	87.0
France	890.0	875.0	704.0	691.2
Germany:				
Bizone	372.4	404.0	348.2	281.8
French Zone	100.0	115.0		
Greece	198.1	170.0	163.5	156.3
Iceland	10.0	7.0	7.3	21.9
Ireland	75.4	64.0	47.0	44.9
Italy	610.1	555.0	407.0	391.0
Netherlands	507.0	355.0	309.2	301.6
Norway	131.8	105.0	94.0	90.0
Portugal	100.6	10.0	33.0	15.3
Sweden	70.7	54.0	48.0	48.0
Trieste	12.8	12.0	14.0	13.6
Turkey	94.2	30.0	61.7	59.0
U.K.	940.0	940.0	962.0	921.0
Totals:	4,690.1	4,202.0	3,776.5	3,510.7

Source: ECA, Recovery Progress and U.S. Aid, 74; and William A. Brown and Redvers
    Opie, American Foreign Assistance (Washington: Brookings Institution, 1953),
    p. 206.

the basic ERP legislation for another year, was passed on April 13, 1949, and signed into law (PL 47, 81st Cong.) six days later. On April 22, the President requested Congress to appropriate $5.272 billion for the ERP—$1.074 billion for the period April–June 1949 and $4.1982 billion for fiscal 1950.[26] This time, however, Congress was not to be rushed, insisting instead on another exhaustive round of hearings and long discussions. Throughout the summer and early fall, Congress debated the matter and finally, in late September, reached its decision: It appropriated the $1.074 billion that had been requested for the second quarter of 1949 but reduced the amount requested for fiscal 1950 to $3.6284 billion.[27] Meanwhile, in late August 1949, the OEEC at last recommended—and the ECA accepted—a set of country allocations totalling $3.7765 billion (Table 8). But, given the amount appropriated by Congress, even this figure soon became irrelevant. Out of the congressionally appropriated funds, the ECA actually allotted only $3.5107 billion during 1949–1950. In all but two cases (Ireland and Sweden), the individual allotments fell below the respective amounts recommended by the OEEC.

There would be no more collective allocations of aid after the summer of 1949. In late October of that year, the ECA called upon its mission chiefs in Western Europe to develop new methods of programming and allocating U.S. aid and urged that the OEEC and its member countries follow suit.[28] One explanation for this change may be found in the enactment, on October 6, 1949, of the Mutual Defense Assistance Act which introduced, for the first time since the end of World War II, a military-aid component into American foreign assistance programs. To be sure, it was not the intention of Congress, in authorizing the Mutual Defense Assistance Program (MDAP), to terminate the ERP at that time. Indeed, in the preamble of the act, Congress "recogniz[ed] that economic recovery [was] essential to international peace and security and must be given clear priority." [29] Still, the very fact that military assistance was to be furnished on a *bilateral* basis and was not contingent on joint economic action by the European countries for which it was intended reduced the potential scope for collective aid allocations by the OEEC. In the words of one European observer: "[When] the military aid program came in, there was need for the United States to have bilateral discussions" with the participating countries.[30] And as military and defense-oriented assistance grew in proportions, so did the basis for bilateral allocations of aid. Collective aid recommendations by the OEEC thus became impractical and, in fact, unnecessary.

Although the growing preoccupation with defense—which had led to the formation of the North Atlantic Treaty Organization (NATO) in April 1949 and which was further intensified after the outbreak of Korean hostilities—did not in itself preclude a continuation of the ERP, it was bound to affect its character and direction. To say this is not to suggest that U.S. policy makers were unaware of such a probability and its likely impact on the course—and costs—of the recovery process. Indeed, as far back as April 1948, Assistant Secretary of State for Economic Affairs Willard Thorp had warned: "To the extent that [European] countries expend their scarce economic resources on armament production they will have proportionally less to devote to civilian production, and their dependence on us for assistance in the form of civilian goods will be thereby increased and prolonged." [31] And in an early December 1948 message to the Office of the U.S. Special Representative in Europe (OSR), Acting Secretary of State Lovett admitted that "a rearmament will require some increase in [Western Europe's] domestic expenditures for military purposes" and "will call for some diversion of resources from recovery programs." Lovett quickly added, however, that "economic recovery must not be sacrificed to rearmament and must continue to be given clear priority"; and he instructed that "Western European countries should not be permitted to formulate a program of rearmament of substantially larger dimensions than the European or U.S. economies could support." [32]

Nevertheless, in late September 1950, barely two and a half years after the start of the recovery program, the Europeans were formally advised by ECA that an increasing portion of U.S. assistance would henceforth be earmarked for rearmament. [33] They were told, moreover, that defense needs may well require a substantial diversion of their own economic resources from civilian to military production, as well as the imposition of controls on the use of such resources. And they were instructed, accordingly, to prepare a careful appraisal of the impact of rearmament programs on their individual economies and of the problems that may arise therefrom. [34] To judge from the evidence, the last quarter (September–December) of 1950 did, in fact, mark the beginning of a basic change in the direction and use of ERP aid. This change was clearly reflected in ECA's own official reports to Congress for the two quarters ending on December 31, 1950, and March 31, 1951, respectively. On these occasions, the agency openly acknowledged that at least part of ERP aid "[was] being used to stimulate defense production in Western Europe" and that the European aid programs were being continuously adapted to the task of securing for Western Europe "the added economic strength needed to advance its defense mobilization [efforts]." [35] And in its last quarterly report (for April–June 1951), it frankly stated that its primary aim was "to help Western Europe rearm within the framework of an expanding economy. . . ." [36]

In any event, if there is one fundamental lesson implicit in the foregoing discussion, it is this: Neither the collective aid allocations by the OEEC nor the increasing emphasis on defense-oriented assistance, from 1950 on, could, in retrospect, be considered a helpful contribution to the efforts aimed at increasing European production. The former because they were geared to overall balance-of-payments considerations rather than to direct requirements of specific production projects; the latter because it implied the diversion of economic resources from the originally stipulated production goals. It is worth observing this lesson, for it bears on the Europeans' commitment to "a strong production effort." That commitment, as noted earlier in this chapter, was to be given concrete expression by the fulfillment of the production targets, set forth in the CEEC report and in subsequent OEEC program reports. But the achievement of the "huge production programme," stipulated in the CEEC report and reiterated later, was predicated on certain assumptions. And as we turn to examine how, and to what extent, the basic commitment would be honored, it must be kept in mind that many of the assumptions on which it was based lost their validity within a fairly short time after they had been made.

Increased Production: 6
Expectations, Constraints, and Accomplishments

In their report on the first annual program, submitted to the ECA in mid-October 1948, the OEEC nations repeated the basic theme by declaring that "increased production is the touchstone of economic recovery."[1] That report, as seen earlier (Table 5), contained a series of projected increases in production during 1948–1949. The participating countries were moved to note, however, that the report, as it stood, "is, no doubt, imperfect" and that, in any event, "the obstacles [to recovery] are such that many of them cannot be disposed of during the period covered by an annual programme."[2] Accordingly, they cautioned against expectations of "rapid results from the application of the European Recovery Programme" and warned that "the expansion of production and the increase of exports, particularly to the Western Hemisphere, will take time."[3] In conclusion, they pointedly stated that, due to the effects of the war, "there are still certain economic weaknesses which will continue to exist . . . over the next four years."[4]

This sober retreat from the seemingly confident pronouncements of the CEEC report a year earlier was, in large measure, a reflection of a much more realistic appraisal of Europe's economic problems and the magnitudes of the efforts needed to overcome them. Yet perhaps a more telling reason behind the cautious tone of the first-year's program report may be found in a European concern that adverse economic or political developments, on one hand, and changing American attitudes and policy considerations, on the other, may well prevent them from fulfilling on schedule the officially declared American expectations— specifically, to achieve, by the year 1952–1953, a viable and healthy European economy, "independent of extraordinary outside assistance." That this concern was real was strongly implied some two and a half months later, when the OEEC submitted its *Interim Report on the Euro-*

pean Recovery Programme. Intended to serve as a basis for the formulation of a long-term joint plan of action, the report identified and critically examined various problems that would have to be tackled in the course of the recovery process. It also projected an aggregate increase, above prewar levels, of 30 percent in industrial production and 15 percent in agricultural production, by 1952. But what distinguished this report from its two predecessors was an explicit reference, at the very outset, to seven basic hypotheses, or assumptions, upon whose validity the achievement of the stipulated goals had been predicated. Four of those assumptions are particularly instructive, for they clearly indicate the Europeans' preoccupation with possible future turns of events and their implications for the recovery program.

Thus, in the report's own words, "the first and most important assumption underlying all the [national] programmes is that there will be peace." Even a continuing deterioration of the international political situation, the report solemnly observed, "would certainly lead to so great a diversion of resources from recovery as would interfere with the programmes and *postpone* the date of their successful execution."[5] Second, the report assumed that "a high level of employment will continue throughout the world and particularly in the United States." All calculations of possible exports to the United States and of the general level of economic activity throughout the world, the report continued, "would be affected by a reduction in the level of demand in the United States." Third, all of the participating countries assumed that "there will be a high level of world trade. . . ." Finally, the participating countries "have assumed that the generous assistance being provided by the United States to assist the recovery of Western Europe will continue for the next three years on a sufficient scale." Without such assistance, the report asserted, "none of the [national] programmes would be possible in their present form."

As will be seen below, quite a few additional assumptions—some specific, others more general—underlined the interim projections submitted by the OEEC countries in late December 1948. But it is worth noting here that even before any of the assumptions could be properly tested, the OEEC had already concluded that "it is improbable" that the national programs "can be implemented in full during the next three and a half years." This was so, the *Interim Report* conceded, because "the total achievements which [are] implied by all the programmes taken together add up to more than is likely in practice to be realized." Hence, the year 1952–1953 should not be regarded as the "end of the recovery story," but rather as "no more than a point on an upward curve."[6]

What was to be the practical nature of this "recovery story" would soon become apparent.

I

Back in April 1948, shortly after the ECA had taken up its duties but before Congress appropriated the funds for the first year of the ERP, an official of the Budget Bureau offered a simple and straightforward working definition of "European recovery." Recovery, he stated in a memorandum to the budget director, can be defined in terms of consumption standards to be reached by 1952.[7] The actual quantities of commodities required to meet those standards, he went on to suggest, could, in turn, be divided between those to be produced domestically in Europe and those that must be imported. Consequently, the specific production goals, set for each participating country, should aim at (1) increasing domestic production to the maximum and (2) providing enough goods for export to pay for the balance of necessary imports.[8] Here, in a nutshell, lay the essential purpose of a "strong production effort" within the context of Europe's economic recovery. It was: To increase the availability of domestically produced consumption goods and thereby reduce European dependence on certain dollar imports; and to increase export earnings so as to progressively bring into balance Europe's external accounts and reduce its sizable payments deficit with the Western Hemisphere (i.e., the dollar area).

There was, of course, an element of irony in this concept of recovery. For, to the extent that increased European production would simultaneously lead to a replacement of dollar imports and an expansion of exports to the United States and third markets, it would pose a potential threat to both U.S. exporters and producers of import-competing goods. Indeed, by aiding Western Europe to modernize and increase its production through the ERP, the U.S. government could well have been open to the charge that it was using American taxpayers' money to undermine their own economic interests. That the point was not lost on special interest groups in the United States is evidenced by the many complaints directed at the ECA by a broad spectrum of American manufacturing interests during the ERP period. Such complaints, moreover, were often augmented by direct queries from members of Congress—queries that the ECA was called upon to answer.[9] Common to most of these complaints and queries was the perceived threat to American producers and exporters from increased European production, made possible and encouraged by the aid program.

But there were those who, after the first year of the ERP, raised a different sort of complaint. "At a time when the U.S. taxpayer is pouring out billions of dollars, in an unprecedented effort to increase Western European production," wrote one American observer in late August 1949, "cutbacks and layoffs are being effected in scores of industries in every country, because—thanks largely to their high price philosophy—Western European producers are not even able to sell the goods they already produce." [10] The implied question was clear: If European producers were having difficulties selling even in Europe itself, how could they be expected to compete effectively with American producers and increase their sales in the U.S. market? This question was explicitly answered, in early 1950, by another thoughtful observer who concluded that "the necessary expansion of United States imports [from Europe] would not be forthcoming," and therefore, the solution to Europe's dollar deficit would have to lie in continued American aid "during the next 5–10 years." [11]

The critical question, then, is: Did the actual performance of the OEEC countries as a group, during the first year of ERP, justify the above-mentioned concerns? Or, to put it quite specifically: Did the Europeans attain, by mid 1949, the production targets that they had set for themselves in the First Annual Program, back in the fall of 1948? In its own report to Congress for the quarter ending June 30, 1949, the ECA appeared to skirt this question. It singled out production accomplishments in a few industries but avoided any mention of most others. Thus, for example, the agency pointed to significant increases in steel and coal outputs during 1948–1949 as well as to great strides made in the production of cotton, rayon, and wool yarns; cement; and motor vehicles. [12] And although it admitted that the actual output of coal fell short of OEEC's goal by five million tons, it did not see fit to inform its congressional readers that steel output, for the same period, was also down by about one million metric tons from the projected target. [13] Nor did it acknowledge that the 8 percent increase in electric power output—to which it drew attention in its report—was actually lower than the OEEC's projected increase of 9 percent.

In retrospect, such omissions are quite understandable. For, judged in terms of OEEC's stipulated targets, the first year's production record was rather mixed. To be sure, by the end of the second quarter of 1949, total output was 15 percent greater than it had been a year earlier, and the overall index of European industrial production had risen by 18 percent above its prewar (1938) level. [14] But a comparison between the projected and actual increases in output for twelve important commodities reveals that only three of the targets had been exceeded; one target had been met head on; and eight targets had not been reached. (See Table 9.) To this it might be added that the hoped-for expansion of European exports to the United States during the same period proved to be short-lived. The record shows that while exports did rise between the second and fourth quarters of 1948, they declined sharply during the first two quarters of 1949. [15]

Given the circumstances under which the First Annual Program had

Table 9   Projected and Actual Increases in Output of Selected Commodities, 1948/49

Commodity	Projected increase over 1947	Actual increase over 1947
Bread grains	45%	42.1%
Coarse grains	12%	16.9%
Sugar beets	26%	40.1%
Coal	14%	12.7%
Pig iron	68%	62.8%
Steel	50%	46.7%
Lead (metal)	78%	61.0%
Zinc (metal)	45%	25.0%
Tin (ores)	38%	52.0%
Aluminum	37%	37.0%
Copper	16%	9.0%
Electric power	9%	8.0%

Source: For figures in column 1, Table 5.   Figures in column 2 have
    been computed from data in ECA, Fifth Report to Congress, p. 21;
    ECA, Country Data Book: All Participating Countries (March 1950),
    Tables IV-I and V-5; and OEEC, European Recovery Program; Second
    Report of the O.E.E.C. (Paris, February 1950), p. 265.

been prepared—as well as the generally recognized unreliability of long-range projections—one need not dwell on the observed discrepancies between the first-year's production projections and actual accomplishments. One may, indeed, be properly impressed by the fact that in five of the cases where targets had not been fulfilled (i.e., bread grains, coal, pig iron, steel, and electric power), the discrepancies were relatively small. On the other hand, it bears noting that the failure to attain many of the production targets for 1948–1949, and to achieve a sustained expansion of exports to the United States, could be partly attributed to the existence of several constraining factors over which the European countries had little or no control. Some of these constraints were temporary, while others turned out to be of long duration. But all of them, as will be seen next, had had an impact on the overall progress of the recovery program.

II

Perhaps the most severely felt constraint during the period covered by the First Annual Program was a product of the first postwar American recession. Between the fourth quarter of 1948 and the third quarter of 1949, the index of manufacturing production in the United States declined by 10 percent, contributing to a 5-percent drop in Gross National Product (GNP) and to a rise in the annual rate of unemployment, from 3.8 percent in 1948 to 5.9 percent in 1949.[16] The consequences of these developments for Europe's dollar-earning prospects can easily be imagined. Having assumed a continuing high level of economic activities in the United States, the Europeans found themselves faced with a shrinking American demand for imports. The aforementioned decline in European exports to the United States during the first and second quarters of 1949 was, of course, an inevitable result of this diminished demand. What might be noted here is that the 5-percent drop in GNP was accompanied by a 30-percent fall in the value of U.S. imports from the OEEC countries.[17] Moreover, while U.S. imports from Western Europe were declining, European imports from the United States were rising, thus widening the gap between Europe's dollar expenditures and dollar receipts. Indeed, the overall quarterly trade deficit of the OEEC countries with the United States rose from $700 million in the last quarter of 1948 to about $1.1 billion in the second quarter of 1949; and the proportion of Western Europe's dollar imports financed by dollar earnings fell from 23 percent for the year 1948 to 16 percent during the first two quarters of 1949.[18]

Interestingly enough, the rise in European imports from the United States was also a partial result of the U.S. recession. Faced with declining sales at home, American producers naturally looked to prospective ERP-financed purchases as the logical means by which to increase their sales abroad. And the ECA, for its part, appeared willing to oblige. Because the effects of the recession were felt more strongly in some parts of the country than in others, U.S. government agencies had been requested by the President to channel their purchases, whenever possible, to those areas where the unemployment rate exceeded 12 percent—so-called preference market areas. Now the ECA was not, strictly speaking, a procuring agency; it merely authorized and financed procurements by foreign governments, the latter presumably being free to choose from among different American suppliers. Yet as late as November 1948, U.S. Special Representative Averell Harriman instructed

ECA mission chiefs in Europe to collate and quickly forward to ECA's headquarters in Washington (ECA/W) information on bid invitations and purchasing intentions of the OEEC governments.[19] They were further directed to transmit to the respective governments the list of "preference market areas" but *not* to mention anything about "labor unemployment." Instead, the mission chiefs were advised to "explain to the foreign government that procurement in these areas might be more advantageous to the foreign purchaser . . . because . . . the companies in these areas are presently not operating at full capacity, and better delivery and better prices may [therefore] be obtained."[20]

The extent to which European governments did, in fact, respond positively to such an explanation is not ascertainable from available records. But the overall beneficial effects of ERP-financed shipments to Europe on the American economy during 1949 had been amply verified. Thus, for example, the ECA frankly admitted that "while the Marshall Plan was not needed in 1948 as a direct stimulant to [U.S.] exports . . . the continuation of the [aid program] in fiscal 1950 was important from the view of maintaining domestic employment."[21] More specifically: The "revival of the U.S. economy," in the second half of 1949, "might not have occurred if, just at the turning point [in the] summer, our exports had been cut back by eliminating Marshall Plan aid."[22] And from the august Federal Reserve Board of Governors came a supporting rejoinder. "One of the factors limiting declines in industrial production during the first half of 1949," the Board stated in January 1950, "was an *expanded* volume of exports under the [European] Recovery Program."[23] What remained *un*stated, however, was the fact that this expansion of exports, though unquestionably helpful to the U.S. economy, was not entirely in the best balance-of-payments interests of the OEEC countries at the time.

A far more lingering constraint on the recovery process stemmed from official U.S. attitudes and policies regarding East-West trade. The basic aim of these policies was to deny the Soviet Union and its satellites access to commodities that might contribute, directly or indirectly, to their military strength. And the main instrument for carrying out this aim was a system of export controls, administered by the U.S. Department of Commerce.[24] The latter was to determine which American products would be subject, at one time or another, to export license and to decide, in each case, whether the required license should be issued. It could thus prohibit altogether the exportation of certain items to specific countries.[25]

A detailed account of the evolvement of the U.S. export-control system during the postwar period falls outside the present discussion. It might merely be observed that, at least initially, the postwar continuation of export controls had been justified by the presumed need to protect the domestic economy from possible injury due to "adverse distribution of materials which continue [to be] in short world supply." (See Section 2(b) of the Second Decontrol Act of 1947.) But with the intensification of the Cold War there came a marked stiffening of congressional attitudes. Through a succession of legislative acts—the Export Control Act of 1949, the Kem amendment to the Third Supplemental Appropriation Act of 1951, and the Mutual Defense Assistance Control Act of 1951—Congress adopted an increasingly tougher posture toward East-West trade, leading to the progressive tightening of American export controls. And, in what was clearly intended as a move to persuade the prospective ERP-aid recipients to adopt export controls of their own, the Economic Cooperation Act had earlier directed the ECA Administrator "to refuse delivery . . . to participating countries of commodities which go into the production of any commodity for delivery to any nonparticipating European country, which commodity would be refused export license to those countries by the United States in the interest of national security." [26] In plain language, Congress served notice that it would not tolerate, much less encourage, the circumvention of U.S.-imposed controls by indiscriminate sales of European-produced goods to the Soviet Union and its satellites.

In order to appreciate the constraining impact of these congressional actions on the pursuit of ERP's main objectives, it is necessary to return briefly to the preparation of the CEEC report. While calculating the magnitudes of their prospective dollar deficits and estimating U.S. aid requirements, the CEEC nations had assumed that a substantial and steady revival of trade with Eastern Europe would occur during the four-year period. Specifically, they had proceeded upon the premise that an increasing portion of their needs for certain products—chiefly timber, coal, grains, meats, and fertilizers—could be obtained from East European sources in exchange for industrial and other manufactured goods. [27] Moreover, they estimated that, through such trade, they would not only be able to conserve dollars, but would actually earn additional dollars by maintaining a favorable balance of trade with the Eastern Hemisphere. [28] As it turned out, the expectations of dollar earnings did not materialize during the ERP period, for it was the East European countries that managed to develop export surpluses with their West European trading partners. (See Table 10 later in this chapter.) Still, the basic assumption of an expanding East-West trade had underlined both the production and the balance-of-payments projections contained in the CEEC report.

A similar assumption was made in 1948 by most of the national programs that provided the basis for OEEC's *Interim Report*. That document put the value of projected OEEC countries' imports from Eastern

Europe in 1952 at $2.2 billion, or two and a half times greater than it had been in 1947. It also singled out timber, coal, nonferrous metals, and several food products as the items in which the largest increases were expected to occur.[29] In its own early reports, the ECA appeared equally cognizant of the importance of Eastern Europe as a source of food and raw material supplies to the OEEC countries and as an outlet for their manufactured products. The agency readily admitted that, should the necessity arise, the United States and other countries could probably provide a great proportion of the raw materials required by Western Europe. But it was quick to point out that failure to maintain East-West trade in Europe would impose an added burden on the OEEC countries and, more importantly, would substantially increase the dollar cost of the recovery program.[30] In sum, both the OEEC and the ECA viewed East-West trade as a viable means of stimulating European production in general and reducing Western Europe's dependence on dollar imports in particular.

Accordingly, during its first year of operations the ECA pursued a deliberate policy of supporting the development of East-West trade in Europe. It did so mainly by issuing to the participating countries procurement authorizations for the purchase of East European commodities. By the end of December 1948, the agency had authorized a total of $31.6 million out of ERP funds for the purchase of coal from Poland, fertilizers from East Germany, and railway transport equipment (mainly freight cars) from Czechoslovakia and Hungary.[31] The latter authorizations, amounting to $20.4 million, were subsequently canceled, thereby reducing the total amount authorized during 1948 to $11.2 million. But during the first half of 1949, the ECA, without publicly mentioning the fact, authorized an additional sum of $4.7 million for the purchase of Polish coal and timber and lead from Yugoslavia.[32] All told, only $15.9 million worth of OEEC's imports from Eastern Europe had been financed through the use of ERP dollars by mid-1949. None were to be so financed during the remainder of the ERP period.

This is not surprising, given the basic economic premise on which the hoped-for expansion of East-West trade had been predicated. Such trade, after all, was supposed to be a means by which ERP dollars could be saved, not expended. And in any event, the bulk of postwar trade between Western and Eastern Europe was conducted within a framework of bilateral trade and payments agreements. Typically, these agreements specified the amounts of various commodities available for exchange and provided for reciprocal financial reimbursements and credit arrangements in the partners' own currencies.[33] Under the circumstances, the mere injection of ERP dollars into this trading system could not in itself have assured a significant expansion of East-West trade. The crucial factor determining the extent of such expansion was not the amount of dollars made available to finance OEEC's purchases of East European goods, but rather the availability of the goods themselves. Or, to put it differently: The magnitude of East-West trade was to be ultimately determined by the *production capabilities* of both East and West European countries and by their *willingness* to supply to each other increasing quantities of respectively desired commodities.

Here, in fact, lay the basic problem. For although East European production of coal, mainly in Poland, recovered fairly rapidly after World War II, that of timber and grains remained substantially below prewar levels as late as 1949. At the same time, increased domestic demand for these products—particularly grains—precluded their large exportation. Thus, two of the major commodities on whose importation from Eastern Europe the OEEC countries had counted were not available in significant amounts.[34] But even a sustained increase of Polish coal production was subject to certain constraints, one of which deserves special mention.

Back in April 1946, the then-provisional government of Poland had received credits totaling $40 million from the Export-Import Bank of Washington, for the purchase of locomotives and freight cars in the United States. In granting these credits, the Export-Import Bank significantly noted that their purpose was "to provide the means of transporting Polish coal to other European countries where coal is a prime requisite for reconstruction."[35] Later that year, Poland applied for a $600 million loan from the World Bank, to finance the reconstruction and expansion of its coal mining, iron and steel, textile, and transport industries.[36] This loan was not granted. But in the spring of 1947, after a series of discussions, Poland applied for a smaller loan, to be devoted exclusively to the reequipment of coal mining. As subsequently reported by the World Bank, a fact-finding mission had been sent to Poland and its visit was followed by further negotiations in Washington. These negotiations, according to the World Bank, failed to produce agreement on the terms of the loan and were suspended in late spring of 1948.[37]

What was not reported, however, was a curious behind-the-scenes maneuver on the part of the Bank's president, John McCloy, and the role played by the National Advisory Council on International Monetary and Financial Problems (NAC) and the ECA in this connection. While still discussing the loan with Polish representatives, McCloy posed a question to the ECA Administrator. Would the ECA, he wanted to know, make dollars available to the OEEC countries to purchase Polish coal, in an amount sufficient to discharge Poland's loan liabilities to the Bank? The matter was promptly taken up by the NAC which "agreed . . . that ECA should answer Mr. McCloy by means of a phone call [and state] that it could not give the assurance requested."[38] Whether such a call was, in fact, made is not publicly known. What *is* known is that ECA's formal reply, when it finally came, was, at best, noncommittal. In a letter to McCloy, written in mid-August, Paul Hoffman stated that "the proposed loan would promote the objectives of the ERP and that, within the limits of its own discretion, the ECA would be willing to provide dollars for the purchase of Polish coal." [39] But he was unable, he confessed, to take a "final position" on McCloy's inquiry at that time.

The practical contribution of this reply to the Bank's decision not to pursue the loan negotiations is obviously open to speculation. Equally speculative would be an attempt to assess the direct (or even indirect) effects of the failure to obtain the loan on future availabilities of Polish coal to the OEEC countries. Still, the record indicates that the impressive recovery of Polish coal production during the early postwar years slowed down between 1948 and 1949. It also shows that Polish coal exports to the OEEC countries during the critical first two years of the ERP were significantly lower than those anticipated by the CEEC report. [40]

The emphasis on coal is not without its reasons. Shortages of coal persisted throughout the ERP period despite great efforts to increase West European coal output. These shortages—and the necessity to import large quantities of high-priced American coal in 1948 and 1949—contributed to the high cost of European production and constituted a major bottleneck in the recovery process. True, in the beginning of

Table 10   Trade of OEEC Countries with Eastern Europe (Including USSR), 1947–52 (in $ millions, current F.O.B. values)

Year	Imports from Eastern Europe	Exports to Eastern Europe
1947	874	827
1948	1,275	768
1949	1,141	994
1950	1,036	925
1951	879	682
1952	991	739

Source: United Nations, Economic Survey of Europe 1948–49, p. 149; U.N. Economic Survey of Europe 1950–51, p. 111; and U.N. Economic Bulletin for Europe (November 1952), p. 37, and (July 1953), p. 28.

1950, the concern over coal shortages briefly gave way to fears that Western Europe might soon be confronted with the problem of disposing of surplus coal.[41] But the growing stress on defense and rearmament during 1950 and 1951 placed new and heavier demands on Western Europe's basic industries; and coal shortages again emerged as a major obstacle to increased production.

By that time, of course, the essential prerequisites for an *expanding* East-West trade had all but disappeared. The progressive tightening of export controls by the United States and its West European allies, matched by a steady integration of the East European economies with that of the Soviet Union, imposed a practical limitation on any expansion of normal commercial transactions between Western and Eastern Europe. Indeed, far from expanding, East-West trade declined after having reached a postwar peak in 1949. As seen in Table 10, the values of OEEC's imports from and exports to Eastern Europe fell during 1950 and 1951. And although a slight recovery occurred in 1952, the total value of East-West trade in that year was less than half of its prewar (1938) value and far below OEEC's earlier projections.

III

While neither the 1949 recession nor the increasingly stiff American position on East-West trade could have been foreseen in 1947 or early 1948, other potential constraints could easily have been inferred from the ERP legislation itself. To say this is not to suggest that Congress had deliberately thrown obstacles in the way of Europe's recovery progress. On the contrary, its intention had been to insure the most efficient use of American aid and a maximum effort on the part of the aid recipients. Indeed, the ECA had been designated as the guardian of this intention; and the agency—mindful of watchful congressional eyes—was often ruthless in requiring of the Europeans the performance promised to Congress. Yet the ECA itself was constrained by various conditions imposed by Congress, which, in turn, affected the very promises the Europeans were supposed to deliver.

Perhaps the most irritating of these conditions were the special-interest provisions noted earlier, in Chapter 4. Thus, for example, the requirement that at least 50 percent of ERP-financed cargo procured in the United States be shipped in American-flag vessels compelled the ECA to monitor, on a quarterly basis, the European countries' compliance with the rule and to impose financial penalties in case of violations.[42] No such violations occurred during 1948. But when Congress authorized the extension of the ERP for another year, it introduced a complication: It distinguished among three types of cargos—dry bulk, dry liner, and tanker—and insisted that the 50–50 rule be applied to each of them individually.[43] Additional paperwork notwithstanding, the ECA was duty bound to follow suit and was almost immediately confronted with the necessity of taking punitive measures.

Until that point, the responsibility for securing compliance with the rule had rested largely with the OEEC and was based essentially on voluntary cooperative measures taken by the participating countries themselves.[44] The ECA had earlier indicated, however, that if such measures did not produce the required results, a rigid system of controls would be instituted, under which percentage quotas for tonnage to be shipped in American-flag vessels would be established for individual countries. Moreover, the agency had made it clear that failure to meet such quotas would result in the disallowance of dollar payments for cargo carried in foreign-flag vessels in excess of 50 percent.[45] And this is precisely what the ECA was forced to do in the latter part of 1949, as a result of the amended version of the 50–50 rule. Ironically, in examining the records of cargo movements during the second quarter (April–June) of 1949, the agency found that 56.5 percent of the total tonnage of ERP-financed goods purchased in the United States had been carried in American-flag vessels—more than enough to meet the overall requirement. It found, moreover, that with respect to dry bulk and tanker cargos, the participating countries had also more than met the 50–50 rule (59.4 percent and 55.3 percent, respectively). On the other hand, the portion of dry liner tonnage carried in American vessels during the same period came to only 47 percent.[46] Accordingly, a quota system for dry liner cargo was shortly put into effect; and seven countries that had been found to be deficient in the utilization of U.S.-flag vessels were requested to reimburse the ECA, in dollars, for the transport cost of 48,395 tons of goods, previously shipped in foreign-flag carriers.[47]

The reaction of the OEEC, upon being informed of this action in early October 1949, was one of surprise and dismay—a reaction, incidentally, that was viewed as unwarranted by ECA/W.[48] What particularly irked the Europeans was the fact that ECA had arbitrarily set a value of $200 per ton as the rate at which reimbursement should be made. But when OEEC representatives took up the matter with ECA/W in late December they were told that this rate was irrevocable. They were advised, moreover, that reimbursement for the cost of 123,000 additional tons, previously shipped in foreign-flag vessels, would soon be requested.[49] Meanwhile, at a December 30 meeting of the OEEC Council, the British representative, Sir Edmund Hall-Patch, argued that the individual countries involved—including the United Kingdom— should refuse to make any payment to the ECA unless a collective decision to do so was reached by the OEEC. But it was soon discovered that Britain had, in fact, already paid its assessment, and the OEEC Council then agreed to instruct the other countries to do the same.[50]

This was the only time that the ECA found it necessary to press the 50–50 rule to such an extent. The lesson must have been well learned, for in all of its subsequent reports, the agency was able to certify that the shipping provisions had been met to its satisfaction. But the point of the story is that, by insisting on special treatment for U.S.-flag carriers, Congress had contributed to the creation of ill feelings on the part of the Europeans and, more importantly, to an inefficient use of dollar aid. Because American shipping charges were generally higher than those of foreign carriers, the substantial shipment of cargo in American vessels added an economically unjustified cost to the program. Indeed, the ECA itself estimated that the use of U.S.-flag vessels had resulted in an addition of $10 million to shipping costs during the first nine months of the ERP.[51] On the same occasion, the agency argued that the imposition of detailed rules and regulations would inevitably interfere with the normal operations of the private market for shipping services and would thus run counter to the congressional intent of maximum utilization of "private channels of trade."[52] But Congress would not budge, and the ECA remained saddled with the responsibility of overseeing the Europeans' adherence to the shipping provisions.

No less irritating than the 50–50 rule were the legislative provisions that governed the procurement of specific commodities in the United States. It may be recalled that Congress had directed the ECA Administrator to minimize the purchase, in this country, of goods considered to be in short supply and to maximize the purchase of surplus commodities. Included among the former were petroleum and petroleum products, farm machinery, steel and steel scrap, various nonferrous metals, and meat. Their exportation to the participating countries, under the ERP, was either specifically limited by law or controlled by the ECA in accordance with its own interpretation of the legislative intent.[53] Procurement of surplus agricultural commodities, on the other hand, was to be strictly confined to U.S. sources of supply—including certified surplus stocks held by the government—and the ECA Administrator was called upon to encourage the use of such commodities by the aid recipients.[54] Moreover, the Economic Cooperation Act authorized the Secretary of Agriculture to pay export subsidies of up to 50 percent of the sales price of surplus agricultural commodities procured for and shipped to the participating countries.[55]

What the Europeans thought of the agricultural procurement provisions was clearly revealed in periodic reports sent from Paris to Washington. Thus, for example, in the latter part of June 1948, having informally discussed with OEEC officials the availability of surplus commodities, Ambassador Caffery saw fit to advise ECA/W that "there is widely existing fear that U.S. wants to dump surpluses [on Europe]." [56] He went on to suggest that, in order to allay such fears, the ECA should make it clear that the intention is not to dump surpluses but "to work out [a] reasonable method of [using] U.S. surplus so as to preserve traditional patterns of U.S. trade without cutting across vital intra-European trade in the same surpluses." [57] Still, fears and suspicions had obviously persisted; for in early September, Averell Harriman circulated to ECA missions the text of a letter from OEEC Secretary-General Robert Marjolin, in which Marjolin expressed distinct reluctance to commit the OEEC countries to automatically buy surplus agricultural products in the United States.[58] And in late December, Harriman frankly acknowledged that "the feature of the [Economic Cooperation] Act viewed with greatest suspicion, is that regarding surplus agricultural commodities." [59] Referring, in this particular instance, to France, he added: "Marked coolness [is] always displayed, even in government circles, when suggestions [are] tactfully made that France may be interested in programming for certain commodities from dollar sources, which are not regarded [by France] as necessities." [60]

Harriman may not have fully realized the significance of his observation, but, in fact, his report inadvertently touched upon the essence of the problem, as perceived by the Europeans. To them, the basic issue was not dumping per se, but the legitimate concern that the procurement provisions mandated by Congress would interfere with and infringe upon their prerogative to plan their own import programs. Thus, any suggestion by the ECA that the Europeans might wish to purchase certain American agricultural products—simply because these had been declared to be in surplus by the U.S. Secretary of Agriculture—was bound to be met with coolness, if not outright resentment. In fact, even the ECA soon came to recognize that its refusal to authorize offshore purchases of commodities declared to be in surplus could on occasion impose undue burdens on individual European countries and limit their freedom of economic action.[61]

It should be clearly understood that neither the shipping nor the agricultural-procurement provisions (and practices) are presented here as major causes of a slower-than-planned recovery progress. In themselves, these provisions did not prevent, or even retard, the eventual achievement of the projected aggregate increases in Western Europe's industrial production. What *is* being suggested, however, is that the continued congressional insistence on safeguarding private American interests imposed an unnecessary constraint on both the ECA and the OEEC governments in the formulation of what they may have perceived to be proper economic decisions and programming needs.

Still another congressionally inspired constraint was the requirement that the ECA consult with the NAC in making certain financial decisions. Specifically, Congress had mandated that the disposition of counterpart funds arising out of ERP grant aid must be approved by the ECA Administrator "in consultation" with the NAC.[62] On its face, this provision appeared harmless enough, but in practice it had serious implications. For by involving the NAC in what were to be day-to-day operational decisions, Congress had imposed an added burden on the ECA. Not only did the agency have to bargain with the participating countries over the merits of particular activities and projects for which release of counterpart funds had been requested or proposed, but it was obliged to secure the consent of the NAC before actually approving such releases. And since the NAC did not necessarily share ECA's views on all matters pertaining to the ERP, its speedy and unqualified consent could not always be taken for granted.[63]

The potential for conflict over the use of counterpart funds, as well as ERP dollar resources in general, may be best considered in light of ECA's own view of its role in aiding Europe's production effort. To many responsible observers, increased production was essentially a function of increased capital formation. Hence, American aid was regarded primarily as a means of enabling the participating countries to sustain high rates of investment without being forced into unacceptable reductions in current living standards. Put differently: To expand their production, European countries would have to continue to undertake capital investment at rates that could not be sustained by existing levels of domestic savings. Dollar grants and loans extended under the ERP would thus provide the supplementary resources needed to acquire both consumption goods and capital goods. Indeed, on the assumption that American assistance would continue on an adequate scale during the four years, the national programs of the OEEC countries had targeted annual investment rates averaging 20 percent of Gross National Product. And during the ERP period itself, some countries, notably the Scandinavian nations, achieved investment rates approaching, and in one case exceeding, 30 percent of GNP.[64]

By late September 1949, however, the ECA had come to the view that the success of the production effort depended not only on the *total* amounts of resources allotted for capital expenditures but, more importantly, on the proper *direction* of investment flows. Consequently, from then on, the agency tried, with varying degrees of success, to influence the flow of investment funds in directions that, in its view, would contribute most to the recovery and expansion of production. And in pursuit of this operational objective, it came to rely heavily on its statutory authority over the disposition of counterpart funds. For, theoretically, its power to approve the release of counterparts could enable the ECA to channel these local-currency funds to projects it deemed desirable or, conversely, to prevent their use for those it considered unsound.[65] Moreover, it could encourage counterpart expenditures on specific projects by initiating proposals of its own and discreetly presenting them to the participating countries for their consideration. Yet all its decisions pertaining to the release and use of counterpart funds were subject to scrutiny by and approval of the NAC.

Out of a total $7.6 billion worth of counterpart funds released by the ECA during the ERP period, some $4.8 billion had been earmarked for investment purposes. Of these, $1.9 billion, or 37 percent, had been approved for the development and expansion of utilities, transportation, and communication facilities; $774.7 million for manufacturing; $693.5 million for agriculture; $584.4 million for housing; $485.6 million for extractive industries; and $378.1 million for other production activities.[66] Technical-assistance and productivity programs had also been partly financed by counterpart funds, although the actual amounts involved were relatively small.[67] These statistics may suggest a certain order of priorities, in ECA's thinking, concerning the most effective use of counterpart funds for the promotion of production. But they mask the fact that about $1 billion worth of accumulated counterpart deposits legally belonging to the participating countries had not been released at all by the time the ERP came to its official end.[68] Nor do they reveal that over 25 percent of the counterparts earmarked for use by the U.S. government (the so-called 5-percent counterparts) had been committed by the ECA either to direct purchases of strategic materials for U.S. stockpiling or to the development of overseas sources of strategic-material supplies—usages that were, at best, peripheral to the main production effort.[69]

But apart from using its authority over the release of counterparts, the ECA sought to influence investment decisions through direct project financing. Introduced in November 1948, the so-called Industrial Projects Program was designed to elicit from the participating countries applications for support of large-scale projects which, if approved by the agency, would be financed by a combination of ERP dollars and local funds.[70] Underlying this approach was the proposition that by holding out the carrot of dollar financing, the agency might induce the participating countries to allocate larger amounts of local resources to projects deemed by it to be critical to the recovery progress. In fact, in early October 1949, ECA missions were instructed by Washington to identify "critical sectors" in individual countries and to influence European investment decisions in these sectors.[71]

Interestingly enough, a critical sector was defined by ECA/W as one "where (a) something really needs to be done with respect to investment, and (b) the ECA can reasonably expect to accomplish something if it concentrates effectively the necessary degree of bargaining power." [72] This was, to say the least, as broad a definition as it was vague. Yet here again the ex post evidence suggests a definite ranking of priorities—a ranking not too dissimilar from the one applied to the release of counterparts. Thus, as of June 30, 1951, the ECA had approved a total of 139 projects under its Industrial Projects Program. The aggregate cost of these projects was estimated at the equivalent of $2.25 billion, of which $565 million represented dollar financing. [73] More than half of the *total* cost was accounted for by manufacturing projects (56 percent), followed by projects in utilities, transportation, and communication (24 percent) and in extractive industries (11 percent). The major portion of ERP-dollar financing was directed to manufacturing projects (61 percent) and to utilities, transportation, and communication (30 percent). [74]

There remains one other aspect of investment activities that should be briefly noted. While authorizing public assistance for European recovery, Congress had also enacted certain measures designed to induce private American investors to add their contributions to those provided by the ECA. The Economic Cooperation Act empowered the ECA Administrator to extend to U.S. citizens and/or business enterprises, "guaranties . . . of investments in connection with projects approved by the Administrator and the participating country concerned as furthering the purposes of [the Act]." [75] But, true to form, Congress introduced two limitations into this provision. It imposed a ceiling of $300 million on the total value of guaranties to be extended, and it limited the amount of local currency earnings that could be transferred back into dollars to the sum initially invested. [76] Still, the investment-guaranty provision could have been viewed at the time as a reasonable attempt to attract private U.S. capital and know-how to Europe and thus provide the participating countries with additional resources that could be channeled, under ECA's influence, to proper usages.

Actual results, however, proved to be quite disappointing—and for good reason. American firms, regarding postwar business conditions in Europe as unsettled, were generally reluctant to risk large amounts of their capital in European ventures. Nor were they particularly anxious to undergo the tedious process of having their projects examined and approved by both the ECA and the respective European governments. In fact, most of the companies to show an active interest in the guaranty program were ones that had already gained considerable business experience in Europe, either through their operation of established plants abroad or by exporting activities. As of the end of December 1948, only one industrial investment guaranty, worth $850,000, had been approved by the ECA. [77] And by the following December, the cumulative value of guaranties issued amounted to a mere $3.8 million.

All told, only thirty-eight industrial guaranties, totalling $31.4 million, were approved and issued during the ERP period, the largest a $13.9 million guaranty to Standard Oil Company, to establish oil refining facilities in Italy.[78] In short, of the $300 million originally authorized by Congress for this purpose, only 10 percent had actually been utilized.

So much for externally imposed constraints. We must now turn to a constraint that was indigenous to Western Europe itself, and the ways in which it was tackled.

IV

It may be recalled that on the basis of the national programs, submitted to it in late 1948, the OEEC projected an aggregate increase above the prewar (1938) level of 30 percent in industrial production and 15 percent in agricultural production, by 1952.[79] When it presented these projections, the Organization cautioned that the achievement of the goals set forth in the national programs was "conditional on an increase of some 15 percent in output per man hour [read: productivity] during the next four years." And it added: "This is a bold assumption. Yet no other assumption is more important."[80]

Bold it was, indeed. For an assumption of a 15-percent aggregate increase in productivity from 1948 to 1952 implied *annual* gains averaging 3½ percent—a rate that was, according to at least one knowledgeable observer, twice as high as the long-term productivity trend in industrial countries.[81] In 1948, moreover, the index of industrial output per man-year in all but two of the OEEC countries was either the same as or actually lower than in 1938.[82] And even by the end of 1949, industrial output per man-year, as measured against the prewar level, was still about the same in four countries and lower in four others. (See Table 11.) Low, or slowly rising, productivity thus constituted the most serious intra-European obstacle to the attainment of the projected expansion of production. It was an obstacle to whose removal the ECA, though somewhat belatedly, would devote considerable attention and energy.

Raising European productivity, however, proved to be a difficult and frustrating task. It required, in addition to investment in plant modernization and reequipment, a concerted effort to change business methods and attitudes. More importantly, it called for fundamental changes in traditional management-labor relationships in Europe, in order to secure their mutual cooperation in overcoming resistance to industrial innovations. Thus, ECA's mission, as it saw it, was to imbue European management *and* labor with a "productivity consciousness" by persuading both of these interest groups that they would stand to gain from increased productive efficiency.

Table 11   Industrial Output per Man-Year, in 1949, for Selected European Countries

Output per man/year compared to 1938	Countries
Higher	France, Ireland, Sweden, Switzerland, Turkey, United Kingdom
About the same	Belgium, Denmark, Greece, Norway
Rather lower	Netherlands
Considerably lower . . .	Austria, Italy, West Germany

Source: OEEC, European Recovery Program; Second Report of the O.E.E.C. (Paris, February 1950), p. 35.

The story of ECA's productivity drive is long and involved. It is a story of a campaign that began uncertainly during the latter part of 1948, did not gain momentum until mid-1949, and reached a significant level of activity only during 1950 and, especially, 1951. It is a story that continued beyond the ERP into the Mutual Security Program (MSP) period, when it acquired new dimension based on specific congressional directives.[83] Yet it is a story that can be summarized by its two operational themes: (1) to demonstrate to the Europeans the virtues of American production techniques and good management-labor relations and (2) to persuade the participating countries to establish national productivity centers, so as to provide concrete frameworks for cooperation between European management and labor.

The first and most visible cooperative venture of this sort—the Anglo-American Council on Productivity (AACP)—was created on the initiative of business and labor leaders from the United States and Great Britain and held its first meeting in October 1948.[84] Its main function consisted of planning, arranging, and evaluating visits of British industrial (or "productivity") teams to the United States. The AACP, it might be noted, was a unique institution; unlike the other productivity centers that were subsequently established on the Continent, its decision-making membership included formal representation by American business and labor.[85] Moreover, although it was neither an agency of the British government nor an official part of the ECA, its operating expenses were financed partly by the U.K. Treasury and partly by ECA's Technical Assistance funds. Its main virtue, however, lay in pioneering the use of what was to become ECA's major instrument of introducing European labor and management to American productive techniques and managerial know-how—namely, the visiting-team program.

Underlying this particular program was an intriguing, if not entirely novel, idea: that a proper appreciation of American productive efficiency and healthy labor-management relations could best be gained through direct on-the-spot observations. This could be accomplished, so went the argument, by organizing groups (or teams) of European managers, technicians, and workers and have them visit American factories. Back in their respective countries, such teams could reflect on their impressions and, wherever possible, apply their newly acquired insights to their own operations. And as more and more teams representing various European industries became exposed to the American experience, their collective impressions might help to break down traditional management-labor antagonism in Europe itself and facilitate the introduction of industrial improvements, leading to increased productivity.

Thus, in early 1949, the program was launched with visits to this country of a twenty-man Danish delegation and of a team representing the British steel foundry industry.[86] Slow and a bit uncertain at first, the pace of the visiting-team program progressively quickened and before long acquired a momentum of its own. A whole apparatus had been created to handle these visits: a field office in New York City, project managers, escort personnel, press and media liaison, and, later on, orientation centers in the United States. By the time the Mutual Security Agency (MSA) took over the administration of U.S. foreign assistance, a fairly solid foundation had been established for the continuation and expansion of this experiment in labor-management education. By that time, over a hundred industrial teams—some sixty from Great Britain alone—had been brought to the United States under the sponsorship of the ECA. In addition, American technical experts had been dispatched to Europe, while European managers and technicians had been brought to this country for special training. And all the while, American organized labor, working through the offices of Labor Advisers both in ECA/W and in ECA missions abroad, had pursued its own campaign of educating European labor in the virtues of collective bargaining as one of the means of increasing productivity.[87]

Yet despite all these activities, the productivity campaign was not to be decisively won during the ERP period. As late as 1951, the ECA was still searching for ways by which to spread its productivity gospel more effectively. The agency, confided an OSR official in January of that year, "can anticipate to be given shortly the responsibility of making a far greater effort to raise the level of industrial productivity in Western Europe than our Technical Assistance has so far been asked or equipped to make."[88] And from ECA/W there followed, two months later, a series of new suggestions for "sustained programs of productivity exhibits and demonstrations" as part of an intensified productivity drive during 1951.[89] But in September of that year, realistic voices within the agency acknowledged that "productivity, being a complex economic concept, may be difficult to dramatize for the European press" and that, in any event, "productivity is difficult to sell because of the opposition of certain segments of management and labor."[90] A much harsher commentary on the difficulties involved had been offered even earlier, in reference to ECA's efforts in Italy. "We have spent hundreds of millions of dollars in Italy," wrote John T. Quinn, "but do not seem to have changed its social structure to an extent which should now permit us to attack and increase its industrial productivity incisively and directly."[91]

Quinn was not alone in decrying ECA's failure to change social structures—or, more precisely, socioeconomic attitudes—in European countries and its impact on the agency's productivity program. In late December 1951, the Director of ECA's Information Program, Robert Mullen, expressed discouragement with the slow progress of the productivity campaign and voiced particular concern about "the apparent inability [of some ECA officials] to grasp how vital it is to work on European attitudes."[92] But barely a month later, he himself was obliged to admit that the attempts to change such attitudes, through ECA's productivity advertising campaign in Europe, had run into "quite a bit of [local] resistance." As a case in point, he cited the clear objections of the British government to, as he put it, "outsiders [coming] in and advertise and talk to their people."[93] Mullen could easily have added, though he did not, that in the fall of 1951 the Belgians, for reasons of their own, had also shown a distinct lack of enthusiasm for the ECA's Productivity Assistance Program.[94] And he might well have explained, though again he did not, that perhaps the major reason for the reluctance of Europeans, in general, to adopt improved productive techniques, à la the American model, lay in their widely held fears that increased productivity would lead to labor unemployment or underemployment.[95] Such fears, as well as the traditional European workers' distrust of overly mechanized production processes, could not easily be overcome. Nor could European producers—accustomed to fairly narrow markets, relatively low volumes of output, and general lack of price competition and subject to a host of government regulations—be readily converted to the American doctrine of increased productivity, based on technological and managerial innovations. Yes, Mullen was quite right: It *was* vitally important for the ECA to work on European attitudes. But a fairly modest informational program—however attractively packaged—could not possibly change deeply rooted attitudes and practices overnight or create incentives where none were perceived to exist.[96]

Indeed, when viewed in retrospect, the entire Technical Assistance Program—including the productivity drive—turned out to be quite modest in scope. It was an undertaking for which a total of $34 million in ERP-dollar funds had been authorized—but only $18 million actually expended—by December 31, 1951.[97] Of these amounts, about $18 million had been authorized (and $7.4 million actually spent) for industrial productivity projects and $5.2 million authorized (and $3.1 million spent) for raising agricultural productivity.[98] It was an undertaking, moreover, that did not get off the ground until well into the second year of the ERP, and moved into high gear only during its last few months.[99] Finally, it was an undertaking that even at its peak level of activities was still beset by conflicting views on desirable tactics, duplication of efforts, hazy lines of operational responsibility, and lack of a clear vision.[100] Such a program could hardly perform a miracle within the space of three and a half years.

V

The measure of the accomplishments of ECA's Productivity Program was perhaps best summed up by the OEEC Secretary-General. "The Marshall Plan," he told an interviewer in late 1952, "has raised productivity during four years. But it hasn't created a basis for permanent increase in productivity." The Europeans, he added, "have not yet created a system in which production is naturally expanding." [101]

"Naturally" or not, European production did, in fact, register a significant expansion during the ERP period; and this expansion was due, in large measure, to impressive gains in productivity.[102] By the end of 1951, the target of a 30 percent aggregate increase in industrial production had actually been surpassed. The index of industrial production for all participating countries, including West Germany, had risen by 35 percent above the 1938 level. Exclusive of West Germany, industrial production surpassed the prewar level by 45 percent. As seen in Table 12, production achievements varied from country to country. Yet in all cases save those of West Germany and Greece, the individual gains, as measured by the index for 1951, exceeded the aggregate target itself.

Expansion of agricultural production, on the other hand, proved to be somewhat slower. To be sure, aggregate agricultural output increased by nearly 30 percent during the three crop years 1948–1949, 1949–1950, and 1950–1951. And in its last quarterly report to Congress, the ECA was able to state that due mainly to this increase in

Europe's domestic production, the prewar levels of food consumption had been virtually reached by 1951.[103] But the target set by the OEEC in 1948—namely, a 15 percent increase in aggregate agricultural production above the prewar level—was not quite reached. In the crop year 1950–1951, the index of agricultural output for human consumption stood at only 11 percent above its prewar level, thus necessitating continued maintenance of substantial food and feedstuff imports. Here,

Table 12   Indices of Industrial Production in Western Europe, 1948/51 (1938 = 100)

Country	1948	1949	1950	1951
Austria	85	114	134	148[a]
Belgium	122	122	124	143
Denmark	135	143	159	160
France	111	122	123	133
W. Germany	50	72	91	106
Greece	76	90	114	130
Ireland	135	154	170	176[b]
Italy	99	109	125	143
Luxemburg	139	132	139	168[a]
Netherlands	114	127	140	147
Norway	125	135	146	153
Sweden	149	157	164	172
Turkey	154	162	165	163[a]
United Kingdom	120	129	140	145
All participating countries	99	112	124	135
All participating countries, exclusive of W. Germany	119	130	138	145

Source: First Report to Congress on the Mutual Security Program, p. 75.

[a] Average of first three quarters of 1951

[b] Average of first two quarters of 1951

Table 13   Indices of Total Agricultural Output for Human Consumption in OEEC Countries, 1948/49–1950/51 (prewar = 100)

Country	1948/49	1949/50	1950/51
Austria	66	79	88
Belgium–Luxemburg	93	116	119
Denmark	92	113	126
France	100	103	111
W. Germany	76	96	106
Greece	79	110	93
Ireland	88	95	103
Italy	95	103	109
Netherlands	93	116	119
Norway	92	112	120
Sweden	111	115	116
Switzerland	98	98	104
Turkey	120	94	106
United Kingdom	111	114	122
All participating countries	95	104	111

Source: OEEC, Statistical Bulletin (Paris, May 1952), p. 66.

too, variations in performance can be observed among the different participating countries. As seen in Table 13, the largest advance, in absolute terms, was made by the United Kingdom, whose agricultural output had climbed to 22 percent above the prewar level. At the other end of the scale were Austria and Greece, whose domestic agricultural production as late as 1951 failed to reach prewar levels.[104]

How is one to assess the significance of this statistical evidence within the context of ERP's basic objectives? An assessment of sorts was offered by a high ECA official not long after the ERP had ended. "Our general conclusion from the Marshall Plan," he observed, "is that we emphasized production—and generally succeeded—but without enough attention to the *composition* of the production."[105] And perhaps that is all that one could say about an objective whose fulfillment was to be measured essentially in quantitative terms. For as originally conceived, the primary economic objective of the recovery program was, indeed, an increase in Europe's production. In monitoring the progress of the program, Congress demanded concrete results; and these could best be demonstrated by quantitative aggregates rather than qualitative details. A commitment to "a strong production effort" had been made by the Europeans. And, to the extent that OEEC's aggregate production targets had been reached or surpassed, by the time the program ended, that particular objective could be said to have been fulfilled.

The Quest for Internal Financial and Monetary Stability

If a strong production effort was to constitute the primary economic element of the recovery program, the creation and maintenance of internal financial stability was to run a close second. The success of the four-year program, the CEEC nations had declared in the fall of 1947, "depends on internal economic financial and monetary stability being restored, or maintained." The production targets, they had gone on to state, "cannot be achieved nor can European co-operation be accomplished unless the economies of all the participating countries are sound and stable." [1] And in the following spring, during the hearings on his nomination, the ECA Administrator-designate appeared to be in full agreement. Having told the members of the Senate Foreign Relations Committee that he would keep his eyes on "one goal, . . . increased production," he hastened to add: "At the same time I want to be sure that the [European] economies are sound from a fiscal monetary standpoint." [2]

I

The preoccupation with fiscal soundness and monetary stability was a reflection of existing realities. In the three years following the end of World War II, practically all of the prospective ERP countries had been plagued by inflationary pressures which reduced the purchasing powers of their currencies, diminished economic incentives, and hampered orderly market relations. Attributed to shortages of consumer goods supplies on one hand and large liquid-asset holdings on the other, these pressures were further reinforced by inflationary methods of financing government budget deficits. Indeed, even before the advent of the ERP, several European countries had already introduced monetary reforms designed to reduce cash balances held by the public and to keep capital expenditures within limits set by balance-of-payments conditions and existing levels of savings. In some countries, part of the money supply was wiped out, blocked, or absorbed by forced loans, in an effort to rid the economy of excess liquidity.[3] Yet by 1948, both wholesale and retail prices in most West European countries had risen well above their pre-war levels (see Table 14), threatening in some cases complete distrust in the national currencies involved.

Table 14   Wholesale Price and Cost-of-Living Indices in 1948 (1948 index measured as percentage of 1938 average)*

Country	Wholesale price index	Cost-of-living index
Austria	469	378
Belgium	389	394
Denmark	227	166
France	1,712	1,250
Germany (Bizone)	155	151
Greece	30,500	215
Iceland	–	322
Ireland	232	182
Italy	5,422	5,844
Netherlands	276	204
Norway	182	159
Portugal	240	190
Sweden	194	154
Switzerland	218	164
Turkey	466	346
United Kingdom	216	172

Source: Tables 32 and 33, in ECA, Recovery Guides, No. 14. June, 1950, pp. 154–55.

*It should be noted that the actual base periods for computing these indices vary for some countries. For details, see the notes following the tables in the original source.

It was a situation whose political, as well as economic, implications were clearly recognized and appreciated by official and private observers on both sides of the Atlantic.[4] And it is not surprising, therefore, that the CEEC nations, under strong American urging, solemnly pledged themselves to carry out stabilization programs "in a spirit of determination." In particular, they promised "to carry out . . . internal measures within their power in fiscal and currency matters, . . . with the purpose of restricting forthwith calls on [their banks] of issue and other inflationary practices."[5] Although the exact nature of these measures was not specified, the intended objective of the stabilization programs was made quite clear: to reestablish an equilibrium between purchasing power and available commodities, and to achieve balanced government budgets. But once again, the attainment of the stated objectives was made conditional on receipt of adequate external assistance. Such assistance, it was reasoned, "will contribute to rapid stabilization by assuring an adequate flow of imports so as to balance the national income and national outlay of the participating countries at a supportable level of consumption." In this way, the CEEC report concluded, "the financial and monetary bases for a sound economy can be rapidly re-established in Europe."[6]

Just how rapidly monetary stability would be restored was a question that neither the Europeans nor the Americans could venture to answer in the fall of 1947. Nor, for that matter, was a precise definition of "stability" even offered at the time. But in formulating the ERP legislation, the Administration, as well as Congress, took care to remind the prospective aid recipients of their obligations in this matter. Thus, in its Statement of Purposes, the Economic Cooperation Act formally called upon the participating countries to "[further] the restoration or maintenance of the soundness of European currencies, budgets, and finances."[7] And shortly after the passage of the legislation—at the insistence of the Administration—the CEEC nations reiterated their previously stated multilateral pledges, this time giving them a legally binding status. Meeting in Paris in mid-April 1948, they signed a Convention for European Economic Cooperation, one of whose provisions obligated each of the contracting parties to "take such steps as lie within its power to achieve or maintain the stability of its currency, and of its internal financial position, sound rates of exchange, and, generally, confidence in its monetary system."[8]

To what extent this obligation would be honored by individual European countries still remained to be seen. But even in the spring of 1948, there were those who felt that the adoption of proper stabilization measures, and especially the prompt balancing of government budgets, could not be left entirely to European initiative and zeal. Hence, whether they liked it or not, the European governments would have to be helped along. "The success or failure of the whole program," observed Professor Gottfried Haberler at the time, "will depend, more than anything else, on the ability of the [ECA] Administrator to push through monetary and financial reforms."[9] And from one of Haberler's close academic colleagues came a similar, though much more blunt, assessment of ECA's potential role in Europe. "If European recovery is to be effectively promoted," wrote Edward Mason, "we shall find it necessary to lay down conditions which will be felt to be extremely onerous. Recrimination on both sides will, therefore, be inevitable."[10]

"Recrimination" may have been too strong a word with which to predict future relations between aid donors and recipients. But it nevertheless captured the flavor of things to come.

II

In late April 1950, at a monthly meeting of the Council on Foreign Relations' Study Group on Aid to Europe, the evening's distinguished guest, Averell Harriman, was asked to comment, among other things, on the following two questions: What do our friends in Europe dislike about the way the Marshall Plan is being handled? and, Do they feel that the United States is going too far in interfering with [their] domestic policies?[11] As recorded by the rapporteur, this was the essence of his reply:

When he had first come to Paris in 1948, Mr. Harriman began, the results of communist propaganda were very much in evidence and "the French feared that we were going to take over their country. Because of this attitude, we started very cautiously and for some time did not take any strong positions." Since then, however, "we have put on pressure—a great deal of it aimed at *forcing sound fiscal policies*—and we have not been entirely free from blame for this pressure."[12]

Coming from no less a person than the U.S. Special Representative in Europe, such a statement was highly instructive. In the first place, it clearly confirmed that the ECA had indeed engaged in deliberate attempts to shape fiscal-monetary policies in ERP countries. Second, it discreetly conceded that these actions had caused a fair amount of resentment on the part of the Europeans. And third, it identified at least one country, France, where political considerations had imposed some constraints on ECA's ability to effect a rapid introduction of what it perceived to be urgently needed fiscal measures. Harriman failed to mention, however, that the pace with which such measures could be realistically implemented had been tempered not only by political exigencies, but also by very real economic problems. Nor did he see fit to acknowledge that despite their supposed reluctance to take "any strong positions" overtly, ECA officials in Paris had, in fact, begun to apply pressures of various sorts on the French government, almost from the very inception of the ERP.

As will be seen shortly, France was, in many respects, a special case. Yet what was true of ECA's campaign to promote monetary and financial stability in that country was also true, in varying degrees, of its activities elsewhere in Europe. For, in a broad *operational* sense, most of ECA's battles against monetary and fiscal excesses rested on one common denominator: local-currency counterpart funds. Specifically, it was the authority to approve the release of counterparts that enabled the agency to exert pressures on European governments in an attempt to influence, directly or indirectly, their monetary and fiscal policies. It may be recalled that in granting this authority, Congress had stipulated that such funds should be "held or used," among other things, "for purposes of internal monetary and financial stabilization." [13] And this, in turn, seemed to imply that before approving the release of counterparts for *any* purpose, the ECA should carefully consider and assess the possible effects of such use on monetary and financial conditions in the country concerned. Thus, the administrative responsibility to approve the disposition of counterpart funds could theoretically become a tactical instrument—a device with which to force fiscal discipline and combat existing or potential inflationary tendencies. How this device was employed in practice may be illustrated by a few examples.

A particularly illuminating example is provided by ECA's initial experiences in France, where the local mission and the French government began negotiations on the use of franc counterpart funds in late June 1948. The French had earlier requested that a portion of previously accumulated counterparts be released to finance the *difference* between the currently required counterpart deposits and current receipts of the French government from the sale of commodities, furnished on a grant basis, in France. [14] This specific request was formally denied on June 3, 1948. [15] On the same occasion, the French were politely advised that the U.S. government "believe[d] that it would be appropriate at this time to review with the French government the steps which [the latter] is taking and plans to take, for the remainder of 1948, toward the creation and maintenance of internal financial stability in France." They were further informed that only on the basis of such a review would the U.S. government and the ECA Administrator "be prepared to consider . . . additional releases of [counterparts]." [16]

So much for diplomatic niceties! Tougher communications would follow later. But it is worth noting here that the negotiations over the utilization of franc counterparts were to be further complicated by another issue—namely, at what rate of exchange should the required local-currency deposits be computed in the first place? That the issue arose at all was due to the fact that, at the time, there existed in France not one but two legally sanctioned exchange rates between the dollar and the franc: an official rate of $1=F214 and a "free" market rate which hovered around a $1=F306 level. Moreover, even the official rate could not be regarded as the *par value* of the franc, as approved by the International Monetary Fund (IMF)—an institution of which France was, at the moment, a member in bad standing.[17] In the absence of an IMF-approved par value for a particular currency, the required counterpart equivalents of dollar grants received were to be computed on the basis of a conversion rate mutually agreed to by the ECA and the government concerned. But in France's case, agreement on such a rate was made doubly difficult by the existing foreign exchange regulations under which the official rate ($1=F214) applied to the purchase of certain imports, while both the official and "free" rate could apply to all other licensed trade transactions.[18] In effect, then, dollar grants, received by the French government, helped to finance the importation of commodities that were subject to different exchange rates when sold to French importers. And under the circumstances, a single conversion rate could not serve to measure the actual local-currency receipts generated by a given amount of dollar grant aid. Nor was this all. For while the French authorities, quite naturally, would have preferred to deposit counterparts on the basis of the official rate, it was clear to all concerned that the higher "free" rate reflected much more realistically the franc's true economic value in relation to the dollar.

A temporary compromise was reached in early June, whereby *two* separate conversion rates would be used to compute the required counterpart deposits: A rate of $1=F214.07 would be used for imported commodities subject to the official exchange rate, and an average between the official rate and the highest prevailing rate on the "free" market would apply to all other commodities.[19] Approved by the NAC, this arrangement was meant to cover only the second quarter (April-June) of 1948, after which a single conversion rate—based on an average between the official and "free" rates—would presumably apply across the board. Such a changeover, however, would have imposed on the French government an obligation to deposit all counterparts at a rate of $1=F262. And to ECA officials in Paris, it seemed clear that the "French at this time would have most serious difficulties in taking steps to deposit at the 262 rate within the framework of [their] commitment to halt recourse to inflationary financing."[20] Accordingly, they recommended to ECA/W and the NAC that the local ECA Mission be authorized "to accept the continuance of the present second-quarter arrangement"; and that the determination of an exchange rate for computing counterparts deposits after June 30, 1948, be simply included as "one of the questions in the [forthcoming] review of plans and programs of the French government in its efforts to achieve monetary stabilization." [21] They further suggested that an agreement to continue the second-quarter arrangement "should [obviously] refer to the desirability of a changeover at a later date." But they themselves, they added, frankly doubted "whether [a change to a rate of] 262 will be actually feasable before the end of the year." [22]

Underlying this assessment was the painful recognition that in order to meet counterpart-deposit requirements at the higher rate, the French authorities would surely have to resort to additional borrowing from the central bank. As it was, current government receipts fell woefully short of current expenditures, creating a serious budget deficit. The deficit would have to be financed either by further government borrowing—which was considered inflationary—or through the utilization of counterpart funds. And throughout the month of June, the French continued to press for release of counterparts to cover current government outlays, as well as to finance long-term investment projects. At first, American officials responded by reiterating their insistence on a "mutual review" of French plans to combat inflation, as a condition for considering the release of counterparts for any purpose. But they soon must have come to realize that neither the French cabinet nor the National Assembly was in a position to devise and adopt the fiscal measures needed to balance the budget within a short time. They, therefore, concluded—and so informed ECA/W—that a certain amount of counterparts would have to be utilized if all government outlays in 1948 were to be covered without recourse to inflationary financing. [23]

This conclusion did not, of course, prevent the ECA from pressing its case for a comprehensive revision of the French fiscal system and for an attack on excessive credit expansion. On the contrary, the agency now possessed an additional argument with which to persuade the French to hurry along: It suggested that the release of counterparts to finance officially planned investment projects—thereby freeing other revenues to cover current budgetary expenditures—would be made contingent on the formulation and adoption of an acceptable program of fiscal and monetary reforms. The alternative, from the French standpoint, would be to increase borrowing from the central bank—a course of action which would not only aggravate inflation, but would require, in the first place, parliamentary approval to raise the existing ceiling on the central bank's advances to the government. Yet precisely because of its concern that such a course might be forced on the French—and also, in part, because it wished to bolster the government's position in the National Assembly—ECA/Paris found itself in a dilemma: Although it kept insisting on a prompt adoption of realistic stabilization measures, it recognized that undue delay in approving counterpart releases may well lead to uncontrollable inflationary consequences.

Thus, in mid-September 1948, while the French National Assembly was debating a series of fiscal-monetary measures submitted by the government, David K. Bruce (Chief of ECA Mission in France) felt compelled to warn ECA/W that the "financial situation in France [is] headed for [a] tragic climax. . . ."[24] Unless checked soon, he continued, "inflation will destroy the gains painfully achieved during [the] first six months of 1948." And he followed this dire prediction by strongly recommending that release of counterparts be promptly approved by Washington (read: the NAC), on the condition that the French government's fiscal plan would be enacted by the National Assembly. His recommendation, Bruce concluded, had been cleared and endorsed by both Harriman and Ambassador Caffery "who join in urging immediate action."[25]

One week later, a much relieved Bruce was able to inform Washington that, "having been passed by the Assembly, fiscal measures now go to the Council and if all goes well should receive Assembly final action [shortly]."[26] In anticipation of such action, Bruce advised, the French had already drawn up an application for the release of counterparts during September and October and had outlined the purposes for which the funds were to be used. Specifically, they had requested that, in each of these months, "a sum not to exceed 45 billion francs" be released and assigned "to finance productive investments, carried out in conformity with the investment and equipment program adopted by the [government]."[27] The French were careful to point out that in determining the amount to be requested by them for October, proper account would be taken of any unanticipated revenues that might accrue to the government. And they formally agreed—no doubt at ECA's insistence—that "before November 15, 1948, the financial and general economic position of France again be reviewed by . . . representatives of the two governments . . . [in order] to provide a basis for determining the disposition . . . of [the remaining counterpart balance in the future]."[28] But perhaps most instructive of all was their explicitly stated recognition that the actual amounts to be released in October (and presumably thereafter) would "be determined in the light of progressive implementation of the measures outlined [by the government]" and adopted by the Assembly.[29]

In agreeing to the release and proposed utilization of the requested counterpart funds, the United States made it clear that its decision had been based on expectation of "the results which should be achieved by the new stabilization program."[30] Indeed, to judge by its declared objectives, the new program appeared fairly impressive. It was designed, the government stated, to assure new financial resources for the French Treasury, to effect substantial economies in the public administration and in the nationalized enterprises, to limit the expansion of bank credit, and to reestablish price-and-wage stability.[31] Yet even a cursory examination of the plan itself must have convinced ECA officials in Paris that few of the measures contained therein could be expected to yield immediate results and that most of them, in fact, could not be implemented at all without future action of the Assembly. This was particularly true with respect to the package of so-called fiscal measures, which consisted of only two items: a bill to raise 80 billion francs in additional tax receipts during the remainder of 1948 and a statement of the government's intention to "[present] a proposal for fiscal reform to the Parliament before December 10, 1948."[32] And in transmitting the outline of the plan to Washington, both the French and ECA/Paris conceded that the effects of such reforms may not begin to materialize until the following year.[33]

But if in the latter part of September the ECA appeared willing to give the French government's fiscal proposals the benefit of the doubt, its patience must have worn thin very quickly. Thus, less than two months later during a discussion with Messrs. Queuille (the Premier) and Petsche (the Minister of Finance), Mission Chief Bruce felt obliged to hint at the "serious difficulties" that ECA anticipated "in seeking to justify aid to France" for the coming year.[34] The most difficult hurdle, he stressed, would be "to present a convincing case to Congress of steps [that the] French government is taking or planning to take, to create internal financial stability and restore confidence to the French franc." He then went on to lecture that inflation could only be tackled "by increasing taxation to permit a large budgetary surplus, and by halting all increases in incomes, profits, and the use of credit. . . ." And he warned that if Frenchmen were unwilling to pay taxes to make French recovery possible, "it will be difficult to ask the American taxpayer to contribute even larger taxes for economic assistance to France."[35]

What must have especially exasperated ECA officials was the French government's obvious procrastination in even formulating the promised fiscal reform measures, let alone presenting them to the Assembly. In fact, at the meeting with Queuille and Petsche, Bruce was advised that such a presentation may have to be postponed beyond December 10 and that "this may mean that final Assembly action would not be taken until January 15 [,1949]."[36] Moreover, as if to take some of the sting out of Bruce's own remarks, the Prime Minister cautioned against too great a reliance on the "mystique" of fiscal reform. "Far reaching reform" he suggested, "could only be implemented gradually" and, therefore, "increases in tax collections would take time."[37] Time, however, was not a commodity the ECA was prepared to dispense generously at that point. On the contrary, the agency was determined to obtain from the French as many commitments as possible before its own next presentation to Congress. And it was undoubtedly with this in mind that Bruce decided to carry his message out into the open.

In a speech delivered in Lille on December 6, 1948, before the French Association of Woolen Manufacturers, he told his audience that, despite the considerable magnitude of American aid, ". . . the greatest contribution to the rebirth of prosperity in [France] must be made by the French people themselves." Many Frenchmen, he bluntly added, "think that France's contribution, since the Marshall Plan came into effect, has not been completely satisfactory." And although he alluded to some accomplishments, he left no doubt that "new and far greater efforts will be necessary if France is to contribute her full share to Europe's recovery."[38] But then came the heart of the message. After pointedly reminding his listeners of France's obligations under Article 7 of the Convention for European Economic Cooperation, he had this to say:

Your cabinet and your Parliament are now deliberating and putting the finishing touches to measures whose purpose is to enable France to fulfill [these] engagements. The United States, naturally, plays no part in these deliberations, but we are intensely interested . . . in what will result from them. It is obvious that substantial sacrifices will have to be made by all French citizens if the country is to create the internal financial stability which will make possible a large increase in production and an expansion of exports. . . . The Congress of the United States will convene in a few weeks, and shortly thereafter will begin consideration of the question of a continued contribution by American taxpayers to the recovery of the French economy. These are fateful days. The measures which the people of France now take . . . may well be a decisive factor in preserving [the] civilization in whose formation and preservation France has always played such a glorious part.[39]

The message must have been sufficiently clear to provoke, in Bruce's own words, "lively comment in the French press."[40] This, however, was an understatement; for, to judge by the sample of press comments that he dutifully cabled home, the reaction was fast and furious. It ranged all the way from outright denunciations of Bruce, by the French Left, for interfering in the internal affairs of France and insulting the country to the more moderate, but just as telling, chiding by Le Figaro which "[had] hoped that Mr. Bruce would have a more subtle view of the problems of the [French] economy." Several newspapers regarded the speech as a warning to France, while others read into it an expression of American refusal to release counterparts to help finance the French budget deficit. Almost alone, the Paris Herald Tribune came to Bruce's defense. The paper noted that "the speech was obviously written with great attention to discretion" and that it "was prepared with great thought." And then, perhaps deliberately, the paper went on to imply that such a speech was necessary, because "among Marshall Plan advisers [in Paris], there has been for some time a feeling that France is not doing as much as it might to support European recovery and that it has permitted internal politics rather than economic reality to chart its course."

In any event, barely ten days after his well publicized criticism of France's "unsatisfactory" performance, Bruce was pleading with Washington for approval to immediately release 20 billion francs from the French counterpart account. Of this sum, 15 billion francs was to finance previously approved investment expenditures and 5 billion francs would be earmarked for the development of strategic materials.[41] He prefaced his request with a fairly long description of the French accomplishments, as well as the legitimate difficulties, in their efforts to achieve financial stability. And he recommended that the only condition attached to such approval would be a French commitment "to reduce, from 200 billion to 175 billion francs, the ceiling on advances from the Bank of France to the government, by March 31, 1949." If this commitment were not kept, he promised, then "all releases of counterparts would automatically stop until the French government obtained new and real [tax] receipts."[42]

The record shows that this particular commitment was actually fulfilled ahead of the stipulated deadline: The legal ceiling on government borrowing from the central bank had been reduced to 175 billion francs at the end of 1948.[43] It also suggests, however, that this lower ceiling could not have been sustained—nor could actual advances be kept, at times, below the legal ceiling—without subsequent releases of counterpart funds to help finance both current and long-term (i.e., investment) government expenditures. Indeed, as late as fiscal 1950, *ordinary* revenues (mostly tax receipts) of the French government amounted to only 86.2 percent of total revenues. Of the 13.8 percent defined as *extraordinary* revenues, counterpart funds accounted for 89.1 percent.[44] In approving such releases, ECA officials must have obviously resigned themselves to existing realities and opted for a pragmatic approach to French fiscal peculiarities.[45] Specifically, they appeared willing to trade off their insistence on a rapid revamping of the fiscal system—so as to increase tax collections and balance the budget—for what they perceived to be less inflationary methods of financing the inevitable budget deficits. The utilization of counterpart funds had made such a trade-off possible. But it did not prevent a rise in the general price level that, as will be seen, persisted, with few exceptions, throughout the ERP period.

III

France was not the only country where the use of counterparts to make up the difference between ordinary tax receipts and total government outlays had been sanctioned by the ECA. In Austria, for example, counterparts withdrawn during fiscal 1950 alone accounted for 89 percent of the government's extraordinary revenues; and in Greece, Italy, and Norway, the comparable figures for the same year were 82.7 percent, 74.2 percent, and 78.3 percent, respectively.[46] Admittedly, these were exceptional cases. But what makes two of these countries—Austria and Norway—especially relevant to the present discussion is the fact that, despite individual differences, the release of counterparts in both of them was intended to serve a very specific purpose: the promotion of monetary stabilization through *debt retirement*. In only three other countries—France, the United Kingdom, and (much later) Denmark— were counterparts directly utilized for this purpose. And it may be useful, therefore, to consider briefly the circumstances under which this particular technique had been employed.[47]

As noted in the preceding chapter, the ECA had approved total withdrawals of $7.5668 billion worth of local-currency counterpart funds during its official life. Of this amount, $2.251 billion, or slightly less than one-third, had been approved for debt retirement.[48] As shown in Table 15, the proportions of total approved withdrawals earmarked for debt retirement ranged from about 7 percent in France to 100 percent in Norway. In Britain, where counterparts had been employed almost exclusively for debt retirement, the proportion was only slightly smaller than in Norway.

The striking similarity in the British and Norwegian experiences is not accidental. Indeed, in both countries ECA's counterpart policy had

Table 15   **Utilization of Counterparts for Debt Retirement, Cumulative, April 3, 1948–November 30, 1951 (in $ millions)**

Country	Total approved withdrawals	Approved for debt retirement	Debt retirement as percent of total
Austria	508.6	85.0	16.6%
Denmark	118.9	88.3	73.9%
France	2,453.3	171.4	6.9%
Norway	200.9	200.9	100.0%
United Kingdom	1,708.8	1,705.3	99.8%

Source: Compiled from Table C-9, in First Report to Congress on the Mutual Security Program, p. 63.

been dictated by a nearly identical combination of circumstances: the existence of large, ongoing government investment programs, largely financed out of tax receipts, and the threat of strong inflationary pressures stemming from excessive purchasing power.[49] In both cases, in fact, the internal monetary condition had been diagnosed by the ECA as one of *suppressed* inflation. Accordingly, the use of counterparts for debt retirement had been conceived of primarily as a means of cancelling—or draining off—part of the money supply. And in Norway, where the ECA had obviously been concerned about "continuing strong inflationary forces," counterparts had not been released for any other purposes.[50]

In sharp contrast, monetary cancellation through debt retirement played a very minor role as an anti-inflationary device in France. As noted above, the release of counterparts in that country had been largely designed to provide sorely needed financial resources with which to finance the ambitious investment programs adopted by the French government (i.e., the so-called Monnet Plan for the modernization and reequipment of industry and agriculture), and, to a limited extent, to help finance part of the ordinary budget deficit. The main attack on inflation, as also noted, was to have consisted of the adoption and implementation of sweeping fiscal measures and the imposition of restraints on private credit expansion. The utilization of French counterparts for debt retirement appears, therefore, to have been largely symbolic. Its sole virtue, to judge by ECA's own account, had been to "enable the government to keep advances from the Bank of France below the legal ceiling, which had been reduced . . . to 175 billion francs."[51]

Still another approach to debt retirement as an anti-inflationary device is illustrated by ECA's counterpart policy in Austria. As of March 1950, nearly two years after the inception of ERP, only $250.7 million of the $408 million worth of local-currency deposits, accumulated in the Austrian counterpart account, had been approved for withdrawal. And of this amount, $85 million was used to reduce the government's debt to the National Bank.[52] It might be noted that this particular debt had been incurred through government borrowings at the time of Austria's liberation. These borrowings had been used to provide a new basis for the Austrian currency (schilling) in place of the previously used German Reichsbank assets. But what is especially noteworthy is that the entire $85 million utilized for the reduction of this debt had been released during the first year of the recovery program and that no other schilling counterparts, arising out of ERP grants, had been approved for withdrawal during the same period.[53] Indeed, only in the second year of the program did the ECA begin to approve withdrawals of ERP-generated counterpart funds to finance investment projects.

The priority initially assigned to debt retirement may be explained largely by ECA's apparent concern about the adverse consequences of strong inflationary forces in Austria. The agency implicitly confirmed this concern by stating that "the use of counterparts to help attain a greater degree of financial stability was considered vital to the economic and political well-being of the country."[54] By early 1950, however, the ECA must have become satisfied that, "despite the persistence of economic weakness, considerable progress has been made toward the attainment of financial stability."[55] Strangely enough, the evidence did not warrant such an optimistic appraisal. On the contrary, during 1948 and 1949, wholesale prices in Austria—in ECA's own words— continued to "rise sharply," and at the end of 1949 they were 30 percent higher than at the end of the previous year.[56] Nevertheless, the order of priorities had evidently changed and other objectives had taken precedence, even before the end of 1949. The record shows that no further releases of schilling counterparts were approved for debt retirement after the first year.

Among the five countries considered here, Denmark constitutes a unique case. As seen in Table 15, about 74 percent of total kroner counterparts approved for withdrawal during the ERP period had been utilized for debt retirement. This was, to say the least, quite a significant proportion. What the table does not reveal, however, is that during the first two years of the Marshall Plan, hardly any Danish counterparts had been released at all.[57] Only in July 1950 did the ECA approve the first—and, as it turned out, the last—major withdrawal of Danish counterpart funds. Of the nearly $119 million released, some $88 million was used for debt retirement—specifically, for the payment of (German) occupation-account claims of the Danish National Bank against the government.[58] But when it recorded this event in its official report to Congress, the agency limited itself to a rather cryptic, if stylistically awkward, comment "The use of these funds for debt retirement," it stated, "makes permanent the anti-inflationary effects exerted by these funds which were allowed to accumulate in the counterpart account during the past two years."[59]

Ultimately, of course, debt retirement must be judged by its actual accomplishments, Thus, one may properly ask to what extent the use of counterparts for debt retirement contributed to the attainment of internal financial stability. Unfortunately, this question is easier posed than answered, for it constitutes only one part of a much larger issue— namely, how effective were counterparts, in general, as an anti-inflationary device. Still, it might be noted that even with respect to the five countries considered above, the record is ambiguous and the evidence inconclusive. What the statistical record does indicate is that in all of these countries prices continued to rise throughout the ERP period.

(See Table 16.)[60] It also shows that the *rates* of price increases differed among the five countries. But, perhaps most significantly, it suggests that such differences cannot be attributed to differences in either the timing of debt retirement or the relative magnitudes of counterparts used for this purpose in each individual case. In other words, monetary cancellation per se did not necessarily yield monetary stability. Continuing inflationary tendencies and debt retirement could—and did—co-exist.

Interestingly enough, such a conclusion had been reached by one of ECA's own top officials who, early in 1950, sharply criticized the heavy use of counterparts for debt retirement in Norway and Britain. The official, none other than Richard Bissell, argued that by approving the release of counterparts for this purpose the ECA had actually missed an opportunity to exercise a much stronger influence over the national economic policies of these two countries. "If we had said to begin with," he stated in an angry memorandum to Hoffman and Foster, "that counterpart was simply not available for debt retirement, counterpart expenditures could have been programmed as part of the [regular] government budget."[61] As it was, he intoned, both the British and the Norwegian authorities persisted in pursuing policies that "lead to a continuous state of inflation that can only be suppressed by rigid government controls."[62] Bissell did not identify the economic policies to which he was alluding. Nor did he offer specific thoughts on how counterpart expenditures could have been programmed within the respective government budgets. But the real target of his remarks—and the main reason for his obvious frustrations—may be inferred from cor-

Table 16   **Wholesale Price Indices for Selected ERP Countries (average 1948 = 100)**

Period	Austria	Denmark	France	Norway	United Kingdom
June 1948	92	101	98	100	99
Dec. 1948	111	104	114	101	101
Dec. 1949	154	107	113	103	110
Dec. 1950	187	129	133	127	133
Dec. 1951	259	151	170	149	151

Source: Compiled from ECA, Thirteen Report to Congress, p. 105; and First Report to Congress on the Mutual Security Program, p. 78.

roborative evidence: His major concern was the ECA's almost total lack of effective control over the use of counterparts in the United Kingdom. The British authorities, according to another ECA official, "didn't even tell the [ECA] Mission what they were doing with [counterparts]" and, in some cases, they simply "created a type of [official] debt in order to retire it with counterpart funds."[63]

British fiscal ingenuities notwithstanding, the fact remains that the United Kingdom was not the only country where ECA's authority over the disposition of counterparts would prove to be more nominal than real. Indeed, Bissell himself implied as much when he observed that "[ECA's] essential bargaining power with most participating countries comes not from counterpart but from dollar aid itself."[64] The practical consequences of this astute observation are noted in Chapter 10. But the point to be reemphasized here is that the specific use of counterparts for the promotion of monetary stability, through debt retirement, was not conclusively justified by the end results.

IV

Less than a year after he had decried the shortcomings of counterparts as a bargaining tool, the same Bissell found himself defending their virtues. The circumstances were, of course, different; for on this particular occasion Bissell was addressing not his colleagues within the ECA, but the members of the NAC. The context was also different: a discussion of policy questions related to the changed character of U.S. foreign assistance—a change directly influenced by the strategic, as well as economic, consequences of the Korean War. In an earlier memorandum the NAC staff committee had stated that while U.S. aid to Europe would continue, it "will [henceforth] be determined basically by defense requirements" and, therefore, "the criteria which in the past have determined the amount and distribution of aid, are no longer necessarily relevant."[65] But then, interestingly, the staff committee added:

There is no reason why, in the period ahead, counterparts might not continue to be used as one of a number of means by which this government might influence the budgetary and monetary policies of foreign countries, and might facilitate the financial, monetary and investment policies appropriate to the military effort. [Indeed, it would be a mistake] to draw a dichotomy between the objectives of re-armament and financial stability.[66]

Four days later, when the issues raised in the staff memorandum were being discussed by the NAC itself, the question of counterparts acquired an added aspect. Representing the State Department, Assistant Secretary of State Willard Thorp expressed the view that, since the nature and purpose of American assistance to Europe were being changed, the counterpart requirements imposed on aid recipients should also be altered. Specifically, he felt that, within the new context of assistance, "it would be desirable" to lower the 100-percent local-currency deposit requirement against grant aid.[67] It was at this point that Bissell, speaking for the ECA, countered by arguing that the 100-percent deposit requirement should, in fact, be continued. "While the usefulness of counterpart", he admitted, "had varied from country to country, it was [nevertheless] a device which had been used at times with *considerable success* in influencing monetary and fiscal policies. . . ." It could prove to be, Bissell confidently added, "a *useful* tool in the future as in the past."[68]

In point of fact, Bissell, who himself had previously questioned the effectiveness of counterparts, was fully aware of disagreements within the ECA about their usefulness as an instrument of financial stabilization. He was aware, moreover, that their very disposition had been the subject of continuing debate and divergent views. He certainly knew of a major division between those in the ECA who advocated the use of counterparts primarily for debt retirement and those who viewed them largely as a means of financing production and investment activities.[69] And, finally, he could not help but know that such differences of opinion had, at times, produced contradictory policy directives that were bound to confuse ECA's country missions, as well as the European governments with which they had to deal.

Consider, for example, a directive to OSR in Paris issued by Deputy Administrator William Foster, setting forth ECA/W's views on investment policy. The main policy objective, as stated by Foster, was to "unify ECA activities with respect to dollar-financed investment projects; management of counterpart; raising productivity . . . ; and review of composition of capital formation in each country and in Europe as a whole."[70] Accordingly, he directed that "all parts of ECA should maximize the degree to which counterpart is used for investment and minimize the use of counterpart for general financial purposes."[71] One month later, OSR dutifully transmitted the essence of Foster's message to ECA missions in the field, but it added a significant qualification of its own. While agreeing with and endorsing the basic objectives and principles laid down by Washington, OSR warned that greater use of counterparts for investment "may create a conflict between the investment and financial stabilization objectives." It therefore instructed that "where an increase in counterpart spending on investment would in fact risk a significant setback to fiscal and monetary stability, the objective of economic stabilization should take precedence."[72]

How, then, were the local ECA missions to interpret these instructions and translate them into operational terms? And, for that matter, how could ECA/W itself reconcile, in practice, the inherent conflict between the financial stabilization objective and the need to stimulate large-scale investments so as to increase production? The answer is that, notwithstanding wishful thinking, such a conflict could not be—and, indeed, was not—truly reconciled. One of the objectives had to be subordinated from time to time (and in different countries) to the other; and the actual choice between the two became increasingly clear from the middle of 1950 on: As the shift to defense-oriented aid and investment accelerated, the practical attention paid to the control of inflation diminished.[73]

To be sure, the concern about monetary stability—or lack thereof—remained and was expressed in a variety of ways. Thus, for example, in a mid-September 1950 dispatch to OSR, Paul Hoffman raised several searching questions concerning the impact of increased defense expenditures on European budget deficits; and he suggested the possibility of imposing direct controls and restricting per-capita consumption levels as means of checking inflation.[74] But even Bissell was subsequently forced to admit that the demands of rearmament, accelerated by the Korean War, had contributed to renewed inflationary pressures that had not been entirely controlled as late as 1952.[75] He cited certain European "structural features" that, he claimed, had greatly "complicated the pursuit of fiscal-monetary policies." And he offered them, in part, as an explanation of "what was not and probably could not have been accomplished by the European Recovery Program."[76] A less well-known member of the ECA staff summed it all up much more bluntly. "I think," he told an interviewer in 1952, "that the question of internal financial stability was not adequately treated in the ERP."[77]

In the general scheme of things, however, numbers often speak more eloquently than words. And in judging the extent to which the restoration and maintenance of internal financial stability had been achieved during the Marshall Plan, the final "word" does belong to the statistical record, as summarized in the following tables.

Reading the figures across each of these tables, one can easily trace the general movement of European prices throughout the ERP period. What one sees serves to confirm the monetary consequences of the change in the character and direction of U.S. assistance, beginning in the second half of 1950. Thus, by December 1951, wholesale prices in all the ERP countries except one (Italy) had risen above their December 1950 levels; and in almost all cases, the increases had been quite significant. Moreover, every single country had experienced increases in retail prices during the same period. But what is especially noteworthy is that European prices had begun their accelerated rise even before the end of 1950. Only in Portugal and Turkey were wholesale and retail prices actually lower in December 1950 than in December 1949; and

Table 17   Wholesale Price Indices for Western Europe, 1948–51
(1948 = 100)

Country	June 1948	Dec. 1948	Dec. 1949	Dec. 1950	Dec. 1951
Austria	92	111	154	187	259
Belgium	101	101	94	113	123
Denmark	101	104	107	129	151
France	98	114	113	133	170
Germany (Bizone)	100	124	126	145	166
Greece	95	114	112	128	134
Ireland	100	99	102	113	123 (Sept.1951)
Italy	94	105	87	100	100
Netherlands	100	103	110	128	144
Norway	100	101	103	127	149
Portugal	97	105	104	102	118
Sweden	101	101	102	118	149
Switzerland	100	100	92	100	105
Turkey	101	105	103	101	106
United Kingdom	99 (March 1948)	101	110	133	151

Source: the same as for Table 16.

only in Germany did the retail price index show a similar decline between these two dates. In all other countries, both the wholesale and retail price indices stood higher in December 1950 than in December of the previous year.

Viewed in its entirety, the three-and-a-half-year history of the ERP featured only one period during which the majority of the participating countries appeared to enjoy relative price stability. That period extended from the beginning of 1949 to the middle of 1950; and, as explained by the ECA at the time, "the principal factor in the restoration of financial stability has been the recovery in [Europe's] industrial and agricultural production . . . , which, in turn, was accelerated by government action curbing inflationary monetary forces." [78] The result of these developments, the agency went on to state, had been "to re-

Table 18   Cost-of-Living Indices for Western Europe, 1948–51 (1948 = 100)

Country	June 1948	Dec. 1948	Dec. 1949	Dec. 1950	Dec. 1951
Austria	88	104	135	158	220
Belgium	101	101	95	97	107
Denmark	99	101	101	113	121 (Oct.1951)
France	–	–	117	127	152
Germany (Bizone)	100	111	103	94	106
Greece	99	112	111	138	149
Iceland	99	101	105	139	165
Ireland	101	100	101	103	114
Italy	100	102	98	103	112
Netherlands	100	104	110	120	127
Norway	100	99	100	112	127
Portugal	96	104	103	98	102 (Nov.1951)
Sweden	101	102	102	108	126
Switzerland	–	–	–	99	105
Turkey	99	103	110	102	106
United Kingdom	102	101	104	108	121

Source: Compiled from Table IX-2 in ECA, Country Data Book: All
    Participating Countries, Op. Cit.; and Table F-9 in First
    Report to Congress on the Mutual Security Program, p. 79.

duce to manageable proportions the powerful inflationary pressures that
had [previously] threatened to escape control. . . ."[79] Perhaps so. Yet
the evidence indicates that even during that period, strong inflationary
pressures—overt or suppressed—continued to plague several countries
(most notably Austria and the United Kingdom).[80]

In any event, the restoration of financial stability proved to be short
lived. For although they may have been successfully curbed during 1949
and 1950, inflationary forces soon gathered strength and were reflected in a sharp upward movement of prices, beginning in the third
quarter of 1950. This upward trend—due, in large part, to the military
build-up programs following the Korean War—was to continue, with
but few exceptions, throughout the remainder of the ERP period. And

by the time the Marshall Plan officially ended, much of the ground gained in the fight against inflation during its first two and a half years had been lost. The quest for a firmly maintained internal financial stability remained largely unfulfilled.

Expansion of Foreign Trade

PART III

Europe's Trade and Payments: Basic Problems and Early Solutions   8

Although the principle of genuine cooperation and joint action on the part of the participating countries had been presumed by Congress to underlie all the economic elements of the ERP, its practical manifestations proved to be fairly limited. Indeed, in formulating and pursuing their national production goals and in implementing domestic stabilization measures, the ERP nations acted pretty much independently of each other. Moreover, for the most part they effectively resisted external attempts to force them into collective planning or regional coordination of economic activities.

Only with respect to one major endeavor were the Europeans—helped by the ECA—induced into what could be said to constitute meaningful cooperation on a regional level. That particular endeavor was directed at the promotion and expansion of Europe's foreign trade. Both the Europeans' and ECA's contributions to the fulfillment of this objective must, therefore, be appraised against a background of the immediate problems that faced European commerce on the eve of the Marshall Plan.

I

It was primarily financial or, more specifically, *payments* difficulties that constituted the main obstacle to an expansion of intra-European trade during 1947.[1] But these difficulties, in turn, were largely rooted in the network of bilateral payments agreements that governed Europe's postwar trade and monetary relations. In fact, in the summer of 1947, Western Europe faced a payments crisis of major proportions—a crisis whose immediate cause was the inability of the bilateral payments machinery to continue to carry the burden of financing intra-

European trade. Put differently: The almost complete exhaustion of bilateral credit margins posed a distinct possibility that intra-European trade would be forced into strict bilateral balancing channels or, worse, would come to a standstill. And in order to appreciate the implications of this threat, as well as European and American reactions to it, it would be useful to consider briefly the nature of Europe's postwar bilateralism and the circumstances under which it arose and functioned.

Simply defined, a bilateral payments agreement consists of a set of provisions for handling financial transactions arising out of mutual economic interchanges between two contracting countries. Such an agreement may cover the settlement of claims involving current-account transactions only or it may allow for capital flows as well. It may require exact bilateral balancing of trade or it may—and most often does—provide for automatic lines of credit with which to finance discrepancies between payments and receipts. It may be limited to present transactions or it may contain procedures for settling previously accumulated debts.[2] Yet whatever are the exact provisions in each case, the essence of bilateral arrangements is that they are concluded between individual pairs of countries and are designed to accommodate their financial problems and/or interests. Hence, to the proponents of universal free trade, a bilateral regime usually connotes selfish and uneconomic trade patterns, inconsistent with the benefits that are ideally associated with a multilateral trade and payments system.[3]

For postwar Europe, however, a simple choice between bilateralism and multilateralism did not exist. The two essential ingredients of multilateralism—generally convertible currencies and realistic exchange rates—were almost totally absent. Most European nations emerged from the war with disrupted economic structures, greatly depleted reserves of gold and foreign exchange, and limited opportunities to earn hard currencies by exporting to the Western Hemisphere. Most of them lacked adequate and acceptable means with which to finance urgently needed imports either from each other or from overseas sources; and in order to conserve their meager financial resources, most governments found it necessary to continue to impose internal economic controls and to maintain strict regulations over external trade and payments. It was, in short, a combination of highly regulated economies, exchange control systems, and overvalued currencies that dominated Western Europe in the aftermath of the war. And under the circumstances, the immediate problem was reduced to finding a financial mechanism to enable a resumption of at least some intra-European trade, in the hope that trade revival would, in turn, help to stimulate general productive activities. Bilateralism—or, more specifically, a series of bilateral trade and payments agreements—appeared to offer the most feasible interim solution in a transition to more normal multilateral trading relationships.[4]

Unlike the exploitative bilateralism imposed during the 1930s by a powerful Nazi Germany on its weaker trading partners, the postwar European bilateral network was essentially "an alliance" of soft-currency countries.[5] Its major aim was to allow countries whose currencies were largely inconvertible—and hence not readily acceptable to exporting countries—to finance trade without the need to draw on their scant gold and hard-currency reserves. Its common denominator was the reciprocal extension of credit lines in the respective partners' own currencies, at fairly fixed and consistent rates of exchange.[6] Typically, the payments agreements specified the amount of bilateral credits to be granted and permitted debit balances, within the specified limits, to be carried by either partner for a considerable period of time. Most agreements, however, also provided that debit balances in excess of the specified limits would have to be settled by payment in gold or convertible currencies.[7]

Herein lay both the major virtue and the fundamental weakness of the bilateral payments machinery. On the one hand it enabled deficit countries to continue importing (and thereby enable other European countries to export) as long as the limits of bilateral credits had not been reached. On the other hand, once credit margins had been used up, net debtors would either have to curtail the level of their current imports or be forced to settle additional imbalances in gold and convertible currencies. Since few countries were willing to risk losses of such reserves for the sake of financing intra-European imports, chronic debtors increasingly opted for the first choice: When bilateral credit margins neared exhaustion, they temporarily cut off imports from their creditors.[8] Nor could creditors utilize their accumulated bilateral-surplus earnings (denominated in their partners' inconvertible currencies) to finance imports from third countries, either in Europe or elsewhere. And as creditors in intra-European trade found it increasingly difficult to obtain gold and dollars to finance purchases from the Western Hemisphere, their willingness and ability to supply additional bilateral credits to their European partners decreased accordingly.[9]

Yet perhaps the most serious defect of the bilateral payments network was its lack of a check-and-balance device—a mechanism that might ensure at least some degree of balance-of-payments adjustments. As a result, the bilateral machinery produced a situation in which European countries quickly became either chronic debtors or chronic creditors. Thus, when debtors reached their bilateral credit limits and creditors found themselves unable to grant additional credits, the entire bilateral structure was threatened with paralysis—a condition that, not surprisingly, was reflected in the stagnation of intra-European trade during 1947.[10] It was a condition of which U.S. policy makers were well aware when they called upon the CEEC countries to "cooperate in facilitating and stimulating an increasing exchange of goods and services" among themselves.[11] Yet neither the Administration nor Congress appeared at first to appreciate that, given existing realities, any European initiative along these lines would require a meaningful and specific support from the United States. Unfortunately, such support was slow in coming; and in its absence the European nations were left groping for solutions that would at best yield half measured and hardly satisfactory results.

II

It was Belgium, supported by its Benelux partners, that took the lead in proposing a new scheme to extricate Europe from the bind of the bilateral payments system. The Belgian proposal, which was endorsed by the Committee of Financial Experts during the CEEC conference in the summer of 1947, sought to combine Marshall Plan aid with *multilateral* clearings (or, offsetting) of intra-European bilateral balances. In its report, the Committee of Financial Experts called for, first of all, the acceptance by European countries of intra-European currency transferability. That is to say, European currencies would be transferred among countries for the purpose of offsetting debits against credits. If this were indeed permitted, a country would be able to use a bilateral credit balance, denominated in one European currency, to offset a debit balance denominated in another. Such an offsetting mechanism, the experts argued, "would reduce to a minimum, payments in gold and convertible currencies which at present European countries are generally required to make to settle [their bilateral] balances. . . ."[12]

However, while transferability might reduce the need to use gold and convertible currencies for settling intra-European balances, it could not eliminate it completely. For, as noted earlier, some European countries occupied—and might continue to occupy—net creditor positions vis-à-vis the group as a whole. And in order to enable net creditors to utilize their excess earnings within Europe to meet payment obligations elsewhere, some gold and/or dollar settlements would still be required. As the leading net creditor in Europe, while at the same time a debtor to overseas countries, Belgium was particularly aware of such a necessity. Accordingly, it proposed (and the Financial Experts concurred) that "American aid should be so arranged as to provide an adequate guarantee for the conversion [into dollars] of the amount due [by debtors] in excess of the credits provided for in the [bilateral] payments agreements." [13] The proposal did not imply an *increase* in the amount of contemplated American aid (which was, in any case, still unknown at the time), but only that "a portion of the aid should be set aside for this purpose; and should be calculated, in the cases of countries having net deficits toward [the ERP group] as a whole, on the basis of these deficits." [14]

In September 1947, following the completion of the CEEC report, a newly-formed Committee on Payments Agreements met in London to consider the proposal further and to formulate concrete recommendations for action. It quickly became apparent that a specific Benelux proposal for multilateral clearings, based on the pooling of all bilateral balances to determine net positions, was an idea whose time had not yet come. [15] Nor was much enthusiasm expressed for intra-European currency transferability suggested earlier. There was, however, sufficient willingness to explore other possible techniques for offsetting debits and credits on a multilateral basis, to be worked out at a later meeting in Paris in mid-October. It is worth noting, in this connection, that although the problem to be resolved concerned *intra*-European monetary arrangements, the Committee on Payments Agreements extended an invitation to the International Monetary Fund to send an observer to the Paris meeting. And it is also worth noting that due to what was subsequently described by the Fund's Managing Director as a "genuine misunderstanding," no such observer actually attended. [16]

In any event, during its Paris meeting the committee hammered out a draft of a multilateral compensations arrangement, in which five countries immediately declared their readiness to participate. On November 18, 1947, Belgium, France, Italy, Luxemburg, and the Netherlands signed the First Agreement on Multilateral Monetary Compensation, thereby agreeing to accept, among themselves, the automatic application of certain offsetting operations. As such, these countries— joined by the Bizone of Germany shortly thereafter—became the "permanent" members of the agreement. Eight other CEEC countries adhered to the scheme as "occasional" members, reserving the right to accept or reject each compensation proposed to them. The agreement provided for each member's monthly reporting to a central office, of its net debit or credit balances with every other member, and for monthly multilateral clearings (or compensations) of such balances to the maximum extent possible. [17] It distinguished, however, between two types of compensations, each of which requires a brief explanation.

Those compensations that would result only in a reduction of existing balances were classified as "first category" compensations. They were to apply automatically to the "permanent" members and could apply to an "occasional" member at the latter's option. Such compensations involved an agreement by each country to cancel its claim on a second country against an equal cancellation of its liability to a third. In practice, therefore, "first category" compensations required the existence of a closed circuit of countries, each of which was a net creditor of the *preceding* country and a net debtor to the *succeeding* one. As an illustration, consider the circuit depicted below, where the Netherlands owes France the equivalent of $4 million; France owes Belgium $6 million; Belgium owes Italy $2 million; and Italy owes the Netherlands $10 million.[18]

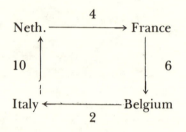

Under the circumstances, "first category" compensations would result in a complete cancellation of Belgium's $2 million debt to Italy; a reduction in Italy's debt to the Netherlands, to $8 million; a reduction in Netherland's debt to France, to $2 million; and a reduction in France's debt to Belgium, to $4 million. Thus, initial debt balances totalling $22 million could be reduced to a new total of $14 million. Or, to put it differently, a maximum of $8 million of debt balances could be cleared without an increase in any of the existing balances in the particular circuit.

"Second category" compensations—those operations that would result in increases in existing balances or the formation of new ones—were left entirely optional by the agreement. Any member, "occasional" as well as "permanent," could entertain but refuse a proposition along these lines. It is not difficult to appreciate this provision once it is realized that "second category" operations presupposed a certain degree of currency transferability. That is to say, such operations would involve payments made by one country to another, utilizing a third currency. As a simple example, consider a case where the Netherlands is a bilateral creditor of both France and England, while France is also a creditor of England. (This means, in effect, that both France and the Netherlands are already holding sterling balances, representing England's bilateral debts.) By using its sterling balances, France could discharge or reduce its bilateral debt to the Netherlands and at the same time eliminate or reduce its bilateral claim on England. However, such an operation would necessarily lead to an increase in the sterling balances held by the Netherlands. Hence, while the British debt to France and the French debt to the Netherlands would be reduced or eliminated, England's debt to the Netherlands would rise.

Although "second category" operations could potentially result in substantial cancellations of outstanding debts, they entailed special considerations for creditors and debtors alike. Thus, in the above example, the Netherlands would have to decide whether it would be in its interest to substitute a larger claim on Britain for a smaller (or no) claim on France. And Britain, for its part, would have to weigh the advantage of owing a smaller (or no) debt to France against a possible disadvantage of incurring a larger debt to the Netherlands.[19] Since the implications of "second category" operations for individual debtors and creditors obviously depended on their respective bilateral arrangements—and current bilateral positions—with the other countries involved, such operations were left to the discretion of each member. Nevertheless, it might be noted that during the lifetime of the agreement, the total debts canceled through "second category" operations far exceeded those cleared through "first category" compensations.[20]

The First Agreement on Multilateral Monetary Compensation entered into force one month before President Truman sent the Administration's ERP message to Congress. While awaiting congressional reaction, eleven European nations participated in the first clearing operation, which took place at the end of December 1947. The results were minimal: Of a total $762.1 million in existing bilateral debts, a mere $1.7 million was cleared through "first category" compensations.[21] But if they were disappointed by these results, the Europeans must have been doubly disappointed to learn that in its message to Congress, the Administration (specifically, the State Department) stated that ERP dollars "will *not* be made available for the specific purpose of settling net debit balances accruing in a multilateral clearing union."[22] Instead, it asked Congress to authorize the ECA to finance certain procurements within Europe with ERP funds. Such offshore purchases, the Administration argued, would help promote intra-European trade by injecting dollars into Europe but would, at the same time, enable the ECA Administrator to exercise "greater control over any U.S. contributions to European multilateral clearing than would be the case if dollars were made available to settle these accounts."[23] Congress subsequently granted this request, and during the last three quarters of 1948, the ECA authorized some $243.9 million for offshore procurements from ERP countries.[24] But in the closing months of 1947 and early part of 1948, the Europeans could draw little comfort from these as yet unknown developments.

III

Throughout the spring of 1948, while Congress labored over the ERP legislation, several European countries continued to search for ways by which American aid could be incorporated into a European multilateral payments scheme. Thus, as early as February 7, 1948, Ambassador Caffery reported to Secretary of State Marshall that the signatories to the Multilateral Compensation accord were planning a meeting, for the twenty-fifth of that month, in order to "initiate a study on the manner in which ERP aid could most effectively promote intra-European trade."[25] He added that before proceeding with final arrangements for this meeting, the prospective participants were anxious to know whether the U.S. Administration "perceives objections to early recommendations on the use of American assistance, or preferably whether [the] U.S. could give some encouragement to [such a] study."[26] Although the Ambassador concluded his message with an urgent request for instructions, Washington took its time replying. Thirteen days later, Caffery was advised that while explorations of various aspects of multilateral clearings could be most useful, "it would not be wise for [the] contemplated meeting to make formal recommendations at this time."[27] He was further instructed to reemphasize, in discussions with the participants, that the "U.S. will not be able to make dollars available for [the] specific purpose of settling debit balances accruing in clearing."[28]

The Europeans, however, persisted in their effort; and during March, financial and technical experts began to formulate and discuss a plan under which counterpart funds, arising out of ERP grants, would be utilized to finance intra-European imbalances. Specifically, the so-called Brussels Plan suggested that a portion of each country's counterpart account be earmarked to finance export surpluses with other ERP countries.[29] In this way, it was argued, some of the ERP dollars, received essentially as gifts, could provide the basis for the extension of credits by European creditors to their European debtors. Put differently, European creditors might be more willing to extend additional credits in their own currencies if such credits arose from previously received dollars that could be used to finance *their* imports from outside Europe. It was quickly realized, however, that the plan, as initially proposed, would not be acceptable to Belgium, the leading European creditor, which stood to receive a large part of its ERP aid in the form of loans rather than grants. For under the circumstances, Belgium, as well as other creditors in a similar position, would have little incentive to continue to accumulate claims in inconvertible European currencies while at the same time incurring dollar liabilities to the United States.[30]

To overcome this dilemma, the technical group then suggested an interesting modification to the plan. It proposed that the use of counterpart funds might be combined with drawings on the financial resources of the International Monetary Fund (IMF). As described in an ECA memorandum written in early May, the plan would have worked as follows: A creditor country, for example England, would transfer, say, £40 million from its counterpart account to France (a debtor).

France would deposit an equivalent amount of francs in its own counterpart account in Paris and would then proceed to draw £40 million from the IMF. As a result, France would be able to finance a deficit totalling £80 million—£40 million being contributed by England and £40 million by the IMF. But, more important, since the IMF's holding of sterling would be reduced by the French drawing, England would now be able to draw dollars from the IMF. If at a future date France's position was reversed and *it* became a creditor of England, similar transactions—involving transfer of counterpart francs to England and subsequent drawings of francs and dollars from the IMF—could take place.[31]

On its face, the scheme was quite imaginative. Its implementation, however, depended on the consent of both the IMF and the ECA. The latter had by then already assumed its administrative duties, and the author of the cited memorandum—an ECA officer in London—felt sufficiently free to criticize the proposal and recommend that it be rejected. He readily conceded that without the key provisions—i.e., drawings on the IMF—neither Belgium nor probably the United Kingdom would accept the plan. But he argued that it was precisely this provision that made the plan unsatisfactory from ECA's standpoint. "Our attitude has been," he stated, "that this problem [of financing intra-European trade imbalances] must be solved by the participants," without recourse to additional dollar resources.[32] "Borrowing from the IMF," he correctly pointed out, "is an attempt to throw this extra credit problem back onto the dollar through the IMF."[33] It was inescapable, he concluded, "that [the Europeans] must solve [their intra-European financial problems] outside the scope of dollar assistance," and hence the plan, as it stood, should be rejected.[34]

Such an attitude, on the part of the ECA, might appear to be quite inconsistent with the objective of encouraging an expansion of intra-European trade. And yet it was not! For, rightly or wrongly, the strongest emphasis of the U.S. Administration, with respect to this particular aspect of the recovery program, was on the principle of self-help and mutual aid. Thus, although the United States was prepared to help finance the *external* dollar deficit of Europe, it was initially opposed to the idea that dollars would be supplied for the purpose of settling *intra*-European imbalances. In fact, the Administration expected that, as a token of their earnest intentions, the European nations themselves would furnish each other with the resources necessary to finance their mutual trade.[35] Much to their dismay, the OEEC countries were to discover that essentially the same attitude—though publicly justified on different grounds—would be taken by the IMF itself.

IV

It can be reasonably argued that the IMF's involvement with the ERP in general, and with the various intra-European payments schemes in particular, was preconditioned by two major factors: (1) its status as a newly evolving international organization and (2) the predominant position occupied by the United States on its policy-making bodies. Created at Bretton Woods in 1944, the IMF was committed, by its Articles of Agreement, to "promote international monetary cooperation" and to "facilitate the expansion and balanced growth of international trade."[36] Underlying these functions was the principle of nondiscriminatory multilateral trade and payments, which, in turn, implied an early reestablishment of freely convertible currencies on a worldwide basis, and the rejection of direct controls as a means of balance-of-payments adjustments. As an alternative to the use of exchange controls, a member country experiencing a payments deficit would be able to draw (borrow) needed currencies from the IMF. The extent of such drawings was to be determined by the respective member's quota (i.e., contribution to the Fund) and by the Fund's current holdings of its currency.[37]

In itself, however, the commitment to an *international* monetary order need not have precluded the possibility that the IMF might assist in the solution of regionally induced payments problems or encourage the formation of desirable *regional* monetary arrangements. That such assistance would have been welcomed was implied in a resolution passed by the CEEC as early as July 31, 1947. That resolution drew "attention to the important part which the International Monetary Fund should be able to play in advising countries on measures of monetary reform and the progressive liberalization of intra-European payments arrangements."[38] But although the Fund's Managing Director, Camille Gutt, was quite anxious to explore the ways in which the Fund might become actively involved in helping to solve Europe's payments difficulties, the IMF Executive Board, for the most part, was not.[39] The majority of the Executive Directors, in fact, opposed the granting of special borrowing privileges to the ERP nations and/or the use of the Fund's dollar resources in an intra-European payments scheme. And in what became known as the "ERP Decision," on April 5, 1948, the Board passed a resolution that stated: "For the first year [of the ERP] the attitude of the Fund and ERP members should be that such members should request the purchase of U.S. dollars from the Fund *only in exceptional or unforeseen cases*."[40]

It is tempting, of course, to justify this attitude on the ground that in its early years, the Fund's dollar resources were fairly limited relative to the demand for them.[41] As an international organization, the IMF was obliged to accommodate the legitimate requests of all of its members. Any special privilege extended to the ERP nations conceivably could have jeopardized its ability to carry out this obligation or, worse, exhausted its dollar resources. Indeed, the Board explained its April 5 decision by suggesting that "the Fund and [its] members participating in ERP should have as their objective to maintain the resources of the Fund at a safe and reasonable level during the ERP period in order that at the end of the period, such members will have unencumbered access to the resources of the Fund." [42] Yet while the concern over potential depletion of the Fund's dollar resources may have been genuine, the explanation offered by the Board for its action was far from complete. A fuller explanation must necessarily take into account the attitude of the United States, as presented by the U.S. Executive Director during the Board's discussions, and the considerable weight this attitude carried with other Executive Directors.

Thus, on January 21, 1948, when the Board met to consider the possible effects of the ERP on the Fund's policies and operations, an interesting argument was put forth to support the suggestion that the ERP members of the Fund "should not count on using the Fund's resources in a normal way." [43] The argument consisted of the proposition that since the amount of ERP aid voted by the U.S. Congress "might implicitly indicate the volume of U.S. production" that Congress thought should be shipped overseas during the program, "there should not be any substantial provision of dollars by the Fund to increase the impact on the U.S. economy." [44] During the same meeting, the U.S. Executive Director, Andrew Overby, stated that, while there might be individual circumstances in which the use of the Fund's resources would be justified, "the general effect of ERP should be to *tighten* the Fund's evaluation" of requests for such use by ERP countries. [45] Following up on this theme during a March 18 meeting, Louis Rasminsky (the Canadian Executive Director) went one step further. The efforts to be made through the ERP, he opined, "should change the favorable presumption, which up to then the Fund had given to all members requesting drawings, to an *unfavorable* presumption for those members receiving ERP aid." [46] Not surprisingly, this view was warmly endorsed by several Executive Directors representing non-ERP members. And it was shortly afterward—following another meeting on March 30—that the Board reached the so-called ERP Decision.

It should be pointed out, however, that during its January 21 meeting, the Board did invite the director of the IMF Research Department to prepare and submit a study on the possible ways in which the Fund might cooperate in the efforts to strengthen Europe's multilateral clearing arrangements. [47] The plan, as subsequently formulated by the Research Department staff, was based on essentially the same idea entailed in the modified Brussels Plan. It proposed that the Fund allow for drawings of European currencies of creditor countries, thereby permitting these countries to have corresponding access to Fund dollars, should their balance of payments require it.[48] But when this proposal came up for consideration, Mr. Overby once again raised objections to any plan that would involve the Fund's providing dollars to ERP countries. The ERP, he pointedly reminded the Board on June 2, 1948, "had been projected as mainly a European self-help program, to be supplemented by U.S. assistance."[49] Any increase in the means of payments available to Europe, he argued, would create a danger of encouraging "non-essential and luxury imports more than the essential trade which was desirable." For this and other reasons, he suggested, the Fund "should not go beyond the limits it had set for the use of its resources, and should not undertake to effect transactions automatically merely because they were within a [multilateral] payments system."[50]

The weight of Overby's argument can be gauged by the fact that, although several Executive Directors felt that "the aim of a multilateral payments system was directly in line with the Fund's aim," the Board turned down the proposal submitted by its own staff. Instead, it merely expressed its hope that "an arrangement can be made for multilateralizing European payments" and that "any increase in the credit margins can be financed by the [European] creditor countries as their further contribution to European recovery."[51] The Board added, however, that the IMF would be willing to place its advice and technical facilities at the disposal of its members in connection with the formulation and administration of any multilateral payments arrangements.[52]

The similarity between the Board's action and the official U.S. position at the time was hardly coincidental. In fact, early in June the National Advisory Council on International Monetary and Financial Problems (NAC) formally advised the ECA Administrator and the U.S. Executive Director of the Fund that "they should favor the active participation of the Fund in rendering technical and administrative assistance in arrangements designed to facilitate European multilateral trade."[53] At the same time, the NAC adopted the view that the "IMF should not be involved *financially* in any intra-European clearing system."[54] Since the NAC had been mandated by Congress to issue general policy directives for the guidance of U.S. representatives on the IMF Board, its expressed views on this matter could be taken as a statement of official U.S. policy. And since the U.S. Executive Director was, in any event, bound to follow closely the NAC's recommendations with respect to the Fund's operations, he spared little effort in persuading his colleagues on the Board to act accordingly. The measure of his success in carrying out his instructions can be attested to by the fact that the language of the Board's official statement was almost identical to that of the NAC-approved advice.

A statement of the Board's position was communicated to all the ERP members of the IMF. The latter had already been prepared for such an outcome and could not have been entirely surprised by it.[55] In any event, shortly thereafter the OEEC countries embarked on a series of negotiations that culminated in the signing, on October 16, 1948, of a more comprehensive payments agreement than the one concluded nearly a year before. The new agreement—formally known as the Agreement for Intra-European Payments and Compensations—did not contemplate any special financial assistance from the IMF. It was, however, predicated on a basic change in American attitude—a change prompted by the realization that any meaningful efforts to liberalize intra-European trade and payments would have to be at least partially financed by ERP dollars, allocated specifically for this purpose.

Bilateralism Challenged: The Intra-European Payments Agreements

This change in attitude had actually begun to take shape shortly before the NAC issued its aforementioned recommendations. Its conceptual origins can be traced to a series of internal ECA staff memoranda, fired in rapid succession in late May 1948, in which a case was made for the creation of an intra-European multilateral payments clearing system based on a limited use of specially allocated ERP dollars.[1] Although few American or European officials may have suspected it at the time, the ideas expressed in these memoranda were to produce a firm conviction, on the part of the ECA, that *regional* trade and payments liberalization was a necessary prelude to the ERP nations' achievement of general currency convertibility and free trade. It was this conviction that made possible the conclusion of the first Agreement for Intra-European Payments and Compensations in the fall of 1948, and for its more ambitious revision one year later. And it was this same conviction that led, within two years, to the establishment of a multilateral payments mechanism in Western Europe—the European Payments Union.

I

Even within the ECA, however, the concept of a multilateral clearing system *cum* directly allocated dollar aid required some time to fully gel. As initially outlined, the scheme called for setting aside a special fund of between $200 and $300 million, to help meet intra-European payment deficits during 1948–1949. For their part, European creditor countries would have to agree to extend additional credits that could be drawn upon by European debtors. When total drawings against a creditor country exceeded the credit margins granted by it, some 70 percent of the overdraft would be converted into dollars, out of the special fund, and would be made available to the creditor.[2] A follow-up memorandum dated two days later carried the idea a step further. It argued that the ECA should urge the establishment of a mandatory multilateral *clearing house* (with overdrafts financed by ECA dollars) for all OEEC countries, tied to a commitment by these countries to eliminate or reduce trade restrictions and discriminatory practices among themselves.[3] The memorandum stressed that the use of dollars in any such payments mechanism should be limited to "a clearly defined *marginal* role."[4] But it nevertheless argued—apparently for the first time—that even a limited use of dollars to support a clearing house arrangement would be superior to offshore procurements as a means of stimulating intra-European trade.[5]

Superior or not, the proposal outlined above could hardly have been advanced formally by the ECA at a time when official U.S. policy, as enunciated by the NAC, still favored the financing of intra-European deficits through offshore procurements.[6] Nor, for that matter, was the ECA itself prepared to propose such a scheme without first exploring other alternatives for easing Europe's payments difficulties. Accordingly, during the early part of June, American officials in Paris were instructed by ECA/W to withhold the clearing house plan from the OEEC until further notice.[7] They were asked instead to undertake informal discussions with the OEEC and to report on the latter's views on the relative merits of several possible devices, including offshore procurements, extension of new intra-European credits, use of local-currency counterparts, compulsory multilateral clearings of bilaterally established balances, and a clearing house mechanism.[8]

The emphasis on informality—which was to recur in subsequent instructions—was not without its reasons. Although it regarded Europe's payments problems with utmost urgency, the ECA had still not committed itself to any one course of action. Moreover, the new agency was reluctant at this stage to openly impose—or even advance—specific proposals of its own. In fact, it much preferred that "the final proposal come from the OEEC and that [the ECA] be in position of accepting it with or without modifications."[9] The ECA was not at all reluctant, however, to formulate a set of acceptable alternatives, discuss them with the Europeans, and invite the latter to submit a proposal along such lines. The purpose of urging the Europeans to draw up an interim proposal of their own, Washington advised, was "to assure that OEEC take the responsibility for initiating whatever arrangements are adopted."[10]

Not surprisingly, the arrangement that was finally adopted, after long and arduous negotiations, turned out to be a far cry from a fully automatic multilateral clearing mechanism. In fact, in at least one respect, noted below, the new arrangement closely resembled the one that had preceded it. Nevertheless, it was unquestionably a more effective instrument with which to tackle the immediate payments problem facing Western Europe. More important still, it embodied an explicit commitment by the United States to a built-in link between ERP aid and intra-European trade and payments liberalization.

II

The Agreement for Intra-European Payments and Compensations (AIEPC), which was signed in Paris on October 16, 1948, but came into force as of October 1, formally terminated the First Agreement on Multilateral Monetary Compensation.[11] But although the latter officially ceased to exist, its main features—i.e., monthly clearings through the Bank for International Settlements (BIS) and the offsetting of certain intra-European credits and debts—were incorporated into the new scheme. The AIEPC, however, extended the principle of offsetting, or compensation, to include all but two of the OEEC countries. It provided for the automatic acceptance of all "first category" compensations by all the signatories except Portugal and Switzerland.[12] But, like its predecessor, it left "second category" operations to the discretion of the countries involved; and it specified that "first category" compensations involving either Portugal or Switzerland would require their respective consent, as well as that of any other affected countries.

Desirable as it obviously was, the extended automaticity of "first category" compensations did not constitute the major innovative feature of the AIEPC. That distinction belonged to a series of provisions that postulated a unique device—a device involving the establishment of so-called drawing rights by European countries, coupled with corresponding allotments of conditional aid, by the ECA. In order to appreciate the significance of this package, it may be helpful to recall that the financial crisis facing Europe at the time was primarily due to the exhaustion of bilateral credit margins and to the unwillingness of persistent creditors to extend additional credits without some recourse to usable dollars. It may also be recalled, however, that the United States placed great emphasis on the need for the Europeans to help each other in financing their mutual trade—an attitude that was hardly appealing to creditor countries. The impass created by these opposing positions could not have been overcome merely by clearing and offsetting operations. What was required, in addition, was the injection of newly created credits into the intra-European trading system. And it was precisely this requirement that the establishment of drawing rights was intended to meet.

Although technically complex, the system of drawing rights rested on two fairly simple operational principles. First, those signatory countries that were expected to be creditors during the year undertook to establish special accounts, in their own currencies, equal in magnitude to their estimated surpluses with each of the other participating countries. These accounts, called "drawing rights," could be used by debtor countries to finance their anticipated trade deficits with the respective creditors.[13] Secondly, having established such drawing rights, creditor countries would be entitled to receive an equivalent allotment of ERP dollar aid, to help finance their own imports from the Western Hemisphere. But any allotment thus made by the ECA would be a conditional one—the condition being that the creditor country concerned had indeed established the necessary drawing rights in favor of its European debtors.

It might be noted that the new form of dollar aid was not meant to entail an increase in the cost, to the United States, of the recovery program. As will be seen shortly, conditional aid was treated as a suballocation of the *total* dollar aid needed to cover the estimated overall balance-of-payments deficit of the ERP countries. Its main virtue, from the ECA's standpoint, lay in the fact that it was to be allotted directly to creditors, rather than to debtors, thereby assuring that the former made their own currencies available to finance intra-European deficits. Thus, unlike the offshore-procurement technique, the new device was expected to reduce the reliance on and use of dollars for the financing of *intra*-European trade. Moreover, it had an important psychological value: Because drawing rights amounted, in effect, to grants-in-aid given by European countries to each other, the ECA could, and did, claim that conditional aid—involving no additional cost to the United States—encouraged the participating countries to fulfill their pledge of self-help and mutual-aid under the ERP.[14]

Be that as it may, the conclusion of the AIEPC necessarily implied a prior agreement on the actual amounts of drawing rights to be established. And this, in turn, required an estimate of Europe's overall payments deficit for the year—a figure consisting of the estimated deficits with the Western Hemisphere and the anticipated intra-European deficits. Quite understandably, it was the latter subset of estimates—which would determine the amounts of drawing rights granted or received, as well as the individual allotments of conditional aid—that proved the most difficult to arrive at. Left to be pursued in a series of bilateral negotiations between each pair of the OEEC countries, the process dragged on for months. And it was only at the prodding of the OEEC Committee of Five, and under "informal" but unmistakable pressure from the ECA, that seventy-eight bilateral payments agreements, in which the anticipated creditor-debtor position of each country vis-à-vis the others was specified, were finally concluded.[15]

As seen in Table 19, the first ECA-approved intra-European payments plan envisioned a combination of ERP dollar allocations and Eu-

**Table 19   ERP Aid and Drawing Rights under the First AIEPC, for the
Year July 1948–June 1949 (in $ millions)**

Country	Total dollar aid	Basic dollar aid	AIEPC Drawing rights granted	Drawing rights received	Total dollar and net European aid
Austria	215	212	3	67	279
Belgium–Luxemburg	248	29	219	11	40
Denmark	109	104	5	12	116
France	981	971	10	333	1,304
Germany:					
Bizone	411	302	109	99	401
French Zone	99	84	15	16	100
Greece	145	145	–	67	212
Iceland	5	5	–	–	5
Ireland	78	78	–	–	78
Italy	555	508	47	27	535
Netherlands	470	458	11	83	541
Norway	83	67	16	48	115
Portugal	–	–	–	–	–
Sweden	47	12	35	10	22
Switzerland	–	–	–	–	–
Trieste	18	18	–	–	18
Turkey	40	11	29	17	28
United Kingdom	1,239	919	320	30	949
Commodity Reserve	13	13	–	–	13
Totals	4,756	3,938	818	818	4,756

Source: BIS, Nineteenth Annual Report, p. 201.   Totals are not exact due
to rounding.

ropean-contributed aid, amounting to about $4.8 billion for the year
July 1948–June 30, 1949. Of this total, drawing rights were to account
for the equivalent of some $818 million, thus giving rise to a corre-
sponding amount of conditional aid.[16] Although the actual amount of
drawing rights finally established during the year differed somewhat
from the above figure, the pattern and aggregate magnitudes of the
anticipated creditor-debtor positions under the scheme are clearly
demonstrated. Thus, every country, with the exception of Greece, actually established some drawing rights in favor of others, and each re-

ceived a certain amount from one or several of them. But it is also clear that two countries—Belgium and the United Kingdom—emerged as Europe's leading net creditors. Between them, they were expected to provide almost 70 percent of all drawing rights while receiving in return slightly over 4 percent of the total. France, on the other hand, was to be the largest net recipient of drawing rights, followed by the Netherlands, Greece, and Austria.

The definitive amounts of drawing rights finally established under the 1948–1949 payments agreement are shown in Table 20. They totalled some $805 million. What is especially noteworthy, however, is the *distribution* of drawing rights among the participants, since it reflects the forecasted patterns of bilateral trade relations within the group. As may be seen, the United Kingdom and Belgium each received drawing rights from only one country: the United Kingdom from Belgium, and the latter from Italy. But whereas Belgium's grants of drawing rights were spread among ten other European countries, the great bulk of the United Kingdom's grants were directed to France. The latter was the recipient of credits from five countries but granted small amounts of drawing rights to only three. The Netherlands granted modest amounts of credit to five countries while receiving drawing rights from three (the bulk of which came from Belgium). Italy's grants were distributed among seven countries, while those established in her favor came from two. And West Germany received some $114.2 million in drawing rights from seven countries (half of which was contributed by the United Kingdom) while granting about $97 million to five (mostly to France).

Equally instructive is the fact that all or nearly all of the drawing rights granted by Belgium, France, Italy, the Netherlands, Sweden, and West Germany were actually utilized during the year; over 70 percent of those granted by the United Kingdom were similarly utilized. In contrast, 70 percent of the drawing rights granted by Austria and 75 percent of those granted by Norway remained unused. France, the chronic debtor, used up nearly 90 percent of the drawing rights established in its favor, while West Germany utilized only about 60 percent of its. Italy used none.[17]

All told, some $667 million in drawing rights was utilized during the life of the 1948–1949 agreement, leaving $128.5 million of unused drawing rights to be disposed of in various ways.[18] The turnover of clearings and compensations amounted to $103.7 million, of which "first category" compensations totalled $99.4 million and "second category" compensations only $4.3 million.[19] Thus, between them, the drawing rights used and the compensation operations contributed some $781 million to the financing of deficits (and surpluses) under the first AIEPC. Inasmuch as the gross amount of surpluses and deficits reported to the BIS by the participants during that period totaled about $1.8 bil-

Table 20 Drawing Rights Finally Established under 1948/49 AIEPC (in $ millions)

Recipient countries \ Amounts finally established for 1948/49	Countries granting drawing rights											Totals
	Austria	Belgium	Denmark	France	Germany	Italy	Netherlands	Norway	Sweden	Turkey	United Kingdom	
Austria	–	4.5	0.1	2.0	29.6	–	1.0	1.5	–	–	2.5	63.7
Belgium	–	–	–	–	–	11.0	–	–	–	–	–	11.0
Denmark	–	6.5	–	2.7	1.2	–	–	–	–	1.5	–	11.9
France	–	40.0	–	–	53.7	11.0	–	5.0	–	–	200.0	309.7
Germany	–	21.0	–	–	–	12.7	2.0	8.0	5.0	13.5	52.0	114.2
Greece	0.4	13.0	2.0	5.0	4.4	7.0	5.0	2.0	5.0	12.3	24.0	80.1
Italy	2.0	–	–	–	–	–	–	–	–	–	25.0	27.0
Netherlands	–	72.5	–	–	8.5	–	–	–	2.0	–	–	83.0
Norway	–	23.0	–	–	–	0.5	2.5	–	21.8	0.5	–	48.3
Sweden	0.7	6.0	3.0	–	–	0.1	–	–	–	–	–	9.8
Turkey	–	2.0	–	–	–	5.0	0.8	–	1.0	–	8.0	16.8
United Kingdom	–	30.0	–	–	–	–	–	–	–	–	–	30.0
Totals	3.1	218.5	5.1	9.7	97.4	47.3	11.3	16.5	34.8	27.8	334.0	805.5

Source: BIS, _Twentieth Annual Report_, p. 225.

lion, it can be seen that roughly 43 percent of this amount was financed through the operation of the payments scheme. The remainder, according to the ECA, was settled by net payments in gold and dollars, or was temporarily financed by the use of credit margins.[20]

III

In judging these results, one must resist the temptation either to exaggerate or to unduly minimize the accomplishments of the 1948–1949 payments scheme. To be sure, despite its more comprehensive membership and innovative feature (i.e., drawing rights), the AIEPC suffered from several basic defects. Thus, it has been suggested elsewhere that the persistent bilateral character of intra-European trade relations, the difficulties of estimating bilateral surpluses and deficits in advance, and the nontransferability of drawing rights gave rise to distorted patterns of trade, under which both creditors and debtors lacked the incentive to readjust their existing balance-of-payments positions.[21] As a result, it has been argued, the AIEPC failed to provide the means by which the basic payments disequilibrium in Europe could be at least partially cured, thereby permitting some progress toward the multilateralization of intra-European trade.[22]

On the other hand, it must be conceded that the payments scheme did provide breathing space at a crucial time. Not only did it help prevent the threatened breakdown of intra-European trade, but it undoubtedly aided in its expansion during 1948 and the first part of 1949. And although the trade directly financed by drawing rights did not necessarily constitute a net increase, there can be little question that the use of drawing rights, in combination with the compensation operations, contributed to the overall trade expansion. Nor should one overlook the less visible, but quite significant, individual cooperative ventures that could be attributed to the signing of the AIEPC itself. As reported by the BIS, the 1948–1949 payments agreement was instrumental in bringing about (1) the conclusion of hitherto nonexisting payments arrangements among several countries, (2) the establishment of new credit margins through renegotiated existing bilateral agreements, (3) the consolidation and realignment of old debts, and (4) the postponement of gold and dollar payments under some existing bilateral agreements.[23]

That the AIEPC failed to accomplish much more than that was primarily due to the economic and political realities that surrounded its negotiations and implementation. The ERP nations were simply unwilling and economically unable, in 1948, to commit themselves to a completely automatic multilateral clearing system.[24] Nor were the majority of them prepared to undertake even limited offsetting operations without the assurance that supplementary resources (i.e., drawing rights for debtors and conditional aid to creditors) would be made available. Drawing rights thus became the central ingredient of the entire payments scheme. But, just as they had previously objected to full *currency* transferability, several key countries—particularly the United Kingdom—now openly rejected the application of transferability to the drawing rights established under the AIEPC. That is to say, they opposed the notion that drawing rights granted by one country to another could be used in part by the latter to finance imports from a third. Had drawing rights been made transferable, an element of multilateralism would have been introduced into the system: The rigidities of bilateral trade relations could have been somewhat softened, and a greater amount of drawing rights might have been utilized. In the absence of unanimous agreement on this issue, however, none of these benefits could materialize.

Not surprisingly, it was prospective creditors, rather than debtors, that largely objected to transferable drawing rights. Yet, quite understandably, individual European creditors had their own specific reasons for adopting this stand. Thus, as far as Britain was concerned, transferability of drawing rights posed a potential threat to its gold and dollar reserves. For while it was expected to, and did indeed, run export surpluses with most of the Continental countries, Britain was a persistent debtor to Belgium (and often to West Germany and Switzerland). Hence, from Britain's standpoint, transferability of drawing rights could mean a possible accumulation of sterling drawing rights by Belgium, to the point that Britain would be obliged, under the term of its bilateral payments agreement with Belgium, to convert them into dollars.[25] Other creditors, more dependent on conditional aid to cover their Western Hemisphere dollar deficits, feared that if drawing rights were transferable, the original contributing countries might not be able to count on their expected share of conditional aid.[26]

In any event, the only concession made to the transferability principle was contained in Article 17 of the AIEPC, which dealt with the procedures for revisions in the amounts and/or distribution of drawing rights. That article provided that, apart from cases of *"force majeure* or catastrophe,"* a debtor wishing to have its drawing rights transferred from the granting country(ies) to others would have to petition and satisfy the OEEC Council that "it has been unable to use the whole or any part of its drawing rights although it has made all reasonable efforts to do so."[27] The record shows that no such requests were made during the lifetime of the 1948–1949 payments agreement. Thus, to all intents and purposes, the drawing rights negotiated under the AIEPC were granted and utilized on a strict bilateral basis.

Transferability, however, was not forgotten. In fact, it became the most heated issue in the negotiations for the extension and revision of the 1948–1949 payments agreement. The new revised agreement, which was to cover the fiscal year 1949–1950, was signed on September 7, 1949. But the negotiations that had preceded its signing proved long and difficult, and the problems encountered along the way appeared at times to be insurmountable.

IV

ECA's dogged insistence on transferability (i.e., multilateralization) of drawing rights—and, for a time, on their convertibility into dollars at the recipients' option—was dictated by two immediate objectives: (1) to foster competition among the European countries themselves and to expose European creditors to some measure of competition from non-European sources and (2) to introduce greater flexibility into intra-European payments and thereby reduce some of the rigidities of strict bilateral trade relationships. Behind these objectives, however, lay a much more fundamental issue—namely, ECA's determination that a revised payments scheme must make meaningful contributions to the overall liberalization of trade and payments in Europe.[28] In order to appreciate the forcefulness of this determination, it is necessary to consider briefly an important change in ECA's conception of the role of trade liberalization within the recovery program as a whole.

Thus, during the first months of 1949, there began to develop several lines of an argument within the ECA, all of them pointing to essentially the same conclusion: If the economic problems facing Europe were to be overcome and the goals of the ERP accomplished by 1952, new institutional arrangements and relationships would have to be established by the OEEC countries.[29] Basic to all these problems, the argument went on, was Europe's trade and balance-of-payments position in the world economy.[30] So basic, in fact, that none of the other important problems (e.g., accelerating productivity) could be effectively solved without a "definite and drastic" change in the structure of Europe's trade and payments.[31] Translating this into concrete policy proposals, the argument explicitly suggested that existing bilateral trade and payments relations in Western Europe must be replaced by mutual convertibility of currencies among the ERP nations, and the progressive elimination of trade barriers.[32] In other words, bilateralism must be replaced by an effective regional free-trade area, whose creation "is not a long run objective which can be put off, [but] must be achieved within the next 3–4 years."[33] The implication was quite clear: If an effective free-trade area in Western Europe was indeed considered essential to the success of the entire recovery program, then the ECA should lose no time in stating this position to the governments of the participating countries.[34]

The record shows that, although they did not express it in quite those terms, ECA officials came fairly close to stating this position when they met with OEEC delegates, in mid-April 1949, to discuss the extension of the AIEPC. At that meeting, the European representatives made clear their reluctance to undertake major revisions of the existing payments scheme.[35] But Richard Bissell, representing the ECA, stuck by his guns. The ECA's objectives, he stressed, were to assure "that the area of international competition should be widened, and that it should be more difficult for Europeans to earn dollars in Europe than by exports to the dollar area." Therefore, he stated, a revised payments plan must provide for "maximum transferability" of drawing rights within Europe and for "convertibility of drawing rights into ECA dollars at the option of debtors."[36] Somewhat taken aback, several delegates suggested that the European economies "are not yet strong enough to be exposed to the degree of competition implied by the ECA proposals."[37] To which Bissell pointedly replied by saying that "if they felt [that] Europe was not ready to be exposed to a small degree of dollar competition as ECA proposed, then he [Bissell] was *extremely concerned* about their notion of the tempo at which necessary adjustments must be made in order to achieve the ultimate objectives of full convertibility and dollar competition by the year 1952."[38] With an unmistakable hint of what might follow, Sir Edmund Hall-Patch then closed the meeting, stating that the OEEC Payments Committee "would attempt to develop proposals to meet ECA objectives, [proposals] which would at the same time be more acceptable to the participating countries."[39]

Yet, as may be surmised, proposals that might be "more acceptable" to some governments would not necessarily be acceptable to others. For while transferability would naturally appeal to prospective net recipients of drawing rights, it could not be said to be in the best interests of each and every prospective contributor. Belgium, confident of her strong competitive position and anxious to convert much of her European surplus into conditional-aid dollars, might have been content to endorse greater multilateralization of drawing rights. The United Kingdom, always fearful of gold and dollar losses and facing a severe drain on its reserves, obviously would not. Moreover, as long as the ECA continued to insist on convertibility of drawing rights into dollars, the potential danger of reserves losses only increased; and neither creditors nor debtors could completely ignore the possible implications of such eventuality. Interestingly enough, at least one ECA official in Paris acknowledged that the insistence on drawing rights convertibility may lead to "undesirable results—e.g., a probable decline in European trade or probable reappearance of unemployment, or else devaluation." [40] He went on to argue that by insisting on convertibility, the ECA "is really demanding the devaluation of the European currencies vis-à-vis the dollar area," and that if this was the case, then "high level discussions should immediately be taken, primarily with the British, in this connection." On the other hand, if the ECA was not prepared to go that far, then "we should abandon our convertibility objective, except insofar as it [may be] used as a bargaining weapon." [41]

It was only in June 1949, when the negotiations appeared to be hopelessly deadlocked, that the ECA finally dropped its insistence on drawing rights convertibility. In retrospect, however, it is doubtful that the course of the negotiations would have been substantially different even if the convertibility proposal had been abandoned earlier. Ironically, a draft plan that might, in principle, have been acceptable to the ECA had actually been drawn up by Belgium, early in May. The plan proposed that in addition to *bilateral* drawing rights, established on the same principle as in the 1948–1949 payments agreement, a pool, from which debtor countries would be granted *multilateral* drawing rights, should be set up. Such drawing rights could be exercised on any creditor country and, when utilized, would entitle the creditor concerned to ECA allocation of conditional dollar aid. [42] In essence, then, the Belgian proposal envisioned a payments plan under which at least a part of the drawing rights—the multilateral—would be fully transferable within Europe. [43] And the evidence suggests that although the ECA still preferred a pool consisting entirely of multilateral drawing rights, it would have been willing to accept a scheme in which even 50 percent of the total drawing rights were transferable. [44]

But as it turned out, the amount of multilateral drawing rights finally agreed upon came to only 25 percent of the total to be established; and even that figure was reached after some two months of hard bargaining. The fundamental issue, as far as some Europeans were concerned, was not simply how *much* multilateral drawing rights should be created, but whether they should be created at all. Thus, when the Belgian plan came for discussion in the OEEC Payments Committee, it was greeted with stiff opposition from Britain—supported by Sweden, Norway, Denmark, and, to a point, France. The British called for "organized flexibility"—i.e., the establishment of bilateral drawing rights, on the same principle as before, with possible transferability left to be settled by negotiations between individual creditors and debtors. The Belgians, supported by the Netherlands, Italy, Greece, Austria, Switzerland, and Portugal, argued instead for "automatic flexibility," under which part of the drawing rights would be bilateral (and nontransferable) and part multilateral (and fully transferable). [45] Had the issue been forced, the Belgian plan would most likely have received the majority's support. But since it was feared that a formal vote at that time would produce a serious and irrevocable split within the OEEC, none was taken. The negotiations simply ground to a halt in early June.

Nor was transferability the only major issue over which the negotiations appeared to falter. Almost equally complex, and difficult to settle, was the matter of Belgium's own position as Europe's largest net creditor. Because it received no grants during the early years of the Marshall Plan, Belgium was anxious to convert as much of its European surplus as possible into a commensurate amount of conditional aid. Yet while the overall surplus with the OEEC countries for the year ending June 30, 1950, was estimated to be around $400 million, Belgium's anticipated Western Hemisphere deficit was calculated at only $200 million. Under ECA rules, no European creditor could be allotted conditional aid—against drawing rights established by it—in excess of what would be needed to cover its own Western Hemisphere dollar deficit. Hence, even if the drawing rights granted by Belgium, under the revised scheme, were to equal the maximum amount of conditional aid that it could expect, only half of the anticipated European surplus could be financed by them. And since the entire uncovered portion of this surplus—which presumably would have to be settled by gold and dollar payments—was expected to result from net exports to France, the Netherlands, and the United Kingdom, it is easy to appreciate Britain's continued fear of dollar losses to Belgium and its adamant refusal to undertake risky experiments involving transferability. For its part, Belgium was no less adamant in insisting that a revised payments scheme, involving transferable drawing rights, must also entail at least some increase in the allotment of ECA dollar aid, or else a prior commitment by Britain to cover part of its expected deficit (with Belgium) in gold.[46]

Concerned as it was over the distinct lack of progress in the negotiations, the ECA nevertheless remained unmoved on the basic issue of transferability. Although its officials were still reluctant, in early June, to openly pressure the OEEC countries into accepting full multilateralization of drawing rights, they began to consider various measures by which to prod them along in that direction.[47] And as the month of June neared its mid-point, they also began to formulate alternative courses of action in the event that a new agreement was not reached by the time the existing one had expired (June 30, 1949).[48] In the end, however, it was the United Kingdom that—albeit unwittingly—took the step that led to an eventual compromise and made the conclusion of a revised agreement possible.

On June 14, the United Kingdom requested a postponement of the OEEC Payments Committee's meeting, scheduled for that very day, on the ground that "no satisfactory agreement could be reached at the technical level, and that therefore the [whole] question should be referred to the ministerial level."[49] Taken at its face value, this action could easily have been interpreted to mean that Britain was unwilling to reach an agreement and was engaged in delaying tactics designed to stall the negotiations.[50] But if that was indeed its intention, the United Kingdom came in for a surprise. Less than ten days later, Averell Harriman, together with Belgium's Foreign Minister Spaak and France's Finance Minister Petsche, was facing Britain's Sir Stafford Cripps in a round of intensive discussions over a meaningful compromise. And shortly thereafter, on June 29, the OEEC Council reconvened for what proved to be a two-day negotiating session, at the conclusion of which an acceptable solution was finally agreed upon: Only 25 percent of the drawing rights established would be transferable, Belgium would advance additional credits to its European debtors, and the United States would increase Belgium's allotment of conditional aid.[51]

Although a formal statement embodying these principles was issued by the OEEC Council on July 2 and publicly endorsed by ECA five days later, the final agreement was yet to be drawn up. Several specific issues still remained to be settled by negotiations. Moreover, as long as congressional appropriations for fiscal year 1950 were not known, the allocation of ECA aid and the exact amount of drawing rights to be established could not be determined. It was not, therefore, until September 7, 1949, that a second revised AIEPC was formally signed, in Paris, by the participating countries.[52]

V

The terms of the 1949–1950 AIEPC have been extensively described and analyzed elsewhere and need not be recounted here.[53] What might be noted instead are the ways in which its provisions were to be implemented. At the time of its signing, the agreement provided for the establishment of drawing rights totaling $802 million, of which $517.1 million was to be bilateral.[54] Once again, every country, with the exception of Greece, was to grant bilateral drawing rights to others, and each (except for Belgium, Italy, Sweden, and West Germany) was to receive some in return.[55] However, three countries—Belgium, the United Kingdom, and West Germany—were scheduled to grant the largest amounts of bilateral drawing rights. Among them they were expected to contribute some $401 million of the total bilateral drawing rights established.

The creation of multilateral drawing rights, on the other hand, involved a different set of calculations. For while they were specifically assigned to individual debtors, multilateral drawing rights were not treated as the contribution of any particular creditors. Instead, they were to constitute a pool, making up 25 percent of the total drawing rights established. In practical terms, this meant that the amount of multilateral drawing rights assigned to each debtor could not exceed one-third of the bilateral drawing rights originally established in its favor.[56] Thus calculated, the total amount of multilateral drawing rights created under the terms of the agreement would have been $172.4 million (equal to one-third of $517.1 million). However, as part of the special arrangements needed to finance Belgium's anticipated surplus, that country established special drawing rights, totaling $112.5 million, in favor of France ($28 million), the Netherlands ($49 million), and the United Kingdom ($35.5 million). And although granted by Belgium, these sums were treated, in the agreement, as multilateral drawing rights assigned to the three countries concerned.[57] Accordingly, the actual total of multilateral drawing rights came to $284.9 million.

The $112.5 million in special drawing rights established by Belgium in favor of France, the Netherlands, and the United Kingdom constituted, in effect, an "extra" contribution—above and beyond some $200 million worth of bilateral drawing rights that Belgium was scheduled to grant under the agreement. Therefore, Belgium made these special grants on the condition that its allotment of ECA dollar aid would be increased by an equivalent amount. In addition, Belgium agreed to extend $87.5 million worth of credits, in the form of loans, to the same three countries.[58] All told, Belgium was scheduled to make available some $400 million worth of financial resources, by which its anticipated European surplus might be covered. In return it would be entitled to a firm allotment of $312.5 million in conditional aid. And as an added inducement, Belgium was formally assured that the total amount of drawing rights exercised on it by all other OEEC countries would not exceed the equivalent of $352.5 million.[59]

The bilateral and multilateral drawing rights originally established under the Agreement, the special resources provided by Belgium, the subsequent granting of $2.5 million in additional drawing rights by France and Italy (to Turkey and Norway, respectively), and the carrying forward of $78.4 million in unused drawing rights from the previous payments scheme all together brought the amount of potential resources available under the 1949–1950 AIEPC to an aggregate of $970 million.[60] As before, France, the Netherlands, and Greece stood to be the largest beneficiaries of the scheme; together these three countries were originally slated to receive over half of the total available resources. At the other extreme stood Belgium, Italy, and Sweden, which were neither scheduled to, nor actually received, any of the drawing rights created. They functioned, strictly speaking, as creditors. Yet both creditors and debtors were affected by changing circumstances during the succeeding months. Thus, for example, the large deficit projected for France turned instead into a sizable surplus. But while France's and, to some extent, Britain's payments positions improved, West Germany's seriously deteriorated. Belgium's European surplus, initially estimated at $400 million, actually amounted to only $302 million during the period. Greece's deficit, on the other hand, exceeded previous estimates and was the largest among the OEEC countries. The Netherlands and Norway also continued to run large deficits, followed closely by Austria and Turkey.

Changing circumstances, in turn, dictated a need for adjustments, and various modifications in the amounts and distribution of drawing rights were made during the lifetime of the 1949–1950 AIEPC. Although the total of multilateral drawing rights remained unchanged at $284.9 million, several reallocations were made within it. The amount of bilateral drawing rights, however, was actually reduced from the original $517.1 million to $499.4 million, bringing the aggregate total of drawing rights, finally established, to $784.3 million. As seen in Table 21, almost half of this total was assigned to France, Greece, and the

Table 21   Total Bilateral and Multilateral Drawing Rights Finally Established under Revised AIEPC (in $ millions)

| Recipient countries | Bilateral drawing rights | Multilateral drawing rights | | | | | Total drawing rights |
		One-third of original bilateral	Special on Belgium	Re-Allocation	Total		
Austria	68.9	21.5	–	+3.0	24.5		93.3
Denmark	17.0	5.7	–	+1.0	6.7		23.6
France	53.4	52.3	28.0	–18.6	61.7		115.1
Germany	60.3	–	–	+12.0	12.0		72.3
Greece	94.7	26.8	–	+8.0	34.8		129.5
Netherlands	39.0	17.4	49.0	–	66.4		105.4
Norway	61.5	19.2	–	+6.0	25.2		86.7
Portugal	14.8	6.8	–	–1.1	5.7		20.5
Turkey	60.9	13.3	–	–	13.3		74.2
United Kingdom*	29.0	9.5	35.5	–10.3	34.7		63.7
Totals	499.4	172.4	112.5	±30.0	284.9		784.3

Source: BIS, Twenty-first Annual Report, p. 216.

*Figures for the United Kingdom include Ireland and Iceland.

Netherlands, though Greece replaced France as the largest recipient. But it should also be noted that France's actual receipts of *bilateral* drawing rights, set originally at $156.3 million, came to only $53.4 million.[61] In contrast, West Germany, which had not been scheduled to receive any drawing rights under the scheme, emerged as the recipient of $60 million in bilateral, and $12 million in multilateral drawing rights.[62]

All of the bilateral drawing rights finally established were utilized by their respective recipients. The record shows, however, that the actual utilization of multilateral drawing rights fell short of the amount available, and that the difference was accounted for by the failure of France, the United Kingdom, and Portugal to make full use of the drawing rights to which they were entitled. Ironically, France, which originally had been assigned some $80 million worth of multilateral drawing

Table 22   Drawing Rights Established and Utilized, 1949/50 (in $ millions)

Established and utilized	Bilateral drawing rights	Multilateral drawing rights			Total bilaterals and multilaterals
		One-third	Special	Total	
Finally established	499.4	172.4	112.5	284.9	784.3
Utilized	499.4	153.3	50.1	203.4	702.8

Source: BIS, Twenty-first Annual Report, p. 217.

rights, used only $15.6 million and exercised none of the special drawing rights granted to it by Belgium.[63] The United Kingdom, though entitled to a total of $45 million in multilateral drawing rights, actually used a scant $1.6 million, of which $1.1 million was drawn on Belgium. And Portugal, whose original allotment of multilateral drawing rights had been set at $6.8 million, used just about half that amount. All other countries fully utilized their shares of multilateral drawing rights; and the Netherlands found it necessary, in addition, to draw on the entire $38 million loan extended by Belgium.[64]

Table 22 summarizes, in aggregate terms, the amounts of drawing rights established and utilized under the second AIEPC. Of the $784.3 million finally established, $702.8 million was actually utilized. The turnover of first- and second-category compensations, during the same period, amounted to $149.3 million.[65] And finally, of the $87.5 million in special credits (loans) advanced by Belgium to France, the Netherlands, and the United Kingdom, some $39.1 million was used up. Together these figures add up to $891.2 million, or to slightly over 10 percent of the total value of intra-OEEC exports during the period.[66]

Although comparisons are at best risky, it might be pointed out that, judged by its results, the revised payments agreement constituted only a slight improvement over its predecessor. During comparable periods of time, roughly the same percentage of intra-OEEC trade was financed by each of the payments schemes.[67] Moreover, the proportion of drawing rights used to drawing rights established turned out to be lower under the revised AIEPC (81 percent) than under the first (83 percent). And while, in absolute terms, the revised agreement provided a larger amount of financial resources—some of which were fully transferable—it was still based essentially on a network of bilateral trade and payments relationships.[68]

A meaningful assessment of the revised agreement's contribution to the promotion of intra-European trade is further complicated by the fact that its formal signing was followed almost immediately by the devaluation of the British pound and nearly all other OEEC currencies. The devaluation of the pound sterling, entailing a 30.5 percent reduction in its dollar value, was announced on September 18, 1949, barely two weeks after the revised AIEPC had been signed. It triggered currency devaluations of similar magnitudes on the part of most countries in the sterling area. And it was followed in short order by devaluations and various exchange-rate adjustments of the currencies of all but two (Switzerland and Turkey) of the OEEC countries.[69]

Although a detailed account of the events and considerations that led to the devaluation of the pound falls outside the present discussion, it might be noted that its immediate causes were (1) a deterioration of Britain's balance-of-payments during the second quarter of 1949, (2) a growing crisis of confidence in the future of the pound sterling, and (3) a substantial decline in British official reserves between June and September of that year.[70] But it should also be noted that the subject of European exchange rates had preoccupied U.S. policy makers long before this round of devaluations actually took place. In fact, as early as March 1949, ECA/W communicated to OSR its view that "positive action" should be taken promptly to achieve "realistic exchange rates" among the OEEC countries and between them and the United States; and it instructed that whenever such action appeared necessary, the concerned participating countries, which were members of the International Monetary Fund (IMF), should be asked to discuss their exchange-rate problems with the Fund.[71] One month later, the Secretary of State himself informed U.S. diplomatic representatives abroad that the IMF Executive Board had recently agreed on the advisability of a thorough review of the exchange-rate structure of Western Europe, and that the Fund's Managing Director would shortly undertake a series of conversations on this matter with West European members of the Fund.[72] And as the summer progressed, the National Advisory

Council on International Monetary and Financial Problems (NAC) added *its* voice to the discussions by suggesting that "a mutual readjustment of exchange rates among the OEEC countries and devaluation against the dollar, particularly of the sterling, would be essential to a successful program for the reduction of trade barriers" and will "assist materially" to stimulate British exports.[73] The evidence indicates, moreover, that throughout the summer of 1949, high-ranking American and British officials held several discussions pertaining to Britain's mounting financial crisis, and that on two occasions—in early July and early September—such discussions were led by senior Cabinet members representing the United States, the United Kingdom, and Canada.[74]

In any event, it should be fairly obvious that the 1949 round of devaluations and exchange-rate adjustments was bound to have its own effects on intra-European trade and on the previously forecasted trade positions of the OEEC countries. Under the circumstances, the actual impact of the revised AIEPC on intra-European trade and payments developments during 1949–1950 cannot be clearly identified. It is even more difficult to assess the role of the revised agreement in furthering the overall objectives of the ERP. To the ECA, which had become convinced that liberalization of intra-European trade was the key to the success of the entire recovery program, the revised AIEPC represented a positive step in the right direction. To John H. Williams, a respected Harvard economist, it seemed that, by insisting on drawing rights transferability (and convertibility), the ECA "had overplayed the importance of intra-European trade in the recovery picture."[75] And to the *internationally*-minded officials of the U.S. Treasury Department, who effectively dominated the NAC, any experiments with *regional* payments multilateralization appeared to pose a serious threat—or worse, a setback—to the attainment of universal free trade.[76]

But if a consensus regarding the virtues of the revised payments agreement was not easily achieved, it did not really matter. For by late 1949 and early 1950, new forces were beginning to exert their own influences on the course of the ERP in general, and the liberalization of Europe's trade and payments in particular. Some of these forces were the inevitable products of changing political and economic conditions in Europe and elsewhere. Others, however, had originated within the ECA itself. And of the latter, none proved more innovative and dramatic than the ideas and efforts that were responsible for the creation of the European Payments Union (EPU).

Toward Multilateralism: Conception and Birth of the European Payments Union

In a narrow sense, the European Payments Union (EPU) could be viewed as a technical device, designed to further facilitate intra-European payments. Its conception, however, had been prompted by and linked to a much broader objective: to foster a greater degree of economic cooperation in Western Europe. Put differently, the EPU was perceived by the ECA not as an end in itself, but as an instrument through which the OEEC nations would formally commit themselves to genuine "cooperative behavior" and eventual economic integration. Accordingly, its formulation was seen as leading to the creation of a central institution, entailing radically new sets of intra-European relationships and obligations. It was to be, moreover, an institution that would outlast the Marshall Plan period itself and would constitute a core around which a regionally integrated economy could be built.

It might be argued, of course, that in pressing the case for the EPU, the ECA was attempting to carry out an explicit, though vaguely stated, congressional mandate—namely, "to encourage the unification of Europe."[1] At least, this was suggested by Paul Hoffman who, during congressional hearings on the Foreign Aid Appropriation Act of 1951, stated: "Now on this matter of unification. There again, that is a goal given to us, that we are to promote the unification of Europe. . . . So the reason we are driving hard for unification is, first, that it is a goal [that Congress gave us]. . . ."[2] But I should like to suggest that the ECA, in effect, did more than merely follow the dictates of Congress. By concentrating its efforts on the establishment of an EPU-like institution, it provided at least a working definition of the term unification or integration. Specifically, it took upon itself to identify "integration" with regional liberalization of trade and payments. And this, in turn, implied that liberalization of intra-European trade had become at once a short-term requisite for economic recovery and a longer term objective of European integration.

The evolution of American views and policies with respect to European integration will be examined, in some detail, in subsequent chapters. For the moment, it might be noted that because the proposed EPU scheme could admittedly be interpreted as an instrument of regional integration in Europe, its development raised a number of complex political and technical issues, and its adoption, by either the ERP nations themselves or the U.S. Administration, could not have been taken entirely for granted. That an agreement for the establishment of EPU was finally reached was thus largely due to the tenacity with which the ECA pursued this goal and to belated support which it was to receive from several unexpected sources.

I

European economic integration was indeed the central theme of a strong signal sent by the ECA to the ERP nations in the fall of 1949. The particular occasion, as is well known, was Paul Hoffman's address to the OEEC Council on October 31, 1949.[3] In it, he argued that "economic integration [was] essential" to the success of Europe's recovery efforts, and he called for "the formation of a single large market within which quantitative restrictions on the movement of goods, monetary barriers to the flow of payments and, eventually, all tariffs are permanently swept away."[4] The ECA Administrator did not elaborate on the precise mechanisms through which these aims should be pursued; nor did he suggest the establishment of specific institutions, such as the EPU.[5] He merely informed his listeners that he expected them to "have ready, early in 1950, a record of accomplishments and a program which together will take Europe well along toward economic integration."[6] Thus, less than two months after they had affixed their signatures to the revised AIEPC, the OEEC representatives were being asked to forge an even more ambitious and, for them, difficult path—and to do so in fairly short order. What they were not told at the time was that less than one week before he had addressed them, the ECA Administrator had actually endorsed, at least tentatively, the establishment of a fully multilateral payments mechanism—i.e., a clearing union, based on a new European settlement currency.[7] Nor could they know that some time during December 1949, the ECA would present them with a fairly comprehensive plan for a clearing union *cum* trade liberalization, together with a timetable for its implementation.[8]

The flurry of activities immediately surrounding Hoffman's speech could be explained by ECA's apparent fear that continued congressional support for the ERP might be jeopardized unless the European countries demonstrated a willingness to proceed toward economic integration. An expression of such concern may be inferred from a cable sent by ECA/W to Paris on October 6, 1949, which called for "a redefinition of ERP and redirection of activities of ECA and of Europeans . . . at this time." [9] What was particularly emphasized, however, was the need for concentrated efforts on the promotion of measures to increase productivity and to "achieve in the short-run" closer form of economic cooperation. "We believe it essential," the cable stated, "that *before next Congressional presentation*, [the] European countries undertake firm commitment to form one or perhaps two integrated economic units which, at a minimum, would involve some surrender of sovereignty to new central agencies. . . ." [10] Underlying this sense of urgency was an ominous note, sounded in an internal ECA memorandum, which advised: "Persons most familiar with attitudes in Congress are afraid that a continuation of ERP at the minimum necessary level of aid cannot be expected unless Western European countries have clearly embarked on a course of economic unity." [11]

Yet while concern about congressional attitudes during the forthcoming round of authorization and appropriation hearings may help explain the *timing* of ECA's emphasis on economic integration, it cannot fully explain the particular form that it took and the process by which it evolved. Indeed, it may be recalled that a strong argument for the creation of an effective free-trade area in Europe had already been made, by some ECA officials, as early as the previous April. [12] Basic to this argument was the proposition that substantial increases in Europe's productivity could not be achieved without a major structural change in Europe's market—a change brought about by mutual convertibility of European currencies and the progressive elimination of trade barriers. This proposition—linking increases in the rate of growth of productivity to trade and payments liberalization—became a dominant theme in policy discussions held within the ECA during the summer and fall of 1949. And this theme, in turn, provided a continuous frame of reference for the formulation of various multilateral payments and trade liberalization schemes.

In fact, barely two weeks after it had acquiesced to the last-minute compromise embodied in the revised AIEPC (i.e., only 25 percent transferable drawing rights), the ECA turned to consider anew a suggestion for automatic transferability of 100 percent of the drawing rights established under the existing plan. [13] But it is worth noting that two additional and more far-reaching suggestions were being considered at the same time. One of these dealt with the creation of a permanent payments mechanism in which, interestingly enough, the pound sterling might conceivably play the role of a key (or settlement) currency. The other called for the establishment of an Intra-European Commerce Commission, modeled after the U.S. Interstate Commerce and Federal Trade Commissions, to oversee the progressive elimination of trade barriers and to prevent their reimposition by European governments.[14] Common to both of these suggestions was the notion of institutional centralization. That is to say, what was being proposed was the creation of institutions endowed with central, or *supranational*, authority over intra-European trade and payments. And while the exact details of such institutional arrangements were yet to be worked out, the "centralization" principle itself had become firmly established in the minds of ECA officials by the early fall of 1949.

This principle was clearly reiterated, in mid-October, in a document summarizing ECA's views on the question of European unification.[15] While stating that "[ECA's] ultimate goal is the creation of an economic and political federation covering the whole of Western Europe . . .," the document conceded that an immediate objective was "the formation of one or more tight economic groupings."[16] It further advised that any approach to the problems of such groupings must be functional and flexible. But it explicitly recommended the creation of three central European agencies—for example, a central monetary authority, a central authority to oversee commercial policies, and a central reserve and dollar pool.[17] Thus, it could be reasonably argued that the principle of institutional centralization had become an agreed-upon ECA policy even before the cited document was actually written, and that the main purpose of the memorandum was not merely to reiterate a principle but to urge its speedy translation into concrete measures.

From ECA's standpoint, time was indeed of the essence; and Hoffman's October 31 speech was obviously designed to impress upon the OEEC countries the importance of prompt action along the lines suggested above. Impressed as they may have been by Hoffman's remarks, the Europeans nevertheless proceeded with caution. To be sure, in an apparent gesture of accommodation the OEEC Council adopted, on November 2, 1949, a decision calling on member countries to remove, by December 15, quantitative restrictions on at least 50 percent of their private imports from each other.[18] But when it came to the formulation of new payments plans, Europe's initial reactions did not quite measure up to ECA's expectations. In fact, Hoffman himself felt sufficiently moved, in late November 1949, to criticize two plans, proposed by France and the Netherlands, as being "weak," adding that "we should not agree to support [a] payments mechanism which has no chance for independent existence after [the] end [of] ERP."[19] And in the meantime, ECA officials in Washington and Paris were busily putting the finishing touches on their own payments scheme, soon to be presented to the OEEC.

II

The plan developed by the ECA during November and early December 1949 called for the establishment of a fully automatic multilateral clearing union and of an effective machinery for direct coordination and review of monetary and exchange rate policies of the participating countries. The latter was to take the form of an Advisory Monetary Committee within the OEEC, with powers to make recommendations on the appropriateness (or lack thereof) of national economic policies pursued by individual member countries. Its main purpose would be to assure—through its recommendations—the existence of conditions necessary for a substantial and permanent elimination of quantitative restrictions among the ERP nations. And while conceding that such a committee could not accomplish a great deal by itself, the ECA nevertheless argued its merits on the ground that its very existence "would tend to lead in the direction of more authoritative central institutions which [were] essential for creating and maintaining a *real free trade area*." [20] Equally, if not more, essential was the creation of a central payments mechanism. Indeed, it may be argued that a reduction of trade barriers could not have been realistically expected without a fundamental change in the structure of intra-European payments arrangements. And it is not surprising, therefore, that the main thrust of ECA's proposed plan was directed at replacing the existing network of bilateral payments relationships with a system of full intra-European currency transferability.

Such a system was to be based on several operational principles, embodied in a central clearing mechanism. [21] Specifically, a clearing union would be established and a common unit of account—i.e., a settlement (or clearing) accounting unit —would be defined. [22] At periodic intervals the participating countries would report to the union the amounts of their respective surpluses and deficits with each other. Although denominated in various national currencies, intra-European surpluses and deficits would be converted into the common unit of account, and the net creditor or debtor position of each country could then be calculated in terms of these units. Each country would have an account with the union, and the clearing of balances would be accomplished through the simultaneous offsetting of these accounts against one another. Inevitably, some countries would emerge from a given clearing process as creditors, and others as debtors, but the settlement of such imbalances would be made between the individual creditors (debtors) and the clearing union itself, rather than between individual pairs of countries.

Since imbalances would indeed require some sort of settlement, the clearing union was to be endowed with financial resources of its own.

Each participating country would, therefore, be assigned a quota—an amount to be contributed by it, in its own national currency—and the ECA would augment these contributions by pledging a certain amount of ERP dollars.[23] In practical terms, the establishment of quotas was intended to serve a dual purpose. Not only would the quotas provide part of the initial capital of the union, but they would also constitute the basis for determining the extent to which imbalances with the union would have to be settled in gold or dollars. Put differently, the size of each country's quota would predetermine the maximum *accumulated* credit it could either receive from or extend to the union. Thus, a debtor would be relieved of making gold payments as long as its accumulated debit balance did not exceed a certain percentage of its quota. Conversely, a creditor could not expect to receive payments in gold as long as its accumulated credit balance remained below a certain percentage of *its* quota. Once these so-called swing margins had been reached, any further accumulation of debt would have to be settled, in varying proportions, by both credit and gold payments.[24]

A moment's reflection will suffice to identify four basic principles inherent in the proposed scheme. First, unlike the offsetting mechanism of the two previous payments plans—in which a distinction had been made between automatic "first category" and optional "second category" compensations—the clearing of balances under the EPU would be fully automatic. Second, the automatic offsetting of deficits and surpluses, converted into a single unit of account, would, in effect, render all OEEC currencies mutually convertible. Third, imbalances would be financed in a completely multilateral fashion—i.e., through credit extended or received by the union. And fourth, settlements at any given accounting period would be based on the cumulative position of each member country vis-à-vis the union. To these might be added a fifth, and conceptually perhaps the most important, principle: The EPU was to provide an automatic mechanism of balance-of-payments adjustment, which would induce both debtors and creditors to move toward intra-European payments equilibrium.[25] It was, in other words, ultimately designed to facilitate a gradual and orderly transition to "a system ensuring the maintenance of free intra-European payments and unrestricted trade, after ECA aid [was] no longer available." [26]

Yet ironically, ECA's continued unwillingness to separate the issue of payments multilateralization from that of trade liberalization was to prove the major source of its difficulty, on both sides of the Atlantic, during the negotiations for the EPU. For on one hand, ECA officials would have to persuade reluctant European countries that an agreement on EPU, without agreement on substantial elimination of quantitative restrictions, "might provide only illusory benefits, or might even be a hindrance to genuine economic integration." [27] And on the other hand, they would have to convince highly skeptical Treasury and State Department officials that *regional* monetary arrangements, such as the EPU, could be compatible with overall U.S. international economic policy, as exemplified by the adherance to the *universalist* principles of the IMF and the General Agreement on Tariffs and Trade (GATT). That the latter task would prove to be especially difficult became evident shortly after the ECA submitted its draft plan for consideration by the NAC.

III

When Paul Hoffman reported to OSR on the NAC staff meeting at which the plan was first presented, he stated: "In general, there was no hostility to [the] plan or any fundamental issue raised in which there was a disagreement between ECA and other members of the NAC staff committee." [28] To judge from the evidence, however, Hoffman's guarded optimism was, to say the least, quite misplaced. He himself admitted in his report that "an atmosphere of skepticism" prevailed during the meeting, and that "considerable efforts" would be required to reconcile all the views of the Executive Branch on U.S. international financial policy. [29] But he was obviously unaware of the intense hostility actually harbored by some U.S. officials toward the proposed scheme. Nor, apparently, was he aware, until a few days later, that several critical questions were indeed being raised by the NAC staff committee, in preparation for a full-dress discussion by the NAC itself. And he would undoubtedly have been quite disturbed to learn that even before the discussion took place, a senior Treasury official had already concluded—and so informed Secretary Snyder—that there was no possible way to reconcile the proposed clearing union setup with U.S. obligations to the IMF. [30]

The tone of the discussions that were to follow was set by an NAC memorandum dated January 16, 1950, titled "Proposed European Clearing Union." [31] In it, the NAC staff chided the ECA for encouraging only "partial steps" toward European integration rather than demanding a "firm commitment to the ultimate establishment of a full economic union." And taking this as its point of departure, the memorandum went on to argue that the proposed scheme might actually lead to the formation of a soft-currency bloc in Europe, a bloc that would discriminate against trade with other areas of the world. The creation of such a bloc would, therefore, run counter to the basic objective of U.S. foreign economic policy—i.e., universal, nondiscriminatory free trade. Moreover, by encouraging and participating in the scheme, the United States might mislead other nations as to its long-run intentions and thus gravely weaken its leading position within the

IMF. As a result, the IMF itself might well lose a major part of its present responsibility.[32]

Given its basic premise—and carried to its logical conclusion—the argument seems to imply that had the ECA proposal called for the establishment of a complete economic union, instead of a mere clearing union arrangement, few if any questions would have been raised against it. Yet this was clearly not the sense of the memorandum. On the contrary, the NAC staff explicitly argued that "if European unification is a goal of U.S. policy, it is necessary to see whether some *modus vivendi* can be reached between the position of the United States toward the management of the European clearing union, and its position in the global institutions, to the support of which [it] is committed."[33] What was in fact being implied by this statement was that the United States' commitments to the principle of *globalism* took precedence over its perceived objective of economic integration under the ERP. And since the IMF represented the global approach to payments liberalization, its preeminent position had to be guarded against any potential challenge from a regional monetary organization.[34]

This argument bore a striking resemblance to the one contained in an office memorandum, also dated January 16, 1950, and written by Assistant Secretary of the Treasury Frank Southard.[35] Addressing his memorandum to the Secretary of the Treasury, Southard sharply criticized the ECA proposal and recommended that it be rejected. His argument, though much more blunt and succinct, was almost identical to the one expounded in the NAC staff memorandum. And it is reasonable to suggest that Southard—himself a member of the NAC senior staff—was actually the author of the NAC document cited above. It is also reasonable to assume that the views expressed therein were, at least tacitly, endorsed by the Secretary of the Treasury. But what is especially noteworthy is that both Southard's memorandum to Secretary Snyder and the NAC staff document were accompanied by a memorandum from the Managing Director of the IMF.[36] In it the latter offered a few recommendations of his own; and it is of some significance that one of those recommendations was subsequently approved by the NAC.

That the NAC should be asked to consider, let alone approve, recommendations emanating from the Fund's Managing Director would have been highly unusual under normal circumstances. In fact, during its formative years the IMF was frequently the recipient of recommendations issued by the NAC, rather than the other way around. But these were not normal circumstances. The preeminence and prestige of the IMF were being challenged by some of its own members. And the Managing Director was accordingly encouraged to seek the help of the NAC on the matter.

This challenge arose during a January 1950 meeting of the IMF Board, at which time the Fund's attitude toward the proposed clearing union scheme was discussed. Stressing the "vital interest" of the Fund in the new arrangement, the Managing Director recommended that the Fund participate in the ongoing OEEC discussions, at both the technical and the policy levels. He also recommended that the ERP members of the IMF consult the Fund before adopting any new plan, and that the Fund set up any new regional monetary organization, if one was actually necessary and desirable.[37] Although they may have been willing to accept the first suggestion, several Executive Directors were clearly offended by the other two. Thus, for example, Ernest deSelliers (the Belgian Executive Director) emphasized that the proposals currently being discussed by the OEEC were the outcome of two years' experience in the workings of intra-European payments. And, recalling the "negative attitude" hitherto taken by the IMF toward Europe's payments plans, he pointedly suggested that "it was *inappropriate* now to request European governments to suspend action pending consultation with the Fund."[38] Another Executive Director then suggested that the views and recommendations of the Managing Director be transmitted to the member countries concerned; the Board quickly agreed. Thus it was that the memorandum from the Managing Director, containing his specific recommendations, found its way into the NAC staff document.

It is against this background that NAC's reaction to the proposed clearing union must be considered. As the appointed guardian of official U.S. international monetary and financial interests, the NAC was duty bound to critically examine any developments that might affect them. Yet because the NAC was lodged in the Treasury Department and its staff was composed mainly of Treasury officials, its views were strongly influenced by those of the Treasury Department itself. And on questions pertaining to the preeminence of the IMF, the Treasury's view was quite adamant: Any development that might conceivably threaten the role or prestige of the IMF must be regarded as detrimental to the self-interests of the United States and inimical to its basic international economic objectives. Accordingly, if the IMF perceived of a European clearing union as a potential rival, then the supposed merits of ECA's proposal must be seriously questioned, and the plan itself either rejected or greatly modified. And, to judge from the record, this was precisely the position taken by the Treasury during the NAC discussions. It was a position, incidentally, that had its advocates in other agencies of the Executive Branch as well.

Thus, when the full NAC met to discuss the proposal on January 19, 1950, Messrs. Hoffman and Bissell found themselves under a constant barrage of questions and comments, most of which implied dissatisfaction with the plan as it stood. To Frank Southard it seemed—and rightly so—that the proposal called for "a permanent institution," and that the NAC must, therefore, consider "whether the possible gains from the proposed institution would adequately offset the risk involved [for the United States]."[39] He felt, as noted earlier, that U.S. sponsorship of and participation in the plan would weaken this country's influence in the global institutions it had helped to create. And he now plainly stated, as he had done before, that "there was no way of reconciling the ECA proposal with [U.S.] obligations to the Fund."[40] William McC. Martin, who would one day head the Federal Reserve Board, also opposed the establishment of a permanent organization, while Thomas Blaisdell, Jr. (Commerce), wanted to see "some modification" so as to make the plan "tenable with respect to relations with the IMF."[41] He was, moreover, concerned about the extent of membership in the organization, wondering "whether Britain, for example, should be included."[42] Under-Secretary of Agriculture Albert Loveland, for his part, objected to the proposal on the ground that it contained a "discriminatory feature" vis-à-vis American exports. And Secretary Snyder, sitting in the chair, wanted to know "how could the European countries have the opportunity of earning dollars if they created a union which kept the United States on the periphery."[43]

All in all, it was a trying opening round for the ECA. Only one agency, the Federal Reserve Board, stood unequivocally on its side. The State Department, unsure of its own feelings, offered merely lukewarm support. Its representative, Willard Thorp, suggested that the EPU should not necessarily be viewed as a permanent institution but should instead be endorsed as "an immediate device [to meet] an immediate situation."[44] In any event, it was finally agreed that the NAC staff should review the various ideas expressed and explore the possibility of alternative approaches to the liberalization of Europe's trade and payments. Rising to the occasion, the staff met on the very next day; and, after considerable give and take with the ECA, they managed to reach agreement on several issues.[45] These, together with issues still remaining to be resolved, were reviewed and considered three days later by the full NAC, at which time a compromise of sorts was at last hammered out.[46]

Underlying this compromise were two explicit principles laid down by the NAC. First, the operation of the clearing union should not conflict with the obligations of the United States and other countries to the IMF. Second, the establishment of such a union should not prevent any participating country from moving as rapidly as possible toward full currency convertibility.[47] From these, there logically followed several additional principles—namely, that (1) the United States should not participate in the management of the union, but should merely have an observer with a veto power over the use of funds contributed by the ECA; (2) the funds contributed by the United States should not be used by the clearing union to make loans in the same way as IMF loans are made; (3) the financing, by ERP dollars, of the union's offsetting operations should not extend beyond June 30, 1952; (4) the ECA should, in any event, fix a maximum limitation on its obligations for such financing; and (5) the IMF should be invited to participate in the discussions of OEEC committees working on the proposal.[48]

Although a compromise had been reached, the NAC did not consider the matter entirely closed. To be sure, the ECA was given a license to proceed with its plan. But since that license was granted reluctantly, it would be subject to frequent reviews and could possibly even be revoked. Thus, what may have momentarily appeared, in ECA's eyes, as the end of a hard fought battle was, in fact, the beginning of a much more intense struggle. And throughout it all the ECA would be faced with an almost impossible task: It would have to strike a proper balance between increasingly hard-nosed demands by the NAC, and Europe's resistance to measures through which these demands could be satisfied.

IV

Indeed, as seen through various European eyes, the ECA proposal was hardly more appealing than it had appeared to the NAC. The reasons, obviously, were different, but the intensity of feeling quite similar. True, the OEEC nations had committed themselves, by the November 2 resolution of the OEEC Council, to explore and adopt measures for closer monetary and economic association among themselves.[49] However, most European countries were not yet prepared to accept the specific terms suggested by the ECA proposal. Particularly irksome to them was ECA's insistence on tying the payments scheme to a code of trade liberalization. But they were equally resentful of the notion of an automatic mechanism for balance-of-payments adjustment, which could conceivably compel both creditors and debtors to correct excessive surpluses and/or deficits by measures contrary to their own national objectives and interests.

Thus, to the Scandinavian countries, especially Norway and Denmark, it appeared that the achievement and maintenance of domestic full employment could well be jeopardized under the proposed scheme. As probable debtors to the union, they naturally feared that the rapid removal of trade restrictions would expose them to an even greater competition from their European partners and would further aggravate their balance-of-payments deficits. In order to correct such excessive deficits they would be forced to adopt deflationary policies at home, with severe consequences to their levels of employment.[50] For other countries, trade liberalization entailed the risk of actually importing unemployment from other participants who might deliberately pursue ex-

cessive anti-inflationary policies. And for countries that viewed inflationary policies as a legitimate means of inducing high levels of
employment, the removal of trade restrictions could certainly spell balance-of-payments deterioration and consequent losses of gold and dollar reserves.

In reply, the ECA would argue that the issue was not whether there
should be full employment but rather how it should be achieved and
maintained.[51] Thus, while declaring itself strongly in favor of high employment levels, it categorically rejected both inflationary policies and
restrictive trade measures as the means toward this end. It opposed
such measures, the ECA stated, because they were inconsistent with the
objectives of the recovery program in general, and constituted the most
serious obstacles to European economic integration in particular. It even
went so far as to suggest that full employment could be considered a
legitimate goal only if it could be achieved by measures that did not
conflict with those essential for the attainment of greater freedom of
trade and payments. And while acknowledging the difficulties of
achieving both goals simultaneously, the ECA nevertheless reiterated
its position that trade liberalization and antiinflationary measures must
proceed hand in hand.

But if potential deflationary pressures and unemployment were of
concern to some European countries, the prospective position and role
of the United Kingdom in the scheme was the concern of them all. In
January 1950, when the OEEC Council outlined the general principles
under which a clearing union might operate, it stated: "If a European
Payments Union of the kind described [here] is to work, it will be necessary to arrive at an agreed method for reconciling both the new system and such existing or additional monetary arrangements as would
remain or come into force. . . ."[52] Such existing arrangements, the
Council went on to say, "include the *multilateral* [payments] facilities
offered by *sterling*. . . ."[53] The pound sterling could indeed have been
considered a multilateral, or international, currency. In 1948, for example, about 36 percent of the total world merchandise trade was financed by sterling, and at the time of the EPU negotiations the British
government estimated that "probably more than 50%" of all international payments (for visible and invisible transactions) were made in
sterling.[54] Moreover, although sterling was subject to an intricate set of
exchange regulations, administered by the Bank of England, the workings of the Sterling Payments System (SPS) actually permitted the free
transferability of the pound sterling within a fairly wide geographical
area.[55] More important still, all of the OEEC countries fell into one or
another of the various groups designated under the SPS, and several
of them enjoyed the privilege of automatic sterling transferability.[56]

The exclusion of Britain from the proposed payments scheme would

have thus been unthinkable to most Europeans. Yet its inclusion raised
two major problems that would have to be resolved if the EPU were to
function successfully. The first of these had to do with Britain's unwillingness to subjugate the management and operations of the SPS to rules
entailed in any central European entity, and its continued fear of potential gold and dollar losses. The second concerned the impact that
the use of credit, extended under the SPS, might have on the operations of the EPU itself—specifically, the possibility that large-scale clearings of sterling balances might impose an undue burden on the EPU
mechanism and might lead to a severe drain on its own resources. Although seemingly independent of each other, these problems required
a common set of solutions. But the search for an acceptable compromise was to be beset by prolonged difficulties.[57]

The nature of these difficulties may be better understood if it is remembered that the proposed plan called for the settlement of *cumulative* payment positions. That is to say, at any given settlement, the debit
or credit position of each country would reflect the cumulative results
of its transactions with all the others, since the beginning of EPU's operations. This, in turn, implied that the calculations of net positions
with the union would have to take into account not only the current
transactions of each member, but also its previously accumulated—and
still outstanding—debit or credit balances. Herein, however, lay a potential problem, both for Britain and for the EPU. From Britain's
standpoint, there existed a danger—real or imaginary—that sterling
balances held by fellow OEEC members may be thrown into the EPU
clearing operations and be treated as other European currencies in the
calculation of positions. These sterling balances—amounting to some
£441 million at the end of December 1949—constituted British liabilities (or debts) to the respective OEEC countries.[58] And the United
Kingdom, quite understandably, feared that their inclusion in the
clearings would adversely affect its own net position and force it to
settle the resulting debt to the EPU through gold and dollar payments.[59] Not surprisingly, therefore, Britain strongly objected to the
automatic transferability of sterling within the proposed EPU system.

Britain's concern about potential gold and dollar losses was shared
by the OEEC Financial Experts studying the ECA proposal. They viewed
the problem from a different vantage point, however. What worried
them was the possibility that the inclusion of sterling balances—or, for
that matter, any other large outstanding debts—in the calculations would
enhance creditors' positions and would result in the weakening of EPU's
own gold and dollar resources. Put differently, if preexisting debts (i.e.,
previously extended credits) were to be liquidated through the EPU
from the very start, its convertible resources might be quickly exhausted and its own credit mechanism would be unable to finance cur-

rent trade transactions. Hence, early in the negotiations the Financial Experts argued in favor of controlling or limiting the use of "existing resources" (read: credits previously extended under the SPS or by other European creditors), so as to avoid "a drain on EPU's resources."[60]

European creditors, on the other hand, were hardly impressed by this argument. Belgium and Switzerland, which looked upon the EPU as a potential source of dollar receipts, naturally favored the inclusion of at least some preexisting debts in the clearing and settlement operations. Belgium in particular was fearful lest its continued extension of large intra-European credits, unmatched by dollar imports, produce inflationary pressures within its economy. Belgium was unwilling to advance credit to the EPU—in fact, unwilling to participate in the scheme—without an assurance that its existing claims on European debtors would be properly and promptly settled. Moreover, when the discussions turned to the actual terms of settlement under the EPU mechanism, Belgium assumed an increasingly tough posture. Whereas the United Kingdom opted for the establishment of fairly liberal credit margins and for keeping hard-currency settlements to a minimum, Belgium argued in favor of hard-currency settlements to the maximum extent possible.[61]

The relative hardness or softness of settlement terms was not the only issue over which the Europeans were divided. Nor was it the only issue separating the United Kingdom from most of the other OEEC members. Thus, for example, throughout the negotiations Britain kept insisting that each country retain the right to reimpose quantitative restrictions *unilaterally*, whenever it deemed such a move necessary to protect its foreign exchange reserves. The Scandinavian countries, for reasons of their own, supported the British position. But other countries, while acknowledging the need to reintroduce trade restrictions in the face of balance-of-payments emergency, were reluctant to entrust such action to a unilateral decision. Even more objectionable, to some countries, was the British-inspired proposal for *collective discrimination* against large creditors. Vigorously supported by the Norwegians, the United Kingdom proposed that the OEEC countries be authorized to collectively impose quantitative restrictions against chronic creditors with large export surpluses.[62] Creditors, of course, were just as vigorous in opposing the proposal. Their main interest in the EPU lay in its held promise that the discrimination to which they had hitherto been subjected would be avoided.[63] They were not about to agree to any measures that might well render such a promise unredeemable; and in the end, the British proposal was indeed rejected.

These and other issues (e.g., the size and use of the quotas, the basis for calculating payments positions, the frequency of settlements, and the composition and powers of EPU's Managing Board) were to occupy the energies of OEEC technical experts and officials—and to tax their endurance almost beyond a breaking point—throughout the winter and spring of 1950. As will be seen later, a reconciliation of divergent views was eventually achieved with respect to most, if not all, outstanding issues. Yet this reconciliation was still quite a way off in the early months of 1950. And both in Washington and in Paris, new moves were being considered by the ECA in order to expedite the negotiation process.

V

Disappointed with what it felt was slow progress on the part of the OEEC nations, the ECA decided to resort to what may be viewed, in retrospect, as a carrot-and-stick approach. The "carrot" was to be a portion of the 1950–1951 ERP appropriations, earmarked as a special incentive fund. The "stick" was the threat to withhold this amount from the actual aid allocations, in the event that the participating countries failed to show sufficient determination to conclude a satisfactory EPU agreement. Interestingly enough, the original suggestion for such a fund was not directly related to the EPU negotiations per se. Indeed, the germ of the idea could be found in a previously cited memorandum, addressed to Paul Hoffman and William Foster by Richard Bissell, in January 1950, in which the latter expressed grave concern over "ECA's failure to influence *internal* economic policies in most participating countries." [64] To Bissell, the single most important reason for this failure had been the very concept of the aid administration—specifically, the principle that each country was somehow entitled to its share of aid and should, therefore, receive it, regardless of the kind of general economic policies it pursued. Ever so much the pragmatist, Bissell argued that the criterion for aid "should progressively move in the direction of *performance* rather than need." As a practical measure, he suggested that "some 20–25% of next year's appropriations" be withheld and be used "frankly and with great toughness as an incentive fund to which the participating countries will have access if, but only if, they perform on a *program of national and supra-national action which [the ECA] will work out with their participation in advance*." [65]

Evidently impressed by the idea, Hoffman sensed in it an opportunity to drive the Europeans to greater effort and speed in their negotiations for the EPU. Accordingly, on February 21, 1950, the ECA Administrator requested Congress to permit him to earmark at least $600 million of the forthcoming appropriation "to encourage the aggressive pursuit of a program of liberalized trade and payments." [66] In making this request, he distinguished between two specific usages to which these funds would be put. Part of this sum, he stated, would be used to support the proposed EPU itself, and the balance would be made available directly to countries that agreed to join the new institution. Countries that refused to join, he added, would simply be denied their share of the fund. In any event, he was confident, Hoffman stated, that "after we hold out these funds . . . we will have a payments union within 90 days." [67]

The Administrator was apparently also confident of favorable congressional action on his request.[68] In early March he announced that "no less than $600 million will be initially withheld from [next year's] country allotments," but that limited restoration of such funds would be made to "countries making major headway on basic policy lines agreed as desirable."[69] To him, "the most clear cut case" of a desirable policy line was "participation in [an] effective Payments Union." And he warned that if no payments union was established, "the funds that would have been used to support it, will not be made available to the ERP nations at all."

The message should have been clear. But if Hoffman hoped to press—or possibly scare—the OEEC negotiators into speedier action, he had not properly reckoned with the difficulties the Europeans faced in attempting to reconcile their own differences, let alone comply with ECA's specific demands. On the other hand, the fact that these difficulties were largely due to Britain's unyielding attitude did not entirely escape the ECA. Thus, in early April, Hoffman himself admitted that "there appears to be a major difference of principle between [the] British position and our own."[70] He was clearly annoyed by Britain's apparent desire "to secure complete freedom to pursue [its] domestic policies and to exploit all the benefits of [its] present bilateral trading relationships." And he instructed ECA representatives abroad to "persuade the UK to accept the major elements of the EPU proposal" and to make clear to that country the consequences of failure to do so.[71]

Britain's attitude, however, was not the only source of Hoffman's growing frustrations. In a message to OSR in early May, he seemed to unleash his anger on the OEEC in general. "We agree," he stated, "that the Europeans may be stalling because they might think that the U.S. may have its back to the wall." But, he bluntly continued, "if there is no satisfactory agreement [on] EPU by June 30, they rather than we, will have their backs against the wall and will suffer the consequences."[72] Still, it was primarily the United Kingdom that had to be nudged from its position if the EPU negotiations were to be brought to a satisfactory conclusion.

Nudged it finally was! But it took the personal intervention of the U.S. Secretary of State to allay Britain's fears and help overcome its lingering reservations. On May 11, 1950, Secretary Acheson personally handed to Foreign Secretary Bevin an *aide memoire* in which he diplomatically "stressed the importance of prompt action" on the part of the United Kingdom.[73] The same document also offered certain safeguards in the event that Britain would experience significant losses of gold and dollar reserves as a result of EPU's operation.[74] As reported by the ECA mission in London, Acheson's intercession with Bevin was absolutely necessary to secure British cooperation. It was necessary, ECA officials claimed, because the matter of Britain's participation in EPU, on terms acceptable to the OEEC experts and the ECA, was now up for a decision by the British Cabinet, "where objections seem to be raised by last-ditch supporters of bilateralism."[75] They were probably right. For, if any objections were indeed raised within the cabinet, they must have been quickly disposed of. And barely four days after the Acheson-Bevin meeting, Averell Harriman, who was in London at the time, was able to inform OSR and ECA/W that the United Kingdom would at last be prepared to join the EPU as a "full and ordinary" member.[76]

Yet while the change in Britain's attitude had removed one major obstacle, Belgium's reluctance to extend liberal credits to the union and its insistence on the liquidation of existing debts posed another.[77] Only in mid-June, less than two weeks before the deadline set by the ECA, was the OEEC Executive Committee able to agree to a series of recommendations presented by the Financial Experts.[78] The latter recommended that the general structure of EPU should consist of (1) country quotas, (2) a 20-percent gold-free swing margin for both debtors and creditors, (3) a rising scale of gold payments by debtors and a 50–50 ratio between extended credit and gold receipts by creditors, once the swing margins had been exceeded, (4) a fully automatic clearing mechanism, and (5) administrative assistance in exceptional and unforeseeable hardship cases. They also recommended that each country's quota should be based on 15 percent of the total turnover of its intra-European trade and payments during 1949. However, as a gesture to Belgium, the experts suggested—and the Executive Committee concurred—that the Belgian quota be set at $360 million.[79] To satisfy Belgium's second demand, they called for the amortization of existing debts within two years, to be arranged either by bilateral agreements or through the good offices of the OEEC. And in recognition of Britain's position, the experts suggested an option: Any participating country would be allowed to substitute bilateral credits for its credit to or from the union, provided its net credit (or debit) position with the EPU did not change as a result. Thus, countries could choose to use the sterling-payments mechanism whenever they deemed it desirable to them and to the British.[80]

VI

Concluding its June 16–17 meeting, the Executive Committee instructed the Financial Experts to prepare a document, embodying their recommendations, for discussion at a subsequent meeting, scheduled for June 30. At that time, final recommendations were to be made on all aspects of the EPU, for presentation to the OEEC Council on July

7. But while OEEC negotiators, under the watchful (but, finally, approving) eyes of ECA officials in Paris, were busily putting together a mutually acceptable agreement, new rumblings were heard in Washington. There, on June 16, the ECA found itself the subject of "quite strong questioning" by the NAC, with regard to the terms of settlement under the proposed EPU.[81] As the NAC saw it, the terms of settlement were "too soft." And although the ECA argued that "harder terms of settlement were simply unobtainable," the NAC senior staff was not entirely satisfied. Nor did it appear to be satisfied with most of the other proposed features of the scheme.[82] Sensing trouble in getting NAC's approval of the plan, Bissell urgently requested his colleagues in Paris to address a personal letter to him, describing the negotiations with the participating countries and "explaining the impossibility of achieving more favorable results." The letter, he subtly hinted, should be so written that it could then be "informally circulated" among the members of NAC.[83]

Such a letter was subsequently sent to Bissell by Henry Tasca, Chief of the Trade and Payments Division of OSR.[84] In this twelve-page document, Tasca very carefully reviewed and analyzed the course of the EPU negotiations, making certain to score as many points as possible in favor of ECA's position. He concluded with the following: "Throughout this letter I have tried to suggest to you what have seemed to us to be the *political* limits to a mutually acceptable EPU arrangements."[85] Tasca's point was well taken. But even before his letter was written, let alone received, the NAC returned to the attack.

On June 29, during a meeting of the full NAC, the ECA was once again criticized for its supposed failure to drive a harder bargain with the Europeans.[86] When ECA Deputy Administrator William Foster suggested "that the arrangement is the best way to the transition to convertibility; that Belgium and the United Kingdom are in it; and that EPU would lead to trade barrier reduction," several voices rose to protest. Both William McC. Martin and Frank Southard repeated their earlier charges that the EPU was likely to turn into a permanent soft-currency area which would constitute a discriminatory bloc. And Southard resurrected his favorite theme—namely, the inherent conflict between the creation of EPU and the United States' obligations to the IMF. According to him, the proposed terms of settlement would allow "too much leeway" to debtors, and hence the soft-currency area would be further strengthened. Even S. M. Szymczak of the Federal Reserve Board, who supported the plan in principle, saw a weakness in it. Given the settlement's terms, he opined, "more rather than less credit might be extended under the plan."

To all of this, Bissell, who had accompanied Foster, could only reply by stating that although the terms might not be ideal, "it was the best the negotiators in Paris could get." But in the course of the discussion, another disturbing question was suddenly raised: Was it true, Thomas Blaisdell asked, that, as an inducement to her participation in EPU, Belgium would be specifically allowed to discriminate against dollar-area exports? Not so, replied Bissell, explaining that such a suggestion, while it perhaps may have originated in the OEEC, would certainly be unacceptable to the ECA.[87] Still, the mood of the NAC meeting remained skeptical. This mood was quite accurately reflected in Secretary Snyder's stern admonition that "a definite stand ought to be taken, to make sure everyone understood that EPU should not be a device for circumventing the main U.S. objectives of non-discrimination and full convertibility." The commitment of U.S. policy to these objectives, he concluded, should be forcefully reiterated "before consumation of the [EPU] plan."

Snyder's admonition did not fall on deaf ears. During the next few days ECA/W hastened to apply last-minute pressure on the Europeans, in an attempt to extract a tighter agreement from them. Two months earlier, by its own admission, the ECA would have been willing to accept—as an absolute minimum, to be sure —an agreement containing "safeguards against the use of bilateral discriminatory tactics by any EPU member.[88] Now it was demanding more specific commitments with regard to trade liberalization. As a condition for "finalizing" the EPU agreement, Bissell informed OSR on July 3, the U.S. government required the Europeans to agree to the following: (1) removal of quantitative restrictions on 60 percent of their mutual imports at the inception of EPU, and (2) a definite commitment to remove such restrictions on 75 percent of their imports by the end of 1950.[89] And on July 6, one day before the OEEC Council was to consider and act on the text of the EPU agreement, William Foster sent an urgent message to OSR, in which he acknowledged receipt of the proposed text but insisted on several additional changes.[90] At least one of the requested changes reflected a concession to NAC's views. In fact, citing a commitment made by ECA to NAC, Foster instructed that the final agreement must provide for a review of EPU's operations "at the end of one year" and not, as previously proposed by OEEC, after two. But in a vein that clearly did *not* reflect NAC's attitude, he also requested that the powers of EPU's management be made "specific and tight" and that the Managing Board have a permanent staff.[91]

"EPU Agreement finally adopted by Council this morning . . . ," OSR cabled Washington, on July 7, 1950.[92] The euphoric cable went on to elaborate:

Full non-discrimination agreed for both liberalized and nonliberalized trade. . . . Financial provisions easily agreed to with requested amendments, [including] full review after one year. . . . Protracted commercial discussion involved [various Europeans'] objections. [But] firm U.S. objections prevented [adoption] of broad escape clause.[93]

It might be noted that the agreement referred to by OSR took the form of a resolution, passed unanimously by the OEEC Council of Ministers.[94] That resolution embodied and approved the principles that would govern the structure and operations of the new institution. It also specified the size of the original quotas assigned to member countries and stipulated the proportions of gold and credit to be used in the settlement of surpluses and deficits with the union. The quotas, totaling nearly $4 billion, were distributed as follows:[95]

Austria	70,000,000
Belgium-Lux.	360,000,000
Denmark	195,000,000
France	520,000,000
Germany	320,000,000
Greece	45,000,000
Iceland	15,000,000
Italy	205,000,000
Netherlands	330,000,000
Norway	200,000,000
Portugal	70,000,000
Sweden	260,000,000
Switzerland	250,000,000
Turkey	50,000,000
United Kingdom	1,060,000,000
Total	3,950,000.000

The terms of settlement, proposed by the Financial Experts and adopted by the Council, provided that net positions with the union be financed partly in gold (or dollars) and partly by credit. The exact proportions agreed to are shown in Table 23.

In effect, the July 7 Resolution (or Decision) signaled the birth of the EPU. Yet several months would pass before the newborn institution was endowed with a proper legal status and needed financial resources. Both technical and legal experts would have to labor over the July 7 document in order to translate its intent into acceptable legalistic language. And even when this task was accomplished, the OEEC, as well as the ECA, would still have to await congressional appropriation of funds for the third year of the recovery program. Not until September 19, 1950, almost one year after Hoffman's famous "integration" speech, did representatives of the OEEC nations formally sign the Agreement for the Establishment of a European Payments Union. By their action

Table 23   Terms of Settlement under EPU

Percent of quota	Debtors		Creditors	
	receive credit from EPU	pay gold to EPU	grant credit to EPU	receive gold from EPU
	Percentages			
1st 20	20	0	20	0
2nd 20	16	4	10	10
3rd 20	12	8	10	10
4th 20	8	12	10	10
5th 20	4	16	10	10
Total utilization of quota*	60	40	60	40

Source: BIS, Twenty-first Annual Report, p. 226.

* Once a member's quota was fully utilized (i.e., exhausted), further settlements would be made in gold only, for both creditors and debtors, except in the case of Switzerland where settlement in excess of its quota would be made on a 50% gold basis.

they committed themselves, for a minimum of two years, to a new experiment in intra-European payments multilateralization. At the same time, they also committed the United States to extend a certain sum of money for the specific purpose of seeing their experiment go through. The challenges and problems that would confront the new institution were still unknown. But for the moment, the assembled delegates could allow themselves a brief feeling of relief—and, perhaps, satisfaction—for having completed the long and hard negotiations. So, presumably, could the ECA. Its own sentiments on this occasion were formally expressed in a message to the Secretary-General of the OEEC "I wish to reaffirm," wrote Milton Katz to Robert Marjolin, "the gratification of my government with the action of the [OEEC] in reaching agreement on a European Payments Union and related principles of commercial policy." [96]

The European Payments Union and Trade Liberalization: Problems and Accomplishments

It would not be long, however, before the feeling of relief gave way to some moments of anxiety. Less than a month after the EPU agreement had been signed, the ECA was called upon to honor part of its financial pledge to the union. Its initial responses on that occasion served only to confuse the Europeans and to heighten their suspicion of some hidden American motives, And in order to appreciate what would indeed appear as a rather curious turn of events, and the circumstances under which it occurred, it is necessary to consider briefly the kind of financial commitments made by the ECA in the course of the EPU negotiations.

I

As noted earlier, Congress had granted ECA its request to earmark a portion of the 1950-1951 ERP appropriations, in order to encourage the "aggressive pursuit" of a program for liberalizing Europe's trade and payments.[1] The Economic Cooperation Act of 1950 provided that $600 million of the funds appropriated for the recovery program for fiscal 1951 would be used "solely" for this purpose. Specifically, the act authorized the ECA Administrator "to transfer funds directly to any central institution . . . , or to any participating country or countries *in connection with the operations of such institution*, . . . in order to facilitate the development of transferability of European currencies or to promote the liberalization of trade by the participating countries. . ."[2] Although the Act did not preclude the use of additional funds to encourage European integration, it imposed a ceiling on the total amount that could be transferred to a central institution such as the EPU. It stipulated that no more than $600 million could be so transferred. And the General Appropriation Act of 1951 later reduced this amount to $500 million.

The 1950 authorization act became law on June 5, 1950, at a time when the EPU negotiations were about to enter their final and most crucial stage. Acting on the authority contained therein, the ECA promised to make available to the EPU a working capital fund of $350 million, which the latter could draw upon if and when it needed dollars to carry out its operations. Such a need would obviously arise whenever EPU gold payments to creditor countries exceeded its gold receipts from debtors. And since under the agreed terms of settlement schedules for gold payments and receipts were not parallel, it was reasonable to expect that at one time or another the EPU could experience net outflows of gold.[3] It was also to be expected that during its early days the EPU would be especially vulnerable to net gold losses, due to the fact that the "initial credit positions," allotted to prospective debtors under the scheme, exceeded the "initial debit positions" assigned to prospective creditors.

These initial positions—or, initial balances—were established by the ECA as a special temporary measure covering the first year of the union's operations.[4] Specifically, initial balances were *additions* to the quotas of several countries; they were designed to serve the special needs of persistent debtors on the one hand, and to augment the resources of EPU on the other. Thus, an initial credit position constituted, in effect, an EPU grant that a debtor country could use to discharge its obligations to the union before utilizing any portion of its quota. An initial debit position, in contrast, required a prospective creditor to extend an initial grant, in its currency, *to* the union, above and beyond its assigned quota.[5] Both kinds of initial balances would have to be exhausted before the members' quotas were to be utilized in the manner provided for by the agreement. However, in consideration of extending grants to the union, creditors were to receive conditional dollar aid from the ECA. Recipients of initial credit balances, on the other hand, would be required to make deposits of local-currency counterparts, as though they were receiving direct ECA grant aid.[6]

As seen in Table 24, six countries were identified by ECA as prospective debtors and three as prospective creditors. It may be observed that the initial credit positions allotted to Austria and Greece were actually larger than their respective quotas.[7] And it may also be noted that part of Norway's initial position and the entire amount allotted to Turkey were to be made as loans, repayable to the EPU. But what is especially noteworthy is that the initial credit positions totaled $314 million, while the initial debit positions amounted to only $215.7 million. In other words, the EPU was to begin its life with more obligations than claims—a prospect that clearly dictated a need for some financial contributions by the ECA. Accordingly, upon the signing of the EPU agreement, the U.S. government obligated the aforementioned $350

Table 24   Initial Balances under EPU (for the year July 1, 1950–June 30, 1951)

Initial debit balances		Initial credit balances	
Prospective creditors	millions of US $	Prospective debtors	millions of US $
Grants by:		Grants to:	
Belgium	44.05*	Austria	80
Sweden	21.2**	Greece	115
United Kingdom	150.00	Iceland	4
		Netherlands	30
		Norway	50
		sub-total	279
		Loans to:	
		Norway	10
		Turkey***	25
Total	215.7		314

Source: BIS, Twenty-first Annual Report, p. 227; also ECA, Tenth Report to Congress, p. 30.

*This amount represented one half of Belgium's ERP aid allotment for 1950/51. Belgium's initial position was later reduced to $29.4 million.

**This amount represented the total ERP aid allotted to Sweden during 1950/51. Sweden's initial position was later reduced to $9.6 million.

***Turkey's initial credit position was not actually allotted until May 1951.

million, "on the books of the ECA," to be made available to the EPU when needed.[8] On the same occasion, the ECA notified the OEEC that an additional sum of $100 million would be made available to provide "special assistance" to individual countries facing particularly serious payment difficulties vis-à-vis the union.[9] And as for the initial positions, the ECA made "firm allotments of conditional aid" to the creditor countries concerned, while simultaneously alloting initial credit balances to the prospective debtors.[10]

II

Armed with these financial assurances, the ERP nations set out to inaugurate the new institution and to test its machinery. As provided by the agreement, a Managing Board consisting of seven members was appointed by the OEEC Council.[11] The Managing Board was to be responsible for supervising the operations of EPU and the management of its funds. Its decisions were to be taken by a simple majority, rather than by an unanimous vote, and normally could not be modified by the Council. The actual execution of operations, however, was entrusted, as before, to the Bank for International Settlements (BIS). The latter, acting as the agent for EPU, was to calculate the members' balances with each other, to carry out the automatic offsetting operations, and to effect the necessary settlement of the resulting net position of each member with the union.

Since the provisions of the agreement had been made retroactive to July 1, 1950, the first operations under EPU were to cover the accounting period July 1-September 30, 1950.[12] Yet even as it prepared for this first round of compensations and settlements, the BIS received a disturbing message from ECA/W—so disturbing, in fact, that it threatened to jeopardize the very beginning of EPU. Accustomed to dealings with as well as between central banks, the BIS had assumed that the funds obligated by the United States could be obtained "in accordance with standard banking procedures"; that is, by a cable drawn directly on the Federal Reserve Bank, New York (FRBNY).[13] Unfortunately, this assumption, which was shared by ECA officials in Paris, was to prove invalid. For on September 29, 1950, the BIS was unexpectedly advised by Richard Bissell that instead of drawing on the FRBNY, the agent would have to draw drafts on the U.S. Secretary of the Treasury.[14] The BIS balked at these instructions, claiming that it was authorized to deal only with central banks, not with governments, and, hence, could not sign a draft on the U.S. Treasury.[15] It also argued that, "owing to the apparent impossibility to draw on the Treasury by cable," such a procedure would cause delays in carrying out the automatic clearing and settlement operations. In sum, the BIS refused to abide by the directive, wryly suggesting that perhaps the Secretary General of OEEC should sign the necessary drafts.[16]

To worried OSR officials the refusal appeared to reflect a genuine feeling of "consternation" on the part of the Europeans, as well as the agent's own "disappointment" with a procedure that "limits access to the line of credit" established by the United States.[17] The "value date"—the date on which settlement of net positions would have to be made—was approaching; and the agent's calculations showed that on that date, October 16, 1950, the EPU would be obliged to pay a total of $42.6 million to creditors.[18] Unless this amount could be drawn upon by the BIS, the new payments scheme might be nipped in the bud. Still, the BIS refused to deal with the U.S. Treasury. And under the circumstances, all that OSR officials could do was to urge ECA/W to reconsider the drawing procedure. Specifically, they urged that a modest agent account be established at the FRBNY and that a sufficient amount of funds be deposited into it in advance, so as "to ensure promptness and full automaticity of [EPU's] operations."[19]

Three days before the value date, ECA/W appeared to have relented. On October 13, 1950, William Foster advised OSR that a Procurement

Authorization (PA) had been signed and immediately handed—together with a voucher and a check for $42.647 million—to the Department of the Treasury.[20] The latter was to instruct the FRBNY, "by telephone," to credit the BIS, as agent for the EPU, by this amount. That message was followed on the next day by another, stating that "P.A. #EPU-1, $42,647,000 will be made available to Agent in FRBNY, Monday morning, October 16."[21] As for future settlements, Foster continued, "the agent could *notify* the FRBNY directly by cable of the funds needed, as late as one day before value date." However, the agent should notify ECA "at least five days before the funds are needed at FRBNY." In this way, he concluded, "agent would deal directly with FRBNY, and ECA/W *would assure* availability of funds as and when needed."[22]

The drama should have ended right there and then. It did not. On the evening of October 16, OSR frantically cabled Washington: "As of 5:30 P.M. Paris time, OSR has not received information cables advising firm allotments to UK, Sweden, and Belgium against [their] initial positions; Agent has not been advised by [these] countries that allotments have been received; and Agent has had no advice from FRBNY of availability of funds."[23] The cable warned that unless the countries concerned "receive words of allotment today" and the agent is advised of availability of funds, it would be impossible to effect settlement before October 18—two days *after* value date. It further informed ECA/W that the EPU Managing Board had called a meeting for October 20, to consider and assess the situation. And it concluded by appealing to Washington "to complete all necessary action urgently today."[24]

The record shows that the first round of EPU's operations did, in fact, take place and that $42.6 million was paid out to net creditors.[25] It also suggests, however, that neither the Europeans nor OSR officials were particularly pleased with the way the procedural matter had been handled by Washington. Obviously baffled, OEEC officials did not hesitate to express their doubts about the "firmness and duration" of U.S. obligations, and to voice their concern over "the procedure for making funds available."[26] And OSR, anxious to reassure the Europeans and to allay their fears, literally pleaded with ECA/W to explore different procedures for the BIS's drawing on the obligated funds.[27] It even offered its own solution for replacing the PA procedure with a more practical and meaningful arrangement. It proposed that a noninterest-bearing Treasury certificate be deposited in advance at the FRBNY, and that it be cashed by the latter whenever the BIS needed dollars for EPU settlements.[28]

Yet while ECA/W appeared willing to acknowledge the desirability of expressing U.S. obligations "in a form more definitive than [the] P.A. procedure," it rejected OSR's suggestion on the ground that the use of a noninterest-bearing certificate, in this instance, would be illegal.[29] Instead, it countered with a proposal of its own: A permanent account should be established on the books of the U.S. Treasury for the remaining balance of the $350 million; it would be debited each time the BIS account at the FRBNY was credited with funds for EPU settlements.[30] But oddly enough, ECA/W chose to ignore the major complaint of the BIS—namely, its inability to draw directly on the FRBNY. In fact, while proposing the establishment of a permanent account for the EPU, the ECA continued to insist that the BIS must either draw drafts on the Secretary of the Treasury—and send them via air mail to the Treasury or the FRBNY—or notify ECA/W by cable of the needed funds, four or five days before value dates. Upon such notification, ECA/W would see to it that the funds were promptly deposited at the FRBNY and made available to the agent.[31] In other words, the drawing procedure itself was to remain essentially the same as before.

What the BIS thought of the proposal is not publicly known, although one may easily guess at its private reaction. What *is* known is that on June 4, 1951—nearly eight months after EPU commenced operations—the remaining balance of the $350 million obligated for EPU was transferred to a separate account, called "Secretary of Treasury, OEEC, EPU." [32] The agent was to draw on this account as needed. But, ECA instructed, should the BIS prefer not to deal with the Treasury itself, it would henceforth have to notify ECA/W of the amounts required "six to eight days before the value date." [33] Ironically, it remains to be noted that except for the first settlement, no drawings were actually made on the obligated funds during the first year of EPU's operations. None were, in fact, necessary. For, beginning with the settlement for the month of October 1950 and continuing through July 1951, gold and dollar in-payments by debtors exceeded out-payments to creditors. As a result, the EPU ended its first year with larger dollar resources than those with which it had started.[34]

On the other hand, during the same period the EPU sustained interest losses amounting to $668,000.[35] These losses ($204,000 for the period ending December 1950 and $464,000 in the first half of 1951) resulted from the fact that interest paid to creditors on credits granted to the union exceeded that paid by debtors on credits received from it. The directives accompanying the EPU agreement had initially fixed the interest rate payable to creditors at 2 percent per annum. Debtors were to be charged interest on a sliding scale: 2 percent for the first year or part thereof; $2\frac{1}{4}$ percent for the second year, and $2\frac{1}{2}$ percent for any period exceeding two years.[36] These rates were to be reviewed by the Managing Board every six months and could be changed by it, with the approval of the OEEC Council. But although the Managing Board was obviously aware of the interest losses incurred up to December 1950, it decided against changing any of the rates at that time. And as credits granted to the EPU continued to rise faster than credits extended by it, interest losses grew commensurately.[37]

Following the settlement for June 1951, OSR was at last moved to act on this matter. Informing ECA/W of the interest losses sustained during the preceding year, it asked Washington to authorize the investment of EPU's dollar funds, on hand with the FRBNY, in U.S. government securities, on a month-to-month basis.[38] Interest earned on the funds thus invested, OSR argued, would help reduce the total interest losses to EPU. But ECA/W was not quite sure that it liked the idea. While agreeing that EPU's interest payments should preferably be balanced by interest receipts, it felt that the investment of funds contributed by the United States in U.S. government securities "would create a bad impression here."[39] Accordingly, it advised OSR that only funds in excess of the $350 million—i.e., funds representing net in-payments to EPU—could be so invested. And as if to underscore the point, ECA/W further suggested that, by lowering interest rates paid to creditors to $1\frac{3}{4}$ percent and raising rates charged to debtors to $2\frac{1}{4}$ percent the EPU would be able to balance its interest account.[40] The message was not lost on the Managing Board, which shortly thereafter decided to raise the interest rates for debtors to an overall $2\frac{1}{4}$ percent.[41]

III

The procedures for drawing on U.S.-obligated funds, and the management of EPU's dollar resources, were not the only issues that seemed to pit the Europeans against Washington during the first year of EPU. Lurking behind these technical problems was a deeply felt policy question. It was a question to which the Europeans—tacitly supported by OSR—would have one answer and ECA/W another. That particular question concerned the prospective relationship between the EPU and the (IMF).

It may be recalled that, much to the displeasure of the Europeans, the IMF had invited itself, with the help of the NAC, to participate in the discussions leading to the formation of the EPU. An IMF staff mission was assigned to Paris for this purpose in the spring of 1950; but although it had been given specific instructions by the IMF Board, the extent of its actual contributions had not been publicly recorded.[42] It may also be remembered that in late June 1950, as the EPU negotiations were nearing their conclusion, the proposed scheme came under severe criticism in the NAC, where Treasury officials continued to attack it as being incompatible with U.S. obligations to the IMF. Thus, it might come as a surprise—though it really should not—that in mid-August 1950 (following the July 7 Council Decision, but before the final EPU agreement had been drafted), ECA/W sent the following message to OSR:

Other agencies of Executive Branch have raised questions concerning relationship between IMF and EPU. [We] doubt that Fund will be prepared to discuss relationship until Annual Meeting. [We] assume that no EPU position will be taken in Paris, that would interfere with appropriate IMF arrangements that may be negotiated later in the year.[43]

To which OSR replied:

OSR knows of no position taken by U.S. participants in EPU negotiations that would interfere with appropriate IMF arrangements.[44]

The significance of this exchange lies not so much in its timing as in its underlying reasons. Having reluctantly accepted the establishment of EPU, the NAC was now determined that the new institution should be brought under the continued observation of the IMF.[45] Not surprisingly, the majority on the IMF Board appeared to share this view. Although its own preliminary discussions of the Fund's association with EPU proved "inconclusive," the Board sought "to ensure that observers on behalf of the Fund might attend meetings of the EPU Management Committee."[46] The Europeans, on the other hand, were not ready to commit themselves to specifics. True, in its July 7 Decision, the OEEC Council acknowledged that "close cooperation and consultation with the International Monetary Fund are desirable."[47] But, it continued, "it will be necessary for the Management Committee to examine and report to the Council what shall be the appropriate relationships."[48] Thus caught between NAC's prodding and OEEC's vague response, ECA/W appeared for the moment to settle on a middle course: While it did not press the Europeans for an immediate decision, it hinted that a proper decision would have to be reached sooner or later.

By April 1951, the gentle hint had been transformed into a specific policy directive. It is "our clear view," William Foster informed OSR, "that [the IMF] should have observer relationship" to the EPU Managing Board.[49] Such observer relationship, moreover, "should be effective for all meetings of managing board."[50] What was being suggested, in effect, was that the IMF be accorded the status of a *permanent* observer at EPU. And OSR was instructed to convey this suggestion to OEEC, presenting it as the official U.S. position on the matter.

This time, however, it was the turn of OSR officials to balk. Reporting on a conversation with IMF representatives in Paris, Robert Triffin (then the ECA observer at EPU) argued that even the IMF itself was still "completely vague and undecided" in its approach to the problem of association with EPU.[51] He went on to suggest that "until the Fund abandons its present passivity and resumes an active role in Europe," no effective and constructive relations could be established between the two institutions. Hence, the question of a permanent Fund observer appeared to him to be "entirely premature at this stage" and might, if pressed, undermine the chances for any fruitful discussions of the is- sue.[52] Quite significantly, one of the reasons cited by Triffin to support his argument tends to suggest that the Europeans themselves under- stood the nature of the proposed "observer relationship" far better than ECA/W or the NAC may have suspected. "There is a general, though unexpressed feeling [in EPU]," wrote Triffin, "that an IMF observer might, in fact, be a U.S. Treasury observer, *in conflict* with the ECA observer, and generally *unsympathetic* to EPU."[53] Expressed or not, this feeling was obviously quite strong. For, as reported by Triffin, the Brit- ish delegate had informed him that *his* government, for one, was "un- alterably opposed" to a permanent IMF observer.[54]

Yet neither the OEEC nor OSR completely ruled out any working relations between the EPU and the IMF. In fact, Triffin himself sug- gested that cooperation between the two institutions might be possible in several areas, and that when such instances arose, an IMF observer might indeed be invited by the Managing Board to attend its meet- ings.[55] He also reported, in late June 1951, that the atmosphere sur- rounding the Managing Board's discussion of relations with the IMF showed "considerable improvement" following a visit of Fund officials to Paris.[56] Still, to judge from the record, the search for "appropriate relations" would stretch over many months to come. Referring to this matter in its *1951 Annual Report,* the IMF Board stated that the "nature of the relationship" was still under consideration at that time.[57] One year later, it reported that such relationships were "being developed."[58] And in its *1953 Annual Report,* it alluded, without elaborating, to rela- tions that "have developed" during the past year.[59] Not until 1954 could the Board explicitly state that the Fund, through its European Office in Paris, had been "represented regularly" at meetings of the EPU Managing Board.[60]

By then, of course, the ECA no longer existed, its functions having been officially assumed by the Mutual Security Agency (MSA) on De- cember 30, 1951. Yet interestingly enough, the changed purpose and character of U.S. aid, under the Mutual Security Program, helped to remove at least one obstacle that had previously stood in the way of a reconciliation between the IMF and its European members. It may be remembered that in April 1948, the IMF Board had adopted the so- called ERP Decision which specifically discriminated against the ERP nations in the use of the Fund's dollar resources.[61] That decision, for which the United States had been primarily responsible, both irked and frustrated the Europeans. But in March 1952, when the question was again raised at a Board meeting, Frank Southard (the then U.S. Executive Director) appeared unusually accommodating. He personally believed, he stated, "that because of *changes in the structure of U.S. assistance to Europe,* the ERP decision had in effect ceased to exist, [and] any European country wishing to use the Fund's resources might apply to do so . . . just like any other member." [62] Southard did not specify the particular changes to which he was referring. But his remarks prompted Ivar Rooth, the then Managing Director, to announce that he "would take it for granted that the ERP Decision no longer applied" and would so inform Fund members. [63]

There can be no question that the rescinding of the ERP Decision constituted the first, though still rather tenuous, move toward the establishment of some relationship between the IMF and the EPU. It was followed, shortly thereafter, by another move that further enhanced such prospects. The occasion was a request by Belgium, made in June 1952, to borrow $50 million from the IMF. [64] What made the request especially significant was the fact that it was explicitly linked to a proposed arrangement for settling Belgium's extreme creditor position in EPU. Specifically, during the negotiations for the first extension of EPU, it was proposed that $50 million of the credit balance due to Belgium be liquidated over a five-year period. In other words, Belgium was asked to extend a loan to EPU, repayable in five equal installments, beginning in June 1953. But before agreeing to do so, Belgium sought an assurance of a corresponding access to the Fund's resources, if this should prove necessary.

With the approval of the United States, Belgium did, indeed, receive such an assurance. It took the form of a stand-by credit arrangement, under which it would be entitled to purchase, with Belgium francs, on a revolving basis, up to $50 million worth of foreign currencies from the IMF. This stand-by credit arrangement, the first of its kind to be negotiated between the IMF and one of its members, was concluded for six months. It was subsequently renewed several times and remained in force until June 1957. Although the IMF Board did not publicly acknowledge any connection between the stand-by arrangement and EPU's financial operations, it implied that such a connection did, in fact, exist. In granting Belgium's request, it stated, it considered the fact that "[its] payments position was the key to a significant part of the payments problems of a number of other Fund's members in Western Europe." [65] Yet, what was not stated in public was recognized in private. Thus, during the Board's discussion of the matter, the Managing Director specifically called attention to the "key position" that Belgium's surplus "held in the EPU." [66] And the Netherlands' Executive Director, who obviously favored the proposed arrangement, expressed the hope that its approval "might bring the EPU and the Fund into closer contact." [67]

Another year was to pass before the hoped-for contacts began to materialize. In June 1953, the Fund's Managing Director traveled to Paris to meet with the EPU Managing Board. The meeting, during which several issues were raised and discussed, would be termed "a success" by a future historian of the IMF.[68] Its immediate accomplishments, however, were relatively modest. In fact, its most concrete result was an agreement to resume the dialogue during the next annual meeting of the Fund, in September. Only after the second round of discussions, which EPU representatives reportedly found "very interesting and useful," did closer liaison begin to develop between the two organizations.[69] It entailed direct working contacts at staff level, official exchange of documentation, and official participation of Fund representatives at meetings of the Managing Board and other OEEC bodies. But, interestingly enough, the IMF, as an institution, was never formally accorded the status of a permanent observer to EPU. Instead, its observer would be referred to, by the Managing Board, as the "personal representative" of the Managing Director of the International Monetary Fund.[70]

IV

Established as a two-year financial experiment, the EPU actually functioned for eight and a half years. In June 1952, the financial commitments embodied in the original agreement were renewed for one year and, thereafter, extended on a year-to-year basis six more times. On most occasions the renewals involved various modifications, designed to accommodate the changing needs of the EPU or the payments positions of individual member countries. Indeed, it may be argued that EPU's staying power lay primarily in its ability—often after long negotiations between its members—to adapt to the changing circumstances under which it operated during its lifetime. And it may also be suggested that its operational success was largely due to the knack of its Managing Board to combine flexibility with determination in facing most of the problems that would be thrust upon it.

Such problems were not long in coming. No sooner had EPU begun operations when two of its members—Germany and the Netherlands—developed extreme debtor positions. Some 54 percent of Germany's quota was utilized in the first settlement operation, in October 1950. By the end of November, its entire two-year quota—originally set at $320 million—was actually exceeded. The Netherlands fared only slightly better. Its initial credit balance with the union was exhausted in the first settlement, and by June 1951, it had utilized 90 percent of the credit to which it was entitled under its regular quota. Three other countries—Austria, Greece, and Iceland—also exhausted their initial credit balances during the first few months of operations and required assistance out of the "special assistance" funds allotted by ECA.[71] Britain and France, on the other hand, were accumulating surpluses at a rate that threatened to absorb their quotas and force 100-percent gold settlement by the union.[72] They were followed, as large creditors, by Belgium, Portugal, and Switzerland, with Belgium registering a cumulative surplus of some $90 million by March 1951.

It was unquestionably the German payments crisis, however, that presented the EPU with its first real challenge. Reacting with speed, the Managing Board agreed to a remedial package consisting of external assistance and internally applied medicines. In mid-December 1950, it offered Germany a special line of credit, amounting to $120 million, on the condition that Germany carry out a series of measures designed to curb domestic monetary and credit expansion.[73] Germany had, in fact, instituted a program of credit restraints in October, by imposing higher reserve requirements on commercial bank deposits, raising the central bank discount rate, and requiring prospective importers to deposit, in their banks, the local currency equivalent of 50 percent of the foreign exchange value of the imported goods. Germany promised to continue the application of these measures and to impose additional ones. And on the strength of this promise, the Managing Board recommended—and the OEEC Council approved—the extension of the special line of credit.[74]

Despite its domestic efforts, Germany's deficit with the EPU continued to rise. By the end of February 1951, it had used over $90 million of the special line of credit and had been obliged, in addition, to pay out about $46 million to the union. Faced with the prospect of exhausting its entire line of credit, Germany suspended trade liberalization and, on the advice of the Managing Board, stopped issuing additional import licenses early in March. The Managing Board also recommended that any future allocations of German import licenses among OEEC suppliers be placed under the direction of a Mediation Group, composed of three independent experts, appointed by the OEEC Council.[75] This group was to ensure a distribution of licenses which, while taking account of the needs of the German economy, would minimize the harmful effects of German import restrictions on other weak members of EPU.[76]

Grim as it appeared in February and early March, the German payments position began to register significant improvements with the clearing operation for March. That clearing marked the transformation of Germany from an extreme debtor to a modest creditor, soon to emerge as a persistently extreme creditor of EPU. By the end of May, the special EPU's line of credit had been fully repaid, and in July, the German quota was revised upward, from $320 million to $500 million.[77] The Netherlands' payments problem, on the other hand, persisted through the spring and summer of 1951. In July, the Dutch quota was also adjusted—from $330 million to $355 million—so as to permit an increase in credit availability. Shortly thereafter, the Dutch government adopted monetary and fiscal measures designed to curtail domestic investment and consumption expenditures. And by the fall of 1951, the Netherlands, too, began to record surpluses with the EPU.

Yet while the German and Dutch payments positions continued to gain strength through the latter part of 1951, those of Britain and France took a drastic turn for the worse. As early as April 1951, both countries began to run monthly deficits with the EPU—deficits that at first merely served to reduce their previously accumulated surpluses. By early fall, however, both countries had been transformed into cumulative debtors. They would continue to run monthly deficits during the remainder of EPU's second year of operations. And although their monthly positions would periodically show improvement, they were to remain net debtors throughout the existence of EPU. In sharp contrast, Belgium—which, like Britain and France, had begun as a substantial creditor—greatly enhanced its credit position during the second year of EPU's operations. It continued to accumulate surpluses at a rapid rate, and by June 1952, the net cumulative surplus amounted to $795.3 million—the largest among all creditors and far in excess of Belgium's quota.[78] Portugal had surpassed its quota toward the end of 1951 and remained an extreme creditor throughout 1951–1952, while Italy, Switzerland, and Sweden (the last initially a modest debtor) also maintained strong creditor positions during the year.

The most visible outcome of all these developments was a severe drain on EPU's convertible assets. The union's dollar and gold resources, which had totaled $352 million after the June 1951 settlement, fell to $179 million in October—their lowest level in the organization's entire history. Less visible, but potentially more serious, was the possibility that a continued imbalance—i.e.., the persistence of extreme debtors and extreme creditors—might deplete the union's resources and threaten its effectiveness. Indeed, as 1951 drew to a close, the Managing Board was quite concerned that EPU's future operations would be severely hampered unless its convertible resources were augmented by additional American aid.[79] The evidence suggests, however, that the implied request for such funds was ignored by the Mutual Security Agency which chose instead to channel dollars directly to various EPU members, through offshore purchases and other defense-related programs.[80] As it turned out, the Managing Board's fears did not materialize. Following the November 1951 settlement, the level of EPU's liquid resources began to rise, due largely to increased gold and dollar payments by debtors whose quotas had been nearly or completely exhausted. After the May 1952 settlement, these resources amounted to some $460 million. And although they declined to $351 million as a result of special adjustments at the time of the June 1952 settlement, they soon rose again and were to remain at a reasonable level from then on.[81]

Nevertheless, the concern about adequacy of the union's convertible resources led to the adoption of two sets of measures when the EPU was extended in June 1952. On the one hand, special arrangements were concluded with four creditor countries, for the settlement of postquota surpluses.[82] These arrangements provided that surpluses arising beyond their quotas during 1952–1953 would be settled, up to specified amounts, on a 50-percent gold/50-percent credit basis, thereby slowing down the rate of potential gold payments by the union to these creditors.[83] Settlement of deficits with the union, on the other hand, was to be accelerated, through a change in the gold/credit schedule applicable to debtors. The latter would no longer enjoy a 20-percent gold-free tranche, but would have to begin making gold payments once their deficits exceeded 10 percent of their respective quotas. Moreover, under the new schedule the proportion of gold payable by debtors in the earlier tranches of the quota was increased, while the proportion due in the last two tranches was reduced.

Commenting on these changes, the Managing Board freely acknowledged that they were designed "to relieve the strain on the convertible assets of the Union."[84] At the same time, it also reported that the members of EPU had undertaken to ensure that the union's gold and dollar resources would not in any circumstances fall below a level of $100 million. Should they threaten to decline below that figure, the Managing Board went on to explain, the agent would call upon members to make temporary gold contributions (i.e., gold and/or dollar loans) in proportion to the size of their respective quotas.[85] Subsequent events, of course, would render this arrangement superfluous. For although the level of EPU's liquid resources continued to fluctuate, it never approached the point at which it would become necessary to call for gold contributions by its members.

In fact, the preoccupation with the adequacy of convertible assets greatly diminished after 1952, its place taken by a concern over the amount and duration of credit extended within the EPU system. By March 1954, debtors had utilized, on the average, 97 percent of their quotas, while creditors had exceeded theirs by an average of 25 percent.[86] By that time, moreover, some 71 percent of the credit granted to debtors by the union and 49 percent of the credit extended to it by creditors had been outstanding for more than two years.[87] In plain terms, most of the initial quota credits had been exhausted, leaving only a meager amount for future EPU settlements. More important still, the persistence of extreme creditors and debtors made it unlikely that outstanding credit (debit) could be quickly amortized through the EPU mechanism itself. What was clearly needed was a new device for reducing the total amount of outstanding credit extended within the union, and for reopening lending and borrowing facilities.

Such a device, consisting of three elements, was incorporated into the EPU scheme on the occasion of its third renewal, in June 1954. First, a series of bilateral repayment and amortization agreements was concluded directly between individual creditor and debtor countries. These agreements provided for the immediate repayment, on a bilateral basis, of $226 million of outstanding debts in EPU and for the progressive amortization of an additional $637 million over a seven-year period.[88] Thus, a total of $863 million in debts (and corresponding claims) was to be settled bilaterally, outside the EPU mechanism but with each payment canceling an equal amount of the debtor's liability to, and creditor's claim on, the union. Second, it was agreed that (1) debtor countries, if their position permitted, could reduce their EPU debts by making voluntary gold and dollar payments directly to the union and (2) the union could utilize part of its own convertible assets to reduce creditors' claims on it. Third, and operationally most important, it was agreed that the reduction of outstanding debts and claims—either bilaterally or through direct payments to and by the union—should entail a progressive reopening of the EPU's credit facilities. That is, in return for the repayment of part of their claims, creditors would accept higher lending obligations to the union, while cash repayments by debtors would entitle *them* to equal amounts of renewed borrowing facilities under their quotas.[89]

This set of principles prevailed throughout the remaining four and a half years of EPU's existence. It led to the conclusion of additional bilateral repayment and amortization agreements at the time of the 1956 renewal, and it prompted voluntary cash repayments to the union by various debtors. Moreover, as part of the 1954 renewal agreement, the EPU itself repaid $130 million of credit previously extended to it by drawing on its own gold and dollar resources. Thus, when the books were closed on EPU's operations in late December 1958, a substantial reduction of the debts outstanding in 1954 had been achieved. By that time, some $843 million of debts (and corresponding claims) had been repaid under the bilateral arrangements, while $207 million had been paid directly to EPU by debtors and used to reduce the union's liabilities to creditors.[90] All told, $1.18 billion of outstanding debts were settled through these various repayment arrangements, enabling the reopening of credit facilities that in many cases had become almost completely exhausted.

V

Occupied as it was with the problems directly related to EPU's operations, the Managing Board did not lose sight of general economic and monetary developments taking place in the OEEC countries. Of particular interest to it were the changes in the balance-of-payments and reserves positions of EPU members—changes that might permit a gradual restoration of currency convertibility and would thus render the EPU, as originally constituted, less and less necessary. Indeed, as overall payments positions of various member countries began to improve in 1953, the Managing Board increasingly turned its attention to possible ways by which the EPU might be modified, so as to enable an effective transition to full convertibility by all or some of its members. And during the negotiations for the 1954 renewal of EPU, it came up with a proposal: It proposed that the graduated schedule of gold payments *within the quotas* be replaced by a uniform settlement basis of 50 percent gold and 50 percent credit, for both creditors and debtors.[91]

Theoretically, this proposal, which was adopted as part of the 1954 revision, was intended to harden the union's settlement terms. In practice, however, its immediate effect was largely formal, since most debtor countries had already reached a quota stage where, even under the graduated-scale formula, they were obliged to pay 50 percent or more in gold, in settlement of their monthly deficits. Moreover, the proposed measure was adopted on the understanding that it would not lead to a reduction in the amount of credit available to each country. Hence, because the original quotas contained a credit element of 60 percent, the new settlement rule (i.e., 50 percent gold and 50 percent credit) required an upward revision of existing quotas by 20 percent. A year later, in August 1955, the terms of settlement were further hardened, to a 75-percent gold/25-percent credit basis, and the quotas then in force were once again increased (in fact, doubled) in order to leave the original credit element unaltered.

Significant as they unquestionably were, the changes in EPU's settlement terms were overshadowed by another series of measures whose main purpose was to insure the continuation and maintenance of monetary cooperation between the OEEC countries once currency convertibility had actually been restored. These measures, adopted at the time of the 1955 renewal, provided for a new payments structure to succeed the EPU, if and when the major OEEC countries returned to full convertibility. They also provided for the termination of EPU, at any time, upon the joint demand of countries representing at least 50 percent of

Table 25   EPU: Original and Revised Quotas (in millions of units of account)

Member-Country	Original quotas*	Quotas as of June 1954	Quotas as of Aug. 1955
Austria	70	84	168
Belgium	360	432	864
Denmark	195	234	468
France	520	624	1,248
Germany	500	600	1,200
Greece	45	54	108
Iceland	15	18	36
Italy	205	246	492
Netherlands	355	426	852
Norway	200	240	480
Portugal	70	84	168
Sweden	260	312	624
Switzerland	250	300	600
Turkey	50	60	120
United Kingdom	1,060	1,272	2,544
Totals	4,155	4,986	9,972

Source: BIS, Twenty-sixth Annual Report, p. 200.

*The original quotas include the upward adjustment in the quotas of Germany and the Netherlands, made in July 1951.

the total quota, and for its simultaneous replacement by a European Monetary Agreement (EMA).[92] The latter contained two major sets of provisions: One of these called for the establishment of a European Fund, with a capital of $600 million, to serve as a discretionary source of short-term credit to countries that might experience balance-of-payments difficulties. The other provided for the institution of a Multilateral System of Settlement, based on 100-percent dollar settlements, to replace the automatic and compulsory clearing mechanism of the EPU.[93]

It bears reemphasizing that the EMA was to come into force only upon the termination of EPU and that the latter, presumably, was to be terminated only if conditions were ripe for the restoration of full convertibility to the major OEEC currencies. In the summer of 1955, it appeared reasonable to hope that such a return to convertibility might not be far off. Most OEEC countries had by then achieved a fair measure of internal monetary stability. The general improvement in Western Europe's balance-of-payments position, which had begun in 1953, continued into 1955. And most OEEC countries had, in fact, already permitted their nationals to carry out certain foreign exchange operations that, in practice, rendered their currencies transferable outside the EPU mechanism itself.[94] It was against this background of auspicious circumstances that the EMA had been negotiated and was formally signed on August 5, 1955.

But shortly after the EMA had been signed, circumstances changed for the worse, as inflationary pressures reappeared in Europe toward the end of the year. Fed by a boom in fixed investment and consumers' durables, as well as a sharp increase in inventories, these pressures persisted into 1956 and placed several countries in serious balance-of-payments difficulties. The resulting disequilibria in the trade and payments positions of major European countries were further aggravated, in the closing months of 1956, by the economic and political repercussions of the Suez crisis, causing uncertainty and jitters in European foreign exchange markets. And these jitters, coupled with fears of continuing inflation in some countries (notably France), prompted large speculative movements of capital that reached crisis proportions in the fall of 1957. It is not surprising that under the circumstances most countries turned their attention to the task of checking domestic inflation, while the EPU concentrated on arranging special ad hoc assistance to countries in severe balance-of-payments difficulties.[95] The drive toward convertibility was, for the moment, relegated to a second place.

Thus, although the termination clause inserted into the EPU agreement in August 1955 could have been invoked any time thereafter, the union continued in operation for another three and a half years. True, its renewals in 1956, 1957, and 1958 did not entail any significant changes in its operating rules.[96] But the very fact that the EPU was renewed three more times, by the unanimous decision of its members, attests to its continued usefulness during that period. Even in June 1958, when it appeared that a return to convertibility of the major European currencies was at long last imminent, the EPU was prolonged for another full year. The termination clause, however, was retained; and before the year was out, it was finally invoked.

The end of EPU came on December 27, 1958, almost exactly seven years after the Marshall Plan itself had ceased to exist. On that date, seven countries, which together accounted for 72 percent of the aggregate quota, notified the Secretary-General of the OEEC of their official desire to terminate the EPU and bring the EMA into force.[97] By their collective action these seven countries had, in effect, brought about the termination of EPU. All that remained was for the Secretary-General to inform all member countries of the fact and to alert the agent to prepare for the union's liquidation. And all that remained for the OEEC Council was to confirm the EMA's coming into operation, which it did on December 30, 1958. The actual liquidation of EPU—consisting of (1) the transfer of its capital assets to the European Fund, (2) the distribution of its excess income over expenditures among the member countries, (3) the distribution of its remaining convertible resources among the creditors, and (4) the conversion of claims on and debts to the union into a series of bilateral claims and debts—was completed shortly thereafter, the value date for these final operations being January 15, 1959.[98]

The story of EPU's successor lies well outside the scope of the present study. It might merely be mentioned that while the European Monetary Agreement remained in force until 1972, it was destined to play a progressively diminishing role in intra-European affairs during its lifetime.[99] What should be noted, however, is that the termination of EPU, and the commencement of the EMA, was predicated on a return to currency convertibility by the major OEEC countries. In other words, the decision to terminate the union necessarily entailed a commitment, by the countries concerned, to restore a meaningful measure of convertibility to their currencies. That commitment led, in fact, to the introduction, at the end of December 1958, of current-account convertibility for nonresidents, by all EPU members except Greece, Iceland, and Turkey.[100] And in the final analysis, it was that particular action that dictated the end of EPU.

VI

EPU's accomplishments may be viewed from several vantage points. In technical terms, it can be argued that EPU's multilateral compensation machinery permitted the settlement of a much larger volume of intra-European payments than could have been possible under the two previous payments schemes, and that it did so at considerable savings in cost. It may be further argued that the payments system embodied in the first and second AIEPCs could not, in any event, have effectively handled the payments imbalances that were to confront the EPU—and would have probably broken down altogether.[101] On both of these scores, the evidence tends to speak well for itself.

Thus, in the twenty-one months preceding the establishment of EPU, bilateral deficits among the OEEC countries totaled the equivalent of

$4.4 billion. Only about one-fourth of this amount, however, could be settled through the (largely bilateral) offsetting mechanism provided for under the two AIEPCs. The bulk of the deficit—over $3 billion— remained to be settled through bilateral gold payments by debtors ($382 million), dollar-financed drawing rights (about $1.3 billion), and additional bilateral credits (about $1.6 billion).[102] Put differently, about 62 percent of the *aggregate* deficit was settled by offsetting operations and intra-European credits, 9 percent by gold payments, and 29 percent by ECA dollar aid. In contrast, during the first twelve months of EPU's operations alone, the gross bilateral deficits amounted to $3.2 billion. Of these, some $2.1 billion—or over two-thirds—were automatically offset through the union's clearing mechanism, leaving slightly more than $1 billion to be settled by other means. The latter amount was covered by gold payments to the union ($225 million), credits granted by it ($547 million), and direct and indirect ECA dollar assistance ($316 million).[103] All told, EPU's offsetting operations and credits were responsible for settling about 84 percent of the aggregate deficit during that first year, while gold payments and ECA aid accounted for 6 percent and 10 percent, respectively.

Useful comparisons need not end here. In fact, when EPU's entire record is considered, the accomplishments of its automatic clearing mechanism seem even more impressive. During the eight and a half years of its existence, the cumulative total of the bilateral positions settled through EPU amounted to the equivalent of $46.6 billion.[104] Nearly $33 billion of these bilateral balances was offset through the union's compensation apparatus, leaving residual balances totaling a little over $13 billion to be covered partly by gold payments and partly by credits. Due to the progressive hardening of the union's settlement rules, as well as the adoption of the special repayment and amortization arrangements noted earlier, these residual balances were settled, on the average, by a ratio of 80-percent gold and 20-percent credit. Yet the predominance of gold payments as a means of settling the *un*compensated balances cannot detract from the overall efficiency of EPU's settlement machinery. For when viewed in the aggregate, gold payments accounted for the settlement of only 23 percent of the total bilateral positions over the eight-year period, compared with 76 percent accounted for by compensating operations and EPU credits.[105]

Lest it be overlooked, it should also be recalled that the original EPU agreement had provided for the consolidation and amortization of old bilateral debts outstanding in June 1950. The terms under which these pre-EPU debts would be repaid were either to be determined by negotiations between pairs of creditors and debtors or referred to the OEEC for a decision. But the repayments themselves were to be effected through the EPU's monthly settlements. Specifically, the periodic installments by which preexisting debts would be repaid were to be counted in the calculation of individual countries' net deficit or surplus positions with the union, to be settled according to the regular settlement rules. Thus, the EPU was assigned double duty—to effect the settlement of future payments imbalances and to help its members discharge their outstanding bilateral debts incurred under previous payments arrangements. And it is another measure of its technical accomplishments that of the $861 million in bilateral debts accumulated prior to the establishment of EPU and still outstanding in June 1950, all but $10 million had been liquidated through the union's settlement system by the time EPU was terminated.[106]

Ultimately, however, the EPU must be judged in terms of its contributions to the liberalization and expansion of intra-European trade. The most obvious of these derived from the operation of the multilateral clearing mechanism itself. For by replacing the previous system of bilateral clearings with single monthly offsettings of each country's deficits and surpluses with all others, the EPU, in effect, rendered all OEEC currencies transferable within its framework. And this—together with the fact that the settlements of imbalances were made, *on a uniformly applied basis,* with the union itself—removed the major incentive for trade discrimination and rigid bilateral balancing among the OEEC nations. Moreover, by providing automatic credit facilities that could be used to finance a substantial portion of net deficits, the EPU also facilitated the removal of quantitative import restrictions on the mutual trade of its member countries.

Nondiscrimination and the progressive removal of quantitative restrictions on intra-European trade were two principles on which the ECA had insisted throughout the EPU negotiations. These principles were embodied in a Code of Trade Liberalization, adopted by the OEEC Council in the summer of 1950.[107] A companion part to the EPU agreement, the Code of Trade Liberalization—together with subsequent Council Decisions—defined the basic goals of a trade liberalization program and charted a course toward their attainment. Essentially, liberalization was to proceed in stages, its progress being measured by the percentage of total intra-OEEC private trade that had been freed from quantitative restrictions at each stage.[108] Although actual progress in reaching the liberalization targets, specified for each stage, varied from country to country, the overall OEEC record turned out to be quite impressive. By the end of 1950, barely three months after the commencement of EPU's operations, some 60 percent of intra-European trade on private account had been freed from quantitative restrictions on a nondiscriminatory basis. By April 1955, the overall percentage of liberalized trade reached 84 percent; and in January 1959, it stood at 89 percent.[109] But the point to be emphasized is that these results could not, in all probability, have been achieved had it not been for the EPU's clearing and credit facilities. In fact, it can be argued that the OEEC countries, especially in the early 1950s, would have been neither able nor willing to contemplate, let alone undertake, the kind of trade liberalization envisioned by the ECA without the underlying support of the EPU payments mechanism.

Herein lay the most significant practical accomplishment of the EPU system: By combining a multilateral payments mechanism with a code of commercial policy, it made possible a substantial liberalization of intra-European trade within a relatively short period of time. It did so, moreover, despite the fact that throughout the same period, most of its members continued to maintain exchange controls and retained their bilateral payments agreements. Indeed, it bears noting that the establishment of EPU could not in itself eliminate forthwith either bilateral payments relations or regimes of exchange controls in Europe. Nor was it expected to do so. Rather, the EPU mechanism was superimposed on a network of bilateral relationships, for the purpose of aiding its members to overcome their inherent constraints. Put differently, the EPU was designed to facilitate trade liberalization by *modifying*, rather than eliminating, existing realities, and thereby encourage an expansion of intra-European trade that might have been impossible otherwise.

To what extent the EPU-Code of Trade Liberalization combination was directly responsible for the ensuing expansion of trade cannot be measured in precise terms. Its impact, however, may be inferred from the observable record. Thus, although trade between the OEEC countries had posted several increases during 1948 and 1949, its *rate* of growth began to accelerate following the establishment of EPU. In 1949, for example, the volume of intra-European trade was 20-percent higher than in 1948. At the end of 1950, it had risen by some 40 percent over its 1949 level; and between 1949 and 1956 it had more than doubled. Equally suggestive was the rapid pace with which intra-European trade outstripped its prewar volume during the early years of EPU's operations. Throughout 1948 and 1949, the volume of intra-European trade remained below its prewar levels.[110] Only in the last quarter of 1949 did it finally rise above it, by a mere 7 percent.[111] In contrast, less than one year later, the volume of intra-European trade stood 24-percent higher than its level in 1938. It rose to 36 percent above it in 1951, and to 40 percent in 1953.[112] The significance of these figures may better be appreciated by reference to OEEC's own forecasts. The OEEC had estimated, in December 1948, that intra-European trade would not regain its prewar volume until 1952–1953.[113] That this goal was achieved—and, in fact, surpassed—some two years ahead of expectations is another reflection on EPU's contribution to the expansion of intra-European trade.

Yet while sympathetic observers could applaud EPU's achievements, its critics could rightly claim that the liberalization of *intra*-European trade entailed an element of discrimination against non-EPU members, particularly the dollar area. There can be no question, of course, that the removal of restrictions on intra-OEEC imports, but not on imports from outside sources, was bound to favor OEEC producers over their non-OEEC competitors. Nor can it be doubted that the availability of EPU credits to finance deficits within the OEEC, but not deficits with the dollar area, provided EPU members with an incentive to maintain and possibly increase their restrictions against dollar imports. But to charge, as the NAC had done earlier and others continued to do, that the EPU would merely serve to perpetuate a high-cost, soft-currency bloc in Europe—and thus impede progress toward the restoration of full currency convertibility and free world-wide trade—is quite another matter. Such a charge may have been justified during the first two years of EPU, when monthly settlements were governed by the original gold/credit schedules. But it increasingly lost its validity with the progressive hardening of EPU's settlement rules, the gradual relaxation of Europe's exchange restrictions, and the steady liberalization, beginning in 1954, of OEEC countries' imports from the dollar area.[114]

A far more valid criticism that might be leveled at the EPU cum trade liberalization program is that it did not prevent periodic relapses into intra-European protectionism by its members. In fact, the Code of Trade Liberalization contained escape clauses that made it possible for member countries to postpone the fulfillment of their liberalization commitments and even to reverse their liberalization progress. Thus, for example, if a country considered that its deficit with the union was increasing at a rate that threatened its reserve position, it could *temporarily* suspend its liberalization measures and reimpose previously removed quantitative restrictions.[115] In practice, however, the term "temporarily" would acquire a more lasting meaning. Countries invoking the escape clause were all too quick to reimpose restrictions but typically slow to remove them again. Restoration of liberalization measures was thus a much more gradual process than the act of their suspension.[116] And as a result, the trade liberalization program itself suffered serious setbacks, particularly during the early years of EPU.

But although the EPU payments mechanism, as such, could not be held directly accountable for these setbacks, it was unquestionably responsible for them at least indirectly. For to the extent that the reimposition of quantitative restrictions could be justified on the grounds of growing deficits with the union, it reflected on EPU's failure to solve the basic problem that continued to plague intra-European trade: the persistence of extreme debtors, as well as extreme creditors. Herein lay EPU's major weakness. Despite its technical superiority over the previous payments schemes, it could not by itself cure Europe's payments disequilibrium. Nor could it prevent the often volatile shifts in its members' balance-of-payments positions—shifts that either intensified existing deficits and surpluses with the union, or transformed creditors into debtors, and vice versa. In short, while the EPU provided its members with an automatic clearing and settlement mechanism, it failed to provide—contrary to ECA's hopes—an automatic mechanism of balance-of-payments adjustment, which would induce both debtors and creditors to move toward an overall payments equilibrium. Its failure to do so may be attributed to many reasons. But perhaps the most important among them was the fact that, as an institution, the EPU lacked both the authority and the proper techniques with which to assume collective responsibility for the national monetary and fiscal policies of its members—policies that, in turn, affected their balance-of-payments positions.

* * *

Summing up the nature and role of EPU, the Managing Board, in its final report, had this to say:

In the immediate post-war period practically all trade between member countries was governed by bilateral agreements and severely limited by quantitative restrictions designed to [conserve] foreign exchange. . . . Thus, one of the earliest tasks of the [OEEC] was to seek to free European trade from the restrictions and bilateralism that had grown up in all member countries. [However,] it was clear that . . . trade liberalization would not be possible without adequate intra-European payments arrangements which would ensure complete transferability of European currencies . . . and also provide short-term credit facilities to carry member countries over temporary periods of [balance-of-payments] difficulties.[117]

The creation of the union, the Managing Board went on to state, was thus "directly linked with OEEC's policy in the trade field; [the EPU] was expressly designed as an international payments mechanism for the promotion of multilateral trade on a non-discriminatory basis."[118]

In so defining the role of EPU, the Managing Board quite aptly gave implicit expression to the central proposition that underlies the story told in the last four chapters—namely, that the obstacles to postwar expansion of Europe's trade were rooted mainly in balance-of-payments difficulties and scarcity of foreign exchange. Thus, the immediate task facing both the ECA and the OEEC was to devise methods and provide the means by which a larger volume of intra-European trade could be financed. This was, in fact, the essential aim of the two intra-European payments agreements—to allow for an expansion of intra-European trade by creating the means of paying for it. There is, however, a more important proposition implicit in the Managing Board's statement—namely, that trade expansion ultimately depended on trade liberalization, and that the main prerequisite for progress in liberalizing trade was the multilateralization of intra-European payments. It is this proposition that, in the final analysis, explains ECA's tactical approach to the task of promoting the growth of Europe's trade.

Indeed, I should like to suggest that the story of ECA's direct contributions to the expansion of Europe's foreign trade is basically a story of its continuing efforts to press the Europeans into adopting a multilateral payments system, based on the principle of intra-European currency transferability. To be sure, ECA policy makers had, from the beginning, insisted on a definite link between *payments multilateralization* and *trade liberalization;* but there can be little doubt that they viewed the former as indispensable to the practical achievement of the latter. Put differently, they correctly recognized that if intra-European trade were to be freed from the constraints imposed by quantitative restrictions and discriminatory bilateral arrangements, it would have to be equipped with a regionally based multilateral payments mechanism. They also recognized that although such a payments mechanism could conceivably exist and function without any accompanying moves by the Europeans to liberalize trade, its ultimate justification would lie in providing a basis for a meaningful commitment to the removal of trade restrictions. Hence their insistence that the EPU agreement and the Code of Trade Liberalization be accepted, by the OEEC, as two integral parts of the same package.

Seen in this light, the EPU was the logical end product of a policy that had begun to evolve, within the ECA, almost as soon as the latter came into existence.[119] As a clearing and settlement mechanism, the EPU was designed to facilitate intra-European payments. But in a deeper sense, it was an instrument whose main objective would be to facilitate trade liberalization *through* payments multilateralization, and thereby stimulate an expansion of intra-European trade. To the extent that the EPU accomplished this objective it vindicated the wisdom of ECA's emphasis on *regional* liberalization of trade and payments, as the most effective means of promoting the growth of Europe's foreign trade under the Marshall Plan.

Development of Economic Cooperation

PART IV

From Cooperation to Integration: Evolving Concepts and Instrumentalities

Thus far, attention has been focused on those elements of the ERP whose essential purpose was to tackle immediate and specific economic problems, and whose main objective was to create the necessary conditions for the attainment of a "healthy [European] economy independent of extraordinary outside assistance" within a reasonable period of time. These three elements—i.e., a strong production effort, the creation and maintenance of internal financial stability, and the expansion of foreign trade—could, therefore, be viewed as the short-term economic goals of the Marshall Plan. But underlying the short-run goals, and at the same time constituting a fourth element of the aid program, was a much broader, long-range objective that must now be examined in some detail. It was an objective based on the proposition that the success of the ERP would require close cooperation among the aid recipients and, more importantly, that Western Europe's economic, as well as political, strength would ultimately lie in European unity.

To say this is not to suggest that the concept of European unity, or unification, was clearly defined or officially endorsed during the formulation of the basic ERP legislation. In fact, it was a concept that took time to evolve and that was not given explicit congressional blessing until the second year of the Marshall Plan. What *is* being suggested, however, is that many influential citizens and some public servants had even earlier come to regard the creation of a European union (or some sort of a European federation) as a desirable goal which should be actively encouraged by the United States.[1] To them, the proposed aid program appeared to offer a legitimate opportunity for initiating actions and processes that may eventually lead to an economically and politically unified Western Europe.[2] And some went so far as to suggest that the United States should insist on a commitment to European unification, or integration, as a condition for ERP aid.[3]

But others, both in the Administration and in Congress, counseled caution and discretion in expressing official American views on the subject of European integration in general, and European political unification in particular. Thus, for example, while acknowledging that "there is a possibility of developing tremendous emotional drive in Western Europe behind the supranational ideal of European unity," an internal State Department memorandum advocated that any American appeal to joint and unifying European actions should be couched in economic rather than political terms. "In our propaganda and our diplomacy," the memorandum argued, "it will be necessary to stress the immediate *economic* benefits which will flow from the joint making of national economic policies and decisions." [4] Similarly, when Senator William Fulbright offered an amendment to the Senate ERP bill, which would have added "political unification of Europe" to the list of policy objectives, he was advised by Senator Henry Cabot Lodge that while the Senate Foreign Relations Committee had been sympathetic to this point of view, it had not thought it expedient to express it in the bill itself. [5]

The Fulbright amendment, which was introduced during the Senate floor debate, found considerable support both in the Senate and among members of the House. [6] But it encountered objections from several influential Senators, including the chairman of the Senate Foreign Relations Committee, Arthur Vandenberg. Both Vandenberg and his fellow committee member, Senator Alben Barkley, were concerned with its impact on public opinion. They were particularly fearful that, if adopted, the Fulbright amendment might be interpreted as political intervention by the United States, and would thus provide communist propaganda with an added excuse to charge that the Marshall Plan was an American device to gain political control of Western Europe. [7] Their arguments eventually carried the day, and the Fulbright amendment was withdrawn. Subsequent efforts by the House to add the adjective *political* at several places in the section on Findings and Declaration of Policy, were fought off by Senate conferees, and all such references were deleted from the Economic Cooperation Act of 1948.

I

But if European unification (political *or* economic) was not explicitly mentioned in the 1948 authorization act, it was nevertheless represented by a proxy of sort. "It is declared to be the policy of the people of the United States," the act stated,

to encourage these countries through a *joint* organization to exert sustained *common* efforts . . . , which will speedily achieve that *economic cooperation* in Europe which is essential for lasting peace and prosperity. . . . It is further declared to be the policy of the United States that continuity of assistance provided by the United States should, at all time, be dependent upon continuity of cooperation among countries participating in the program.[8]

Thus, at least initially, *economic cooperation*, rather than *European unification*, became one of the four declared objectives of the European recovery plan. And although Congress chose not to elaborate on this point, it offered at least one clue as to what it may have had in mind. It called attention to the advantages that the United States had enjoyed through the existence of a large domestic market, devoid of internal trade barriers; and it prescribed that the development of economic cooperation should include "all possible steps to establish and maintain equitable rates of exchange and to bring about the progressive elimination of trade barriers."[9]

It might be presumed that, in singling out these particular actions, Congress had actually intended to define economic cooperation largely in terms of trade and payments policies, and to identify it specifically with the adoption of measures designed to facilitate the growth of Europe's trade. But I should like to suggest that Congress had much more in mind when it called for the development of economic cooperation. In fact, when it spoke of "common efforts" by the participating countries, the Economic Cooperation Act explicitly referred to (without enumerating, however) those undertakings that had been "set forth in the report of the Committee of European Economic Cooperation signed in Paris on September 22, 1947."[10] In other words, Congress appeared to serve notice that the participating countries should be guided by and would be held to *all* the multilateral pledges and obligations that they had undertaken in the CEEC report.

That report contained a chapter titled "Economic Co-Operation," and in it the participating countries identified several areas where joint and cooperative actions would be necessary, useful, and desirable.[11] Thus, besides resolving "to abolish as soon as possible the abnormal restrictions which [hampered] their mutual trade" and to aim at "a sound and balanced multilateral trading system" with the rest of the world, the signatories of the report specifically promised to (1) progressively relax both import and export restrictions, (2) explore ways and means of adopting a system of currency transferability, (3) consult with each other on steps for the liberalization of their trade, with the view toward the eventual elimination of quantitative restrictions, (4) play their full part in the efforts to secure reductions of tariffs on a multilateral basis, (5) explore, by means of a special Study Group, the possibility of forming customs unions between groups of European countries, (6) adopt measures to promote free movement of labor across their national borders, (7) encourage greater volume of tourism between them, and (8) collectively pool resources and exchange technical information in such endeavors as the development of new sources of electric power, steel production, and transportation.[12] Last, but certainly not least, the signatories declared themselves ready to set up, by mutual agreement, a joint organization to coordinate the execution of the recovery program and to review the progress achieved by it.[13]

By spelling out in the report the potential framework for mutual economic cooperation, the CEEC countries may have saved Congress from the need to spell it out for them. But the point to be made here is that the spelling out of what economic cooperation *may* mean was not quite the same as the carrying out of specific cooperative plans and projects. Ultimately, the achievement of economic cooperation would have to be judged by its results. And these, in turn, would depend on the kind of machinery by which joint planning would be pursued and collective decisions reached. Put differently: Regardless of how they were initially defined, the measures of economic cooperation would be largely a function of the instrumentality charged with their execution. Such an instrumentality was to be provided by the joint organization that the participating countries had agreed to establish. And it would be the nature of that particular organization that, in the final analysis, would determine the practical meaning of economic cooperation and the extent to which its goals could and would be achieved.

II

On April 16, 1948, two weeks after Congress passed the Economic Cooperation Act, the CEEC countries, meeting in Paris, signed the Convention for European Economic Cooperation. With the signing of this document, the participating countries formally bound themselves to work in close economic cooperation and created the Organization for European Economic Cooperation (OEEC). As specified by the convention, the new organization was to consist of (1) a decision-making governing body—the Council of Ministers—on which each of the participating nations would be represented; (2) a seven-member Executive Committee, chosen by the Council, to direct the day-to-day activities of the OEEC; (3) several Technical Committees; and (4) a Secretariat, staffed by international civil servants and headed by the Secretary-General, to assist the Council, the Executive Committee, and the Technical Committees in their tasks and to perform various housekeeping services. The major aim of the OEEC, the convention stated, was "the achievement of a sound European economy through the economic cooperation of its members." And to that end, the organization was assigned a variety of functions, ranging from the preparation of "general production, export and import programs," to the preparation of reports on the "execution of the European Recovery Program and the use of external aid."[14]

What was not stated, though well known by all concerned, was the fact that the drafting of the convention was attended by a sharp difference of views about the desired structure of a joint European organization and the powers with which it should be endowed. Or, to put it in a more fundamental context, the delivery process that brought the OEEC into the world was characterized by a conflict between alternative approaches to the very concept of European unity. The proponents of Europeanism, represented primarily by the French, saw in the OEEC a legitimate vehicle for the realization of common economic plans and policies within Europe—in a word, an instrument of European economic unification. To them, European unity—even cooperation—necessarily entailed acceptance of limitation on national sovereignty and the establishment of common institutions possessing some measure of supranational authority. Accordingly, they argued for an organization whose structure would allow for considerable power at the center, and whose officials would have the authority to coordinate the economic activities of member countries and take major policy initiatives. Had they won their argument, both the Executive Committee and the Secretariat would have emerged as the decision-making bodies within the OEEC.

But the British, as would be the case on many other occasions, viewed matters differently. They rejected out of hand the notion of limitation on sovereignty and proposed instead that the OEEC should be placed under the control of its member countries, rather than the other way around. As far as they were concerned, the leading role in OEEC should be played by the national delegations to the organization, and the decision-making powers should be vested in the Council, whose members belonged, of course, to the national cabinets of their respective countries. In essence, then, the British conceived of the OEEC as an instrument for *inter*governmental consultations and negotiations, rather than as a supranational machinery that could initiate and execute collective projects of its own. And in the end, their view—supported by the Scandinavians—prevailed. For, at least structurally, the OEEC was drawn along lines suggested by the British rather than the French model.[15]

Yet while the British managed to mold the structure of the OEEC, they had not reckoned with ECA's determination to mold the behavior of its member countries and, if need be, force them into meaningful cooperative actions. This determination, as previously noted, was to be manifested in a variety of ways throughout the Marshall Plan period; but its earliest manifestation came almost as soon as the OEEC commenced its life. Thus, less than a month after the Convention for European Economic Cooperation had been signed, the OEEC was informed that it would have to work out, and recommend to the ECA, the division of American aid among the participating countries.[16] Since the amount of aid allocated to each country would have to be based on its own estimated requirements, the OEEC, in effect, was handed the task of analyzing and passing collective judgment on the national programs to be drawn up and submitted by its members. And this, in turn, implied that the OEEC—and not the governments of its members—would have to formulate and adopt a policy on which the division of aid would be based. More important still, in the process of drawing up a recommended distribution of aid, the OEEC would be obliged to modify, reconcile, and consolidate the individual national plans into a well-integrated *joint* recovery program—a program designed to assure the most effective use of resources by the participating countries and to extract from each of them the maximum contributions to the common recovery effort. In other words, the determination of how the aid should be distributed would have to involve the preparation of a common program—an undertaking that, at least to some extent, would place the OEEC, as a collective institution, above the national governments of its member states.

Quite understandably, when the nature of the expected task was communicated to the OEEC, it was met with a distinct lack of enthusiasm by the majority of its members.[17] By its own subsequent admission, the OEEC had accepted the ECA's request "with some hesitation," because it was considered by many to be "too early to place such a severe strain upon the corporate life of the Organization."[18] This, however, was a polite understatement whose real sentiment is suggested only by implication. To judge from the evidence, the Europeans had anticipated—and, in fact, preferred—that the division of aid would be determined by the ECA itself. Such a course, they reasoned, would offer each country the opportunity to present its case directly to the aid agency and literally bargain for what *it* considered its rightful share of the aid pie. Indeed, notwithstanding their solemn pledges to cooperate with one another in a joint recovery program, most governments were, to say the least, reluctant to allow the supposed needs of the group as a whole to take precedence over the perceived requirements of its individual members. Hence, when the ECA presented its request (read: direction) for a collective scrutiny of such requirements, the initial European reaction was not exactly one of hesitant acquiescence; it was, in fact, a mixture of shock, disbelief, and strong reservation.[19] It was a reaction, moreover, whose forcefulness could hardly have been expected to diminish, given the pressure of time under which the OEEC was obliged to prepare both the quarterly supply program for the third quarter of 1948 and the First Annual Program for the year 1948–1949.

III

The first of these assignments—i.e., the preparation of the quarterly supply program—was handed to the OEEC in early May; and by the middle of the month, an OEEC committee had drawn up a time table that allowed barely two weeks for the screening of the individual national estimates. These estimated requirements were to be submitted to the Organization, on special questionnaires, by May 22, and the OEEC Council was to forward them, with its own recommendations, to the ECA by June 5.[20] Incredible as it may seem in retrospect, the record shows that this particular assignment was completed on schedule and its results promptly transmitted to ECA/W.[21] The record also indicates, however, that ECA officials were not entirely pleased with the actual outcome of the exercise. W. Averell Harriman, who forwarded the OEEC report to Washington, found the overall results "disappointing." He frankly felt, he stated, that the "[OEEC] has not done a genuine job of screening, in [the] sense of *joint* review on the basis [of] some economic standards and comparisons."[22] He blamed the "pressure of time," the "lack of necessary information," and "inadequate directives from the OEEC Council" as the main reasons for these disappointing results. But he was also astute enough to recognize that at least a partial explanation lay in the "general attitude, held in [the] past by OEEC, that ECA should and would do [the] screening."[23]

This "general attitude," however, was not a thing of the past, as implied by Harriman, but a fairly persistent phenomenon that manifested itself in various ways in the early days of OEEC's existence. Thus, for example, during the preparation of the third-quarter program, the Greek delegate to the Organization informed U.S. Ambassador Caffery of his country's great reluctance to have *its* national program screened by the OEEC, and formally requested that any such screening be done by the ECA.[24] Around the same time, an official Irish delegation paid a visit to ECA headquarters in Washington to personally argue that Ireland was unwilling and unable to accept any ERP aid in the form of loans.[25] And when, upon the completion of the quarterly program, the OEEC turned to the task of preparing the First Annual Program and formulating the 1948–1949 intra-European payments scheme, the British proceeded to pull an obstructionist trick of their own. In late June, Sir Edmund Hall-Patch informed OSR officials that it would be "impossible" for his government to even formulate a national requirements program, or to commit itself on payments arrangements with other participating countries, "without first knowing the loan/grant ratio" contemplated in the aid allocation to the United Kingdom.[26] His understanding was, he added, that a recipient country would, in any event, "have the right to reject all or any part" of sums offered by the United States as loans.[27] To which Harriman replied by stating that ECA "could not permit individual countries to exercise unilateral option on acceptance [or rejection] of the loan part of aid while maintaining [the] right to receive grants in amount originally coupled with loans."[28] Just the same, Harriman was sufficiently concerned about the implications of the British attitude, and its possible effect in delaying OEEC's work, to recommend to Washington that "tentative loan/grant figures" be given to Thomas Finletter for "transmittal to [Sir Stafford] Cripps verbally." Similar information, he urged, should be made available to ECA mission chiefs in other countries, if required for planning and programming purposes.[29]

Other countries, meanwhile, were playing other, if less obstructive, games. The Turks, for example, took the position that they were entitled to a larger amount of third-quarter aid than the OEEC was initially prepared to recommend. Specifically, they laid claim to an additional $10 million on the grounds that a "U.S. commitment had been given to [them] in this amount."[30] Obviously impressed by the argument, the OEEC Council approved the increase and included it in its report to the ECA. The latter, however, was decidedly unimpressed. Upon receiving the report and noting the increase, ECA/W cabled OSR that the Turkish position was based on a "complete misunderstanding," and instructed that the "situation created by the Turks in [the] OEEC Council" be corrected.[31] But what is particularly instructive here is that the so-called misunderstanding, according to ECA/W, may have been due to direct conversations between the Turks and the State Department, during which the latter "has *informally* advised the Turkish representatives in Washington that they could expect a revision in the [estimated] figures."[32] Informally or not, the moral was quite clear: In carrying their case directly to the State Department, the Turks, in effect, had gone over the heads of both the OEEC and the ECA, and succeeded in turning whatever assurances they may or may not have received into their own advantage with the OEEC.

The Danes, for their part, sought an advantage of a different kind. Nearly a year earlier, they had secured from the World Bank a $40 million loan, whose stated purpose was to "assist Danish economic recovery."[33] The twenty-five-year loan, which was designed to finance imports of essential capital goods and raw materials during 1947 and 1948, carried an interest rate of $3\frac{1}{4}$ percent per annum plus a special commission charge of 1 percent.[34] Its effective date was October 17, 1947, and for some time thereafter the Danes proceeded to draw parts of it as needed. However, once ECA came into existence, they stopped further drawings, asking instead for repeated extensions. Their behavior greatly irked John McCloy, at the time president of the World Bank, who suspected—and so informed ECA/W—that the Danes were merely waiting to see whether they could get credit from the ECA on more attractive terms.[35] He was prepared to insist, McCloy told ECA Deputy Administrator Howard Bruce, that Denmark either utilize the entire World Bank loan forthwith or cancel it altogether. And Bruce, tacitly supporting this position, suggested to Paul Hoffman that ECA should make sure that it did not encourage the Danes "into the thought that they can get cheaper money from us."[36] But as it turned out, Denmark *was* able to obtain ECA-authorized credit on cheaper terms. In the fall of 1948, it received from the Export-Import Bank a $25 million loan, repayable in thirty-five years and carrying an interest rate of only 2½ percent.[37]

Whatever else may be concluded from the above sample, at least one conclusion is inescapable: Despite their membership in a joint organization, and pledged to mutual cooperation, most OEEC countries either did not fully comprehend the doctrine of cooperative behavior, as preached by the ECA, or else chose to ignore it. Each of them, in fact, sought to protect and promote its own national interests, paying scant regard to the notion of collective well-being. Consequently, when they were literally forced to prepare a joint program and collectively recommend a division of aid, most countries resorted to various tactics in order to maximize their own individual gains within the program. And under the circumstances, it was hardly surprising that the third-quarter recommendations submitted by the OEEC would be considered disappointing by the ECA. Nor is it surprising that the OEEC was unable to proceed to its next assignment—the preparation of the First Annual Program—as rapidly as the ECA would have liked to see it do. For, given its structure, the ability of the Organization to carry out its functions to ECA's satisfaction ultimately depended on the willingness of its members to adopt and follow a course of behavior in which the needs of the group would indeed transcend the desires of its individual parts. Or, to put it differently: Before the OEEC could truly function as a joint organization, "a proper sense of corporate responsibility" would have to be created in the Council and accepted by the national governments represented on it.[38] But in the spring and summer of 1948, this was easier said than done.

IV

Obviously aware that the slowness of OEEC's programming progress was due mainly to the nationalistic attitudes of its members, the ECA nevertheless continued to push for joint and collective action. "We are inclined to believe," ECA/W cabled OSR in mid-June, "that our attitude has been too complacent toward OEEC's reluctance to assume adequate programming responsibilities."[39] There was a danger, the cable continued, that unless steps were taken to toughen this attitude, the Organization might degenerate into a "mere post office." Accordingly, OSR was instructed to "press vigorously" for the OEEC's prompt assumption of its assigned functions. The OEEC was to be told, in no uncertain terms, that it was expected to produce a "realistic" program without undue delays.[40]

Yet practically in the same breath, ECA/W entered a reservation that was bound to have a demoralizing effect on OEEC's efforts and to increase its difficulties. In conveying Washington's message, OSR was to emphasize that while the "ultimate responsibility" for OEEC's operation rested with the OEEC itself, "the United States should always be given adequate opportunity to comment on and *recommend changes* in proposed OEEC programming principles and procedures." This was necessary, ECA/W explained, "in order that information and programs submitted by the OEEC, can in fact be useful to ECA."[41] Whatever its merits, the explanation could hardly have impressed the Europeans. If anything, it could have been regarded by them as a slight; for it implied that the OEEC was not to be entirely trusted to formulate an adequate program on its own.[42] Worse still, the message could have led to the conclusion that, since the ECA reserved the right to suggest changes anyway, the programming procedures and aid allocations recommended by the OEEC need not be taken seriously by its individual members. And such a conclusion could undoubtedly encourage some of the participating countries to eschew the collective effort in the hope of securing larger gains for themselves by dealing directly with Washington.

Nor was this the only handicap confronting the OEEC. One month after they had supposedly begun working on the First Annual Program, the Europeans were given, "for planning purposes," a tentative figure of the total amount of ERP aid for 1948–1949.[43] What they were told must have come as a rude surprise, for the figure given—$4.875 billion—turned out to be some $500 million less than what they had expected.[44] And if, as one observer aptly put it, the cutting of the aid cake was difficult to begin with, the task of reducing the portions would be harder still.[45] It was a task that, given the prevailing mood of most participating countries, could not possibly have been accomplished through open and detailed discussions at the meetings of the sixteen-member OEEC Council.

The story of how the first division of aid was finally resolved need be only briefly outlined here. On July 16, after "much backstage fighting," the Council appointed a Committee of Four, whose members were drawn from the national delegations of Britain, France, Italy, and the Netherlands, and empowered it to review the national programs and recommend a provisional allotment of aid. At the same time, the Council drew up a set of principles to guide the Committee in its work.[46] Each country, in turn, submitted its program to the committee and was given the opportunity to explain and defend its virtues. Armed with this information, as well as with advice from the ECA, the four experts proceeded to review the material and formulate their recommendation in seclusion. On August 12, they presented their report to the Council where, according to an eyewitness, "pandemonium broke loose."[47] Some delegations frankly questioned the wisdom of even discussing the report; others questioned the specific allotments recommended for them, and several delegations declared themselves unable to accept the committee's recommendation until the matter of intra-European payments had been settled.

This last point was, in all fairness, well taken. For although the Committee of Four had based its recommendations on the assumption that part of the participating countries' import requirements could be satisfied through intra-European trade (i.e., nondollar sources), it had not concerned itself with the specific ways in which that trade would be financed. Put differently, the committee had taken as given that an intra-European payments scheme would be in operation, but had not dealt with the prospective debit/credit positions of the European countries vis-à-vis each other. Yet, as noted earlier, the anticipated intra-European surpluses and deficits were to provide the basis for determining the drawing rights contributed and received under the intra-European payments arrangement; and the contributions of drawing rights, in turn, were to determine the allotments of conditional dollar aid to which creditor countries would be entitled.[48] Thus, it could indeed be argued that a final decision on how aid should be distributed required an estimation of prospective intra-European credit and debit balances and a determination of how they would be financed.

That particular task, however, was to be accomplished through bilateral negotiations between pairs of OEEC countries, assisted and guided by another independent committee: the Committee of Five. That committe was to supervise the negotiation of the bilateral agreements, to ensure that the figures agreed to by the respective parties were realistic, and to make its own recommendations when the figures were in dispute.[49] Seventy-eight bilateral payments agreements, covering the period July 1, 1948–June 30, 1949, were ultimately concluded by the participating countries. But even while the negotiations were still in process, the Committee of Five submitted to the Council a report recommending the amounts of drawing rights to be established. The two reports—the one by the Committee of Four and the other by the Committee of Five—were considered together by the Council which then empowered its chairman to draw up composite proposals based on both sets of recommendations.

These proposals were approved by the Council on September 11; but certain matters still remained to be worked out before a final agreement could be reached. Previously submitted national programs had to be revised and resubmitted, many bilateral payments agreements still had to be concluded, rules of commercial policy had to be drafted, and the exact terms of the intra-European payments plan had to be agreed upon by both the OEEC and the ECA. A whole month would pass before these remaining hurdles were overcome. On October 16, 1948, the OEEC Council, meeting at the ministerial level, finally approved all the elements of the 1948–1949 program and forwarded them to the ECA.[50] Thus, six months after it had been created, the young Organization could boast of having passed its first test. Despite their differences, its members managed to muster the necessary cooperative will to produce a "joint statement of their views and intentions" concerning the first year's progress toward Europe's economic recovery.[51]

The joint statement, however, did not quite constitute a joint program—a fact that was not lost on either the OEEC or the ECA. Nor could subsequent rounds of programming and aid-allocation efforts be said to produce joint programs in the strict sense of the word. Indeed, any hopes that the OEEC would be able to formulate a truly integrated recovery program—a sort of a long-range master plan—must have been quickly recognized as impractical, if not altogether futile.[52] For, apart from the technical difficulties of projecting and coordinating the national plans and policies of sixteen different countries, a much more serious obstacle stood in the way: the unwillingness of the participating countries to accept a centrally instituted planning and coordinating authority over their individual economies. Put differently, while they agreed to cooperate in economic matters, the Europeans refused the degree of economic *unity* that the formulation and implementation of a long-range integrated program would have required.

In any event, early in 1949, the idea of a joint four-year master plan was allowed to fall quietly by the wayside.[53] In its place, the OEEC Executive Committee, aided by a ministerial Consultative Group, drew up a set of principles for cooperative and parallel actions by the participating countries. These principles formed the basis of a Plan of Action for 1949–1950, which was approved by the Council on March 26, 1949. Their essential purpose was to guide the participating countries, singly and collectively, in adopting specific steps designed to solve specific problems that stood in the way of economic recovery and the reestablishment of intra-European equilibrium.[54] But it is worth noting that while the Plan of Action implied continued cooperation, and explicitly called for coordination of policies and activities in certain areas, it did not envision a jointly planned and coordinated approach to the solution of Europe's economic problems. Nor did it contemplate the integration of the separate national economies of the OEEC countries into a single regional entity. Cooperation, in other words, was still to remain largely a function of *inter*governmental consultations and negotiations, rather than of the dictates of a supranational central authority.

V

However perceived by the Europeans, "economic cooperation" was soon to acquire a new dimension. Less than a month after the OEEC Council had approved the Plan of Action, Congress passed, and the President signed into law, the act extending the ERP for another year.[55] In its section on general objectives and purposes, Congress declared it to be "the policy of the people of the United States to encourage the *unification* of Europe."[56] Yet while the encouragement of European unification thus became an officially stated objective of U.S. policy, the meaning of the term was not made clear by either Congress or the Administration. Nor did Congress indicate at the time whether unification should be couched in economic or political terms.[57] And a year later, when it came to consider the third authorization bill (i.e., the Economic Cooperation Act of 1950), Congress again declined to be specific. It turned down a proposal that would have conditioned the continuation of ERP aid on a timetable of accomplishments and progress toward unification; and it eliminated, in conference, a House-inspired amendment calling for the economic unification and political federation of Europe.[58] Instead, it merely reiterated its general sentiment by stipulating, as an objective of the act, the encouragement of "further unification." Under the circumstances, it fell largely to the ECA to interpret the newly added congressional mandate and to devise the tactical means by which it could be implemented.

Actually, even while Congress was deliberating over the 1949 authorization act, a working definition of the term *integration* began to take shape within the ECA. But unlike congressional proponents, who envisioned unification as a broad and long-term objective, the essence of ECA's approach was focused on immediate problems. In fact, as early as March 18, 1949, an internal ECA memorandum had already argued that slogans such as "self-support by 1952" or "greater European economic integration" must be given content and meaning in terms of specific institutional arrangements and relationships.[59] That same document, as noted earlier, stressed Europe's trading position as the basic problem facing the recovery program; and it prescribed, as a remedy, the development of a system of mutual convertibility among European currencies and the progressive elimination of intra-European trade barriers. And barely a week before the 1949 authorization act became law, another ECA staff memorandum had proposed the creation of a large West European free-trade area, to be achieved within the next three to four years.[60] During the next several months, these lines of thought were to develop into an operational concept that defined integration in terms of regional liberalization of trade and payments. In other words, the movement toward integration was to be identified with the progressive removal of intra-European trade barriers and the multilateralization of intra-European payments. Its ultimate measure of achievement would be the formation of a "single large market" throughout which goods and payments could move freely.[61]

Thus conceived, the thrust of ECA policy was to be directed at the encouragement of *economic* integration rather than political unification.[62] And it was essentially this message that Paul Hoffman sought to convey to the OEEC Council in his famous "integration" speech in late October 1949. In subsequent months, the ECA remained generally faithful to *its* notion of economic integration and pursued it along two main routes: (1) the push for the establishment of the European Payments Union (EPU) and (2) the insistence on the rapid removal of intra-European quantitative restrictions. Still, toward the end of 1949, the ECA came to be involved in and lent its strong support to a proposal that could clearly be interpreted as political in nature and design.

That particular proposal, whose declared purpose was to revitalize the OEEC and strengthen its authority as an institution, called for more frequent, and possibly even continuous, meetings of the Council at the ministerial level; and the creation of a permanent position—Director-General of OEEC—to be filled by an outstanding European political figure. Interestingly enough, the idea for such a post appears to have originated in an "informal suggestion," made by French Foreign Minister Robert Schuman to Harriman, sometime in 1948.[63] Underlying this suggestion was the view, reportedly shared by both France and Belgium and increasingly subscribed to by the State Department and the ECA, that the slowness of OEEC's strides toward integration stemmed from "the organizational lack of a leader with sufficient authority, stature and international prestige to influence the member governments toward greater European cooperation."[64] The attainment of greater cooperation, in other words, would require sustained political leadership in the OEEC. And such leadership, the argument implied, could best be provided by a full-time permanent head of the Organization, who would continue to hold his office regardless of political changes in his home country.[65]

By late July 1949, the State Department had come to settle on a likely candidate—Belgium's Foreign Minister Paul-Henri Spaak, who was serving at the time as the Chairman of the OEEC Council. "Given Spaak's outstanding qualities of statesmanship," Secretary of State Acheson cabled Paris on July 29, "he would unquestionably give much additional strength to the OEEC during the coming critical period." [66] A few days later, the Secretary of State received assurances from the U.S. Chargé d'Affairs in Brussels that Spaak himself had "confirmed his desire" to accept such a post and thought that the time was indeed ripe for "altering the organization of OEEC." [67] All that presumably remained for the Americans was to take up the matter with other European leaders, particularly Robert Schuman (who reportedly favored Spaak's candidacy anyway) and Britain's Foreign Secretary, Ernest Bevin, whose government's support for the move the Americans sought to enlist. But as it turned out, the British proved a tough nut to crack, and in the end even the French became somewhat less enthusiastic about the idea than they had originally appeared to be.

What the British thought of the proposal, in general, and Spaak's candidacy, in particular, may easily be surmised. Given their initial stand on the structure and powers of the OEEC, they were, to put it mildly, opposed to any increase in the authority of the Organization (or to its politicization), especially under the leadership of a continental European. Nor were they inclined to support—much less lead—a move designed to tie them closer to the continental economies under any kind of an integration scheme. But although U.S. officials seemed aware of this attitude, and even acknowledged that the British were "holding back on many vital economic aspects of their own involvement with western Europe," they continued to insist that without Britain's active participation, "western European integration [would] have little if any value." [68] It is hardly surprising, therefore, that when the matter was formally taken up, there followed what might be described as a contest of wits from which, as will be seen shortly, neither side emerged a complete winner.

On October 18, 1949, having that day delivered a personal message from Acheson to Bevin, Ambassador Douglas reported to Washington on his meeting with the British Foreign Secretary. In his message, Acheson had urged Bevin to assume, together with Sir Stafford Cripps, a leading role in persuading the other OEEC countries to agree to "significant further steps which will make for greater European cooperation." [69] He had also urged that serious consideration be given to Spaak's candidacy for the newly proposed position. But Bevin's reaction, according to Douglas, indicated "little likelihood" that either he or his cabinet colleagues would agree to Spaak's appointment to any position of real authority in the OEEC. [70] Bevin, in fact, did not mince any words. "The Labor Government," he pointedly told Douglas, "could not, under American pressure, accept the appointment of Spaak, or *any other continental*, to a position of control in the OEEC." [71] He was, he added, "fearful" that an attempt might be made to "clothe the OEEC with political power." And as if to leave no doubt where he stood, Bevin stated that, in his view, "the function of OEEC was economic and factual, and should not drift into the political sphere." [72]

But Acheson persisted. "We will certainly not acquiesce," he cabled Paris on October 19, 1949, "in any British attempt to obstruct integration." On the contrary, he continued, "we will use our influence with the U.K. to secure its cooperation and collaboration along all lines." [73] A few days later, Bevin responded with a personal message of his own. In it, he assured Acheson that his government had "neither the desire nor the intention to impede any sound scheme of closer European union." [74] He cautioned, however, that Britain "could not accept obligations, in relation to western Europe, which would prevent or restrict the implementation of [its] obligations elsewhere." Accordingly, if proposals for closer economic grouping in Europe were to be put forward, he stated, his government would be quite prepared to "consider them sympathetically." [75]

Acheson may have been somewhat mollified, but not entirely satisfied. "I would hope that your government could indicate a more positive role," he replied to Bevin on October 28. "We believe," he added, "that there can be no unity of Europe . . . without the strong support of the U.K., backed by the rest of the Commonwealth." [76] But for the moment, Bevin held his ground. To Ambassador Douglas, who had been instructed to call on him again, he remarked dryly that "perhaps Washington did not fully comprehend that Great Britain could not accept integration in Western Europe on a scale which would impair its other responsibilities." [77] And shortly thereafter, he proceeded to demonstrate that despite its seeming aloofness, Britain had not lost its persuasive powers among the continental members of the OEEC.

As subsequently reported by an irate Harriman, Bevin—disregarding an understanding previously reached with both Harriman and Hoffman—quietly met with the majority of foreign ministers from the other OEEC countries and managed to "play down" the importance of the proposed organizational change. [78] To Harriman, who personally favored such a change, it seemed clear that the United States could "no longer tolerate this type of maneuver by the British." He was convinced, he continued, that as long as the OEEC structure remained as it was, "there [was] no hope for cooperation on *as significant and effective basis as American policy requires*." [79] And he argued that ways must be found to bring the members' "governments, rather than officials, into the direction of OEEC affairs." [80]

The State Department obviously concurred; and during a Paris meeting with Messrs. Bevin and Schuman on November 9–10, Acheson once again brought up the subject of the new OEEC post and Spaak's appointment to it. [81] This time, however, his hand was forced; for Bevin asked that the U.S. government address a formal letter to all the member countries, "setting forth just exactly what was wanted [in order] to strengthen the OEEC." What he specifically desired, he told Acheson, was an outline of the duties to be assigned to the head of the Organization, rather than a "discussion of personalities involved." [82] Quite understandably, the Secretary of State was taken aback. The last thing *he* desired was to openly dictate—or to give the impression that the United States was trying to dictate—to the Europeans the specific institutional changes they should adopt. Accordingly, when confronted with Bevin's request, Acheson merely promised to take up the issue with the government upon his return to Washington.

It did not take long, however, for Bevin to receive his answer. On November 16, a draft of a proposed message to the OEEC countries was sent by Acheson to Ambassador Douglas in London. [83] In it, the Americans suggested that, in the intervals between meetings of the OEEC Council of Ministers and the Consultative Group, the person occupying the newly proposed position would

(1) sharpen the issues before the Organization and facilitate agreement on them among the member governments; (2) work with the ministers of the participating countries and officials of the U.S. government in coordinating activities and developing and carrying out policies; and (3) assist in presenting the purposes and objectives of the Organization to the public. [84]

Douglas, who had been instructed to transmit the draft to Bevin for his comments and reactions, did so on November 17, adding, "I hope you can support this proposition." But all he got in return was a noncommittal assurance that "[the U.K.] would offer no opposition." [85] Noncommittal, indeed! For Bevin's reaction implied that Britain would presumably remain neutral in any subsequent discussion of the proposal; it would neither openly oppose nor endorse it.

The OEEC Consultative Group was scheduled to meet on December 20, 1949. And while Douglas, in London, was endeavoring—unsuccessfully, it might be added—to secure a "more positive" British support, Harriman, in Paris, decided that the time had come to look for support elsewhere. In late November, he suggested to Acheson and Hoffman that Paul Van Zeeland, Belgium's new Foreign Minister and Spaak's successor as Chairman of the OEEC Council, be approached and persuaded to endorse Acheson's draft message. [86] The Belgian had reportedly prepared a similar proposal for consideration by the Consultative Group at its forthcoming meeting. He was, therefore, presumed to be sympathetic to the American conception of the new OEEC post. In fact, during an early December meeting with Robert Murphy, newly appointed U.S. Ambassador to Belgium, Van Zeeland expressed satisfaction with Acheson's draft message and agreed that it should be transmitted, with minor changes, to the entire OEEC membership.[87] Moreover, during the same meeting he professed to favor Spaak's appointment to the contemplated post.

Encouraged by Van Zeeland's accommodating response, the State Department made its next move. On December 13, 1949, Acheson instructed the American diplomatic representatives in the OEEC countries to deliver his slightly amended message to the respective foreign ministers and to urge that it be given serious considerations.[88] But if he had hoped that the Europeans would be swayed by his appeal, the Secretary of State was in for a disappointment. Within one week after Acheson's message had been sent, U.S. officials were rudely awakened to the fact that Britain's strong reservation about the politicization of the OEEC was shared by other OEEC members as well. Indeed, during the December 20 meeting of the Consultative Group, an obviously angry Harriman was confronted with what was later described as an attempt to "completely emasculate the Secretary's proposal."[89] As reported by Harriman's deputy, Milton Katz, the move was led by, of all people, French Foreign Minister Schuman, who proposed that a new OEEC head should only have representative functions outside the Organization—that is, in relations with the U.S. government, nonmembers, and other international organizations. But what particularly irked the Americans was the fact that Sir Stafford Cripps, whose government had promised to remain neutral in the matter, strongly supported Schuman's proposal during the meeting.[90] Nevertheless, Harriman managed to salvage at least two things: an agreement that after January 1950 the Consultative Group would meet on a regular monthly basis, and a promise by the group to consider a working paper based on the Acheson and Schuman proposals.[91]

Nor was the suggested redefinition of the new post's nature the only source of aggravation to U.S. officials. During January 1950 it became increasingly clear that Spaak's candidacy—though favored by the Americans—lacked wide support within the OEEC. In addition to the British, who found him unacceptable, he was opposed by Portugal and the Scandinavian countries. In fact, early in January the Norwegians, acting on behalf of the Scandinavian group, approached Dirk Stikker, the Dutch Foreign Minister, and tried to interest him in becoming a candidate for the contemplated position.[92] At first Stikker appeared reluctant, and for a time the Americans continued to push for Spaak.[93] But by late January Acheson had finally come to see the light. "I believe," he cabled Harriman on January 24, 1950, "it would be a mistake to push candidacy of Spaak."[94] Acheson cited the flat opposition of Britain and the varying degrees of opposition of other countries as the reason for his conclusion. But it is also reasonable to suggest that he himself may have become somewhat disenchanted with the outspoken

Spaak who, on several occasions, appeared almost totally oblivious to the provocative nature of his public utterances.[95]

Thus, in the end, Spaak's candidacy was dropped and Stikker's took its place. On April 4, 1950, the Dutch Foreign Minister was elected Chairman of the OEEC Council, a post he would combine with that of Political Conciliator.[96] The latter position was defined in terms that closely resembled Schuman's proposal, made at the December 20 meeting of the Consultative Group; that is, the duties of the Political Conciliator were primarily external: to insure liaison between the OEEC and the U.S. government and, where appropriate, with nonmembers and other international organizations. But in an apparent deference to American wishes, he was also allowed to make direct contacts with members of the OEEC itself, either on his own initiative or at the request of the Council's chairman. The purpose of such contacts would be to facilitate agreements between members and to coordinate activities aimed at accomplishing agreed ends. Finally—and borrowing directly from the language of Acheson's draft message—the Political Conciliator was to actively assist in presenting the objectives of the OEEC to the public.

There can be little question that American efforts to politicize the OEEC and thereby hasten progress toward European unification bore little immediate results. In fact, both the State Department and the ECA would have been well advised, in late 1949, to heed the opinion of the Council on Foreign Relations that "too fast a push on integration [was] neither feasible nor particularly beneficial."[97] The ECA, at least, seemed to have learned its lesson. During the spring and early summer of 1950, it concentrated its greatest attention on matters pertaining to intra-European trade and payments liberalization. Moreover, throughout the remainder of its own official life the aid agency refrained from becoming directly and openly involved in the question of European political unification. The State Department, on the other hand, continued its efforts to strengthen the political posture of various European institutions.[98] And Congress, meanwhile, was preparing itself for yet another piece of aid legislation that would reinforce its previously expressed sentiment with regard to European unification.

VI

By the summer of 1951, when Congress began to consider the Administration's request for next (fiscal) year's foreign aid appropriations, European unification had become a well-established goal of U.S. foreign policy, strongly supported by a majority of American public opinion. To be sure, a new element had been introduced into official discussions of the subject—namely, a perceived need for European unity in order to maintain and increase the security of Western Europe. And to judge from the evidence, the Administration had little difficulty in mobilizing authoritative voices to play this theme before American and European audiences. Thus, for example, on July 3, 1951, shortly before Congress began hearings on the Mutual Security Act of 1951, General Dwight D. Eisenhower, then Supreme Allied Commander in Europe, addressed the English-Speaking Union in London. In a widely publicized speech, a draft of which had been submitted to and cleared by the State Department, he told his listeners: "We cannot reach maximum security without a united Europe." And although the General did not elaborate, he called for "the establishment of a workable European federation."[99] Some seven months later, Eisenhower returned to the same theme. On January 22, 1952, during a press conference at his headquarters outside Paris, he opined that Europe "cannot gain strength and stability if it remains split up in a number of independent economies." He saw, he declared, "no acceptable alternative to a union, an economic union between the states of Western Europe." And he added, "I can't see how an economic union can be successful unless there is political union."[100] By then, of course, the Mutual Security Act of 1951 had been law for several months, and the General was essentially adding his own voice to that of Congress.

Indeed, in the Mutual Security Act, Congress went further than it had done before in expressing itself on the subject of European integration. Whereas in the previous two years it had limited itself, without elaboration, to the term *unification*, it now declared that one of the purposes of the new aid program—the Mutual Security Program—was to encourage "the economic unification and political federation of Europe."[101] Still, no specific definition was given to either of these terms; and in the absence of clear congressional guidelines, the newly formed Mutual Security Agency (MSA) proceeded cautiously. "Only Europeans can make a decision to federate their nations," declared Acting Special Representative Paul Porter, shortly after the passage of the act. "But our backing," he added, "can be a powerful boost."[102] Porter's words were uttered in late October 1951, during the transition from the ECA's administration to that of the MSA. By early 1952, however, a much more specific set of suggestions concerning American "backing" had been put forward by some MSA staff members.

Not surprisingly, the basic rationale for unification, from MSA's standpoint, lay in the contributions an integrated European economy would be expected to make to both productivity and defense. Simply stated, the doctrine to be expounded was this: Defense requires increased productivity; "and the only incentive to productivity," wrote an MSA official in an internal memorandum, "is the creation of a single large market, for which unification is necessary." Hence, "once achieved, integration would provide consequent solutions to the problems of defense and productivity." [103] The author of this rather sweeping conclusion went on to claim that public polls in Europe indicated a strong *popular* support for unification. The main task before the MSA, he argued, was to "sell" the idea of integration to the European governments themselves. In carrying out this task, he suggested, the OSR should work primarily through the offices of the European Movement. Specifically, OSR should help to set up, in each participating country, "action committees," composed of prominent citizens, which would be supplied with informational material and propaganda techniques. Thus armed, the action committees, with the assistance of the local MSA missions, should undertake "an informational program that would have one theme—that the people of Europe are *far ahead of their elected governments* in supporting a European Union." The ultimate objective of such a program, he stated, would be to pressure "[the respective] governments to act in accordance with the will of the electorate." [104] This, then, was to be a bold and decisive course of action. But even the author of the document himself undoubtedly appreciated the implications of his proposal; for he cautioned that any assistance rendered by the MSA must be "extremely discreet." And he concluded by suggesting that "competent guidance should be sought from the CIA in these matters." [105]

Whether or not CIA's guidance was actually sought, or freely given, is not a matter of public record. Nor is it known to what extent the specific proposals noted above were carried out. [106] What *is* known, however, is that in the spring of 1952, during hearings on the extension of the Mutual Security Program, Secretary of State Acheson stated before the Senate Foreign Relations Committee that the U.S. government's efforts to "speed up" the unification of Europe had been "sound and good." [107] And Congress, apparently satisfied, passed the Mutual Security Act of 1952, in which it formally welcomed "the recent progress in political federation, military integration, and economic unification in Europe." At the same time, it reaffirmed "its belief in the necessity of further vigorous efforts toward these ends as a means of building strength, establishing security, and preserving peace in the North Atlantic Area." [108]

* * *

Soon after the passage of the Mutual Security Act of 1952, the two major political parties in the United States began to gear themselves for the forthcoming presidential election campaign. In their respective party platforms, both Democrats and Republicans pledged their support and encouragement of continued progress toward European unification. The Democrats spelled out their position by declaring: "We encourage the economic and political unity of free Europe and the increasing solidarity of the nations of the North Atlantic community. We hail the Schuman Plan and the European Defense Community. We are proud of America's part in carrying these great projects forward and we pledge our continuing support until they are established." [109] The Republicans, though somewhat more succinct, appeared just as committed to the idea. In their platform, they stated that the United States would use its "friendly influence . . . for ending the political and economic divisions which alone prevent [Western Europe] from being strong on its own right." [110]

When these statements were made, the ECA no longer existed; and with the end of the ECA had come the official termination of the Marshall Plan itself. Strictly speaking, therefore, any actions and measures to further the cause of European unification, which were undertaken by the U.S. government from 1952 on, fall outside the scope of the present study. On the other hand, during the ERP period several attempts were made by the Europeans themselves to give the concept of integration a more concrete meaning than had been offered by either Congress or the Administration. Some of these attempts never got off the ground, others reached the discussion stage, and at least one was carried to full fruition. And inasmuch as the United States had lent its support to most of the European initiatives along these lines—both during and after the end of the Marshall Plan—it would be useful to accord them at least some consideration. Indeed, the story of ERP's contributions to the development of economic cooperation in Western Europe would not be complete without a critical look at the various *European* approaches to economic integration and the methods proposed for its implementation.

European Economic Integration: Methods and Forms 13

"Of all the obscure and uncomely words with which the study of economics clutters up one's language," wrote François Perroux in 1954, "the term integration ranks among the uppermost." [1] His seeming frustration may readily be appreciated if it is considered within the specific context of *European* integration. For even in the early 1950s, after several years of continuous and increasing U.S. efforts to reshape Western Europe into a closely knit economic and political entity, there still remained many unanswered questions concerning the nature and scope of an integrated European economy. Nor were there signs to indicate that the American conception of a Western European federation—with one army, one market area, and perhaps even one currency—would be embraced with enthusiasm, if at all, by the OEEC countries. [2]

In a strict economic sense, however, the term *regional integration* can be quite clearly defined to mean the removal, by two or several countries, of barriers to the flow of economic activities across their national borders. Such barriers include tariffs, quantitative restrictions, exchange controls, and immigration restrictions. But which of these barriers are to be removed, and to what extent, are matters left to the discretion of the countries involved. Their decisions will determine how closely the respective economies are to be brought together; in other words, what form the particular integration scheme will take.

Four types of regional economic integration may be distinguished: (1) the free-trade area, (2) the customs (or tariff) union, (3) the common market, and (4) the economic union. The least binding of these is the free-trade area—an arrangement that provides for the removal of barriers on the trade between the participating countries, but allows each of them to deal independently with nonparticipants. In other words, while committing themselves to free trade vis-à-vis each other, the individual members of a free-trade area may pursue either liberal or restrictive commercial policies in their relations with nonmembers. Thus, the formation of a free-trade area requires little mutual cooperation in matters that do not relate directly to the reduction and eventual elimination of barriers to intra-area trade.

A somewhat greater degree of cooperation is exemplified by a customs union. In this case, the participating nations must agree not only to eliminate restrictions (typically tariffs) on their mutual trade, but to pursue a common commercial policy vis-à-vis the rest of the world. Hence, the formation of a customs union necessarily entails the establishment of a common schedule of external tariffs, to be levied on goods entering the area, and the creation of a central agency to collect and distribute duty receipts. Moreover, the members of a customs union must agree to act as one unit in negotiating tariff and trade agreements with nonmembers. Finally, the existence of a customs union implies at least some degree of coordination of its members' domestic economic policies.

If, in addition to the removal of trade barriers, the members of a customs union agree to allow free flows of productive resources (i.e., labor, capital, etc.), the resulting agreement is referred to as a common market. Indeed, as the term suggests, a common market constitutes a single unified market area, throughout which goods and services, as well as labor and capital, can move freely across national borders. As such, a common market represents a more closely knit economic bloc than the customs union and, consequently, entails a higher degree of cooperation.

The highest degree of regional economic integration is represented by the economic union, or economic community. For although its members may still constitute separate political entities, an economic union implies an almost complete unification of economic institutions throughout the union area. Thus, it usually involves the setting up of supranational agencies whose decisions are binding on the union members and whose powers may supersede, in part or in whole, those of national decision-making authorities. But even when institutional unification is less than complete, the satisfactory operation of an economic union demands close coordination and harmonization of its members' economic policies.

The need for such coordination may be easily appreciated if it is noted that the removal of trade barriers among previously protected national economies is bound to make each of them more susceptible to economic fluctuations originating outside its own borders. It may also result in severe dislocations of domestic resources. Hence, the formation of a regional economic bloc requires that its members agree to coordinate, or at least cooperate, in pursuit of national policies designed to combat recession, prevent excessive inflation, and facilitate balance-of-payments adjustments. And the higher the degree of integration, the greater the need to create central institutions through which such coordination could be carried out. The creation of central, or supranational, institutions also implies a willingness, on the part of the countries involved, to surrender part of their national autonomy over economic matters. Thus, in the final analysis, the *technical* form of a particular integration arrangement is largely a reflection of the degree of national sovereignty its members are willing to surrender. It is reasonable to argue, therefore, that the ambiguity about European integration—so lamented by Perroux—was due, not so much to a misunderstanding or obscurity of the basic concept, as to a lack of consensus over the specific form it could or should take.

I

When, in late October 1949, Paul Hoffman called for the formation of a "single market" within which trade and payments barriers would be "permanently swept away," he was addressing himself to what he perceived to be the *substance*, rather than the *form*, of an integrated European economy. His deliberate omission of any reference to a specific integration model was largely based on State Department advice, to "let the Europeans themselves develop the institutions necessary to handle the problems of integration."[3] In part, however, this omission must have been dictated by a recognition of existing realities. The ECA Administrator was fully aware that during the preceding two years, a specific approach to European economic integration had been discussed, studied, and finally abandoned by the Europeans. To resurrect it at this date would have served no useful purpose. Besides, even the Americans, who had initially urged the adoption of this approach, had by now become resigned to its demise.

That particular approach—the formation of an OEEC-wide customs union—may be said to have originated, on the American side, in Will Clayton's famous "European Crisis" memorandum, handed to Secretary of State Marshall on May 27, 1947.[4] In arguing the need for a three-year grant to Europe, Clayton proposed that this grant be based on a plan to be worked out by the principal European nations, headed by the United Kingdom, France, and Italy. "Such a plan," he continued, "should be based on a European economic federation, *on the order of the Belgium-Netherlands-Luxembourg Customs Union*."[5] Two months later, a similar recommendation was put forward by the Policy Planning Staff (PPS) of the State Department. In a document dated July 23, 1947, the PPS stressed the importance of intra-European trade liberalization and called for "the eventual formation of a European customs union" as "a long-term objective."[6] By then, of course, the CEEC nations had already begun work on their report; and Clayton, serving as one of America's "friendly advisers," did not miss any opportunity to impress upon the CEEC conferees that a commitment to form a West European customs union would be the sort of cooperative undertaking that would "catch American public opinion and imagination" and would greatly improve the chances of congressional approval of American aid.[7]

As it were, Clayton was not the only or even the first one to broach the subject of customs unions during the CEEC deliberations in that summer of 1947. On July 15, some two weeks before Clayton's own arrival in Paris, the CEEC delegates were treated to a passionate address by the Italian Foreign Minister, Count Carlo Sforza, who concluded by proposing the formation of a customs union between Italy and France. Such a venture, he stated, would be the first step on the road, to be followed sooner or later by the whole of Western Europe.[8] Nor was Sforza's dramatic pronouncement the only evidence of European initiatives to which the CEEC delegates were exposed. The formation of the Benelux—a customs union consisting of Belgium, the Netherlands, and Luxembourg—had actually been agreed upon as early as September 5, 1944, when the governments-in-exile of these countries signed the Benelux Convention in London. In April 1946, the same three countries had agreed to broaden the aims of the Benelux, from a customs union to an economic union. And with the ratification of the convention by their respective parliaments in July 1947, the Benelux tariff union was scheduled to take effect on January 1, 1948.[9]

With the example of Benelux before their eyes and Sforza's words ringing in their ears, the CEEC delegates were bound to give at least some consideration to a European-wide customs union, as a possible instrument of European economic cooperation. Under the circumstances, Clayton's role was mainly one of prodding them toward that particular objective, while dissuading them from pursuing less ambitious projects—such as, for example, the creation of a preferential tariff area (or areas) in Europe.[10] And as if to underscore the point, Clayton and his fellow American advisers made it quite clear that mere exchanges of intra-European tariff preferences would be unacceptable to the U.S. government unless accompanied by a definite commitment to the eventual formation of a European customs union.[11]

Actually, both the Europeans and their American advisers were cognizant of an inherent conflict between any measure to create a European preferential tariff bloc and one of the cardinal tenets of postwar American foreign economic policy—namely, equal treatment and nondiscrimination in trade relations. Known as the General Most-Favored Nation (MFN) Treatment, this principle was embodied in the then-evolving draft charter for a proposed International Trade Organization (ITO).[12] It specified that any tariff concessions granted by one ITO member to another must be "immediately and unconditionally" extended to all other members.[13] As originally drafted, however, the charter did provide for two exceptions to the General MFN Treatment principle: It allowed members to accord preferential concessions to adjacent countries, "in order to facilitate frontier traffic," and it permitted the formation of customs unions between two or more members.[14] What was *not* provided in the early draft of the charter was an allowance for an exchange of preferential tariff concessions that *might* eventually lead to the formation of a customs union by the countries concerned. That is, the draft charter seemed to imply that while an overnight commitment to the creation of a customs union—which by definition entails 100-percent preference for members and 100-percent discrimination against outside countries—was in conformity with its provisions, any preferential tariff arrangements, short of a customs union, were not.

Quite understandably, it was the Europeans who first sought clarification of this point, while searching for ways by which to satisfy the American demand for a commitment to intra-European economic cooperation. In late July 1947, Sir Oliver Franks raised the issue with Clayton, subtly informing him that several CEEC delegates were "honestly perplexed" as to how a program of reducing intra-European trade barriers could be adopted without violating the proposed ITO charter. To which Clayton replied by assuring him that if the CEEC conference did indeed come up with a plan that provided for "a series of definite, overall percentage [tariff] reductions, culminating in the elimination of [trade] barriers at a definite time," then he, Clayton, was confident that the proposed charter could be modified to accommodate such a plan.[15] The message should have been clear: If the Europeans agreed to proceed toward a customs union in several stages, each involving preferential reductions of intra-European tariffs, the Americans would be prepared to adjust their own position and endorse such a move. And, true to their word, the American representatives at the charter negotiations in Geneva shortly proceeded to amend Article 38 of the London draft, so as to allow for "the formation of a customs union" as well as "the adoption of an *interim* agreement necessary for the attainment of a customs union; provided that any such agreement shall include a definite plan and schedule for the attainment of such a customs union within a reasonable length of time."[16]

As is well known, the proposed ITO never saw the light of day. For although the so-called Havana Charter was signed on March 24, 1948, by the representatives of fifty-three nations—including all but one of the CEEC countries—it was never ratified.[17] But the charter's provisions relating to the conduct of commercial policy, including the General MFN Treatment principle, had been incorporated earlier into another international document, the General Agreement on Tariffs and Trade (GATT). The latter, negotiated and concluded in Geneva in the fall of 1947, also contained the above-noted exceptions to the General MFN Treatment principle, and added yet another. It allowed the contracting parties to form either customs unions *or* free-trade areas, and to adopt interim agreements necessary for the attainment of either one of such projects.[18] In a word, the definition of what might constitute legitimate departures from the equal-treatment principle had been further relaxed to include free-trade areas. But in the end, neither the creation of a European customs union nor the formation of a European free-trade area appeared as a formal commitment in the CEEC report.

Indeed, the report approached the subject of customs unions very cautiously. It declared that "the advantages which the United States has enjoyed through the existence of a large domestic market with no internal trade barriers, are manifest"; and it conceded that the decision of Belgium, the Netherlands, and Luxembourg to form a customs union "is an instructive example of mutual cooperation."[19] It took note of developments with respect to the Benelux, and it cited declarations, made during the CEEC conference by various governments, of their intentions to explore the possibilities of forming individual customs unions among themselves.[20] At the same time, however, the report was careful to point out that "no customs union can be brought into full and effective operation by a stroke of a pen," and that the formation of a customs union, "particularly between several large and highly industrial countries," necessarily involves complex technical negotiations and adjustments "which can only be achieved by progressive steps over a period of years."[21] Still, the signatories of the report were prepared to conclude, somewhat innocuously, that, on balance, "the idea of a customs union, including as many European countries as possible, is one which contains many possibilities for the economic future of Europe, and it is in the general interest that the problems involved should receive careful and detailed study. . . ."[22]

Accordingly, on September 12, 1947, the governments of thirteen CEEC nations agreed to create a European Customs Union Study Group. Its purpose, in the words of the report, was to "examine the problems involved and the steps to be taken" in the formation of a customs union or customs unions between all or any of the governments concerned and any other governments invited to participate in the work of the Study Group.[23] And to help launch the Study Group properly, the governments of the Benelux countries agreed to act as the sponsoring powers and to convene its first meeting. Two months later, having settled in Brussels, the Study Group began work; and by March 1948, it was ready with its own first report. But if the Americans, or anyone else for that matter, had expected the Study Group to render a fast and unequivocal judgment in favor of customs unions, they were in for a disappointment. For although that first report seriously considered both the difficulties that stood in the way of a European customs union and the benefits that might accrue from it, its verdict was, at best, inconclusive and, at worst, outrightly evasive. "It is not practical at this stage," it stated, "to pronounce definitely on the merits and disadvantages of a Customs Union." And while it leaned toward the presumption that "such a Union would in the long run make for greater prosperity of the countries composing it," the report stopped short when it came to specifics. "How far [a customs union] would do so," it vaguely suggested, "would depend on the proper solution of a great many problems and the nature of the compromise reached." [24]

So much for the Study Group's first published effort! Yet despite the noncommittal nature of the initial report, the work begun in November 1947 continued for several years to come. In fact, at its very first meeting the Study Group had established a Tariff Committee, later known as the Customs Committee, to deal with matters relating to tariff nomenclatures, definitions of values, and customs procedures. [25] And in the spring of 1948, it appointed an Economic Committee, to study the various production and industrial problems to which a customs union may give rise.

None of these committees' studies and reports to the parent group contained an a priori commitment to the formation of a European customs union. To be sure, the General Report, submitted by the Economic Committee in October 1948, distinguished between several possible methods by which a customs union *might* be formed. But the impasse created by that particular report caused the permanent suspension of the committee's work. Nor did the Study Group itself ever manage to achieve a consensus on the desirability of establishing an OEEC-wide customs union, though the evidence seems to suggest that it made at least one attempt in this direction, in November 1949. [26] The attempt failed, and thenceforth the Study Group confined its work largely to the sphere of tariff nomenclatures and related problems. By the end of 1949, the European customs union project had, to all intents and purposes, been given up.

II

A similar fate befell all but one of the other potential customs union projects cited in the CEEC report.

Not an official word was to be subsequently heard about the declared intention of the Greek and Turkish governments to "devote all their attention to the study of a regional customs union between their two countries." Although commissions were set up in both countries to explore this possibility, it soon must have become apparent that there existed no real basis on which to negotiate a customs union agreement between them; and none was ever concluded. Nor did the declaration made by the Scandinavian countries of *their* intention to examine the possibility of eliminating "customs frontiers" between them produce any concrete results. In February 1948, a Joint Scandinavian Commission for Economic Cooperation began work on this matter. But after two years of discussion, it reported that a Scandinavian customs union would not be feasible in the near future, and the subject was accordingly dropped from further consideration at the time.[27]

In contrast, the proposal for a Franco-Italian customs union appeared, at least initially, destined for rapid fulfillment. Before the year 1947 was out, a Mixed Commission appointed by the two governments had completed a report that concluded ambitiously that a customs union between the two countries was not only feasible but should, in fact, be regarded as the first step toward the formation of an economic union. In March 1948, the two governments signed a protocol in which they declared their formal desire to establish a Franco-Italian customs union, and created a new commission to devise the ways and means of accomplishing this goal. The latter completed *its* report in January 1949; and on March 26, 1949, France and Italy—with the blessings of ECA—signed a customs union treaty that provided for the mutual reduction and eventual elimination of trade barriers over a six-year period.

But that was as far as the Franco-Italian customs union project ever got. The treaty—signed in March and further revised in June and July—drew strong opposition from various interest groups in both countries and was never ratified by their respective parliaments. In late 1949, following Hoffman's "integration" speech, an attempt was made to breathe life into the Franco-Italian project by combining it with the Benelux. A proposal, known as Fritalux or Finebel and eagerly supported by ECA at the time, envisioned the creation of a five-country economic bloc whose members would commit themselves to (1) remove quantitative restrictions from a greater percentage of their mutual trade than was called for by the OEEC, (2) permit a higher degree of currency convertibility among themselves, and (3) allow exchange rates to fluctuate, so as to maintain an approximate balance in intrabloc payments. The Benelux countries, though interested in the proposed scheme, favored mutual reductions of tariffs, as well as the removal of quantitative restrictions; but France and Italy objected. Moreover, the Netherlands strongly urged that Germany be included in the bloc, while the French and the Italians were, at best, reluctant to see this happen.

In any event, in early December 1949, technical experts from the five countries reached, and submitted to their governments, a tentative agreement on the first steps in the formation of such a bloc. These included a very limited provision for currency convertibility, a limited allowance for exchange rate adjustments, an agreement in principle on coordination of internal financial policies, and a commitment to free 60 percent of total intrabloc private trade from quantitative restrictions.[28] Modest as it was, the plan embodied in the tentative agreement was not acted upon by the governments concerned during the remainder of 1949; and the push for the project itself slackened considerably when the United States brought forth its proposal for the European Payments Union. Interest in Finebel, however, was shortly revived when it became all too apparent that an agreement on EPU could not be quickly reached in the OEEC. But the continued Dutch insistence on the inclusion of Germany, and the strong French objection to it, brought the negotiations on a newly prepared draft agreement to a standstill. Ironically, several months later, when the French appeared finally to have overcome their reluctance to enter into collaborative economic ventures with Germany, the Finebel project had lost its raison d'être. For by then, the EPU negotiations—encompassing the OEEC trade liberalization program—had progressed so far as to render a Finebel-like scheme superfluous. And it, too, was discarded.

Indeed, the only effort to create a subregional customs union that bore fruit was the one undertaken by the Benelux countries; and even *their* experiment with economic integration had had its share of difficulties. A Benelux tariff union—under which all customs duties on intragroup trade were eventually abolished and a common tariff imposed on imports from outside—took effect on January 1, 1948. Progress toward a full economic union, however, proved slow, and the ultimate goal was never reached. Initially planned for January 1, 1950, the commencement of the economic union was postponed, first to July 1950 and then to January 1951, at which time it was again postponed— indefinitely. The diversity of internal economic structures and policies between Belgium and the Netherlands, the great disparities in their balance-of-payments positions; and differences in customs classifications and procedures—all of these contributed to the difficulties that stood in the way of rapid integration of the Benelux economies.[29] Yet despite the frustrating delays, the three countries persisted in their efforts and in 1954 managed to reach an agreement allowing for movements of workers between them. This was followed, some two years later, by an agreement dealing with the free movement of capital. By that time, the Benelux countries, in partnership with France, Germany, and Italy, had already been involved in another ongoing integration project, to be discussed below. But the point to be emphasized here is that from 1948 to 1950, the Benelux symbolized the only persistent effort toward integration in Western Europe. In fact, it constituted the only *operating* customs union during the entire period of the Marshall Plan.

Viewed in retrospect, the general failure of the customs union approach, under the ERP, should not be surprising. For, notwithstanding the lofty declarations made in the CEEC report, existing political and economic realities at the time made such a course of action extremely unlikely. An OEEC-wide customs union would have had to count as its members a mixture of ex-allies, ex-enemies, and ex-neutrals. It would have consisted of former colonial powers with lingering ties to their overseas spheres of influence, and of small nations; of countries that believed in and pursued central economic planning, and those that espoused free-market economic liberalism; of war-shattered and strained economies, on the one hand, and largely untouched and prosperous ones on the other; of countries experiencing galloping inflation, and others enjoying relative monetary stability. The mutual removal of tariff protection by such a diverse group of countries would have inevitably exposed most of them to serious economic problems over which, by definition, they would have had a lesser degree of national control. Hence, if such a customs union were to function properly, its prospective members would have had to commit themselves in advance to a very close coordination of their internal economic policies—something few European countries were willing or able to do throughout most of the ERP period.

The difficulties inherent in the formation of an OEEC-wide customs union could be said to apply—though on a smaller scale—to the formation of subregional customs unions as well. There was, however, an additional complication that bore directly on these latter efforts. Once the notion of a European customs union was abandoned, the main thrust of OEEC's trade liberalization program became directed at the progressive elimination of quantitative restrictions by all its members. A customs union, on the other hand, is basically a device for the mutual removal of tariffs. Since both tariffs and quotas were being used by European countries to restrict and regulate their imports, the removal of quantitative restrictions would, in effect, leave the tariff to assume a greater role as an instrument of national commercial policies. Put differently, with the progressive removal of quantitative restrictions, existing tariffs would become increasingly more important as the means by which a domestic economy could be protected from competing imports. Under the circumstances, the mutual elimination of tariffs by members of a subregional customs union could prove especially hazardous to those members whose economies were not sufficiently strong to withstand competition from their partners. And because all of the proposed subregional customs unions would necessarily be composed of countries that were simultaneously members of the OEEC—and hence obliged to follow its quota liberalization program—it was only to be expected that none of these projects could be easily negotiated, let alone implemented.[30]

Yet if the formation of customs unions—either on a regional or a subregional basis—did not prove to be a viable approach to European economic integration, other European-inspired schemes were soon being offered as possible alternatives. In mid–1950, as the negotiations for the EPU were nearing completion, three proposals for trade liberalization were presented to the OEEC by the Netherlands, France, and Italy, respectively. Common to all three was an underlying conviction that the creation of a single European market must entail not only the removal of quantitative restrictions but also the reduction and elimination of tariffs, and that even the removal of quotas on intra-European trade, beyond the 75-percent goal demanded by the Americans, could not be achieved on the basis of the provisions contained in the Code of Trade Liberalization.[31] The plans differed, however, with respect to timing and the procedures to be followed in pursuing the ultimate objective.

Boldest of the three was the proposal submitted on behalf of the Netherlands by its Foreign Minister, Dirk Stikker.[32] This so-called Stikker Plan proposed the nondiscriminatory removal of quantitative restrictions on 75 percent of private intra-OEEC trade by December 31, 1950, and the subsequent removal of such restrictions on the remaining 25 percent of trade, to be accompanied by the elimination of tariff (and other trade barriers) on *all* trade. The real novelty of the plan, however, lay in its proposed industry-by-industry approach. That is, liberalization measures would be applied, in turn, to one industry (or sector) of the European economies after another, as each was studied and agreed to by the OEEC. As such, the Stikker Plan represented the so-called sector or functional approach to integration. Recognizing, moreover, that a particular industry in a given country might not be able to adjust easily to the impact of freer trade, the plan envisaged the establishment of a European Integration Fund. Such a fund would extend assistance to governments for the purpose of retooling and reequipping industries adversely affected by liberalization measures. It could also be drawn upon to finance new investments in other suitable industries and to retrain workers displaced from the adversely affected ones.

The French proposal, known as the Petsche Plan, constituted a variant on the sector approach. It called for the development, by the OEEC members as a group, of a common list of identical products, on which quantitative restrictions would be relaxed.[33] Second, it proposed the establishment of a European Investment Bank, to finance industries producing for the European market. The proposal did not limit the bank's activities to only the financing of industries that might be confronted with the repercussions of liberalization—i.e., industries whose products were included in the common list. Nor did it restrict its lending sphere to governments alone. In fact, unlike the Integration Fund proposed in the Stikker Plan, the European Investment Bank was envisioned as a permanent institution, whose general purpose was to assist in financing efficient production ventures, capable of earning commercial returns in a unified and unrestricted European market. The bank could, and presumably would, lend to both private and state enterprises, as well as to governments.[34]

In contrast to the Stikker and Petsche plans, the Italian plan, named after Italy's Finance Minister Giuseppe Pella, rejected the sector approach as being rigid and difficult to implement. It proposed instead the formation of a preferential tariff zone in Europe, to be accomplished through multilateral negotiations among the members of OEEC. Tariff rates (or margins of preference) agreed upon through these negotiations would remain in force for a given period but would be subject to further reductions—both automatic and renegotiated—from time to time. Carried to its logical conclusion, the Pella Plan could be said to have aimed at the eventual formation of a free-trade area, or possibly even a customs union, in Europe. But because of the fairly long period of time over which this process might have to stretch, the adoption of the Italian proposal by the OEEC would have required the consent of the United States, as well as the other signatories of GATT.[35]

What American officials thought of the Pella Plan might be partially inferred from the fact that, in its *Tenth Report to Congress*, the ECA devoted exactly one sentence to its description.[36] On the same occasion, the agency went into some length in describing the Dutch and French plans.[37] Still, the ECA refrained from commenting publicly on the relative merits of any of the proposals. Instead, it limited itself to expressing the hope that "agreement might be reached on a single plan, the implementation of which would make possible the creation of a wider, freer European market."[38]

The OEEC, upon being presented with the three proposals, reacted in a predictable manner: It turned them over to its Technical Committees for study and recommendations. And there the matter came to rest. Several months later, the ECA informed Congress that during the quarter ending on December 31, 1950, committees of the OEEC "continued their study of the Petsche, Pella and Stikker plans."[39] But this laconic statement proved to be the last official reference made by the agency to any of them. None of the three proposals passed beyond the committee-discussion stage; and by the fall of 1951, they had all been dropped from active consideration.

III

The "sector" approach, however, did not die with the Stikker and Petsche plans. On the contrary, it was to be effectively embodied in the most dramatic and far reaching integration project initiated during the ERP period. In fact, even before the Stikker Plan was presented to the OEEC, the French government—in the person of Foreign Minister Robert Schuman—had startled both Americans and Europeans by unveiling a proposal for placing the coal and steel industries of France and Germany under a common authority and creating a common organization (a coal-steel pool) which other European countries were invited to join. This so-called Schuman Plan, which was announced on May 19, 1950, led, within less than a year, to the signing of a treaty establishing a European Coal and Steel Community (ECSC), composed of six OEEC countries: France, Germany, Italy, and the three Benelux countries.[40] The treaty was signed on April 18, 1951, and by late June 1952 had been ratified by the parliaments of the six signatories. It came into force on July 25, 1952; and on August 10, the High Authority—the Community's executive body—formally began to function.

Given the continued American emphasis on the theme of European integration, it is not surprising that Schuman's proposal, when announced, was greeted with enthusiastic support from official quarters in the United States. President Truman hailed it as "an act of constructive statesmanship" and said the United States welcomed it. Other Administration officials followed suit by publicly expressing similar sentiments.[41] But it is also worth noting that the first American official who had been made privy to the outline of the plan prior to its public disclosure expressed initial reservation, if not outright skepticism. By his own account, Secretary Acheson, who had arrived in Paris on his way to a Big Three conference in London, was informed by Schuman of the proposal and its impending announcement on May 7, 1950. His gut reaction, as he subsequently related, consisted of the view that the Schuman Plan was "the damndest cartel I have ever heard of in my life. . . ."[42] Yet it obviously did not take him long to be sold on the virtues of the plan. For later that day, having been additionally briefed by Jean Monnet (the true architect of the plan), both Acheson and John McCloy "[became] convinced that this was a darn good thing; this was all right; it might turn out badly, but the chances were pretty good for it."[43]

The clue to the official American support of Schuman's proposal may be found not so much in economic as in political and strategic considerations. Indeed, the overall significance of the proposal may be better appreciated if it is viewed in political rather than economic terms. To be sure, the proposal envisioned joint steps being undertaken to modernize and expand production in the industries concerned; to pool and coordinate coal and steel resources; to assure adequate supplies of these products and equal access, to all consumers, to their sources of production; to improve and equalize the living standards of industrial workers in the participating countries; and to remove trade restrictions on coal, iron, and steel products traded among them. On its face, then, the ultimate objective appeared to be economic in nature: The creation of a large single market, covering the coal and steel industries of the participating nations, within which greater gains to economic efficiency and well-being could be realized.[44]

Underlying this objective, however, was a more fundamental purpose: to cement closer relationships between France and Germany through the fusion (or merger) of national interests in the basic sectors of their economies. Such a fusion presumably would minimize the risk of future wars between these two ancient enemies, and would help create a more viable basis for cooperation between Germany and the other Western European countries. Thus, in announcing his proposal, Schuman dramatically stated that the pooling of coal and steel production would mean that a war between France and Germany "[would] become not only unthinkable but materially impossible." And U.S. policy makers, who for some time had been pushing for the restoration of West Germany to an acceptable and useful position in Europe—and who would soon be pushing for German rearmament—were quick to perceive of the Schuman Plan as just the kind of instrument by which this goal might be accomplished. Echoes of such perceptions naturally found their way into unofficial pronouncements, though not always in a complimentary fashion. The Schuman Plan, observed one skeptical critic at the time, is a "convenient self-delusion, permitting the French to cajole themselves into accepting the rearmament of Germany."[45] Another, more restrained observer nevertheless agreed that there were definite "motives of political expediency" in the plan.[46] Still a third referred to it as "a political action in the form of an economic innovation."[47]

In its own official commentaries, the ECA understandably tried to maintain a proper balance between the economic and the political-strategic virtues of the plan. Thus, when reporting to Congress in mid-1950 the agency stated, practically in the same breath, that the proposal "affords additional opportunities for the fuller participation of Western Germany in European affairs" and that, if carried out according to announced objectives, the plan "could contribute markedly to more efficient production, increased liberalization of trade, and lower prices."[48] And shortly after the ECSC treaty had been signed, the agency returned to the same theme. "Apart from the anticipated economic gains," it stated, "the operation of the Schuman Plan will mean a significant step toward the integration of Germany into the family of free European nations." [49]

Yet while it warmly endorsed the Schuman Plan, the U.S. government refrained, at least initially, from taking an active and overt role in the negotiations for the ECSC. This was in line with a deliberate policy decision that reflected a correct assessment of existing realities. The French proposal represented a *European* initiative, and it was, therefore, considered politically and psychologically important that its details should be worked out by the Europeans themselves. Moreover, there existed a distinct danger that a significant U.S. effort to shape—or reshape—the proposed project might make it appear as yet another American push for European unification and would doom its prospects to failure. Thus, in contrast to their customary presence (as advisers, observers, experts, or cajolers) in the councils and committees of the OEEC—and particularly, their active involvement in the ongoing negotiations for the EPU—American officials in Paris maintained a low profile during the first months of the treaty's negotiations. [50] These negotiations began on June 20, 1950, and for some time thereafter only the U.S. Ambassador to France, David Bruce, and William Tomlinson (the U.S. Treasury's representative in Paris and Monnet's good friend) maintained regular contact with the European negotiators. [51] At least until the late fall of 1950, the U.S. government had deliberately kept itself in the background, looking, in the words of one seasoned observer, "benignly but unobtrusively" on the progressing negotiations. [52]

Several developments, however, conspired to alter this state of affairs. The first of these was the invasion of South Korea by North Korean forces in the summer of 1950, and the ensuing changes in the international political atmosphere and economic climate. Strengthening the defense of the West, and particularly the defense of Western Europe, soon emerged as an explicit U.S. policy objective. And this policy shift, with its corollary emphasis on defense production needs, was bound to heighten American desire to speed up the integration of West Germany into the Western European community. Germany, in the official U.S. view, was simply too important—nay, indispensable—to the common defense effort; its return to autonomy and equality, free of existing Allied controls over its coal and steel production, was imperative.

The likely impact of such an American attitude on the Schuman Plan negotiations may be readily appreciated. The original French proposal had held the promise that, by agreeing to join the coal-steel pool, West Germany would indeed accelerate the pace of becoming a full-fledged member of the European community and would, in the process, rid itself of the various economic restrictions and controls imposed by the occupying powers. [53] It was precisely such a promise that had been calculated to induce the Germans to accept the French idea of a supra-national authority over the coal and steel industries of the participating countries. Yet by urging German integration into a common European *defense* system, the United States could be seen to present Germany with a possible alternative by which to achieve its desired objective. And this, in turn, could well enhance the Germans' bargaining position vis-à-vis France in negotiating the terms of the ECSC treaty. At worst, Germany might even decline to participate in the Schuman Plan altogether.

Much to their dismay, the French were soon confronted with what they perceived to be exactly that kind of a possibility. For, in September 1950, just as the treaty's negotiations were about to enter their most difficult phase, the United States began to press its key European allies for an agreement on a limited rearmament of Germany within the framework of the North Atlantic Treaty Organization (NATO).[54] France objected. Still fearful of the resurgence of a powerful Germany unless its heavy industries were subject to supranational controls, the French opposed German rearmament in any form, so long as the ECSC treaty had not been signed. In private, they expressed thinly veiled annoyance at what they considered "lack of comprehension by the United States on the whole question of rearming Europe and, above all, Germany" and felt that the United States "stirred up a hornets' nest by presenting the issue of German rearmament in an inept fashion."[55] Yet, quite obviously, their objections and frustrations were based on a fear that any German incentives to accept the Schuman Plan, on terms the French considered essential, would disappear once an agreement on German rearmament was reached.

Their concern was not entirely without foundation. For at the same time that the rearmament issue was being injected into the picture, the Schuman Plan began to encounter growing opposition from German industrial circles. Although the German government itself still professed strong support for the project, various economic interests—especially steel producers—openly criticized it as a device calculated to protect higher cost French steel production.[56] Particularly disturbing to the French, however, was the intransigence of German industrialists on the question of decartelization and deconcentration. Traditionally accustomed to cartel arrangements, the Germans vehemently opposed any proposals that would lead to the elimination of their central coal sales agency and would compel the Ruhr steel companies to divest themselves of their extensive ownership of coal mines. The French, on the other hand, had insisted all along that a genuine "single market" in coal and steel could not be achieved unless decartelization and deconcentration measures were vigorously applied under the coal-steel pool.[57]

Their insistence on this point was just as strong as the Germans' objections to it.

It was over these two issues—German opposition to decartelization and French opposition to Allied decontrols of German industry, as well as to German rearmament, before the treaty had been signed—that the negotiations threatened to falter. And it was under these circumstances that the United States felt obliged—largely at the behest of the French—to step into the breach. On November 6, 1950, President Truman publicly reiterated his endorsement of the Schuman Plan, hoping thereby to revive the stalled negotiations. But the real efforts of U.S. officials centered on persuading the Germans to modify their stand on decartelization, and to agree to a reorganization of the Ruhr industries along lines acceptable to the French. During the next several months, a tireless John McCloy (U.S. High Commissioner for Germany) and his staff took on the main burden of this task; and by March 1951, they had managed to hammer out a compromise that appeared to satisfy both the German and the French governments.[58] On March 19, 1951, delegates of the six countries initialed the ECSC treaty. Formal signatures, by the respective foreign ministers, followed one month later.

Thus, in the final analysis, it was active American diplomatic intervention that brought about the conclusion of the negotiations. Given the situation that it had itself created by proposing German rearmament, only the United States possessed the necessary weight to wrestle meaningful concessions from Germany and to persuade the French to accept them. Only the United States, moreover, was in a position to obtain agreement from the other occupying powers on extensive decontrols of German industry, as a quid pro quo for German acceptance of the Schuman Plan. And finally, only the United States could provide a strong mixture of moral support and subtle pressure, at crucial moments, in an effort to guide the negotiating governments toward finding a basis for a mutually acceptable agreement.

IV

The treaty establishing the European Coal and Steel Community provided for the creation of a fairly elaborate institutional-organizational structure. It was to consist of a High Authority, a Council of Ministers, a Consultative Committee, a Common Assembly, a Court of Justice, a Secretariat, and several working committees. The drafters of the treaty took pains not only to create this institutional framework, but to assure a system of checks and balances within it. To that end, they went to great length in specifying the functions and spheres of activities of the Community's major bodies, and in prescribing definite relationships between them.[59] Yet neither the Treaty itself—containing one hundred articles and supplemented by several annexes—nor the organizational structure it had created should obstruct sight of what was, at bottom, the fundamental character of the new venture. Political and strategic considerations aside, the formation of the ECSC was essentially an exercise in the creation of a regional economic bloc in Western Europe. When launched, the ECSC constituted a concrete example of regional economic integration: Based on the "sector" approach to integration, it conformed to the general specifications of a common market.

In the prevailing scheme of things there was, of course, more to the ECSC than a mere common market for coal and steel products. The very creation of the coal-steel pool, comprising six pivotal European countries, represented a significant measure of economic cooperation, far exceeding any others previously undertaken through the OEEC. As such, the establishment of the ECSC could have been said to reflect an effort to give a concrete impetus to the process of closer economic cooperation, on which the American government had predicated the ERP. But more important: To the proponents of European unification, the formation of the Community symbolized a decisive first step toward the ultimate attainment of that goal—"the first step," in Schuman's own words, "in the federation of Europe." And it was primarily this acclaimed feature of the Schuman Plan—i.e., the promise that it held as an instrument of Western European integration—that invited wholehearted American approval and support.

Official U.S. endorsement of the ECSC manifested itself in several ways during the Community's formative period. Thus, shortly after the High Authority settled into office, a U.S. diplomatic mission, headed by an ambassador, was accredited to the Community and sent to Luxembourg.[60] Moreover, the United States formally stated that henceforth it would deal with the Community (read: the High Authority), rather than with its individual members, in matters relating to coal and steel. And even before the Community actually began to function, Congress had offered its own version of encouragement and support. In the Mutual Security Act of 1952, which was passed on June 20, 1952, Congress specifically named the ECSC as a potential recipient of American aid. It authorized the Administration, if it saw fit, to use funds appropriated under the act to furnish direct assistance to the ECSC, as well as to NATO and to any organization that might evolve from the proposed European Defense Community (EDC).[61]

Close support of a third kind did not lag far behind. In the fall of 1952, the six members of the Community applied for a waiver of their obligations under GATT. Their action was necessitated by the fact that some of the measures by which the treaty was to be implemented could be viewed as violations of certain of their obligations as GATT signatories. In particular, the provisions calling for the mutual elimination of tariffs and quantitative restrictions on coal and steel traded among the Community's members, but not between them and nonmembers, stood in direct conflict with GATT's rules of MFN treatment and nondiscrimination.[62] Such conflict could be legally resolved only if the ECSC members were to obtain a waiver from their fellow signatories of GATT, permitting them to depart from these rules.

During GATT's discussions of this matter, the U.S. delegation played a crucial role in supporting the waiver application and persuading other GATT members to vote for it.[63] It was also instrumental in devising the terms of the waiver, which not only exempted the Community's members from the application of the MFN treatment principle, but permitted them several additional departures from the rules.[64] Granted on November 10, 1952, the waiver stressed, however, that if the creation and progressive development of the ECSC were to contribute to the general objectives of GATT, then the removal of intrabloc trade barriers must be accompanied by appropriate trade policies vis-à-vis third countries. In other words, while granting the waiver, the GATT membership wished to impress upon the Community's members that their experiment with intrabloc trade liberalization must take into account the economic interests of outside countries as well. And as an added reminder, the waiver stipulated that during the Community's transitional period (i.e., five years), the governments of its members would have to report to GATT annually on the measures taken by them toward the full implementation of the ECSC treaty. But the point nevertheless remains: Had it not been for the strong American backing of the Community's application, the waiver—even with its qualifiers—may well have been denied.

Some four years later, another GATT gathering again afforded the United States an opportunity to demonstrate its high esteem of the ECSC. The occasion was the 1956 session of GATT's tariff negotiations, to which, for the first time, the High Authority came prepared to bargain on behalf of the Community as a whole. During that particular session the United States and the High Authority concluded a reciprocal tariff agreement, under which the United States agreed to lower its duties on certain products (including steel bars and tubes) imported from the Community's countries. In return, the Community offered some reductions in French and German duties on special steel products, and in Italian duties on both ordinary and special steels.[65] But while the concessions exchanged were, in themselves, fairly modest, the symbolic significance of this transaction was quite important. For by undertaking to negotiate with the High Authority, rather than with the individual governments, the United States undoubtedly helped to enhance the prestige of that supranational body and, by implication, the prestige of the Community as an entity in the arena of international negotiations. Indirectly, its action may also have served to bring about greater cooperation between the governments of the ECSC members on matters pertaining to external trade and to strengthen liberal trade elements within the group.

Yet perhaps the most visible measure of official American support had actually come two years earlier. On April 23, 1954, the U.S. government and the High Authority signed a loan agreement under which the former lent to the latter the sum of $100 million. Funded out of foreign aid appropriations, the twenty-five-year loan was to be administered by the Export-Import Bank, acting as the agent for the U.S. Foreign Operations Administration. It carried an annual interest rate of 3⅞ percent and was subject to fairly elaborate and detailed security and repayment provisions.

From a strictly financial standpoint, the loan was not really crucial to the successful operation of the Community at the time. Its main economic justification rested on the argument—or, more correctly, the expectation—that such a financial commitment by the U.S. government would greatly improve the High Authority's prospects of obtaining additional loan capital from other (both public and private) sources.[66] The real motive behind the loan agreement, however, was undeniably political: an official desire to demonstrate, in a tangible and useful way, American interest in and encouragement of any concrete steps toward European integration. The formation of the ECSC could clearly be viewed as constituting such a step. Thus, it is not surprising that, during testimony before Congress, Assistant Secretary of State Livingston Merchant openly acknowledged a sentiment that must have already been well appreciated by all concerned. The loan had been largely granted, he admitted, on "straight political justifications."[67] He might reasonably have added that justifications of a similar nature could explain practically all the measures of support that the U.S. government had already extended and would in the future extend to the Community.

* * *

Chronologically, Schuman's proposal came at about the midpoint of the ERP period. Its practical implementation—i.e., the formation of the ECSC—did not begin until after the Marshall Plan per se had ceased to exist. Yet even while it was still being formulated, the Schuman Plan could already be perceived as the most ambitious and far-reaching integration project initiated by the Europeans up to that time. It represented, in fact, the only approach to integration that explicitly envisaged the establishment of a supranational authority over economic processes and activities carried within and between sovereign nation-states. As such, it constituted the first serious attempt to introduce new institutional structures into the European economy, for the expressed purpose of furthering the cause of European unification. So drastic did this step appear at the time that at least one American observer was moved to assert that "the Schuman plan experiment in coal and steel is perhaps as much European unification as Western Europe can digest in a decade." [68]

Subsequent events, of course, proved this assertion wrong. In early June 1955, less than three years after the launching of the ECSC, a foundation was laid for further economic integration among its members. Meeting in Messina, Sicily, the foreign ministers of the six countries formally agreed on the desirability of creating a common organization to develop nuclear energy for peaceful use, and of initiating a "common European market, free from all customs duties and all quantitative restrictions." The Messina Conference also went on record as favoring the establishment of "appropriate institutional means" by which such an enlarged economic organization could be realized and operated. And, as a first step toward the implementation of these declarations, the conference created an intergovernmental committee, chaired by Belgium's Paul-Henri Spaak, and charged it with the task of "drafting the relevant treaties or arrangements." [69]

What followed next is well known. In late May 1956, having completed work on the technical details involved, the Spaak Committee presented its preliminary proposals for the creation of a common market and a European atomic energy organization. At their May 29–30 meeting in Venice, the six foreign ministers accepted the Spaak report as a basis for negotiating the two proposed institutions. Tedious negotiations ensued, and finally, on March 25, 1957, two treaties—one establishing a European Economic Community (EEC) and the other a European Atomic Energy Community (EURATOM)—were signed in Rome. [70] Ratified by the six national parliaments during the same year, the so-called Rome treaties went into effect on January 1, 1958. The first round of mutual tariff reductions under the EEC treaty took place twelve months later. Thus, long before the ECSC even reached its first decade—digestion difficulties notwithstanding—a second and more comprehensive experiment in European economic integration had been undertaken by its members.

The story of that experiment (i.e., the EEC) and its continuing accomplishments to the present day falls outside the scope of this study. So does the chronicle of another European initiative—namely, the formation in late 1959 of the European Free Trade Association (EFTA), consisting originally of Austria, Denmark, Norway, Portugal, Sweden, Switzerland, and the United Kingdom. [71] If there is, however, a lesson to be drawn from the narrative of the last two chapters, it is this: European economic integration, no more than European political unification, could hardly have been accomplished by the application of external pressure from Washington or OSR in Paris. The pursuit of European unification, with an emphasis on reshaping or scrapping existing institutional structures, had been persistently preached by the Americans, during and after the ERP period.[72] But the most that such preachings accomplished, within the framework of the Marshall Plan itself, was to gain European acquiescence to pursue economic cooperation by traditional means—i.e., through *inter*governmental machineries for consultation and bargaining. "If one asks the extent to which the Marshall Plan has achieved [its] aims in changing the structure of the European economy," stated the eminent French writer Raymond Aron in 1952, "the answer must be absolutely negative."[73] He may have been unduly harsh with his words, but he was not far off the mark in his verdict.

Indeed, when supranational (or quasi-supranational) organizations did emerge in Europe, they sprang outside the institutions of the Marshall Plan; and then only because the governments concerned were finally ready to accept them. Seen in this light, it is quite clear that the formulation and implementation of the ECSC was a European-initiated (*and* executed) venture, not an ECA-imposed project. And it is equally clear that the EEC had had its roots mainly in the ECSC experiment rather than in either the Marshall Plan or the Mutual Security Program. There is, of course, truth to the proposition that the OEEC experience "was vital" for the development of such institutions as the ECSC and the EEC and that, "had it not been for the Marshall Plan and the OEEC, a basis [would not] have existed" for them.[74] But it is also true that, despite its encouragement and support, it was not the U.S. government—and certainly not the OEEC—that constituted the major instrument of European economic integration. It was the European governments themselves.

A Summing Up   14

The Marshall Plan, observed Charles Kindleberger some years ago, "never came to an end but was swallowed up in defense activity which developed under the North Atlantic Treaty Organization. . . ." [1] In a sense, he was right. For when viewed as a process, Europe's economic recovery extended well into the 1950s, increasingly fed by congressionally appropriated expenditures on rearmament and defense-related production. Indeed, the retrospective observer may find it difficult, if not altogether impossible, to pinpoint an exact date by which Western Europe as a whole could be said to have returned, in Secretary Marshall's words, to "normal economic health." Nor is it possible, especially from mid–1950 on, to separate, in a precise and meaningful way, the respective contributions of "defense" and "non-defense" American assistance to Europe's overall recovery progress. [2] In an *economic* sense, the recovery program was, in fact, a continuous process.

Still, in an *administrative* sense, the ERP officially ended on December 30, 1951—some forty-five months after it had been launched. During that period, nearly $12.4 billion, mostly in the form of grants, had been allotted by the ECA to the participating countries. [3] This amount represented approximately 1.2 percent of total U.S. Gross National Product (GNP) for the calendar years 1948–1951. Computed on a yearly basis, the shares of ERP aid in U.S. GNP ranged from 1.9 percent in 1948 to 0.5 percent in 1951. But during the first fifteen months of the program (April 1948–June 30, 1949), ECA's allotments to Western Europe amounted to 2.3 percent of total U.S. GNP for the same period. In themselves, these figures may have little meaning three decades after the fact. Their significance—and, by implication, the significance of the Marshall Plan itself—lies in the actual results the extension of U.S. aid helped to bring about. Put differently, the success or failure of the

Marshall Plan must ultimately be judged by the extent to which the aims and expectations of its planners had been fulfilled.

What were these aims? As noted in the beginning of this book, the ERP could be viewed as a political effort couched in economic terms: foreign policy initiative whose main objective was to help create viable and stable national economies in Western Europe, strong enough to resist communist subversion and encroachment. Economic viability, it was reasoned, would promote the political strength and stability needed to secure the survival of a community of free nations in Europe. Moreover, economic viability would enable Western Europe to become an active participant in a workable international economic system, based on unrestricted trade and payment relationships. Hence, if the Marshall Plan is to be judged by its economic accomplishments, the verdict must rest on one central question: To what extent was European economic viability achieved by the time the ERP was administratively terminated?

In attempting to answer this question, one must briefly consider two others: How was viability perceived by the planners of the ERP, and what measures were prescribed as the means toward its attainment? Although Congress, in authorizing the aid program, did not offer precise definitions, the Economic Cooperation Act of 1948 seemed to suggest that Western European viability should imply the achievement of a "healthy economy independent of extraordinary outside assistance." To that end, Congress—following the specific undertakings stipulated in the CEEC report and reiterated in the Administration bill—mandated a recovery program based on four economic endeavors: (1) a strong production effort, (2) expansion of foreign trade, (3) the creation and maintenance of internal financial stability, and (4) the development of (European) economic cooperation. These endeavors, then, were to constitute the means by which the declared goal of the ERP—i.e., a West European economy sufficiently strong to stand on its own feet without continued American support—could be reached within four years. And it is these endeavors that must, therefore, be translated into some measurable terms in order to judge the success or failure of the Marshall Plan as an economic program.

To the economist, several terms of measurement readily suggest themselves. They include GNP growth rates, production and consumption indices, price indices, and trade and balance-of-payments statistics. Thus, for example, when one comes to gauge the extent of Europe's "strong production effort" under the Marshall Plan, one may begin by noting the impressive growth of Europe's Gross National Product. As seen in Table 26, Western Europe's combined GNP rose from $119.6 billion in 1947 to almost $159 billion in 1951—an overall increase of 32.5 percent with annual increases ranging from a high of 10 percent during 1948 to 4.7 percent during 1951. This continued growth—al-

Table 26   Western Europe's Gross National Product, 1947–51

Year	West Europe's GNP ($ billion)	Percent increase of GNP over previous year (%)
1947	119.6	
1948	131.6	10.0
1949	140.8	7.0
1950	151.4	7.5
1951	158.5	4.7

Source: OEEC, Europe--The Way Ahead, p. 112.

beit at a diminishing rate—was attributed, in large part, to the high rates of investment undertaken by most of the participating countries. From 1948 to 1951, the aggregate value of gross domestic capital formation in Western Europe rose by 30.1 percent, yielding an average annual increase of over 9 percent.[4] But it should be pointed out that such high rates of investment in all probability could not have been sustained, especially during the early years of the program, without the financial resources provided through ERP aid.[5] The provision of such resources, at a relatively small real cost to the United States, may thus be regarded as the key contribution of the Marshall Plan to Europe's industrial recovery.

An equally instructive measure of Western Europe's productive accomplishments lies in the increases in industrial and agricultural production during the ERP period. It may be recalled that in its *Interim Report* (December 1948), the OEEC had projected, for 1952–1953, aggregate increases above prewar (1938) levels of 30 percent in industrial production and 15 percent in agricultural output. The record shows that by the end of 1951, the projected target for industrial production had been significantly surpassed, while the target for agricultural production had almost been reached. Specifically, in the last quarter of 1951, the index of Western Europe's industrial production (excluding West Germany) registered an increase of 40 percent above the 1938 level; and for the year as a whole, it averaged a 45-percent increase.[6] During the same year, the index of agricultural output rose to 11 percent above the prewar level, somewhat short of the projected target.

Between them, these two measures—GNP growth rates and aggregate production indices—point to a clear and obvious conclusion: The primary economic element of the Marshall Plan had largely been fulfilled by the time the aid program was officially terminated. Judged in terms of their own projections, the Europeans' commitment to a "strong production effort" had been amply demonstrated by the aggregate results. Both the phenomenal growth of GNP and the rapid rise in industrial production attest to the success of the Marshall Plan in helping to rebuild Europe's productive capacity and thereby induce a sizeable increase of Western Europe's total production.

A similar conclusion can be reached with respect to the second element of the ERP—namely, expansion of Europe's foreign trade. Here, too, the results point to accomplishments far exceeding initial expectations. In late December 1948, the OEEC had estimated that intra-European trade would not regain its prewar volume until 1952–1953. The actual record shows that in 1950, the volume of intra-European trade was already 24 percent above its 1938 level. A year later it stood at 36 percent above the prewar level; and by 1953, it had risen to 40 percent above it. Moreover, between 1948 and the end of 1951, the volume of intra-European trade expanded by over 70 percent; and during the same period, Western Europe's exports to and imports from the rest of the world had increased by 66 percent and nearly 20 percent, respectively.

Yet while intra-European trade, as well as trade with the rest of the world, had registered a significant expansion, Western Europe as a whole had not been rid of serious balance-of-payments difficulties by the time the ERP ended. In fact, the second half of 1951 and the first half of 1952 marked a sharp deterioration of Western Europe's external trade balance. The combined monthly trade deficits of the OEEC nations with the rest of the world, during that period, ranged between $440 million and $590 million—compared with deficits averaging $280 million per month at the end of 1950—causing serious depletions of Western Europe's gold and dollar reserves. Meanwhile, intra-European trade, notwithstanding the facilities offered by the European Payments Union, continued to be governed by bilateral payments arrangements, exchange controls, and quantitative import restrictions. A persistent balance-of-payments *dis*equilibrium was still the prevailing condition in Western Europe when the Marshall Plan came to an end.

And so, for that matter, was inflation. Although the efforts to restore internal financial and monetary stability had borne some fruit by early 1950, the gains made were soon eroded by the demands of rearmament and defense production programs. Expanded government defense budgets (especially in the post-Korean War period), larger imports of high-cost raw materials, and the diversion of domestic resources from civilian to defense production—all of these contributed to renewed inflationary pressures, which were reflected in accelerated increases of both wholesale and retail prices from mid–1950 on. By late 1951, the ground gained in the fight against inflation during the first two years of the ERP had been largely lost. By late 1951, moreover, private consumption was barely higher than its prewar level, and per capita agricultural production remained below the prewar level. Western Europe was still dependent on the rest of the world for about 30 percent of the food it consumed, and on the United States for many specialized tools and machines, as well as coal, steel, and other industrial parts.

Nor was there, in late 1951, any sign of real progress toward European-wide economic intergration, much less political unification. With the exception of the Benelux customs union and the newly emerging European Coal and Steel community, regional economic cooperation was still largely confined to intergovernmental consultations and bargaining within the framework of the OEEC. The basic structure of Western Europe's economy *and* polity, in other words, remained essentially the same as it had been at the start of the ERP.

In sum, the beginning of 1952 marked, true to OEEC's earlier prediction, not the "end of the recovery story" but merely "a point on an upward curve."

With hindsight wisdom, it is possible to suggest that the goal set by Congress had been unrealistic from the outset. Indeed, it may be argued that even under the best of circumstances, Western Europe could not have attained economic viability in four years' time. For, at bottom, economic viability, as implicitly defined by the Administration and Congress, required the fulfillment of two conditions: the achievement of a sustainable balance-of-payments equilibrium and the maintenance of adequate per capita real incomes, through sufficiently high levels of domestic production. Given Europe's economic posture in 1947–1948, neither one of these conditions could possibly have been achieved by 1952 without drastic—and, hence, politically unacceptable—sacrifices of current living standards. It was, after all, the American perceptions of the political implications of such imposed sacrifices that prompted the offer of assistance to Europe in the first place. But the congressional stipulation of the particular terminal date, however politically expedient, failed to take into proper account the enormous task facing the European nations in attempting to achieve simultaneously external balance, internal stability and adequate growth, all in a relatively short period of time. Nor did it allow for the added constraints imposed by the increasing emphasis on military and defense build-ups following the Korean War. Moreover, neither the Economic Cooperation Act of 1948 nor, particularly, the subsequent aid-authorization acts seemed to appreciate fully the economic and political obstacles that lay on the road toward European integration, or even the development of genuine regional cooperation. That the congressional timetable had not been fully met is, in retrospect, quite understandable.

But while the Marshall Plan did not enable Western Europe as a whole to achieve economic viability by 1952, it certainly laid a firm basis from which the OEEC nations could generate their own economic momentum. Despite balance-of-payments difficulties and continued dependence on U.S. assistance, most of the West European economies had reached a point of self-sustaining growth when the ERP ended. This growth continued throughout the decade of the 1950s and well into the 1960s. It was accompanied by a gradual relaxation of trade and payments restrictions within Europe and the liberalization of trade with the rest of the world. In late 1958, current-account currency convertibility was restored by all, except three, of the OEEC nations. A year and a half earlier (in March 1957), six OEEC countries had committed themselves to the establishment of a European Economic Community which took effect two years later, and which was enlarged, during the 1970s by the addition of three more former OEEC members. In 1961, the OEEC itself was transformed into the Organization for Economic Cooperation and Development (OECD) which initially included, in addition to the OEEC countries, the United States, Canada, and Japan. One of the new organization's declared objectives was to "contribute to sound economic expansion" in the less developed countries of the world; and in line with this objective, several members of the OECD had already created, in 1960, a Development Assistance Committee (DAC). Thus, by 1960, some of the recent aid recipients had become, in effect, prospective aid donors. But then, by 1960, Western Europe had become the second most important industrial and trading center in the world.

Viewing these post-ERP developments, one may well argue that the Marshall Plan should be judged not so much by its short-term economic results as by what it had enabled Western Europe to achieve during the first decade following its termination. Such an argument has considerable merit, for it allows the economic significance of the Marshall Plan to be cast in a much broader perspective than the one dictated by the program's own official life span. To be sure, the Marshall Plan was not intended as a long-range development program. Rather, it was created to address specific and immediate economic problems, and to provide financial resources with which to induce a fairly intensive, short-term effort on the part of the aid recipients. Still, its planners had stipulated, and expected, the fulfillment of certain economic goals. And when these expectations are tested against existing realities in Europe in 1952, the Marshall Plan as an economic program must be judged to have been only a qualified success. On the other hand, if one is permitted to project beyond 1952 and to measure the economic distance traveled by Western Europe in less than ten years after the aid program had ended, then one can, indeed, hail the Marshall Plan as one of the great economic success stories of modern time.

Notes

CHAPTER 1

1. See "European Initiative Essential to Economic Recovery: Remarks by the Secretary of State," U.S. Department of State, *Bulletin*, XVI (June 15, 1947).

2. See Scott Jackson, "Prologue to the Marshall Plan: The Origins of the American Commitment for a European Recovery Program," *Journal of American History*, Vol. 65, No. 4 (March 1979), p. 1046; also Charles P. Kindleberger, "Memorandum For the Files: Origins of the Marshall Plan," July 28, 1948 (Document 23, Misc. Documents), Harry S. Truman Library. This document is also printed in *Foreign Relations of the United States 1947*, Vol. III, pp. 241–47. *Foreign Relations of the United States* is cited hereafter as *FRUS*, followed by year and volume number.

3. See James H. Johnson, "The Marshall Plan: A Case Study in American Foreign Policy Formulation and Implementation," unpublished Ph.D. dissertation (University of Oklahoma, 1966), p. 147.

4. See Jackson, *op. cit.*, p. 1046.

5. Notably Joseph Jones. See his *The Fifteen Weeks* (New York: Viking Press, 1955), where he states that on March 5, 1947, "Acheson formally initiated a survey . . . to determine which countries [other than Greece and Turkey] might in the months ahead urgently require United States aid to preserve their integrity and independence," p. 159.

6. Among them, Harry B. Price, *The Marshall Plan and Its Meaning* (Ithaca: Cornell University Press, 1955), p. 21. The date of these instructions was April 29, 1947; they led to the famous George F. Kennan memorandum, dated May 23, 1947.

7. Ellen Garwood, *Will Clayton: A Short Biography* (Austin: University of Texas Press, 1958). These notes formed the basis of a memorandum, dated May 27, 1947, which Clayton submitted to Acheson and via him to Marshall. "This memorandum and the conversations that ensued had a powerful impact both upon the content of Secretary Marshall's Harvard speech and probably upon his decision to make it." See Jones, *op. cit.*, pp. 246–47.

8. For a fuller discussion of these and other considerations that led to Marshall's speech, see Jackson, *op. cit.* See also Michael Hogan, "The Search for a 'Creative Peace': The United States, European Unity, and the Origins of the Marshall Plan," *Diplomatic History*, Vol. 6, No. 3 (Summer 1982).

9. See William C. Cromwell, "The Marshall Non-Plan, Congress, and the Soviet Union," *Western Political Quarterly*, Vol. 32, No. 4 (December 1979), p. 429.

10. See Economic Cooperation Act of 1948, Section 102(a). The Economic Cooperation Act of 1948 is cited hereafter as 62 Stat. 137.

CHAPTER 2

1. See, for example, Jones, *op. cit.*, pp. 253–54.

2. See Cromwell, *op. cit.*, p. 442.

3. Interview with William Clayton, Marshall Plan Project, Oral History Research office (OHR), Columbia University, p. 29.

4. See Cromwell, *op. cit.*, pp. 429–30.

5. The full text of the revised *aide memoire* is printed in *FRUS 1947*, Vol. III, pp. 284–88.

6. See *Ibid.*, pp. 285–86 and p. 288.

7. *Ibid.*, p. 289.

8. See, for example, David Wightman, *Economic Co-Operation in Europe* (New York: Praeger, 1965), pp. 33–34.

9. *FRUS 1947*, Vol. III, pp. 288–89.

10. Actually, Bidault's proposal was based on an agreement reached during the Bevin-Bidault talks of June 17–18.

11. See Wightman, *op. cit.*, p. 40 and pp. 41–42.

12. See *Ibid.*, p. 40.

13. See *FRUS 1947*, Vol. III, p. 302 and p. 304.

14. At least this is how Bevin assessed the situation as early as June 30. See *Ibid.*, p. 301.

15. Bevin's account of the meeting is reproduced in *Ibid.*, pp. 306–7.

16. In fact, to all the countries of Europe except Spain and the Soviet Union.

17. They were: Austria, Belgium, Denmark, France, Greece, Iceland, Ireland, Italy, Luxembourg, the Netherlands, Norway, Portugal, Sweden, Switzerland, Turkey, and the United Kingdom. In addition, the Bi-Zone and French Zone of Germany were represented by the respective occupation powers.

18. See *FRUS 1947*, Vol. III, p. 317.

19. See telegram from Lovett to Clayton, July 11, 1947, 840.50 Recovery/7-1147, National Archives.

20. Thus, for example, in a position paper dated July 21, 1947, the Policy Planning Staff stated at the very outset: "We have no plan." See *FRUS 1947*, Vol. III, p. 335.

21. That is, the sixteen CEEC countries plus the Western zones of Germany.

22. Interview with Paul Nitze, Marshall Plan Project, OHR, Columbia University, p. 5 (italics added).

23. Ernest Gross Papers, OHR, Columbia University, p. 478.

24. See Clayton to Marshall, "Confidential Memo on the European Crisis," May 31, 1947, William L. Clayton Papers, Box 42, Harry S. Truman (HST) Library. This is the same memorandum referred to in Chapter 1, footnote 7. Note, however, the curious difference in dates.

25. See "Memorandum on the Marshall Plan," undated, William Clayton Papers, Box 42, HST Library.

26. *Ibid.*

27. Clayton to Lovett, August 25, 1947, *FRUS 1947*, Vol. III, p. 377.

28. *Ibid.*

29. See *Ibid.*

30. Minutes of September 9, 1947, meeting of the Interdepartmental Committee on Marshall Plan, Clark Clifford Papers, Box 4, HST Library (italics added).

31. Also known as the Harriman Committee, this advisory committee of distinguished citizens was appointed by President Truman on June 22, 1947. For details of its assigned tasks and membership, see Price, *op. cit.*, pp. 39–42, and also Chapter 3.

32. For a more complete presentation of the four-year estimates and an interesting commentary on the Harriman Committee Report, see Bert Hoselitz, "Four Reports on Economic Aid to Europe," *Journal of Political Economy*, Vol. 56, No. 5 (1948), pp. 109–23.

33. See Committee of European Economic Cooperation, Vol. I, *General Report* (Paris, 1947), Chapter V. Cited hereafter as CEEC, *General Report*.

34. See *Ibid.*, Table XI.

35. See *European Recovery and American Aid: Report by the President's Committee on Foreign Aid*, November 7, 1947 (Washington: Government Printing Office, 1947), p. 79.

36. See C. T. Wood to Acheson, "Plans for Organization and Operation of United States Relief Program," April 7, 1947, OF426 (Foreign Relief), HST Library.

37. The specific provisions contained in these bilateral agreements are noted in Chapter 4. However, it might be interesting to note here that one of these provided for the sale of raw materials by the ERP countries to the United States. Said Gross: "This was put in because we wanted to be sure that we did have the *right* to obtain raw materials which we wanted for our own stockpiling." Ernest Gross Papers, OHR, Columbia University, p. 412 (italics added).

38. Among them: the U.S. Treasury; the departments of Commerce, Agriculture, Interior, War, and Navy; the Budget Bureau, and the Harriman committee.

39. That even Great Britain entertained such thoughts is clearly suggested by the following entry, dated July 4, 1947, in Hugh Dalton's (at that time Britain's Chancellor of the Exchequer) private diary: "Bevin thinks [that] it will make it easier to get the Americans to produce the dollars now that the Russians have behaved so unreasonably." Dalton Diaries, 1945–48 (folder 32–36), Special Collection, London School of Economics.

40. For details of the discussion during this meeting, see Memorandum by Wesley Haraldson, "Paris Discussion on the Marshall Plan, August 4–6, 1947," *FRUS 1947*, Vol. III, pp. 345–50.

41. Lovett to Marshall, August 24, 1947, *FRUS 1947*, Vol. III, p. 374 (italics added). Marshall approved the suggestion, and Kennan and Bonesteel arrived in Paris in late August for discussions with American officials and CEEC delegates.

42. For details of these proposals, see Lovett to Caffery and Clayton, August 26, 1947, *FRUS 1947*, Vol. III, pp. 383–89.

43. "Kennan Report on Paris Trip," September 4, 1947, *FRUS 1947*, Vol. III, p. 398.

44. *Ibid.*, p. 401.

45. *Ibid.*, p. 402 (italics added).

46. Caffery to Marshall, September 5, 1947, *FRUS 1947*, Vol. III, p. 407.

47. *Ibid.*

48. *Ibid.*

49. Lovett to U.S. Diplomatic Representatives accredited to countries participating in CEEC, September 7, 1947, *FRUS 1947*, Vol. III, pp. 412–15.

50. Clayton, Caffery, and Douglas to Marshall and Lovett, September 11, 1947, *FRUS 1947*, Vol. III, p. 421.

51. Marshall to Douglas, Clayton, and Caffery, September 11, 1947, *FRUS 1947*, Vol. III, p. 424.

52. Caffery to Marshall and Lovett, September 12, 1947 (1:00 P.M. and 4:00 P.M. Paris time), *FRUS 1947*, Vol. III, pp. 426–27.

53. Caffery to Marshall, September 17, 1947, *FRUS 1947*, Vol. III, p. 436.

54. *Ibid.*

55. Clayton and Douglas to Marshall, September 23, 1947, *FRUS 1947*, Vol. III, p. 446.

56. See CEEC, *General Report,* p. 1 (italics added).

57. See Franks to Lovett, *Aide-Memoire,* October 22, 1947, *FRUS 1947*, Vol. III, pp. 446–47.

58. *Ibid.*, p. 447 (italics added).

59. See "Record of Meeting between Advisory Steering Committee and CEEC Delegation, November 4, 1947," *FRUS 1947*, Vol. III, p. 468.

60. *Ibid.*, p. 465.

61. Lovett to Marshall, December 7, 1947, *FRUS 1947*, Vol. III, p. 484.

CHAPTER 3

1. This was four days after Congress had passed the European Interim Aid Act of 1947, authorizing emergency U.S. aid to Austria, France, and Italy.

2. The full text of the message can be found in *Public Papers of the Presidents: Harry S. Truman 1947* (Washington: Government Printing Office, 1963), pp. 515–29.

3. See *Ibid.*, pp. 520–21.

4. *Ibid.*, p. 523. But shortly thereafter, in a letter to Secretary Marshall, Senator Vandenberg suggested that the reference to a specific four-year authorization (i.e., the $17 billion) be removed, and the State Department quickly accepted the suggestion. See letter from Vandenberg to Marshall, dated December 31, 1947, and a reply by Robert Lovett, dated January 2, 1948. These are reproduced in Appendix I of U.S. Senate, Committee on Foreign Rela-

tions, 80th Cong., 2d Sess., *Foreign Relief Assistance Act of 1948, Hearings Held in Executive Session on European Recovery* (published in 1973), pp. 520–21, cited hereafter as Senate Committee on Foreign Relations, *ERP Hearings in Executive Session*, 1948.

5. See Department of State, Office of Public Affairs, "Popular Opinion on Aiding Europe: Main Findings of an October Public Opinion Survey," October 29, 1947. Office Files of the Assistant Secretary of State for Economic Affairs (Clayton-Thorp), Folder: Memoranda, July 1-December 31, 1947, HST Library.

6. Thus, for example, an opinion survey undertaken by the highly conservative Committee for Constitutional Government claimed that the overwhelming majority of those polled strongly opposed both the concept of the ERP and the amounts requested for its support. The results of this survey, together with a covering letter, were sent by Frank Gannett, president of the Gannett newspapers, to many Senators in early March 1948. See letter from Frank Gannett to Senator J. Howard McGrath, March 5, 1948, Papers of J. Howard McGrath, HST Library. For an interesting analysis of anti-ERP themes in American newspapers during that period, see Kimball Young, "Content Analysis of the Treatment of the Marshall Plan in Certain Representative American Newspapers," *Journal of Social Psychology*, Vol. 33 (May 1951).

7. Among the latter were former President Herbert Hoover and former Vice-President Henry Wallace.

8. See, for example, Hadley Arkes, *Bureaucracy, the Marshall Plan and the National Interest* (Princeton: Princeton University Press, 1972), p. 56; also Arthur Vandenberg, Jr. (ed), *The Private Papers of Senator Vandenberg* (Boston: Houghton Mifflin, 1952), p. 377.

9. See Price, *op. cit.*, p. 42.

10. For supporting evidence on this point, see Harold L. Hitchens, "Influences on the Congressional Decision to Pass the Marshall Plan," *Western Political Quarterly*, Vol. 21, No. 1 (March 1968), p. 65.

11. "Statistical and Economic Background to the Marshall Plan," prepared by the Research Department, National Association of Manufacturers (mimeographed and undated, but suggestive of having been written during the summer of 1947), p. 3 (italics added).

12. *Ibid.*, p. 11.

13. Among the groups that offered recommendations along these lines were the Committee for Economic Development, the National Planning Association, the United States Associates of the International Chamber of Commerce, and the National Lawyers Guild.

14. W. R. Burgess to Richard M. Bissell, Jr., October 28, 1947, Records of the President's Committee on Foreign Aid, HST Library (italics added).

15. Per Jacobsson to W. R. Burgess, October 22, 1947, Records of the President's Committee on Foreign Aid, HST Library, p. 1 (italics added).

16. *Ibid.*, p. 3. Jacobsson's view on this issue is quite understandable. It largely reflected the view of the Basel-based Bank for International Settlements (BIS), with which he was associated at the time. In fact, as early as July 1947, the Monetary and Research Department of the BIS drew up a memorandum in which it argued that inflation and monetary instability must be most urgently

tackled. For details, see "The Marshall Proposal of Assistance to Europe, July 10, 1947," prepared by the Monetary and Research Department of the BIS, John Snyder Papers, HST Library.

17. Per Jacobsson to W. R. Burgess, p. 3 (italics in the original).

18. *Ibid.*, pp. 4–5.

19. *New York Times*, June 16, 1947 (italics added).

20. See memorandum from George Elsey to Clark Clifford, October 16, 1947, George Elsey Papers, HST Library.

21. See Executive Committee of the International Chamber of Commerce, "European Recovery Statement of the Executive Committee of the ICC." Doc. No. 8105-Rev., February 25, 1948, John Snyder Papers, HST Library.

22. See *Ibid.*

23. Friedrich A. Lutz, *The Marshall Plan and European Economic Policy*, Essays in International Finance No. 9 (Princeton: Princeton University Press, Spring 1948), p. 19.

24. See *Ibid.*, p. 20.

25. Interestingly enough, at least two American economists took exception to the views expressed above. Thus, in his "Four Reports on Economic Aid to Europe," *op. cit.*, p. 122, Bert Hoselitz stated: "In spite of the contrary opinion of the Harriman Committee, this writer believes that too ambitious a program of monetary stabilization will produce severe political tensions, possibly endangering the ultimate success of the whole foreign-aid program." And from Harvard, Seymour E. Harris added: "By insisting upon an early stabilization of exchange rates . . . the sponsors of the ERP may not be furthering their objective of obtaining 'realistic' rates." See Seymour E. Harris, *The European Recovery Program* (Cambridge, Massachusetts: Harvard University Press, 1948), p. 112.

26. See *Public Papers of the Presidents: Harry S. Truman 1947*, *op. cit.*, p. 526.

27. *Ibid.*, p. 527.

28. An excellent account of these discussions is given by Hadley Arkes in his *Bureaucracy, the Marshall Plan and the National Interest, op. cit.*

29. For a sample of the Budget Bureau's views and arguments, see R. P. Bramble to Phillips, "Use of Separate Agency or Corporation to Administer Operation in ERP," August 11, 1947; Harold Seidman to Carl Schwartz, "Proposed Federal Charter for the International Trading Corporation," September 15, 1947; Arnold Miles and Harold Seidman to Blanford, "Use of a Government Corporation for Administration of European Recovery Program," October 28, 1947. Typewritten copies of these are among the private papers of Harold Seidman, Storrs, Connecticut. Bureau of the Budget, "Staff Memorandum: Use of a Government Corporation for Administration of European Recovery Program," November 3, 1947, dittoed copy among the private papers of Harold Seidman. And Bureau of the Budget, "Staff Memorandum concerning Administration of the Program for European Recovery," November 4, 1947, copy in James Webb Papers, HST Library.

30. Aldrich's proposal was contained in his address before the seventy-third annual convention of the American Bankers Association held in Atlantic City, New Jersey, on September 30, 1947.

31. See "The General Principles and Administration of the Marshall Plan," a joint statement by the National Planning Association (adopted at a meeting,

December 8–9, 1947), copy in the Secretary of State File, the George C. Marshall Library. And CED, *An American Program of European Economic Cooperation*, February 1948.

32. For details, see *Administration of United States Aid for a European Recovery Program*, Report to the Committee on Foreign Relations, U.S. Senate (submitted at the request of the chairman of the committee by the Brookings Institution, January 22, 1948).

33. See letter from Herbert Lehman to Isidore Lipschutz, January 8, 1948, Herbert H. Lehman Papers, Rare Book and Manuscript Library, Columbia University Libraries.

34. See, however, Harold L. Hitchens, op. cit., who states: "During the development of the Marshall Plan . . . there was an extensive propaganda campaign for it, *participated in by all* of the Executive departments," p. 67 (italics added).

35. These were Harry Bullis, president of General Mills, Inc., and Leo Burnett of the Leo Burnett Advertising Company. On the basis of the notes they had taken, these two executives prepared confidential reports for their own respective firms. Copies of these reports (the one by Bullis dated October 29, 1947, and the one by Burnett dated November 3, 1947) were sent to John Steelman. They are available in OF 426—Aid for the Reconstruction of Europe (folder #3), HST Library.

36. In his report, Burnett attributed to Secretary of Agriculture Anderson the prediction that the shortage of grain would be greater in 1948 than it was in that year.

37. These quotes come from Bullis' report and are attributed by him to John McCloy (re.: communism) and to Secretary Marshall.

38. *Ibid.*

39. Those attending were Robert Patterson, Arthur Page, Herbert B. Swope, Herbert H. Lehman, Alger Hiss, Philip D. Reed, Clark M. Eichelberger, James B. Carey, William Emerson, Hugh Moore, Herbert Feis, and Frederick C. McKee. See Minutes of the Organizing Meeting of the Committee for the Marshall Plan to Aid Europe, October 30, 1947, Records of the Committee for the Marshall Plan, HST Library.

40. See *Ibid.*

41. See Price, *op. cit.*, pp. 55–57.

42. Interestingly, the CMP refused to finance the distribution of a strongly pro-ERP pamphlet titled "America's Great Hope: Recovery in Europe," which had been prepared by the Public Affairs Institute and offered to the CMP at printer's cost. For details, see Dewey Anderson to Herbert Lehman, February 20, 1948; Herbert Lehman to John Ferguson, February 24, 1948; and John Ferguson to Dewey Anderson, February 25, 1948, Herbert H. Lehman Papers, Rare Book and Manuscript Library, Columbia University Libraries.

43. In other words, the draft bill submitted by the Administration, as distinguished from the bill submitted by Congressman Herter and the one drafted by the Senate Foreign Relations Committee.

44. Minutes of the December 11, 1947, meeting of the CMP Executive Committee, Records of the Committee for the Marshall Plan, HST Library (italics added).

45. Minutes of the January 8, 1948, meeting of the CMP Executive Com-

mittee, Records of the Committee for the Marshall Plan, HST Library (italics added).

46. *Ibid*.

47. Minutes of the January 16, 1948, meeting of the CMP Executive Committee, Records of the Committee for the Marshall Plan, HST Library.

48. *Ibid*.

49. A copy of the CMP's first public statement on the essential principles of the Marshall Plan is in the William Clayton Papers (Alphabetical File 1948–49. Marshall Plan, Committee for), HST Library.

50. Minutes of the January 16, 1948 meeting of the CMP Executive Committee, Records of the Committee for the Marshall Plan, HST Library.

51. CMP Press Release, January 25, 1948, a mimeographed copy in Herbert H. Lehman Papers, Rare Book and Manuscript Library, Columbia University Libraries.

52. Minutes of the January 16, 1948 meeting of the CMP Executive Committee, Records of the Committee for the Marshall Plan, HST Library.

53. *Ibid*.

54. See Memorandum for the President and the Cabinet by the Secretary of State, March 5, 1948, Papers of Harry S. Truman, President's Secretary File (PSF), HST Library.

55. *Ibid*.

56. Minutes of the February 20, 1948, meeting of the CMP Executive Committee, Records of the Committee for the Marshall Plan, HST Library.

57. Hitchens, *op. cit.*, p. 53.

58. *Ibid*.

59. See J. Barabash, *The Practice of Unionism* (New York: Harper and Row, 1965), p. 287; also J. P. Windmuller, *American Labor and the International Labor Movement 1940 to 1953* (Ithaca: Cornell University Press, 1954), p. 35.

60. For details, see Windmuller, Chapters 2–6.

61. The AFL's international activities were carried out mainly by the Free Trade Union Committee (FTUC), under the direction of its Executive Secretary, Jay Lovestone. The FTUC was established in 1944 as a subunit within the Labor League for Human Rights, an earlier creation and the financial beneficiary of the International Ladies Garment Workers Union.

62. See Windmuller, *op. cit.*, p. 35. For a more recent account of the AFL's anti-Communist attitudes and activities, see Peter Weiler, "The United States, International Labor, and the Cold War: The Breakup of the World Federation of Trade Unions," *Diplomatic History*, Vol. 5, No. 1 (Winter 1981), pp. 1–22.

63. See Weiler, p. 7 and p. 16.

64. *Ibid*., p. 13.

65. Reporting on European attitudes toward the proposed U.S. aid, John McCloy stated: "I travelled through Europe and due largely to the constant din of Soviet propaganda, even the potential recipients of United States aid were ascribing the most sordid motives for it." See Memorandum to Charles Ross from John McCloy, November 14, 1947, OF 426-Foreign Relief, HST Library. To appreciate the Administration's concern over the possible impact of the anti-ERP propaganda on European labor, it might be noted that under the ERP Steering Committee there was included a Foreign Labor Group. The lat-

ter was responsible for (a) analyzing the possible reaction of organized labor in Europe to the ERP, (b) assessing the probable tactics of the Communist elements in the labor movement in certain countries and the probable effectiveness of such tactics, and (c) examining the problem of maximizing broad support by European labor to the ERP. See Bonesteel to Murphy, October 20, 1947, and an attached document titled "Organization of the Executive Branch: U.S. Support for European Recovery," Charles Murphy Files, HST Library.

66. Editorial in *American Federationist*, February 1948, p. 17.

67. See Phillip Murray, "Memorandum on Basic Principles Which Must Govern a Foreign Aid Program, Submitted to the President of the United States," p. 1 and p. 11. Phillip Murray Papers, Labor History Collection, Department of Archives and Manuscripts, Catholic University of America.

68. Thus, for example, during the January 8, 1948, meeting of the CMP Executive Committee, Jay Lovestone, sitting in for David Dubinsky, in effect offered to the CMP the use of the AFL's Sunday radio national hook-up for discussion of the Marshall Plan. During the same meeting, Harry Read, sitting in for James Carey, reported on the CIO's plans for launching a nationwide campaign for support of the ERP. See Minutes of the January 8, 1948, meeting of the CMP Executive Committee, Records of the Committee for the Marshall Plan, HST Library.

69. Minutes of the March 18, 1948 meeting of the CMP Executive Committee, Records of the Committee for the Marshall Plan, HST Library.

70. See AFL Information and Publicity Service, Press Release, November 13, 1947. It has recently been suggested that the idea for such a conference had actually originated in the U.S. State Department. See Weiler, *op, cit.*, p. 6 and p. 16.

71. See CIO, circular from Michael Ross to all International Unions, Industrial Union Councils, and Regional Directors, October 20, 1948, Phillip Murray Papers, Labor History Collection, Department of Archives and Manuscripts, Catholic University of America.

72. For full details, see Windmuller, *op. cit.*

73. The conveners were the British TUC, the N.V.V. of Holland, the F.G.T. of Belgium, and the C.G.T. of Luxemburg. See *Report of the International Trade Union Conference, Held at Transport House, London, March 9–10, 1948*, p. 3. For a list of the participants, see pages 47–48 of the report. It should be noted, in this connection, that the TUC's intentions to call such a conference had actually been reported to Washington as early as January. See Gallman (Chargé in the United Kingdom) to Secretary of State, January 13, 1948, in which he states: "Britain's Trade Union Congress will convene International Trade Union Conference on Marshall Plan shortly after WFTU meeting in February," *FRUS 1948*, Vol. III, p. 362. This clearly suggests that even before its request for the special WFTU meeting was rejected, the TUC had already made plans for the London conference.

74. The interested reader may wish to consult Windmuller, *op. cit.*, Chapters 8–10, and Weiler, *op. cit.*, pp. 18–22.

75. The full text of the declaration is given in Appendix C of the *Report of the International Trade Union Conference, op. cit.*

76. *Ibid.*, p. 43.

77. *Ibid.*

78. *Ibid.*, p. 44.

79. *Ibid.*

80. *Ibid.*, p. 43–44.

81. *Ibid.*, p. 44. The ERP/TUAC did, in fact, call two additional sessions of the conference; one took place in London on July 29–30, 1948, and the other in Rome on April 18–20, 1950.

82. See, for example, AFL Information and Publicity Service, Press Release, November 13, 1947.

83. For more details concerning public opinion trends about the Marshall Plan at that time, see Price, *op. cit.*, pp. 58–60.

CHAPTER 4

1. A case in point are the remarks of W. Randolph Burgess, a former member of the Harriman Committee, during a discussion meeting of the Council on Foreign Relations. At that particular meeting, which incidentally was also attended by Congressman Herter, Burgess expressed dissatisfaction with the Administration's presentation to Congress, saying that it "seemed oblivious of what the Harriman Committee had thought to be the important points." See Council on Foreign Relations Files, Records of Groups, Vol. XIV, the Marshall Plan, Digest of Discussion of the Second Meeting, January 12, 1948.

2. See Chapter 3, footnote 4.

3. See Senate Committee on Foreign Relations, *ERP Hearings in Executive Session*, 1948, p. 2 and p. 4.

4. For details and analysis of the political-bureaucratic processes that produced the Economic Cooperation Act of 1948, the reader may wish to consult Hadley Arkes, *Bureaucracy, the Marshall Plan, and the National Interest* (Princeton: Princeton University Press, 1972).

5. See Memorandum for the President from James Webb, received on December 1, 1947, "Subject: Transfer of Ships to Foreign Countries under the European Recovery Program"; a copy in the Papers of Harry S. Truman, President's Secretary File (PSF), HST Library.

6. *Ibid.*

7. See *Ibid.*

8. *Ibid.*

9. Administration draft bill, Section 7(b).

10. *Ibid.*, Section 8(c).

11. U.S. Senate, Committee on Foreign Relations, 80th Cong., 2d Sess., *Hearings on European Recovery Program*, 1948, p. 40. Cited hereafter as Senate Committee on Foreign Relations, *ERP Hearings*, 1948.

12. *Ibid.*

13. *Ibid.*

14. *Ibid.*

15. *Ibid.*, p. 41 (italics added).

16. See, in particular, the testimony of Joseph Curran, J. R. Gormley, and Harry Lundenberg in *Ibid.*, pp. 1314–23, 1211–13, and 1282–87, respectively. It might be noted that both Curran and Gormley also demanded that at least

60 percent of the supplies extended under the ERP should be carried in U.S.-flag merchant vessels. During his own testimony before the Foreign Relations Committee, James Carey presented a formal statement by CIO President Phillip Murray, in which the latter also urged Congress to provide for the carrying of relief cargoes in U.S.-flag vessels. Murray, however, did not specify any particular percentage. See *Ibid.*, pp. 1303–4.

17. In fact, even before the Foreign Relations Committee began its hearings in executive session, the Senate, with eight members present, passed a resolution prohibiting the sale *or* charter of U.S. vessels. The Administration was obviously aware of this resolution, which was passed on February 5, 1948.

18. See Senate Committee on Foreign Relations, *ERP Hearings in Executive Session*, 1948, pp. 257–58.

19. *Ibid.*, p. 263.

20. *Ibid.*, p. 256.

21. *Ibid.*, p. 264.

22. *Ibid.*, p. 262.

23. *Ibid.*

24. *Ibid.*, p. 263.

25. *Ibid.*, p. 271.

26. Section 11(a)(4) of the committee bill, cited hereafter as S.2022.

27. See U.S. Senate, Committee on Foreign Relations, 80th Cong., 2d Sess. Report No. 935, *Report. European Recovery Program*, 1948, p. 36.

28. *Ibid.*, p. 37.

29. *Ibid.*

30. See, for example, AFL Information and Publicity Service, Press Release, March 8, 1948, urging prohibition on the charter of ships.

31. 62 Stat. 137, Section 111(a)(2).

32. In his testimony before the Senate Foreign Relations Committee, Secretary Anderson freely conceded that the ERP may provide markets for cotton, wheat, tobacco, rice, fruits and vegetables. See Senate Committee on Foreign Relations, *ERP Hearings*, 1948, pp. 312–25. When asked by Senator Vandenberg if the ERP is supported by "intelligent American self-interest," Anderson replied: "Yes, it is," and then continued: "Yes. We feel that agriculture needs a market . . . and that agriculture is able to put itself in a position to help now and then subsequently enjoy that market." *Ibid.*, p. 316.

33. Among these were meats, eggs, fats, and oils.

34. See, for example, Senate Committee on Foreign Relations, *ERP Hearings in Executive Session*, 1948, pp. 227–28.

35. S.2202, Section 12(a).

36. *Ibid.*, Section 12(b).

37. *Ibid.*, Section 12(c).

38. The provisions dealing with agricultural surplus are in 62 Stat. 137, Sections 112(d), (e), and (f).

39. *Ibid.*, Section 112(c).

40. Foreign Aid Appropriation Act, 1949, Secton 203.

41. Administration draft bill, Section 10(a).

42. See *Ibid.*, Sections 10(b) and (c).

43. Administration draft bill, Section 15, as modified by the staff of the

Senate Foreign Relations Committee in collaboration with experts from the State Department.

44. See, for example, the report of the Committee on International Law and Relations of the National Lawyers Guild, titled "The European Recovery Program and American Foreign Policy," which stated: "The imposition of such [bilateral] conditions . . . [establishes] that the [ERP] necessarily and inescapably involves interference by the United States in the internal economic and political affairs of the participating countries." A copy of this report is in the Papers of J. Howard McGrath, HST Library. Also among the McGrath Papers is a letter to the Senator from Charles Boss, Executive Secretary of the Commission on World Peace of the Methodist Church. The letter, dated March 15, 1948, states that the Methodist Church "affirms [its] support of ERP, but hopes that the program will not be an extension of American imperialism in Europe. . . ."

45. Senate Committee on Foreign Relations. *ERP Hearings in Executive Session*, 1948, p. 147.

46. *Ibid.*, p. 145.

47. *Ibid.*

48. *Ibid.*, p. 146.

49. S.2202, See Section 15(b).

50. See *Ibid.*, Section 15(b)(5).

51. *Ibid.*, Section 16.

52. 62 Stat. 137, Section 115(b)(5).

53. *Ibid.*, Section 115(b)(9).

54. Administration draft bill, Section 10(c)(6).

55. See Senate Committee on Foreign Relations. *ERP Hearings in Executive Session,* 1948, p. 247 and p. 250.

56. *Ibid,* p. 248.

57. *Ibid.*, p. 251.

58. *Ibid.*

59. S.2202, Section (b)(6). It would be useful at this point to identify the National Advisory Council on International Monetary and Financial Problems (NAC). The NAC was created in July 1945 by the same legislative act (the Bretton Woods Agreements Act) that authorized U.S. participation in the International Monetary Fund (IMF) and the International Bank for Reconstruction and Development (World Bank). It was set up as an interagency body, consisting of the Secretary of the Treasury (chairman), Secretary of State, Secretary of Commerce, the chairman of the Board of Governors of the Federal Reserve System, and the chairman of the Board of Directors of the Export-Import Bank. Its main function was to coordinate U.S. foreign lending and credit programs and to integrate American policies with the operations of the IMF and the World Bank.

60. Senate Committee on Foreign Relations. *ERP Hearings in Executive Session*, 1948, p. 248.

61. *Ibid.*, p. 283.

62. *Ibid.*, p. 284.

63. For details of the rather extended discussion, see *Ibid.*, pp. 285–301.

64. 62 Stat. 137, Section 114(c).

65. Senate Committee on Foreign Relations. *ERP Hearings in Executive Session*, 1948, p. 309.

66. *Ibid.*

67. *Ibid.*, p. 310 and p. 311. It might be noted that the fiscal 1948 surplus was estimated, at the time, to be between $7.5 and $8 billion.

68. *Ibid.*, p. 314.

69. *Ibid.*, p. 313.

70. *Ibid.*, p. 314.

71. See *Ibid.*, p. 317, for details.

CHAPTER 5

1. Senate Committee on Foreign Relations. *ERP Hearings in Executive Session*, 1948, p. 501 (italics added).

2. See CEEC, *General Report*, pp. 14–15, and tables on pp. 16, 19, and 21.

3. *Ibid.*, p. 25.

4. As subsequently stated by a knowledgeable European observer: "The choice of a period of four years was more a political decision than it was based on concrete economic data and plans." See E.H. van der Beugel, *European Integration as a Concern of American Policy: From the Marshall Plan to Atlantic Partnership* (Amsterdam: Elsevier, 1966), p. 166.

5. See Memorandum To: Mr. Hoffman, Mr. Bruce—From: Richard M. Bissell, Jr., "Subject: Handling of First Annual Program by ECA," October 4, 1948, ECA Files, Federal Records Center (FRC), Accession No. 53A–405, Box 29.

6. See *Ibid.*, p. 1. Actually, as noted in Chapter 12, the OEEC was to be informed much earlier that the ECA reserved the right to change its programming recommendations.

7. *Ibid.*, p. 2.

8. *Ibid.*

9. *Ibid.*, p. 4.

10. *Ibid.*, p. 2.

11. *Ibid.*, pp. 2–3.

12. Economic Cooperation Administration, *A Report on Recovery Progress and United States Aid* (Washington, D.C., 1949), p. 66, cited hereafter as ECA, *Recovery Progress and U.S. Aid*.

13. *Ibid.*

14. *Ibid.*, p. 67.

15. A brief explanation is in order here. In presenting its initial dollar requirements for 1948–1949, the British government did not include the dollar needs of the self-governing sterling countries (referred to as Rest of Sterling Area, or RSA), deciding instead to meet those needs out of Britain's own current dollar receipts. The evidence strongly hints at the possibility that this decision was influenced by the advice of sympathetic U.S. officials who were fearful of congressional opposition to the inclusion of the RSA within the framework of ERP financing. Later on, however, the OEEC recommended that the dollar requirements of the RSA be included in the calculation of ERP aid required by Britain, in exchange for an understanding that the needs of Continental coun-

tries for sterling-area currencies would be met by the United Kingdom and other members of the Sterling Area. This recommendation was apparently endorsed by the National Advisory Council (NAC) and may partly explain the increase in the actual allotment to Britain. On this matter, see Memorandum, "The Dollar Problem of the Self-Governing Sterling Area Countries" (unidentified author, undated, but circa May 1948), and a letter from Secretary of Treasury John Snyder to Paul Hoffman, September 27, 1948. Both documents are in John Snyder Papers, Box 12, HST Library.

16. This was done in the 1949 authorization act, which was enacted in April 1949. More on this below.

17. See ECA, *Fifth Report to Congress*, pp. 28–29, and p. 106.

18. The two largest recipients were the United Kingdom ($1.6197 billion) and France ($1.3134 billion) which between them accounted for almost half of the total allotment. Italy, the Netherlands, and the Bizone of Germany came next with $668 million, $571.1 million, and $496 million, respectively.

19. The ECA, in fact, admitted as much. It was not until the first quarter of 1949, the agency stated, that it was able to appraise "more carefully and accurately" the aid needs for the year. See ECA, *Recovery Progress and U.S. Aid*, p. 66.

20. Although the agency did not go into full detail in describing its analytical methods, its account suggests that the method used consisted of a mixture of microeconomic and macroeconomic projections, and that the resulting two sets of estimates were then reconciled with one another. See *Ibid.*, pp. 57–63.

21. *Ibid.*, p. 104.

22. ECA, *Recovery Progress and U.S. Aid*, p. 73.

23. See *Ibid.*

24. *Ibid.*, p. 71. In addition, the agency asked for authorization of $150 million in unallocated reserves for fiscal 1950, that is, a sum with which to authorize the purchase of goods and services by the participating countries, on which disbursements would not be made and for which an appropriation would not be requested until fiscal 1951.

25. The 1949 authorization act, Section 8(a)(1).

26. These downward-revised requests were based on price declines in the United States.

27. See Foreign Aid Appropriations Act of 1950.

28. To judge from the evidence, this call came during a meeting of ECA mission chiefs, which took place in Paris on October 20, 1949, and was addressed by Messrs. Richard Bissell and Lincoln Gordon. See REPTO Circular A–134, October 22, 1949 (from Harriman), ECA Files, FRC, Accession No. 53A–278.

29. See Section on Findings and Declaration of Policy, Mutual Defense Assistance Act of 1949.

30. See interview with H. M. Hirschfield, 1952, Harry B. Price Oral History Interviews, HST Library.

31. See Memorandum by Assistant Secretary of State for Economic Affairs to the Secretary of State, April 7, 1948, *FRUS 1948*, Vol. III, p. 560.

32. See Acting Secretary of State to the United States Special Representative in Europe, December 3, 1948, *FRUS 1948*, Vol. III, p. 305.

33. See "Statement of Mr. Bissell before the Economic Committee of OEEC, on September 29, 1950," in Records of the Policy Series of the Assistant Administrator for Programs, ECA 1949–1951, ECA Files, FRC, RG 286, S.5, R.46, Sec. 15, cited hereafter as *ECA Policy Series*.

34. See *Ibid*. Specifically, they were asked to devote the bulk of the Third Annual Report of the OEEC to such an appraisal.

35. See ECA, *Eleventh Report to Congress*, p. ix, and ECA, *Twelfth Report to Congress*, p. ix.

36. ECA, *Thirteenth Report to Congress*, p. ix.

CHAPTER 6

1. OEEC, *Report to the Economic Co-operation Administration on the First Annual Programme* (Paris, October 1948), p. 21.

2. *Ibid*., p. 15 and p. 20.

3. *Ibid*., p. 20.

4. *Ibid*., p. 67.

5. OEEC, *Interim Report on the European Recovery Programme*, Vol. I (Paris, December 1948), pp. 11–12 (italics added), cited hereafter as OEEC, *Interim Report*. (All quotes in this paragraph come from the pages cited here.)

6. *Ibid*., p. 121.

7. See "To the Director, from Alvin Roseman. Subject: ERP Appropriation Estimate, April 11, 1948," copy in Papers of Frederick J. Lawton, HST Library.

8. See *Ibid*. Such imports, it was recognized, would obviously have to cover both direct consumption requirements and the capital goods and raw materials needed to achieve the production goals.

9. For an illustrative sample of such exchanges between ECA officials and members of Congress, see C. Tyler Wood to Hon. Frances Bolton, December 22, 1949; James Fulton to Paul Hoffman, January 25, 1950, and Paul Hoffman to Hon. James Fulton, February 7, 1950; Paul Hoffman to Hon. Gordon Canfied, February 13, 1950; William Foster to Hon. Cecil King, February 27, 1950; C. Tyler Wood to Hon. Frances Bolton, March 23, 1950; and William Foster to Senator Alexander Smith, March 17, 1950. All of these documents are in ECA Files, FRC, Accession No. 53A–405 (Folder: General—ECA Export Policy).

10. See Patrick McMahon, "Report on ERP: Summary of Observations," August 24, 1949 (mimeographed), p. 12, copy in Clark Clifford Papers, HST Library.

11. See Seymour E. Harris, *Foreign Aid and Our Economy* (Washington, D.C.: Public Affairs Institute, 1950), pp. 29–30.

12. See ECA, *Fifth Report to Congress*, pp. 20–21, 24–25. Interestingly enough, none of the last three—yarns, cement, and motor vehicles—had even been targeted by the Europeans in their first annual program report.

13. The target for steel had been set at 45.3 million metric tons, while actual output amounted to 44.4 million tons. The figures given by ECA for coal are not quite accurate. The target had been set for 419.7 million tons and

actual output reached 416 million, yielding a difference of slightly less than 4 million, not 5 million, tons.

14. See ECA, *Fifth Report to Congress*, p. 18 and p. 90.

15. See *Ibid.*, p. 24 (more on this below).

16. The reasons for this, the first substantial post war economic decline in the United States, need not be detailed here. Suffice it to say that it has been attributed to two major developments: (1) a reduction in business inventories and (2) a sizable reduction in output of machinery and other producers' equipment. For more details, see Federal Reserve Board, *Bulletin*, January 1950, p. 3.

17. This requires some elaboration. According to ECA data, the decline was from $279.8 million in the fourth quarter of 1948 to $190 million in the second quarter of 1949, which is slightly more than 30 percent. (See ECA, *Fifth Report to Congress*, p. 104.) The OEEC gave 30 percent as the percentage of overall decline in the value of U.S. imports from *both* the participating countries and the nonparticipating sterling area countries. (See OEEC, *European Recovery Programme: Second Report of the O.E.E.C.*, pp. 83–84.) In 1953, Averell Harriman distinguished between a 20-percent reduction in U.S. imports from the OEEC countries and as much as a 40-percent reduction from certain raw-material exporting countries of the sterling area, which averages out to 30 percent. (See transcript of October 10–11, 1953, meeting, "Princeton Seminars," Acheson Papers, HST Library.)

18. See ECA, *Fifth Report to Congress*, p. 6 and p. 9.

19. See Repto-Circular A–157, from Harriman to All Missions, November 30, 1949, ECA Files, FRC, Accession No. 53A–278.

20. *Ibid.*

21. Richard Bissell, Jr., to Phillip Arrow, December 2, 1949, ECA Files, FRC, Accession No. 53A–405, Box 33 (Folder: Organizational Units—Labor Division).

22. *Ibid.*

23. Federal Reserve Board, *Bulletin*, January 1950, p. 8 (italics added).

24. Later on, other governmental agencies were to become involved in the export controls program, sharing responsibility with the Department of Commerce.

25. These prerogatives derived from the powers and duties conferred upon the Secretary of Commerce by the Second Decontrol Act of 1947, which was passed on July 15, 1947.

26. 62 Stat. 137, Section 117(d).

27. This, in fact, had been the prewar pattern and composition of East-West trade. See, for example, William Diebold, "East-West Trade and the Marshall Plan," *Foreign Affairs*, Vol. 26, No. 4 (July 1948), pp. 709–10.

28. See an internal ECA memorandum prepared by L. C. Beechever, "The Significance and Development of East-West Trade" (mimeographed, undated), p. 2.

29. See OEEC, *Interim Report*, pp. 55–56.

30. See ECA, *Recovery Progress and U.S. Aid*, p. 219. A similar observation had been made earlier by Diebold, *op. cit.*, p. 715.

31. See ECA, *Third Report to Congress*, pp. 37–38.

32. See "The Significance and Development of East-West Trade," *op. cit.*, p. 14.

33. More is said about the nature and working of bilateral agreements in Chapter 8. Here it might be noted that as of 1950, some ninety-three bilateral agreements covering East-West trade were in operation. The ECA, in fact, preferred that goods be obtained from Eastern Europe through direct trading governed by such agreements.

34. Prewar imports of East European grains, by the countries making up the OEEC, averaged 4 million tons annually. In 1948–1949 and 1949–1950, the quantities of such imports were only 1.5 million and 2.5 million tons, respectively. Prewar imports of timber averaged 19 million cubic meters per year, in 1948, they were only 5.4 million. See "The Significance and Development of East-West Trade," *op. cit.*, p. 22 and p. 24.

35. Export-Import Bank of Washington, *Second Semi-Annual Report to Congress for the Period January-June 1946* (Washington, D.C.), p. 24.

36. See International Bank for Reconstruction and Development, *Second Annual Report 1946–47*, p. 19.

37. See International Bank for Reconstruction and Development, *Fourth Annual Report 1948–49*, p. 27. It might be noted that the loan was never granted, and that in early 1950 Poland withdrew altogether from the International Monetary Fund and the World Bank.

38. See Minutes of Meetings of NAC, Meeting #15 of NAC Alternates, August 3, 1948.

39. Paul Hoffman to John McCloy, August 14, 1948, ECA Files, FRC, Accession No. 53A–405, Box 28 (Folder: I).

40. The CEEC report had estimated that prospective coal imports from Poland would amount to 16 million metric tons in 1948 and 24 million in 1949. (See Diebold, *op. cit.*, p. 715.) Actual imports were 11.9 million tons in 1948 and only 12.6 million in 1949. (See "The Significance and Development of East-West Trade," *op. cit.*, p. 19.)

41. William A. Brown and R. Opie, *American Foreign Assistance* (Washington: Brookings Institution, 1953), p. 252.

42. More on this below.

43. See ECA, *Fifth Report to Congress*, p. 59.

44. The OEEC, however, was obliged to submit to ECA monthly reports on movements of ERP-financed cargo, and was charged with formulating cooperative plans that would insure compliance with the law. See ECA, *Recovery Progress and U.S. Aid*, p. 244.

45. See ECA, *Fifth Report to Congress*, p. 59. In practice, this took the form of requiring the individual countries to reimburse the ECA for payments already made by the agency.

46. See *Ibid.*

47. The details leading to this particular action, including the apportionment of tonnage deficiencies among the seven countries, are given in TOREP #8203, to OSR from Washington (Hoffman), September 30, 1949, ECA Files, FRC, Accession No. 53A–177, Box 156.

48. See TOREP #9541, ECA/W (Foster) to OSR, November 23, 1949, ECA Files, FRC, Accession No. 53A–177, Box 156.

49. See TOREP #10423, to Katz from Foster, December 27, 1949; also Memorandum to: R. L. Cumming, from: Chief, Transport Section, January 16, 1950. Both documents are in ECA Files, FRC, Accession No. 53A–177, Box 156.

50. See letter from Addison Foster to Arthur Syran, January 20, 1950, ECA Files, FRC, Accession No. 53A–177, Box 156.

51. See ECA, *Recovery Progress and U. S. Aid*, p. 246.

52. *Ibid.*, pp. 243–44.

53. As noted earlier, 62 Stat. 137, Section 112(a), dealt with procurement of petroleum and petroleum products, while the Foreign Aid Appropriation Act of 1949 placed a specific limit of $75 million on exports of farm machinery to the participating countries during the first year of the program. From April 3, 1948, to April 2, 1949, the ECA issued authorizations for $48.9 million worth of farm machinery (see ECA, *Fourth Report to Congress*, p. 49), and it closely monitored the procurement, in this country, of other scarce commodities. (See, for example, ECA, *Third Report to Congress*, p. 56.)

54. 62 Stat. 137, see Sections 112(d)(1) and (e).

55. 62 Stat. 137, Section 112(f).

56. TOECA #198, to Secretary of State from Caffery, June 26, 1948, ECA Files, FRC, Accession No. 53A–278.

57. *Ibid.*

58. See Repto Airgram #22, to U.S. Diplomatic Missions in Participating Countries, from Harriman, September 2, 1948, ECA Files, FRC, Accession No. 53A–278. In his own reply to Marjolin, however, Harriman must have reinforced European fears, for he stated: ". . . It is clearly the intention of Congress that surplus products in the United States should be used whenever feasible to assist European recovery."

59. TOECA #542, to ECA Administrator from Harriman, December 23, 1948, ECA Files, FRC, Accession No. 53A–278.

60. *Ibid.*

61. This recognition undoubtedly played a part in the decision to permit Britain, in September 1949, to use ERP funds to finance wheat purchases in Canada. The ECA justified this decision by explaining that if ERP dollars could not be used to meet British contractual commitments to Canada, the United Kingdom would have to divert its own dollars to finance the wheat procurement, which would result in a serious drain on its already depleted dollar reserves. For more details, see ECA, *Sixth Report to Congress*, pp. 57–58.

62. 62 Stat. 137, Section 115(b)(6). It may be recalled that the participating countries were required, as part of their *bilateral* obligations (see Chapter 4), to deposit in a special account the local-currency equivalents of U.S. aid in the form of grants. Of these deposits, 5 percent was to be earmarked for use by the United States, and 95 percent legally belonged to the respective European countries. All subsequent references to the amounts of counterpart funds accumulated and approved for release by the ECA apply to the 95-percent portion.

63. The restraining role played by the NAC in connection with other aspects of ECA's activities—particularly, the development of intra-European monetary arrangements—are discussed in Part III of this book.

64. For projected investment targets of various countries, see OEEC, *Interim Report*, p. 98. For actual investment rates attained, see OEEC, *Europe— The Way Ahead: Fourth Annual Report of the OEEC* (Paris, December 1952), p. 120; also, International Monetary Fund, *International Financial Statistics*, March 1954, Vol. VII, No. 3.

65. There was, of course, another consideration that governed the approvals or disapprovals of counterpart releases—namely, the impact of their use on internal financial stability. This issue is discussed in the next chapter.

66. See U.S. President, *First Report to Congress on the Mutual Security Program* (December 31, 1951), p. 63.

67. As of June 30, 1951, only about $20 million in counterpart funds had been authorized for Technical Assistance projects. See ECA, *Thirteenth Report to Congress*, p. 128 and p. 129. (More on technical assistance and productivity projects below.)

68. See *First Report to Congress on the Mutual Security Program, op. cit.*, p. 62.

69. For details of cumulative expenditures on strategic-material purchases and projects, see *Ibid.*, p. 63, and ECA, *Thirteenth Report to Congress*, pp. 86–87. In all fairness to the ECA, it must be said that the agency was extremely reluctant to engage in procurements and development of strategic materials. It did so only under pressure from Congress and other U.S. governmental agencies. (This statement is based on personal interviews with former ECA officials.)

70. See ECA, *Third Report to Congress*, pp. 72–73. Local funds were to include the use of counterparts, as well as the countries' own financial resources.

71. See TOREP #8349, to Embassy Paris from ECA Administrator (Hoffman), October 6, 1949, copy in *ECA Policy Series*.

72. TOREP #8489, to Embassy Paris from ECA Administrator (Foster), October 12, 1949, copy in *ECA Policy Series*.

73. See ECA, *Thirteenth Report to Congress*, p. 53.

74. Computed from data in *Ibid.*, pp. 120–21.

75. 62 Stat. 137, Section 111(b)(3). These guaranties were intended to protect prospective investors from exchange controls, imposed by the participating countries, that might prevent the transfer of their foreign incomes or assets back into dollars. The guaranties were to be authorized by ECA but were issued by the Export-Import Bank.

76. See *Ibid.* The second limitation was subsequently removed by the 1949 authorization act, which permitted guaranties to cover the conversion of actual earnings or profits arising from the initial investment. Accordingly, from then on, the ECA offered to guarantee conversions of up to 175 percent of the sum invested. See ECA, *Fifth Report to Congress*, p. 37.

77. See ECA, *Third Report to Congress*, p. 47. The American company involved was Godfrey L. Cabot, Inc., and the project entailed the construction, in England, of a plant to produce carbon black, a product used in making tires.

78. See Export-Import Bank of Washington, *Thirteenth Semi-Annual Report to Congress for the Period July-December 1951* (Washington, D.C.), pp. 70–71. Of the thirty-eight guaranties issued, thirteen were for projects in England and twelve for projects in France; Germany, Italy, and the Netherlands were the only other countries involved in the investment guaranty program.

79. OEEC, *Interim Report*, p. 25 and p. 32. For summaries of the national

programs, see pp. 131–92. (The complete programs are contained in Volume II of the *Interim Report*.)

80. *Ibid.*, p. 45.

81. See Lincoln Gordon, "ERP in Operation," *Harvard Business Review*, Vol. 27, No. 2 (March 1949), p. 145.

82. For details, see OEEC, "Report on the Progress of Western Europe Recovery," June 1949 (mimeographed). The two exceptions were Sweden and the United Kingdom, where the index stood at 10 percent above the 1938 level.

83. Thus, for example, the Mutual Security Act of 1951 contained the so-called Benton amendment which declared that American assistance to Europe should be used so as to encourage free enterprise and free labor unions, and to discourage restrictive business practices. And the Mutual Security Act of 1952 actually authorized specific expenditures of funds for the promotion of these objectives. Consequently, in *its* productivity drive, the MSA laid great stress on an *equitable* distribution of the benefits of increased productivity and production among management, labor, and consumers.

84. Paul Hoffman and Sir Stafford Cripps have generally been credited with initiating the idea of such a body, during a meeting in London in late summer of 1948. Hoffman, however, often mentioned W. H. Joyce, Jr., an American industrialist from California, as being the originator of the idea. See Memorandum for Files, by Neil Dalton, dated September 8, 1949, ECA Files, FRC, Accession No. 53A–441, Box 114.

85. The AACP consisted of a U.K. Section and a U.S. Section, each with an almost equal representation of business and labor. Coordination of activities was entrusted to a group of Joint Secretaries from both sections.

86. The Danish team came in February and the British team in mid-March. See ECA, *Fourth Report to Congress*, pp. 55–56.

87. A detailed account of U.S. labor's involvement in the productivity drive is beyond the scope of the present study. What might be noted, however, is that American organized labor viewed the ERP in general (see Chapter 3) and the productivity program in particular as a made-to-order framework within which to carry *its* message to trade unions in Europe. As related to this writer by two former MSA's Labor Advisers, the productivity drive provided the best vehicle by which to "export" the notion of collective bargaining. It is in this context that the role of ECA's Labor Advisers, as well as the Labor Information Officers, must be perceived. Their official responsibility was to advise the ECA on such matters as European labor conditions, manpower utilization, etc. But their ultimate mission, from U.S. labor's standpoint, was to pass on the conviction that collective bargaining and free-trade unionism were absolutely necessary to the rebuilding of strong economies. An interesting though biased account of labor's formal association with the ERP and MSP is provided in William Gomberg's "Labor's Participation in the European Productivity Program: A Study in Frustration," *Political Science Quarterly*, Vol. 74, No. 2 (June 1959), pp. 240–55.

88. Memorandum: To E. M. Flaherty from John T. Quinn, January 29, 1951, ECA Files, FRC, Accession No. 53A–177, Box 156 (Folder: Industrial Technical Assistance).

89. For details, see ECATO Circular E-A 16, To All European Missions

from ECA Administrator, March 9, 1951, ECA Files, FRC, Accession No. 53A–441 (Folder: Productivity).

90. Memorandum from Labor Information, OSR, to All Missions, "Subject: Productivity Drive Information Program," September 1, 1951, ECA Files, FRC, Accession No. 53A–441 (Folder: Productivity).

91. To E. M. Flaherty from John T. Quinn, *op. cit.*

92. See letter from Robert Mullen to W. H. Joyce, Jr., December 28, 1951, ECA Files, FRC, Accession No. 53A–441 (Folder: Productivity Drive).

93. See transcript of remarks made before a workshop organized by the Public Relations Society of America on January 30, 1952, ECA Files, FRC, Accession No. 53A–441 (Folder: Productivity Drive).

94. See Memorandum of interview with J. Jacque Errera, October 3, 1951 (by W. H. Joyce, Jr.), ECA Files, FRC, Accession No. 53A–441 (Folder: Productivity Drive).

95. During the Marshall Plan period there was, in fact, substantial unemployment in Greece, Italy, and West Germany, and, to a lesser extent, in Belgium.

96. According to Robert Mullen, the initial productivity advertising campaign had been prepared for the ECA by the advertising agency J. Walker Thompson Co. See his remarks to the Public Relations Society of America's workshop, *op. cit.*

97. *First Report to Congress on the Mutual Security Program, op. cit.*, p. 61.

98. See *Ibid.*

99. It was only in late March 1950, for example, that a Productivity Section was established in OSR, in Paris.

100. As late as August 1951, in reference to the recruitment of new staff members for the productivity program, W. A. Nielsen (Director of the European Information Division) confessed that he was "not clear as to the precise skills we need, largely because the final shape of the Productivity Drive itself is not determined." See W. A. Nielsen to Robert Mullen, August 27, 1951. In November 1951, Mullen himself complained of serious overlapping and duplication of efforts in connection with the productivity information program. See Memorandum: To Richard Bissell from Robert Mullen, November 1, 1951. Both documents are in ECA Files, FRC, Accession No. 53A–441 (Folder: Productivity).

101. Interview with Robert Marjolin, November 14, 1952, Harry B. Price Oral History Interviews, HST Library.

102. According to a subsequent United Nations study, output per worker in Europe's mining and manufacturing industries had shown an average annual rate of growth of 6.2 percent between 1948 and 1953. See United Nations, Department of Economic and Social Affairs, *Patterns of Industrial Growth 1938–1958* (New York, 1960), p. 84. When computed for the period 1948–1952, this annual rate yields an aggregate increase of 27 percent in output per man—well above the 15 percent increase considered imperative by the OEEC in 1948.

103. ECA, *Thirteenth Report to Congress*, pp. 22–23.

104. It must be noted, however, that both the individual-country figures and the aggregate figure in Table 13, which are taken from OEEC, *Statistical Bulletin* (May 1952), are at odds with the figures for agricultural production given

in the fourth annual report of the OEEC. According to the latter, the aggregate agricultural output for human consumption in crop year 1950–1951, was 16 percent above the prewar level. See OEEC, *Europe—The Way Ahead, op. cit.*, pp. 105–6.

105. Interview with Harlan Cleveland, September 29, 1952, Harry B. Price Oral History Interviews, HST Library (italics added).

CHAPTER 7

1. CEEC, *General Report*, p. 26.

2. Senate Foreign Relations Committee, *ERP Hearings in Executive Session*, 1948, p. 501.

3. For two illuminating accounts of European attempts to cope with postwar inflationary pressures, see Fred H. Klopstock, "Western Europe's Attack on Inflation," *Harvard Business Review*, Vol. 26, No. 5 (September 1948); and John G. Gurley, "Excess Liquidity and European Monetary Reforms, 1944–1952," *American Economic Review*, Vol. 43, No. 1 (March 1953).

4. See Chapter 3.

5. CEEC, *General Report*, p. 27.

6. *Ibid.*, p. 28.

7. 62 Stat. 137, Section 102(b).

8. Article 7 of the Convention for European Economic Cooperation (signed in Paris on April 16, 1948).

9. Gottfried Haberler, "Some Economic Problems of the European Recovery Program," *American Economic Review*, Vol. 38, No. 4 (September 1948), p. 507.

10. Edward Mason, "The New Approach to the Role of the United States in European Economic Stabilization," in Seymour E. Harris (ed.), *Foreign Economic Policy for the United States* (Cambridge, Mass.: Harvard University Press, 1948), p. 297.

11. See Council on Foreign Relations Files, Records of Groups, Vol. XVIII-A, "Aid to Europe," Digest of Sixteenth Meeting, April 24, 1950, p. 2.

12. *Ibid.*, p. 3 (italics added).

13. 62 Stat. 137, Section 115(b)(6).

14. France, as well as Italy and Austria, had earlier begun to receive American assistance, authorized by the European Interim Aid Act of 1947, which was passed in December 1947. That assistance had also generated counterpart deposits which could not be used without the approval of the United States.

15. See TOECA #74, for Taylor and Southard from Tomlinson, June 3, 1948. ECA Files, FRC, Accession No. 53A–278.

16. *Ibid.*

17. In January 1948, France had devalued the franc and established the two-tier exchange rate system in open defiance of an explicit disapproval of the IMF. Accordingly, the IMF refused to recognize the new official exchange rate as the *par value* of the franc. For details, see International Monetary Fund, *Annual Report 1948*, pp. 36–37.

18. That is, for most licensed imports, French importers were permitted to

obtain half of their authorized foreign exchange needs at the official rate and to buy the other half on the "free" market. See *Ibid.*, pp. 37–38.

19. This compromise was suggested by ECA/Paris and accepted by the French. See TOECA #83, from Tomlinson to Southard and Taylor, June 5, 1948, and TOECA #101, June 9, 1948. Both documents are in ECA Files, FRC Accession No. 53A–278.

20. NIACT #3335, from Paris to Secretary of State, June 23, 1948, ECA Files, FRC, Accession No. 53A–278.

21. *Ibid.*

22. *Ibid.* Actually, the issue was resolved *before* the end of the year. For details, see International Monetary Fund, *Annual Report 1949*, p. 60.

23. See TOECA #250, from Paris to Secretary of State, July 9, 1948, ECA Files, FRC, Accession No. 53A–278.

24. TOECA #358, Personal attention Hoffman from Bruce, September 14, 1948, ECA Files, FRC, Accession No. 53A–278.

25. *Ibid.*

26. TOECA #375, from Paris to Secretary of State, September 20, 1948, ECA Files, FRC, Accession No. 53A–278.

27. See *Ibid.* For details of the French investment program, see Annex B of this document.

28. *Ibid.*

29. See *Ibid.*

30. *Ibid.*

31. For details, see Annex A of TOECA #381, from Paris to Secretary of State, September 23, 1948, ECA Files, FRC, Accession No. 53A–278.

32. See TOECA #381, *op. cit.* As stated in this document, the French government at the time was "putting the finishing touches on a program which tends to simplify the obligations of the taxpayers . . . and makes possible improvement in tax enforcement."

33. See *Ibid.*

34. TOECA #475, from Paris to ECA Administrator, November 18, 1948, ECA Files, FRC, Accession No. 53A–278.

35. *Ibid.*

36. *Ibid.*

37. *Ibid.*

38. TOECA #52O, from Paris to ECA Administrator, December 10, 1948, ECA Files, FRC, Accession No. 53A–278.

39. *Ibid.*

40. TOECA #517, from Paris to ECA Administrator, December 10, 1948, ECA Files, FRC, Accession No. 53A–278. All the quotes in this paragraph come from this document.

41. See TOECA #536, to: ECA Administrator (Attention Bissell and Southard) from Bruce, December 16, 1948, ECA Files, FRC, Accession No. 53A–278.

42. *Ibid.* Bruce's request *was* approved by Washington, and the French accepted his stipulation. This is indicated by an exchange of letters between Bruce and Queuille, as reported in TOECA #544, to ECA Administrator from Bruce, December 27, 1948, ECA Files, FRC, Accession No. 53A–278.

43. See ECA, *Local Currency Counterpart Funds: Midpoint Review*, April 1950 (Washington, D.C., April 27, 1950), p. 9. Cited hereafter as ECA, *Counterpart: Midpoint-Review*.

44. See ECA, *Country Data Book: All Participating Countries* (March 1950), Table XI–3.

45. "Pragmatic" may, in fact, be too generous a term with which to describe ECA's counterpart policy in France. As related to this writer by a former ECA official in 1976, the routine for releasing counterparts had worked for the most part as follows: Under an agreement reached earlier between Richard Bissell and the U.S. Treasury Representative in Paris, William Tomlinson, the latter would confer periodically with Jean Monnet (the head of the French Central Planning Office) to consider the various purposes for which counterparts should be used. On Tomlinson's subsequent recommendations, which nearly always reflected Monnet's ideas, the ECA would approve the release.

46. Computed from ECA, *Country Data Book: All Participating Countries, op. cit.*, Table XI–3.

47. It must be clearly noted that "debt retirement" in this context took the form of the repayment of debt owed by the government to the central bank, *not* to the public at large. Or, to put it differently, it consisted of a reduction of claims by the central bank against the government.

48. See *First Report to Congress on the Mutual Security Program, op. cit.*, p. 63. These figures are actually the cumulative totals through November 30, 1951, one month before the official termination of the ERP.

49. See ECA, *Counterpart: Midpoint Review*, pp. 8–9.

50. See *Ibid.*, p. 17. ECA's counterpart policy in Britain, Norway, and Denmark (see below) may well have been motivated by another consideration—namely, a desire to *force* on these countries an anti-inflationary discipline to which they were not inclined to subscribe on their own. As stated by Professor Gurley: ". . . Where Keynesian doctrine in Europe was particularly strong—in England and the Scandinavian countries—either no steps to reduce excess liquidity were undertaken or else only token gestures in this direction were made." See Gurley, *op. cit.*, p. 76. Although Sweden also fell into this category, the ECA could do very little there, since ERP aid to that country took the form of loans that did not generate local-currency counterparts.

51. See footnote 43 above.

52. See ECA, *Counterpart: Midpoint Review*, p. 22.

53. See *Ibid.*, p. 11. However, a portion of the counterparts generated by the Interim Aid received by Austria was released during the first year for certain investment projects.

54. *Ibid.*, p. 9.

55. *Ibid.*, p. 11.

56. See ECA, *Country Data Book: All Participating Countries, op. cit.*, p. 6.

57. Of the $95 million worth of local-currency funds accumulated in the Danish account by March 1950, less than $50,000 had been released to finance technical assistance projects. See ECA, *Counterpart: Midpoint Review*, p. 23.

58. See ECA, *Tenth Report to Congress*, p. 54.

59. *Ibid.*

60. In France, however, the wholesale price index in December 1949 was one percentage point *lower* than in December 1948.

61. See Memorandum to: Paul G. Hoffman and William C. Foster from Richard M. Bissell, Jr., January 20, 1950, "Subject: Counterpart and Investment Policy," copy in *ECA Policy Series*.

62. *Ibid*.

63. Interview with Robert Oshins, 1952, Harry B. Price Oral History Interviews, HST Library.

64. See Memorandum to: Paul G. Hoffman and William C. Foster, January 20, 1950, *op. cit.*

65. See NAC Document #1081, December 22, 1950, "Financial Policy Questions Re: Foreign Assistance Programs Proposed for Fiscal Year 1952."

66. *Ibid*.

67. See Minutes of Meetings of NAC, Meeting #168, December 26, 1950.

68. *Ibid*. (italics added).

69. For details about this division between the so-called fiscal and physical schools within the ECA, see interview with Robert Oshins, *op. cit.*, and interview with Herbert Rees, 1952, Harry B. Price Oral History Interviews, HST Library.

70. See TOREP #8489, to Embassy Paris from ECA Administrator (Foster), October 12, 1949, *op. cit.*

71. *Ibid*.

72. Repto Circular D–29, to All ECA Missions from OSR, November 16, 1949, copy in *ECA Policy Series*.

73. Thus, except for Britain, Norway, and Denmark, counterpart funds were increasingly utilized for defense-related production and investment activities from mid–1950 on.

74. See TOREP #7999, from ECA Administrator to OSR, September 15, 1950, copy in *ECA Policy Series*.

75. See his "European Recovery and the Problems Ahead," *American Economic Review, Papers and Proceedings*, Vol. 42, No. 2 (May 1952).

76. See *Ibid*, pp. 316–24, and p. 325.

77. Interview with Richard Birnberg (ECA economist), 1952, Harry B. Price Oral History Interviews, HST Library.

78. ECA, *Country Data Book: All Participating Countries, op. cit.*, p. 7.

79. *Ibid*.

80. For monthly price movements during 1949 and 1950, see *Ibid.*, Tables IX–1 and IX–2; and ECA, *Thirteenth Report to Congress*, p. 105.

CHAPTER 8

1. For such a diagnosis, see Per Jacobsson's letter to W. Randolph Burgess, cited in Chapter 3.

2. For a more detailed description of bilateral payments arrangements, see Imanuel Wexler, *Fundamentals of International Economics*, 2d ed. (New York: Random House, 1972), Chapter 11.

3. See, for example, Howard S. Ellis, *Bilateralism and the Future of International Trade*, Essays in International Finance No. 5 (Princeton: Princeton University Press, Summer 1945).

4. For a complete list of bilateral payments agreements in postwar Europe, and a detailed description of their provisions and operations, the interested reader may wish to consult Merlyn N. Trued and Raymond Mikesell,

Postwar Bilateral Payments Agreements, Studies in International Finance No. 4 (Princeton: Princeton University Press, 1955).

5. See Judd Polk and Gardner Patterson, "The Emerging Pattern of Bilateralism," *Quarterly Journal of Economics*, Vol. 62, No. 1 (November 1947), p. 138.

6. This was accomplished through the actual sales of currencies by one central bank to another.

7. Most of them also provided for periodic settlements, in gold, of outstanding debit balances.

8. Thus, for example, at the end of 1947, France was compelled for a time to cease importing from Belgium and Switzerland. In March 1948, Sweden placed a temporary ban on further imports from Belgium; and Britain found it necessary to postpone for several months its agreed schedule of imports from Belgium. See Robert W. Bean, "European Multilateral Clearing," *Journal of Political Economy*, Vol. 56, No. 5 (October 1948), p. 404.

9. Some additional credit was nevertheless extended during 1946 by Belgium, the United Kingdom, and Sweden. Moreover, in February 1947, Belgium, the leading European creditor, was allowed by Britain to convert current sterling earnings into dollars, to help finance its deficit with the Western Hemisphere.

10. See ECA, *Recovery Progress and U.S. Aid*, p. 205.

11. This, as noted in Chapter 4, was one of the bilateral undertakings to which the CEEC countries were asked to agree before becoming eligible for ERP aid.

12. Committee for European Economic Cooperation, Vol. II, *Technical Reports* (Paris, 1947), Appendix B, p. 531.

13. *Ibid.*, p. 532.

14. *Ibid.*

15. For a brief account of this particular Benelux proposal, see William Diebold, Jr., *Trade and Payments in Western Europe* (New York: Harpers & Bros., 1952), pp. 22–23.

16. See J. Keith Horsefield, *The International Monetary Fund 1945–1965. Volume I: Chronicle* (Washington, D.C.: International Monetary Fund, 1969), pp. 214–15. More on the relations between the Fund and the CEEC nations in a later section.

17. The Bank for International Settlements (BIS) was designated as the agent for the group. The full text of the agreement is reproduced in BIS, *Eighteenth Annual Report*, pp. 167–68.

18. For simplicity's sake, it is assumed that the net bilateral balances between the Netherlands and Belgium and between France and Italy are zero.

19. A problem may well have arisen for Britain if its bilateral agreement with the Netherlands specified that sterling held by the latter, beyond a certain amount, must be converted into dollars by Britain.

20. Total clearings, during the period of operations under the agreement, amounted to the equivalent of $51 million. Of these, $5 million was cleared through "first category" compensations and $46 million through "second category" operations. See BIS, *Twentieth Annual Report*, p. 224.

21. These figures are given by Bean, *op. cit.*, p. 408, and are repeated by

Diebold, *op. cit.*, p. 25. On the basis of his own calculations, Bean argues that if all possible "first category" compensations had actually been carried out at the first clearing, a total of $39.2 million could have been cleared.

22. Department of State, *Outline of European Recovery Program* (Washington, December 1947), p. 50 (italics added).

23. *Ibid.*

24. Compiled from ECA, *First, Second, and Third Reports to Congress.*

25. Caffery to the Secretary of State, February 7, 1948, *FRUS 1948*, Vol. III, p. 380.

26. *Ibid.*

27. See Department of State, Outgoing Telegram #537, February 20, 1948, for Embassy and Tomlinson from State and Treasury, copy in National Archives, 840.50 Recovery/2–748.

28. *Ibid.* It is of interest to note that this telegram was drafted on the basis of recommendations made by the U.S. Treasury. See Memorandum to: Mr. Ness (State) from: H. J. Bittermann (Treasury), National Archives, 840.50 Recovery/2–748.

29. It was also referred to as the Ansiaux-Playfair Plan, after Hubert Ansiaux of Belgium and Edward Playfair, an official of the United Kingdom Treasury. They, together with Guillaume Guindey of France and Pietro Stoppani of Italy, were the main architects of the plan.

30. Nor could counterparts be used in such cases, since loans, unlike grants, would not generate counterpart funds.

31. See Memorandum from: W. L. Hebbard (ECA Mission in the United Kingdom) to: Ambassador (Douglas), London, May 1948, "Subject: OEEC Plan for Financing European Trade," *FRUS 1948*, Vol. III, pp. 439–42.

32. *Ibid.*, p. 440.

33. *Ibid.*, p. 441.

34. *Ibid.*, p. 442.

35. Thus, as early as November 1947, the National Advisory Council (NAC) had stated that "the *voluntary* adoption of a multilateral clearing mechanism on the part of some or all of the participating countries, would be regarded favorably by the United States as a *significant effort* toward *self-help* on the part of these countries." See Minutes of Meetings of NAC, Meeting #73, November 8, 1947 (italics added).

36. Article I of the *Final Act* of the Bretton Woods Conference.

37. The specific rules and regulations governing the use of the Fund's resources by its members were laid out in Article V of the *Final Act*. For a brief account, see W. M. Scammell, *International Monetary Policy*, 2d ed. (London: Macmillan & Co., Ltd., 1961), pp. 157–60.

38. Quoted in Horsefield, *op. cit.*, p. 213.

39. However, the Board authorized Mr. Gutt to attend meetings of the CEEC Financial Committee during August 1947.

40. IMF, *Annual Report 1948*, p. 74 (italics added).

41. As of April 30, 1948, the total quota amounted to the equivalent of $7.976 billion, of which the U.S. quota was $2.750 billion. See *Ibid.*, Appendix X, pp. 102–3.

42. IMF, Press Release No. 45, April 20, 1948.

43. Horsefield, *op. cit.*, p. 217.

44. *Ibid.*

45. *Ibid.*, pp. 217–18 (italics added).

46. *Ibid.*, p. 219 (italics added).

47. *Ibid.*, p. 218.

48. See *Ibid.*, p. 220.

49. *Ibid.*, p. 221.

50. *Ibid.*

51. IMF *Annual Report 1948*, p. 35.

52. *Ibid.*

53. See ECATO #48, for Harriman, Marget, Lindsay, Tomlinson from Maffry, June 3, 1948, ECA Files, FRC, Accession No. 53A–278.

54. See ECATO #53, for Marget from Maffry, June 4, 1948, ECA Files, FRC, Accession No. 53A–278 (italics added). This message came as a reply to a question raised earlier by Hubert Ansiaux concerning the possible use of the IMF in connection with intra-European financial plans. See TOECA #67, for Maffry from Marget, June 1, 1948, ECA Files, FRC, Accession No. 53A–278.

55. On the reasonable assumption that they had been informed of the content of ECATO #48 and ECATO #53.

CHAPTER 9

1. For details, see next section.

2. See Memorandum, "Intra-European Clearing System," dated May 25, 1948, by Theodore Geiger and Franklin A. Lindsay, ECA Files, FRC, Accession No. 53A–405.

3. See Memorandum, "Intra-European Payments Clearing System," dated May 27, 1948, by T. Geiger and F. Lindsay, ECA Files, FRC, Accession No. 53A–405.

4. *Ibid.*

5. See *Ibid.*

6. See ECATO #48, *op. cit.*, in which the NAC is quoted as stating: ". . . the United States is prepared . . . to arrange the financing of offshore procurement in the participating countries in a manner which will give full recognition to the importance of facilitating essential intra-European trade."

7. See ECATO #52, to Amembassy Paris from Hoffman, June 4, 1948, ECA Files, FRC, Accession No. 53A–278.

8. See ECATO #60, to Amembassy Paris from Hoffman, June 8, 1948, ECA Files, FRC, Accession No. 53A–278.

9. See ECATO #92, to Amembassy Paris from Hoffman, June 14, 1948, ECA Files, FRC, Accession No. 53A–278.

10. See *Ibid.*

11. Article 26 of the AIEPC. The full text of the agreement and its three annexes is reproduced in BIS, *Nineteenth Annual Report*, pp. 232–45.

12. It may be recalled that under the First Agreement on Multilateral Monetary Compensation, only the five permanent members had agreed to automatic "first category" compensations.

13. On the supposition that these would be deficits, for the financing of which no other resources or credit margins were available.

14. See "Intra-European Payments Plan," dated October 15, 1948, authors identified as JCC, WFS, PMP in ECA Files, FRC, Accession No. 53A–405.

15. As will be noted in Chapter 12, the negotiations for and conclusion of these bilateral agreements were a necessary ingredient in the overall negotiations over the OEEC-recommended division of U.S. aid for the first year of the ERP. Put differently, the agreement on the AIEPC was part of the agreement on the division of aid itself.

16. According to Annex C of the AIEPC, the drawing rights, as initially established, totaled only $810.4 million. Subsequently, however, the United Kingdom granted Turkey $8 million in drawing rights, thus bringing the total to $818.4 million.

17. For fuller details, see BIS, *Twentieth Annual Report*, pp. 299–300.

18. Some $78 million of the unutilized drawing rights were carried forward to be utilized during 1949–1950; $25 million were to be used under a special protocol, and $45.7 million were simply canceled. See *Ibid.*, p. 224 and p. 298.

19. See *Ibid.*, p. 226, and ECA, *Fifth Report to Congress*, p. 13.

20. ECA, *Fifth Report to Congress*, p. 13.

21. For an elaboration on this theme, see Diebold, *op. cit.*, pp. 53–62, and Scammell, *op. cit.*, p. 284.

22. Scammell, p. 284.

23. Moreover, the AIEPC made it easier for several European countries to import raw materials from the sterling area (using sterling supplied by Britain), thus reducing Europe's dollar deficit with the Western Hemisphere. See Diebold, *op. cit.*, pp. 52–53.

24. See "Intra-European Payments Plan," October 15, 1948, *op. cit.*

25. In this sense, drawing rights transferability would not be substantially different from full currency transferability. In fact, during the life of the 1948–1949 AIEPC, Britain was obliged to transfer $175 million in gold to Belgium. See Diebold, *op. cit.*, p. 47.

26. *Ibid.*, p. 60.

27. Article 17(b)(ii) of the AIEPC. The same article also allowed for the transfer of drawing rights if a *creditor* certified that "the whole or any part of drawing rights established by it, are no longer required by a debtor for the purpose for which they were established."

28. See Memorandum to Henry Tasca from Hubert Havlik, May 26, 1949, "Subject: Salient Points for Discussion on Trade and Payments," ECA Files, FRC, Accession No. 53A–177.

29. See "First Draft of Long Range Proposals," dated March 13, 1949, by T. Geiger, copy in *ECA Policy Series*.

30. *Ibid.*

31. See "The Problem of Convertibility and a Free Trade Area in Western Europe," dated April 13, 1949, by H. van B. Cleveland, copy in *FCA Policy Series*.

32. See both Geiger's paper and Cleveland's paper, cited in notes 30 and 31.

33. "The Problem of Convertibility and a Free Trade Area in Western Europe," *op. cit.*

34. See *Ibid.*

35. As reported in an ECA memorandum: [Sir Edmond] Hall-Patch stated that he understood none of the delegations wished to make any major changes in the [1948] Payments Agreement. . . . The [other] Europeans indicated concurrence in this statement." See "Notes on Meeting on April 14, 1949, at OEEC" (by Dechert), ECA Files, FRC, Accession No. 53A–177.

36. *Ibid.* Bissell's stated position during this meeting had been developed earlier in the office of Milton Katz, Deputy Special Representative in Europe. See "ECA Objectives on Principles in Revision of Payments Agreement," draft dated April 13, 1949, by Kingman Brewster and Hubert Havlik, ECA Files, FRC, Accession No. 53A–177.

37. "Notes on Meeting on April 14, 1949, at OEEC," *op. cit.*

38. *Ibid.* (italics added).

39. *Ibid.*

40. See Memorandum, "Argument against Convertibility," dated May 5, 1949, by M. Levv-Hawes, ECA Files, FRC, Accession No. 53A–177.

41. See *Ibid.*

42. See Memorandum, "Comments on the Draft Belgian Payments Plan," dated May 12, 1949, by M. Levy-Hawes, ECA Files, FRC, Accession No. 53A–177.

43. The draft plan also proposed that unused drawing rights held by debtors would be converted into *unconditional* dollar aid. See *Ibid.*

44. See Memorandum for Mr. Harriman, June 13, 1949, by Hubert Havlik, ECA Files, FRC, Accession No. 53A–177.

45. See "ECA Observer's Report on OEEC Payments Committee," dated June 9, 1949, by M. Levy-Hawes, ECA Files, FRC, Accession No. 53A–177.

46. See Belgian Proposal (Draft), dated June 4, 1949, ECA Files, FRC, Accession No. 53A–177.

47. One suggestion, made along these lines, was to make it clear to the Europeans that if no acceptable agreement was reached by the time of the aid allocations for 1949–1950, a certain amount will be subtracted from the total appropriated funds. See Memorandum, "The Important Policy Decisions Necessary to Implement OSR Program on Trade and Payments," dated June 1, 1949, by an unidentified author, ECA Files, FRC, Accession No. 53A–177.

48. See Memorandum to H. Havlik from K. Brewster, dated June 14, 1949, "Subject: Possible Course of Action in the Event No Agreement on Trade and Payments for 1949–1950," and Memorandum from Havlik to Tasca, dated June 16, 1949, "Subject: Methods of Financing Intra-European Trade in the Absence of a Payments Agreement," ECA Files, FRC, Accession No. 53A–177.

49. This was immediately reported in a telephone conversation to Hubert Havlik of OSR. See Memorandum from Havlik to Tasca, dated June 14, 1949, ECA Files, FRC, Accession No. 53A–177.

50. In fact, this was precisely how the Chairman of the OEEC Payments Committee had interpreted the British request and so informed the ECA. See *Ibid.*

51. See "Notes—June 30, 1949 Evening Meeting," dated July 1, 1949, by

the ECA observer at the OEEC Council, ECA Files, FRC, Accession No. 53A–177.

52. In the meantime, the monthly compensations continued under the rules of the first AIEPC.

53. The full text of the revised AIEPC and its annexes is reproduced in BIS, *Twentieth Annual Report*, pp. 263–81. For discussion and analysis of the revised agreement, see BIS, *Twentieth Annual Report*, pp. 226–41; also Diebold, *op. cit.*, pp. 70–84, and Scammell, *op. cit.*, pp. 285–88.

54. See Table II, Annex C of the 1949 AIEPC in BIS, *Twentieth Annual Report*, p. 278.

55. Switzerland did not participate in the drawing-right system, while Portugal, which did become a full participant, granted only a small amount (equaling $750,000) of bilateral drawing rights to only one country, Greece.

56. In fact, multilateral drawing rights were to be calculated by taking the total of drawing rights to which a debtor was entitled and subtracting 75 percent of these, to be assigned to various contributors. The remaining 25 percent (or, one-third of 75 percent) was earmarked as multilateral drawing rights.

57. Their use, however, was to be governed by special agreements concluded between Belgium and each of the three countries.

58. As follows: $21.5 million to France, $38 million to the Netherlands, and $28 million to the United Kingdom.

59. The 1949 AIEPC, Article 20(a).

60. See BIS, *Twentieth Annual Report*, p. 228 and p. 233.

61. The figure $156.3 million is from Table II, Annex C, of the 1949 AIEPC. The drop was accounted for by the cancellation of the entire amount of bilateral drawing rights originally granted to France by Britain, and by a reduction in the amount granted by Germany.

62. The $60 million in bilateral drawing rights was part of the $78.4 million in unused drawing rights carried forward from the 1948 AIEPC.

63. Nor did Britain utilize the special Belgian loan of $28 million. See note 58 above.

64. For details, see BIS, *Twenty-first Annual Report*, p. 218.

65. Of which $63.0 million was "first category" and $86.4 million "second category" compensations. See *Ibid.*, p. 219.

66. Estimated at $8.6 billion. See Diebold, *op. cit.*, p. 84.

67. During the twelve-month period July 1948-June 30, 1949, about 9.5 percent of total intra-OEEC trade had been financed by drawing rights and compensation operations under the first AIEPC, compared with slightly more than 10 percent, during the life of the revised AIEPC.

68. According to the BIS, only 9 percent of the total drawing rights was used in a truly multilateral fashion. For details, see BIS, *Twenty-first Annual Report*, p. 217.

69. For fuller details, including the magnitudes of the respective devaluations and exchange-rate adjustments, see International Monetary Fund, *Annual Report 1950*, pp. 28–54 and pp. 88–89.

70. See *Ibid.*, pp. 30–31.

71. See TOREP #3893, from Washington (Bissell), March 17, 1949, in *FRUS 1949*, Vol. 1V, pp. 377–80.

72. See Secretary of State to Certain Diplomatic Offices, April 12, 1949, in *FRUS 1949*, Vol. IV, pp. 382–83.

73. See NAC Document #851, June 29, 1949, and NAC Document #876, August 24, 1949. Also Minutes of Meetings of NAC, Meeting #131, June 28, 1949; Meeting #132, June 30, 1949; and Meeting #134, August 11, 1949.

74. For documentation relating to American concern and views about Britain's financial crisis, and details of the bilateral and tripartite discussions and consultations, see *FRUS 1949*, Vol. IV, pp. 781–839.

75. Remarks made by John H. Williams during dinner given by the Council on Foreign Relations, in honor of Sir Edmund Hall-Patch, Robert Marjolin, and Sir Eric Roll, on February 23, 1950. See Council on Foreign Relations Files, Records of Meetings, Vol. X.

76. More is said about the Treasury's attitudes in the next chapter.

CHAPTER 10

1. This congressional mandate was first introduced in the authorization act of 1949 (i.e., the amended Economic Cooperation Act of 1948) and was reiterated a year later in the Economic Cooperation Act of 1950. More on this in Part IV.

2. U.S. House of Representatives, Subcommittee of Committee on Appropriations, 81st Cong., 2d Sess., *Hearings on Foreign Aid Appropriations for 1951*, 1950, p. 2.

3. See, for example, Price, *op. cit.*, pp. 270–72.

4. As quoted by the *New York Times*, November 1, 1949.

5. This was in line with customary ECA policy of not publicly proposing schemes of its own. In this particular case, moreover, the ECA had been specifically advised by the State Department to "let the Europeans themselves develop the institutions necessary to handle [the] problems of integration." See cable to Paris (for Perkins) from Acheson, October 19, 1949, ECA Files, FRC, Accession No. 53A–177.

6. *New York Times*, November 1, 1949. Interestingly enough, Hoffman's use of the word integration rather than unification, which he had originally planned to use, came at the suggestion of the State Department. See cable from OSR (Hoffman) to Secretary of State, October 30, 1949, ECA Files, FRC, Accession No. 53A–177.

7. See TOREP #8769, from ECA Administrator to Bissell, October 25, 1949, copy in *ECA Policy Series*.

8. See REPTO #7717, from OSR to Secretary of State, December 3, 1949, ECA Files, FRC, Accession No. 53A–177.

9. TOREP #8349, to Embassy Paris from ECA Administrator, October 6, 1949, *op. cit.*

10. *Ibid.*, (italics added).

11. Quoted in Price, *op. cit.*, p. 121, and attributed by him to a memorandum prepared by H. Van B. Cleveland and Theodore Geiger, in the fall of 1949.

12. See preceding chapter.

13. See "The Problems of Western Europe Competitive Position in the World Economy and Its Remedies," by T. Geiger, H. van B. Cleveland, and John Hulley (transmitted to E. T. Dickinson and James McCullugh by Harlan Cleveland on July 19, 1949), *ECA Policy Series*.

14. See *Ibid*. It might be noted that Paul Hoffman subsequently rejected the notion of the pound sterling as a settlement currency (see TOREP #8769, *op. cit.*) and that nothing came out of the suggestion for an Intra-European Commerce Commission.

15. See "The Economic Integration of Western Europe," dated October 15, 1949, by T. Geiger, H. van B. Cleveland, and R. M. Bissell, *ECA Policy Series*.

16. *Ibid.*

17. *Ibid.*

18. See Diebold, *op. cit.*, pp. 162–63. The Council also called for the exploration of "further measures of cooperation."

19. TOREP #9656, from ECA Administrator, November 29, 1949, *ECA Policy Series*.

20. TOREP #9606, from ECA/W (Foster) to OSR, November 26, 1949, ECA Files, FRC, Accession No. 53A–177 (italics added).

21. The pertinent documents on which the following account is based are (1) TOREP #9606; (2) an undated memorandum to Harriman and Katz from Lincoln Gordon, "Discussions with State Department Representatives on European Economic Integration," ECA Files, FRC, Accession No. 53A–177 (these discussions took place on November 11–12, and a rough draft summarizing the views exchanged was attached to the memorandum); and (3) a draft working paper, "Intra-European Currency Transferability and Liberalization of Trade," dated December 9, 1949, *ECA Policy Series*. The third document also appears as NAC Document #942, dated December 20, 1949.

22. The accounting unit subsequently adopted, the "EPU Unit of Account," was equivalent in value to one U.S. dollar.

23. The quotas, as initially established, are given in Section VI. For the amounts contributed by the ECA, see next chapter.

24. For details, see Table 23.

25. On the assumption that the automatic-settlement mechanism, involving a graduated scale of gold and dollar payments, would impose a certain degree of balance-of-payments discipline on the participating countries.

26. See "Intra-European Currency Transferability and Liberalization of Trade," *op. cit.*

27. See TOREP #2543, from Washington (Foster) to OSR, March 28, 1950, ECA Files, FRC, Accession No. 53A–177.

28. See TOREP #263, from Washington (Hoffman) to OSR, January 10, 1950, ECA Files, FRC, Accession No. 53A–177.

29. See *Ibid*.

30. See office memorandum, from Frank Southard to Secretary Snyder, dated January 16, 1950, "Subject: ECA Proposal for a European Clearing Union," John Snyder Papers, Box 11, HST Library. More details below.

31. This memorandum appears as NAC Document #948.

32. *Ibid.*, pp. 2–3.

33. *Ibid.*, p. 6.

34. In fact, the NAC staff cited an earlier NAC opposition to a proposed clearing union for Latin America on similar grounds. See *Ibid.*, p. 5.

35. Cited in note 30.

36. A copy of this memorandum, which is titled "Proposed New Financial Institution for Europe," is in John Snyder Papers, Box 11, HST Library.

37. See Horsefield, *op. cit.*, p. 289.

38. *Ibid.* (italics added).

39. See Minutes of Meetings of NAC, Meeting #146, January 19, 1950.

40. *Ibid.*

41. *Ibid.*

42. *Ibid.* It might be noted that the representative of the Federal Reserve Board was also concerned about the participation of the United Kingdom and the sterling area in the proposed plan, but was not opposed to the plan as such.

43. *Ibid.*

44. *Ibid.* This, incidentally, appears to have been the official view of the State Department at the time. Thus, during a discussion meeting of the Council on Foreign Relations in mid-February, George Perkins, Assistant Secretary of State for European Affairs, was asked whether the EPU was something that the State Department—as distinguished from the ECA—was "keen about." Mr. Perkins answered: "It is regarded, not as the ultimate solution but as another necessary intermediate step." See Council on Foreign Relations Files, Records of Group, Vol. XIX(B), Digest of Discussion of the Third Meeting, February 14, 1950.

45. See Minutes of Meetings of NAC Staff, Meeting #46, January 20, 1950.

46. The next paragraph, summarizing the points agreed to, is based on the Minutes of NAC Meeting #147, January 23, 1950.

47. These two principles were also expressed in NAC, *Semi-annual Report to the President and the Congress*, for the period October 1, 1949–March 31, 1950 (Washington, 1950).

48. This last point, as noted earlier, was one of the recommendations submitted by the Fund's Managing Director.

49. See note 18.

50. See, for example, a report by the ECA mission in Norway in late April, which stated that the Norwegians are "definitely convinced that the automatic dollar payments-and-receipts feature of EPU will have serious tendency to spread deflationary pressures." See TOREP #190, from Oslo (Nordness) to OSR, April 28, 1950, ECA Files, FRC, Accession No. 53A–177. This concern on the part of the Norwegians and Danes had been continuously expressed since early January 1950.

51. The following is based on TOREP #340, from ECA Administrator to Amembassy Paris, January 24, 1950; and TOREP #2637, from ECA Administrator to Amembassy Paris, April 4, 1950, *ECA Policy Series*.

52. OEEC, *European Recovery Programme: Second Report of the OEEC* (Paris, February 1950), p. 232.

53. *Ibid.* (italics added).

54. See Joel Bernstein, "The Integration of the Sterling Payments System and the Intra-European Payments Arrangements, Embodied in the European

Payments Union," unpublished Ph.D. dissertation (University of Chicago, 1956), p. 1.

55. An excellent description of the evolution and operations of the Sterling Payments System is given in *Ibid.*, pp. 104–21. A more succinct account is to be found in BIS, *Eighteenth Annual Report*, pp. 149–51.

56. The latter were Iceland, Ireland, the Netherlands, Norway, and Sweden.

57. As early as February 1950, Britain's Foreign Secretary Ernest Bevin, warned Secretary of State Acheson that "some serious difficulties emerged from the expert examination in Paris, [concerning] the relationship between the European Payments Union and the Sterling System." He continued: "We are anxious to cooperate, and we shall make every effort to devise proposals which will enable the Sterling Area to play its part in a satisfactory scheme of European Payments." See British Secretary of State for Foreign Affairs to the Secretary of State, February 11, 1950, *FRUS 1950*, Vol. III, p. 628.

58. See Diebold, *op. cit.*, p. 105.

59. Moreover, Britain was fearful of the potential impact of *future* acquisition of sterling by OEEC countries from other parts of the sterling area.

60. Quoted in Bernstein, *op. cit.*, p. 23.

61. See NAC Document #1009, dated June 29, 1950, "Subject: European Payments Union," p. 2.

62. Parallel proposals were also made for collectively sanctioned discrimination in favor of extreme debtor countries.

63. See Bernstein, *op. cit.*, p. 83.

64. See Memorandum to: Paul G. Hoffman and William C. Foster, from Richard M. Bissell, Jr., January 20, 1950, *op. cit.*

65. *Ibid.* (italics added).

66. See Diebold, *op. cit.*, p. 191.

67. U.S. House of Representatives, Committee on Foreign Affairs, 81st Cong., 2d Sess., *Hearings on Extention of European Recovery*, 1950, p. 73.

68. His confidence proved justified, for Congress did earmark the requested sum. More on this in the next chapter.

69. See TOREP #1839, from ECA Administrator (Hoffman) to Amembassy Paris, March 9, 1950, *ECA Policy Series*. The rest of the quotations in this paragraph are from the same document.

70. See TOREP #2647, from Hoffman to OSR, April 5, 1950, *ECA Policy Series*.

71. See *Ibid.*

72. TOREP #3730, from Washington to OSR (Personal for Harriman), May 4, 1950, ECA Files, FRC, Accession No. 53A–177. These consequences would include (1) ECA's ceasing to finance any intra-European payments along present arrangements, (2) withholding the entire $600 million incentive fund, and (3) henceforth financing only offshore purchases out of remaining aid allotments.

73. This was reported in TOREP #493, from London to OSR, May 11, 1950, ECA Files, FRC, Accession No. 53A–177. The full text of the *aide memoire* is reproduced in *FRUS 1950*, Vol. III, pp. 655–57.

74. These included a special guaranty of $150 million, to be granted to the

United Kingdom by the ECA, to cover any large dollar and gold payments to the EPU. In addition, the United Kingdom would be allowed to automatically reimpose quantitative restrictions, in the event of its experiencing significant losses of reserves.

75. See TOREP #494, from London to OSR, May 11, 1950, ECA Files, FRC, Accession No. 53A–177.

76. See TOECA #587 (repeated, Paris TOREP #500), from London (Harriman) for Hoffman, Foster, and Bissell, May 15, 1950, ECA Files, FRC, Accession No. 53A–177. This cable contained the final text of the British paper on sterling participation in the EPU, to be submitted to the OEEC Payments Committee. In it, the United Kingdom declared, for the first time, its willingness to allow the use of sterling balances, held by other OEEC members as of June 30, 1950, for the settlement of cumulative deficits with the EPU.

77. On these points, see Albert O. Hirschman, "The European Payments Union: Negotiations and Issues," *The Review of Economics and Statistics*, Vol. 33, No. 1 (February 1951), pp. 49–55. See also TOREP #198, from ECA, Brussels, to OSR, June 9, 1950, ECA Files, FRC, Accession No. 53A–177, in which the Belgians were reported unwilling to extend large credits to the EPU without assurance of additional dollar aid in the form of direct (and *un*conditional) grants.

78. The meeting of the Executive Committee and the agreed-upon recommendations were reported in REPTO Circular #136, from OSR to all ECA missions (and Secretary of State), June 20, 1950, ECA Files, FRC, Accession No. 53A–177. The present paragraph draws on this document.

79. Based on the actual turnover of its intra-European trade in 1949, the Belgian quota should have been $433 million. By setting it at a lower figure, the Financial Experts, in effect, reduced the amount of credit that Belgium would have to advance to the union. The Executive Committee also recommended that one-half of ECA aid to Belgium during 1950–1951 should be in the form of direct grants, and one-half in the form of conditional aid.

80. However, the use of sterling balances held as of June 30, 1950, was allowed only to overall cumulative debtors.

81. See TOREP #5091, from Washington (Bissell) to OSR (Personal for Katz, Tasca, and Gordon), June 17, 1950, ECA Files, FRC, Accession No. 53A–177.

82. Thus, in an office memorandum, "The Outcome of the EPU Negotiations," dated June 16, 1950, an unidentified Treasury official criticized the EPU and stated: "There is no basis whatsoever for regarding the EPU which is now emerging, as a step toward economic integration." A copy of this document is in John Snyder Papers, Box 11, HST Library.

83. See TOREP #5091, *op. cit.*

84. See Henry Tasca to Richard M. Bissell, Jr., July 3, 1950, ECA Files, FRC, Accession No. 53A–177.

85. *Ibid.* (italics added).

86. See Minutes of Meetings of NAC, Meeting #158, June 29, 1950.

87. This exchange, which appears in the Minutes of NAC Meeting #158, was also reported to ECA officials in Paris, in TOREP #5798, from ECA/W to OSR, July 9, 1950, ECA Files, FRC, Accession No. 53A–177.

88. See TOREP #3730, *op. cit.*

89. See TOREP #5657, from ECA/W (Bissell) to OSR, July 3, 1950, ECA Files, FRC, Accession No. 53A–177.

90. See TOREP #5692, from ECA/W (Foster) to Katz, July 6, 1950, ECA Files, FRC, Accession No. 53A–177. The text referred to by Foster was contained in OEEC Document TP(50)71, dated June 28, 1950, a document prepared by the Financial Experts for consideration by the OEEC Executive Committee.

91. See TOREP #5692, *op. cit.*

92. See REPTO #3793, from OSR (Stokes) to Secretary of State (Personal for Foster and Bissell), July 7, 1950, ECA Files, FRC, Accession No. 53A–177.

93. *Ibid.*

94. OEEC Document C(50)190(Final); also published as OEEC, *A European Payments Union and the Rules of Commercial Policy to be Followed by Member Countries* (Paris, July 7, 1950).

95. The following amounts are denominated in EPU Units of Account (1 U/A = $1). For each country, except Belgium and Switzerland, the quota represents approximately 15 percent of its intra-European trade in 1949. The Belgium quota, as noted earlier, is smaller; the Swiss quota was set higher. See BIS, *Twenty-first Annual Report*, p. 225; also ECA, *Ninth Report to Congress*, p. 28.

96. See Milton Katz to Robert Marjolin, September 18, 1950, ECA Files, FRC, Accession No. 53A–177. Note that this letter, to which additional references are made in the next chapter, was dated one day before the actual signature of the EPU agreement. According to the records, it was hand-delivered to Marjolin.

CHAPTER 11

1. See Chapter 10, note 68.

2. 64 Stat. 198, Section 103 (italics added).

3. It may be recalled, from Table 23, that the first two portions of the quota, *after* the gold-free tranche, favored debtors more than creditors. That is, debtors were to pay proportionally less gold to the union than creditors stood to receive from it. It might also be noted here that "gold payments" refers to payment in either gold or dollars, or any other currencies acceptable to creditors.

4. These initial positions were actually set as early as July 1950, shortly before the OEEC Council approved the EPU arrangements. They were detailed in a letter from Milton Katz to Robert Marjolin, dated July 4, 1950, ECA Files, FRC, Accession No. 53A–177.

5. The exception was Belgium, whose initial debit position was considered part of its quota during 1950–1951. See *Ibid.*

6. However, $10 million of Norway's initial credit balance and the entire $25 million subsequently allotted to Turkey took the form of loans and hence did not require counterpart deposits.

7. Austria's and Greece's quotas had been set at $70 million and $45 million, respectively. Because their initial credit positions were larger, these countries were not permitted to draw on their quotas until the end of 1951.

8. See Katz to Marjolin, September 18, 1950, *op. cit.* This amount was later increased to $361 million.

9. See *Ibid.*

10. See *Ibid.* The exact amounts of the initial debit balances assigned to Belgium and Sweden, however, were specified in a letter from Milton Katz to Robert Marjolin, dated October 17, 1950. See BIS, *Twenty-first Annual Report*, p. 227.

11. See REPTO Circular A–353, to all ECA Missions from OSR (Katz), September 26, 1950, in which the names of the members of the Managing Board, as well as those of the ECA observers on the board, were detailed, copy in ECA Files, FRC, Accession No. 53A–177.

12. The second accounting period was to cover the month of October 1950, and from then on, operations would be effected on a monthly basis.

13. See Memorandum, "Re: First EPU Settlement," dated October 5, 1950, by Robert Triffin, ECA Files, FRC, Accession No. 53A–177.

14. See *Ibid.*

15. See Memorandum, "Signature of Drafts for EPU on Secretary of the Treasury," dated October 10, 1950, by Robert Triffin, ECA Files, FRC, Accession No. 53A–177.

16. See *Ibid.*

17. See *Ibid.*, and also the October 5, 1950, memorandum, cited in footnote 13.

18. The exact figure was $42.647 million of which $40.809 million would be due to France and $1.838 million to Portugal. See REPTO #5545, from OSR to Washington, October 11, 1950, ECA Files, FRC, Accession No. 53A–177.

19. This suggestion had actually been made earlier by Robert Triffin, in his October 5, 1950, memorandum, *op. cit.*

20. TOREP #8832, from ECA/W (Foster) to OSR, October 13, 1950, ECA Files, FRC, Accession No. 53A–177.

21. TOREP #8842, from ECA/W (Foster) to OSR, October 14, 1950, ECA Files, FRC, Accession No. 53A–177.

22. *Ibid.* (italics added). Note, however, that *notification* of needed funds is not the same as direct drawing.

23. REPTO #5656, from OSR (C. T. Wood) to Washington, October 16, 1950 (9:00 P.M. Paris time), ECA Files, FRC, Accession No. 53A–177.

24. *Ibid.*

25. See BIS, *Twenty-first Annual Report*, p. 232. Yet interestingly enough, neither the BIS nor the Managing Board, in its *First Annual Report*, mentioned the actual date on which the first settlement was finally effected. My own guess is that it was not before October 18, 1950, since the allotments of initial balances to Belgium and Sweden were not specified until October 17. See note 10.

26. See REPTO #387, from OSR (Wood) to ECA/W (for Bissell), January 24, 1951, ECA Files, FRC, Accession No. 53A–177.

27. See, for example, REPTO #6878, from OSR (Katz) to Secretary of State, December 16, 1950, ECA Files, FRC, Accession No. 53A–177.

28. See REPTO #387, *op. cit.*

29. See TOREP #1682, from ECA/W (Bissell) to OSR (for Katz), March 12, 1951, ECA Files, FRC, Accession No. 53A–177.

30. See *Ibid.*

31. See *Ibid.*

32. See TOREP #3809, from ECA/W (Foster) to OSR, June 6, 1951; also TOREP A–1717, from ECA/W (Foster) to OSR, July 20, 1951, ECA Files, FRC, Accession No. 53A–177. The sum involved was $307.353 million.

33. See TOREP A–1717, *op. cit.*

34. During the first year of operations, EPU's liquid resources reached their highest level ($448 million) after the November 1950 settlement; they stood at $352 million, or $2 million more than at the beginning, after the June 1951 settlement. See BIS, *Twenty-second Annual Report*, p. 241.

35. See *Ibid.*, p. 244.

36. See BIS, *Twenty-first Annual Report*, p. 226.

37. For the actual amounts of credits granted and received by the EPU during its first year of operations, see BIS, *Twenty-second Annual Report*, p. 241.

38. See REPTO #3420, from OSR (Katz) to Secretary of State, July 17, 1951, ECA Files, FRC, Accession No. 53A–177.

39. TOREP #5118, from ECA/W (Foster) to OSR, July 19, 1951, ECA Files, FRC, Accession No. 53A–177.

40. See *Ibid.*

41. See BIS, *Twenty-second Annual Report*, p. 244. It might be noted that ECA's calculations proved quite accurate. During the second half of 1951, the EPU's interest account showed a profit of $630,000, which all but offset the previous losses.

42. The specific instructions are described by Horsefield, *op. cit.*, pp. 289–90. The IMF Board itself described the supposed contributions of its staff mission as follows: "During the formative stages of the European Payments Union, the Fund took part in the formal and informal discussions held among the participating countries of the OEEC in Paris." See IMF, *Annual Report 1951*, p. 70.

43. TOREP #6919, from ECA/W (Foster) to OSR, August 14, 1950, ECA Files, FRC, Accession No. 53A–177.

44. REPTO #4755, from OSR (C. T. Wood) to Secretary of State, August 25, 1950, ECA Files, FRC, Accession No. 53A–177.

45. On the supposed assumption that constant observation would, in fact, entail some measure of control over EPU's operations and would reduce the risk that the EPU would usurp the Fund's functions. See Diebold, *op. cit.*, pp. 410–12, for some interesting observations on this point.

46. See Horsefield, *op. cit.*, p. 290.

47. OEEC Document c(50) 190 (Final), *op. cit.*, par. 82.

48. *Ibid.* According to Robert Triffin, this paragraph was inserted into the July 7 document at the expressed request of the IMF. See his *Europe and the Money Muddle* (New Haven: Yale University Press, 1957), p. 136.

49. See TOREP #2498, from ECA/W (Foster) to OSR, April 17, 1951, ECA Files, FRC, Accession No. 53A–177.

50. *Ibid.*

51. See Memorandum, "Re: Relations between IMF and EPU. Private Conversation with Mladek and Bertrand," May 11, 1951, by Robert Triffin, ECA Files, FRC, Accession No. 53A–177.

52. See *Ibid.*

53. See Memorandum, "Possible Outline of IMF-EPU Cooperation," May 11, 1951, by Robert Triffin, ECA Files, FRC, Accession No. 53A–177 (italics added).

54. See *Ibid*.

55. Such instances might involve consultation on matters of exchange-rate adjustments, exchange controls, or the sale, by the IMF, of one EPU currency against the other. See *Ibid*.

56. See REPTO #3004, from OSR to Washington, June 25, 1951, ECA Files, FRC, Accession No. 53A–177.

57. IMF, *Annual Report 1951*, p. 71.

58. IMF, *Annual Report 1952*, p. 81.

59. IMF, *Annual Report 1953*, p. 89.

60. IMF, *Annual Report 1954*, p. 125.

61. See Chapter 8.

62. Horsefield, *op. cit.*, p. 362 (italics added).

63. *Ibid*.

64. It should be noted that the request was for $50 million *in addition* to Belgium's regular gold tranche position in the IMF.

65. IMF, *Annual Report 1952*, p. 44.

66. Horsefield, *op. cit.*, p. 329.

67. *Ibid*., p. 330.

68. See *Ibid*., p. 351.

69. See *Ibid*., p. 352.

70. See OEEC, *European Payments Union, Final Report of the Managing Board* (Paris, 1959), p. 25.

71. For details, see OEEC, *European Payments Union, First Annual Report of the Managing Board* (Paris, 1951), pp. 24–26.

72. By March 1951, Britain's net cumulative surplus position with the EPU was $633.9 million, while France's net cumulative surplus was $271.3 million, which in both cases represented more than half of the respective quotas. See BIS, *Twenty-first Annual Report*, p. 231.

73. Specifically, the arrangement was designed to cover Germany's deficit with the EPU up to a total of $180 million in excess of the German quota, as follows: $60 million in gold payments by Germany and $120 million by the special line of credit.

74. See Diebold, *op. cit.*, pp. 114–16.

75. See Triffin, *Europe and the Money Muddle, op. cit.*, p. 182.

76. See *Ibid*.; also Diebold, *op. cit.*, p.123.

77. The decision to increase the German quota was actually reached by the Managing Board in mid-June, after some opposition from France. See REPTO #3004, *op. cit.*, in which Triffin reported on that particular meeting of the Managing Board.

78. Belgium's quota had actually been exceeded as early as August 1951. See OEEC, *European Payments Union, Second Annual Report of the Managing Board* (Paris, 1952), p. 31.

79. See *Report of the Managing Board of the European Payments Union on the Operation of the Union after 30th June 1952* (Paris: OEEC, 1952).

80. See Gardner Patterson and John M. Gunn, Jr., *Survey of United States*

International Finance 1952 (Princeton: Princeton University Press, 1953), pp. 246–47. However, during 1951–1952, the United States provided $109 million directly to the EPU, under the "Special Resources" procedure, to cover deficits of Austria, Greece, Iceland, and Turkey. See BIS, *Twenty-second Annual Report*, p. 227.

81. EPU's liquid resources reached their highest level—$544 million—after the June 1954 settlement; they stood at $404 million at the time of EPU's termination in December 1958. For additional data on this point, see BIS, *Twenty-ninth Annual Report*, p. 209.

82. These countries were: Belgium, Italy, Portugal, and Switzerland.

83. Previous arrangements for settlement of postquota surpluses had been made with Belgium, Italy, and Portugal. For details, see OEEC, *European Payments Union, Second Annual Report of the Managing Board, op. cit.*, pp. 43–46.

84. *Ibid.*, p. 48.

85. *Ibid.*

86. See BIS, *Twenty-fourth Annual Report*, p. 212.

87. See *Ibid.*, p. 211. By June 1954, these percentages were 76 percent and 60 percent respectively. See Triffin, *Europe and the Money Muddle, op. cit.*, p. 194.

88. For details, see BIS, *Twenty-fifth Annual Report*, pp. 173–74.

89. See *Ibid.*, pp. 176–77, for specific provisions.

90. See *European Payments Union, Final Report of the Managing Board, op. cit.*, p. 24.

91. See *Ibid.*, p. 24.

92. This particular provision took the form of a "termination clause" inserted into the EPU agreement.

93. For details, see BIS, *Twenty-sixth Annual Report*, pp. 211–14; also Triffin, *op. cit.*, pp. 220–29.

94. See Triffin, *op. cit.*, pp. 212–16; also Randall Hinshaw, *Toward European Convertibility*, Essays in International Finance No. 31 (Princeton: Princeton University Press, November 1958), pp. 22–26.

95. Particularly France and Italy.

96. Although, as noted earlier, additional bilateral repayment and amortization agreements were concluded at the time of the 1956 renewal.

97. They were: Belgium and Luxemburg, France, Germany, Italy, the Netherlands, and the United Kingdom.

98. For details, see *European Payments Union, Final Report of the Managing Board, op. cit.*, pp. 53–62; also BIS, *Twenty-ninth Annual Report*, pp. 216–20.

99. Since the BIS was designated as the agent for the EMA, the details of the latter's operations may be found in the annual reports of the BIS, beginning with the *Twenty-ninth Annual Report*.

100. Finland, though not a member of OEEC, also made its currency convertible for nonresidents at that time.

101. Such an assertion was, in fact, made by Robert Triffin when summarizing EPU's first year. See "Summary of Robert Triffin's Statement on the First Year of EPU," August 2, 1951, ECA Files, FRC, Accession No. 53A–117. Interestingly enough, this particular assertion was eliminated from the revised memorandum on the subject, which was subsequently sent to Washington. See

REPTO #4008, from OSR to Secretary of State (for Ambassador Wood), August 14, 1951, ECA Files, FRC, Accession No. 53A–117.

102. See REPTO #4008, *op. cit.*

103. See *Ibid.*, p. 2.

104. See *European Payments Union, Final Report of the Managing Board, op. cit.*, p. 19, and Table II of Annex.

105. *Ibid.*, p. 39. EPU credits accounted for only 6 percent of the cover of the total bilateral positions, the bulk of which (70 percent) was settled through the multilateral compensations.

106. *Ibid.*, p. 40. The bulk of these outstanding debts was repaid during the first two and a half years of EPU's operations. Interestingly enough, the evidence suggests that ECA officials in Paris had been quite concerned lest excessively fast rates of amortization, negotiated in the bilateral agreements, might impose an undue burden on the newly established EPU. See, in particular, "Amortization Agreements and EPU," dated October 3, 1950, by Robert Triffin, and a memorandum from Thomas Schelling to H. Havlik, dated October 13, 1950, ECA Files, FRC, Accession No. 53A–177.

107. This was part of the July 7 decision, noted in Chapter 10; it came into effect on September 19, 1950, at the same time as the EPU agreement.

108. It may be recalled that the liberalization targets, insisted upon by the ECA, were to be 60 percent at the inception of EPU and 75 percent by the end of 1950. The 75 percent target was subsequently changed, by the OEEC Council, to August 1951. In the beginning of 1955, the Council called on member countries to raise their overall liberalization level to 90 percent in the course of the year. See BIS, *Twenty-sixth Annual Report*, p. 121.

109. See *Ibid.*, p. 123, and BIS, *Twenty-ninth Annual Report*, p. 161. These figures are based on the composition of intra-European imports in the base year 1948, for most OEEC countries. Liberalization levels achieved by the individual countries, as well as commodity-group breakdowns, are given in the same source.

110. Taking as the base 1938 = 100, the volume index of intra-European commodity trade was 79 in 1948 and 95 in 1949. See ECA, *Eleventh Report to Congress*, p. 110.

111. *Ibid.*

112. See ECA, *Thirteenth Report to Congress*, p. 103; also *Mutual Security Program for FY 1953, Basic Data Supplied by the Executive Branch*, p. 64; and Robert Marjolin, "The European Trade and Payments System," *Lloyds Bank Review*, No. 31 (January 1954), p. 2.

113. See OEEC, *Interim Report*, p. 82.

114. By January 1956, some 54 percent of OEEC imports from the United States and Canada had been liberalized; by January 1958, the figure had risen to 64 percent and by January 1959, it stood at 73 percent. See BIS, *Twenty-ninth Annual Report*, p. 161.

115. For other exceptions allowed under the escape clause provisions, see Diebold, *op. cit.*, pp. 172–73.

116. Thus, for example, in 1951 and 1952, Germany, France, and the United Kingdom withdrew previous measures of liberalization. France, which suspended liberalization in March 1952, began to restore it from October 1953

onward, until it reached an 86 percent level. But in June 1957, France again reverted to quantitative restrictions on all imports. See BIS, *Twenty-eighth Annual Report*, p.143.

117. *European Payments Union, Final Report of the Managing Board, op. cit.*, p. 17.

118. *Ibid.*, p. 18.

119. See Chapter 9.

CHAPTER 12

1. For specific examples, see Max Beloff, *The United States and the Unity of Europe* (New York: Vintage Books, 1963), pp. 20–21 and pp. 100–101; also Armin Rappaport, "The United States and European Integration: The First Phase," *Diplomatic History*, Vol. 5, No. 2 (Spring 1981), and Hogan, *op. cit.*

2. Thus, for example, during his testimony before the Senate Foreign Relations Committee on January 22, 1948, Robert Patterson (Chairman of the Executive Committee of the Committee for the Marshall Plan) stated: "One of the most encouraging features of the European Recovery Program is the impetus it should provide toward achieving economic unity of the sixteen nations, with European political unification as the ultimate goal." A copy of this statement is in the Papers of J. Howard McGrath, HST Library. See also a comment by John Foster Dulles, made during a discussion meeting of the Council on Foreign Relations, to the effect that the ERP "should induce [the Europeans] toward unity." Council on Foreign Relations Files, Records of Groups, Vol. XIV, The Marshall Plan, Digest of Discussion of the Third Meeting, February 2, 1948.

3. Among them, Congressman Hale Boggs from Louisiana. See Rappaport, *op. cit.*, p. 128.

4. This memorandum was authored by Messrs. Charles Kindleberger, H. van B. Cleveland and Ben T. Moore. See Beloff, *op. cit.*, pp. 23–24. The memorandum actually contained the term *economic and functional unification of Europe*, but did not define it.

5. See Beloff, p. 38.

6. In fact, the staff of the House Select Committee on Foreign Aid (the Herter Committee) was subsequently credited as being the first to suggest and urge that European integration be made one of the aims of the ERP. See Interview with Theodore Geiger, 1952, Harry B. Price Oral History Interviews, HST Library.

7. See Hadley Arkes, *Bureaucracy, the Marshall Plan and the National Interest, op. cit.*, pp. 136–37. It may be of interest to note, however, that several months earlier, when the Senate Foreign Relations Committee considered the European Interim Aid Act of 1947 (which became PL 389 on December 17, 1947), the issue of American intervention had already come up. On that occasion, Senator Lodge, in his usual blunt way, made the following statement: "I think this whole question of interfering in [Europe's] internal affairs is going to come up all the time, and God knows this Marshall Plan is going to be the biggest damned interference in internal affairs that there has ever been in history. It doesn't do any good to say we are not going to interfere. . . . I don't think we

have to be so sensitive about interfering in the internal affairs of these countries . . . , and almost everybody except a few political leaders will be damned glad to see us interfere!" See U.S. Senate, Committee on Foreign Relations, 80th Cong., lst Sess., *Foreign Relief Aid: 1947. Hearings Held in Executive Session*, 1947, pp. 153–54.

8. 62 Stat. 137, Section 102(a) (italics added).

9. *Ibid.*

10. *Ibid.* The reference to such undertakings was repeated in Section 115(b) of the act.

11. See CEEC, *General Report*, Chapter V.

12. See *Ibid.*, pp. 30–38. More will be said about customs unions in the next chapter.

13. *Ibid.*, pp. 39–40. At that point in time, however, the signatories still resisted the idea of a permanent organization. "The organization," they stated, "will be of a temporary character and will cease to exist when the special aid necessary for the recovery of Europe comes to an end."

14. For a list of these functions, see ECA, *Recovery Progress and U.S. Aid*, p. 91.

15. It might also be noted that the Council's decisions were to be subject to the rule of unanimity, presumably to assure the sovereignty of small, as well as large, countries.

16. As will be seen below, there were to be two sets of aid-distribution recommendations during the first year of the ERP.

17. In fact, when Harriman put the division of aid up to the OEEC, only the Dutch appear to have supported him. See Interview with H. M. Hirschfield, 1952, Harry B. Price Oral History Interviews, HST Library.

18. OEEC, *Interim Report*, p. 110.

19. See Harry B. Price, *The Marshall Plan and Its Meaning, op. cit.*, p. 82; also Richard Mayne, *The Recovery of Europe* (New York: Harper and Row, 1970), p. 118.

20. A detailed step-by-step account of this timetable was reported to ECA/W in TOECA #13, from Paris (Caffery) to Secretary of State (for Hoffman), May 13, 1948, ECA Files, FRC, Accession No. 53A–278.

21. TOECA #88, from Paris (Harriman) to Secretary of State (for Bissell), June 7, 1948; and TOECA #99, from Paris (Caffery) to Secretary of State, June 8, 1948, ECA Files, FRC, Accession No. 53A–278.

22. TOECA #88 (italics added).

23. *Ibid.*

24. TOECA #42, to Secretary of State from Caffery, May 24, 1948. The Greek request was rejected by Hoffman, in ECATO #34, May 27, 1948. Both documents are in ECA Files, FRC, Accession No. 53A–278.

25. See Urgent Memorandum, from A. Muffrey to Hoffman, H. Bruce, Bissell, and Wayne Taylor, May 28, 1948, ECA Files, FRC, Accession No. 53A–405. It may be noted that under the ERP grant-loan classification, drawn up earlier by the NAC, Ireland had been designated as 100-percent loan country.

26. TOECA #187, from Paris (Harriman) to Secretary of State, June 24, 1948, ECA Files, FRC, Accession No. 53A–278.

27. *Ibid.* As reported by Harriman, the same points were raised by Sir Staf-

ford Cripps in London, in conversation with ECA Mission Chief Thomas Finletter.

28. *Ibid*.

29. *Ibid*.

30. ECATO #76, from ECA (Hoffman) to AmEmbassy Paris, June 10, 1948, ECA Files, FRC, Accession No. 53A–278.

31. *Ibid*.

32. *Ibid*. (italics added).

33. International Bank for Reconstruction and Development, *Third Annual Report 1947–48*, p. 21. The loan was approved on August 22, 1947.

34. See *Ibid*.

35. See Memorandum, from Howard Bruce to Hoffman, June 25, 1948, ECA Files, FRC Accession No. 53A–405.

36. *Ibid*.

37. See Export-Import Bank of Washington, *Seventh Semiannual Report to Congress, July-December 1948*, p. 12.

38. OEEC, *Interim Report*, p. 110.

39. ECATO #82, to AmEmbassy Paris, from Hoffman, June 11, 1948, ECA Files, FRC, Accession No. 53A–278.

40. *Ibid*.

41. *Ibid*. (italics added).

42. Whatever the implication, the fact is that in mid-June, ECA/W raised the suggestion of sending to Paris a small group of technical experts to assist the OEEC during the preparation of the annual program. The suggestion was warmly embraced by ECA/Paris five days later. See ECATO #122, to AmEmbassy Paris, from Hoffman, June 17, 1948; and TOECA #171, from Caffery to Secretary of State, June 22, 1948, ECA Files, FRC, Accession No. 53A–278.

43. According to the OEEC, this was done on July 4, 1948. See OEEC, *Report to the Economic Co-operation Administration on the First Annual Programme, op. cit.*, p. 26. Actually, however, the message containing the tentative aid figure was ECATO #171, dated June 21, 1948, in which OSR was instructed to communicate the information to the OEEC.

44. The Europeans had asked for nearly $6 billion; the Economic Co-operation Act of 1948 authorized a total of $5.3 billion ($4.3 billion to be appropriated and $1 billion authorized for loans), which the Europeans had assumed would be available during the first year.

45. Richard Mayne, *op. cit.*, p. 118.

46. For details, see OEEC, *Report on the First Annual Programme, op. cit.*, p. 26.

47. Quoted in Mayne, *op. cit.*, p. 119.

48. See Chapter 9.

49. OEEC, *Report on the First Annual Programme, op. cit.*, p. 28; also OEEC, *Interim Report*, p. 111.

50. These are listed in OEEC, *Report on the First Annual Programme, op. cit.*, p. 7.

51. *Ibid*.

52. While the ECA may have been unwilling to admit this at the time, other

observers did not feel constrained in expressing their own reactions. Commenting on OEEC's efforts to draw up a long-range four-year program, which he had been invited to observe, John H. Williams called particular attention to the great deal of "confusion prevailing in Paris." See his remarks of December 9, 1948, "The Marshall Plan: Long-Term Program as Seen from Paris," in Council on Foreign Relations Files, Records of Meetings, Vol. IX.

53. For the apparent rationale behind this move, see Brown and Opie, *op. cit.*, pp. 200–201.

54. For a list of these principles and suggested measures by which they could be followed, see OEEC, *Plan of Action for 1949–50* (Paris, 1949); also ECA, *Fourth Report to Congress*, pp. 23–25.

55. The 1949 authorization act was signed into law (P.L. 47, 81st Congress) on April 19, 1949.

56. *Ibid.*, Section 102(a) (italics added).

57. It might be noted, in passing, that Senator Fulbright once again tried, unsuccessfully, to attach the adjective *political* to the word *unification*.

58. This may be partly explained by the attitude of the State Department. Thus, during the House-Senate Conference on the 1950 authorization act, when Congressman Vorys pressed for the inclusion of "encouragement of political federation in Europe," Acting Secretary of State James Webb sent an urgent cable to Acheson, who was in London at the time. In it, Webb suggested that it would be most helpful if Acheson cabled his views on this issue, to which Acheson replied the next day, urging that the conference committee oppose the inclusion of this provision in the act. See *FRUS 1950*, Vol. III, p. 654, for this exchange of cables.

59. See "First Draft of Long Range Proposals," by T. Geiger, *op. cit.*

60. See "The Problem of Convertibility and a Free Trade Area in Western Europe," by H. van B. Cleveland, *op. cit.*

61. This was first mentioned publicly by the ECA in its *Sixth Report to Congress*, p. 23 (a report covering the quarter ending September 30, 1949); it was reiterated in ECA, *Seventh Report to Congress*, p. 15.

62. Yet, as noted earlier, some ECA staff members argued that the ultimate objective should be the "creation of an economic *and* political federation covering the whole of western Europe." See "The Economic Integration of Western Europe," dated October 15, 1949, *op. cit.*

63. See Memorandum by Assistant Secretary of State for European Affairs (Perkins) to the Secretary of State, September 9, 1949, in *FRUS 1949*, Vol. IV, pp. 421–23.

64. *Ibid.*, p. 421.

65. As opposed to an office holder who would cease to represent his country on the OEEC Council if his own political party would be turned out of the government at home.

66. See Secretary of State to Embassy in France, July 29, 1949 in *FRUS 1949*, Vol. IV, p. 409.

67. See Chargé in Belgium (Millard) to Secretary of State, July 31, 1949, in *FRUS 1949*, Vol. IV, pp. 415–16.

68. See Ambassador in France to Secretary of State (for Secretary, Webb, and Hoffman) from Perkins, October 22, 1949, in *FRUS 1949*, Vol. IV, p. 343.

69. See Secretary of State to Embassy in United Kingdom (for Holmes), October 14, 1949, in *FRUS 1949*, Vol. IV, p, 430.

70. See Ambassador in United Kingdom (Douglas) to Secretary of State, October 18, 1949, in *FRUS 1949*, Vol. IV, pp. 430–31.

71. *Ibid.*, p. 431 (italics added).

72. *Ibid.*

73. See from: Washington, to: Paris (for Perkins), October 19, 1949, ECA Files, FRC, Accession No. 53A–177.

74. See Personal Message to Secretary of State from Mr. Bevin, October 25, 1949, in *FRUS 1949*, Vol. IV, p. 348.

75. *Ibid.*

76. See Secretary of State to Embassy in United Kingdom, October 28, 1949, in *FRUS 1949*, Vol. IV, p. 349.

77. See Ambassador in United Kingdom (Douglas) to Secretary of State, October 26, 1949, in *FRUS 1949*, Vol. IV, p. 436.

78. See U.S. Special Representative in Europe to Secretary of State (for the Secretary and Hoffman) from Harriman, November 6, 1949, in *FRUS 1949*, Vol. IV, pp. 440–43.

79. *Ibid.*, p. 442 (italics added).

80. *Ibid.*

81. A brief account of this meeting, which dealt primarily with questions relating to Germany, is given in *FRUS 1949*, Vol. IV, pp. 447–48.

82. See *Ibid.*, p. 447.

83. The text of this message is contained in Secretary of State to Ambassador in United Kingdom, November 16, 1949, in *FRUS 1949*, Vol. IV, pp. 448–50.

84. See *Ibid.*, pp. 449–50.

85. See Ambassador in United Kingdom (Douglas) to Secretary of State, November 23, 1949, in *FRUS 1949*, Vol. IV, p. 452.

86. See U.S. Special Representative in Europe to Secretary of State (for the Secretary and Perkins, personal for Hoffman) from Harriman, November 29, 1949, in *FRUS 1949*, Vol. IV, pp. 453–54.

87. See Ambassador in Belgium (Murphy) to Secretary of State, December 2, 1949, in *FRUS 1949*, Vol. IV, pp. 455–56.

88. See Secretary of State to Certain Diplomatic Representatives, December 13, 1949, in *FRUS 1949*, Vol. IV, p. 459.

89. See Katz to Hoffman and Foster, December 21, 1949, in *FRUS 1949*, Vol. IV, p. 464.

90. See *Ibid.*

91. See *Ibid.*, pp. 466–67. The text of the working paper was communicated to Washington in REPTO #8111, December 22, 1949, and to ECA mission chiefs in REPTO Circular #428. Both documents are in ECA Files, FRC, Accession No. 53A–278.

92. See Ambassador in Belgium (Murphy) to U.S. Special Representative in Europe, January 5, 1950, in *FRUS 1950*, Vol. III, pp. 611–12. In reporting this development, Murphy opined that the approach to Stikker was probably made at the suggestion of the United Kingdom.

93. In fact, toward the middle of January, Harriman, purportedly on the

advice of Foreign Minister Schuman, suggested to Washington that pressure be applied on Portugal to drop its opposition to Spaak's candidacy. See U.S. Special Representative in Europe to Secretary of State, January 12, 1950, in *FRUS 1950*. Vol. III, pp. 612–13.

94. See Secretary of State to U.S. Special Representative in Europe, January 24, 1950, in *FRUS 1950*, Vol. III, p. 616.

95. One such occasion was a speech given by Spaak at the University of Pennsylvania, on January 14, 1950, in which he was quite critical of Britain's attitudes toward European unity. The speech was published by two British newspapers—the *Daily Telegraph* and *Morning Press*—on January 17, 1950, and drew severe criticism from the United Kingdom.

96. See Editor Note, in *FRUS 1950*, Vol. III, pp. 645–46.

97. See Council on Foreign Relations, Study Group on Aid to Europe, Digest of Eleventh Meeting, December 20, 1949, in Council on Foreign Relations Files, Records of Groups, Vol. XVIII-A.

98. Thus, for example, in late June 1950, President Truman, undoubtedly at the urging of the State Department, signed an executive order designating the OEEC as a Public International Organization, entitled to the privileges, exemptions, and immunities conferred by the International Organizations Immunities Act. See OF426K, Box 1280, Folder 3, HST Library.

99. The full text of the speech appeared in the *New York Times*, July 4, 1951. The quotes here come from C. L. Sulzberger's *A Long Row of Candles* (New York: The Macmillan Company, 1969), p. 653. According to Sulzberger, the final draft of the speech was being prepared on the afternoon of July 2 and was submitted to the State Department. See *Ibid.*, p. 652.

100. See *New York Times*, January 23, 1952.

101. Mutual Security Act of 1951, Section 101(a).

102. This quote comes from "Our New Job," A Personal Message to All ECA Employees in Europe, From the Acting U.S. Special Representative; copy in Cecilia Martin Collection, Book 10, George C. Marshall Library.

103. See "European Integration," a policy paper (undated) drafted by Thomas K. Hodges of the MSA Employment Information Program; copy in Cecilia Martin Collection, Book 10, George C. Marshall Library.

104. *Ibid.* (italics added).

105. *Ibid.*

106. It may nevertheless be noted that the Mutual Security Agency, as well as a private group called the American Committee on United Europe, did finance, through subscriptions, the journal of the European Movement. See Beloff, *op. cit.*, p. 104.

107. See U.S. Senate, Committee on Foreign Relations, 82d Cong., 2d Sess., *Mutual Security Act of 1952. Hearings on a Bill to Amend the Mutual Security Act of 1951. . .*, 1952, p. 99.

108. Mutual Security Act of 1952, Section 2(b).

109. *New York Times*, July 24, 1952.

110. *Ibid.*, July 11, 1952.

CHAPTER 13

1. François Perroux, *L'Europe sans Rivages* (Paris: Presses Universitaires de France, 1954), p. 419.

2. In fact, Britain and the Scandinavian countries continued to remain aloof to any serious attempt to federate, or integrate, Europe; and the hopes pinned by the Americans on the formation of a European Defense Community (EDC) were dashed when the French National Assembly rejected the EDC treaty in late August 1954.

3. See Chapter 10, footnote 5.

4. This memorandum is cited in Chapter 2, footnote 24.

5. *Ibid.* (italics added).

6. Quoted in Beloff, *op. cit.*, p. 33. The document itself, "Certain Aspects of the European Recovery Program from the United States Standpoint," is referred to, without being reproduced, in *FRUS 1947*, Vol. III, pp. 337–38. Its location in the State Department Archives is given as Lot 64 D 563, Box 1 (20027), Envelope "Foreign Assistance 1947–50."

7. See Mayne, *op. cit.*, p. 124.

8. See Diebold, *Trade and Payments in Western Europe, op. cit.*, p. 354.

9. More on the Benelux, as well as the Franco-Italian customs union proposal, below.

10. *Preferential tariff areas* typically refer to arrangements whereby a number of countries accord each other selective tariff concessions. That is, import duties are reduced—though not necessarily eliminated—on certain commodities. Needless to say, such concessions apply only within the group and are not shared with outside countries. Hence, preferential tariff arrangements have been considered discriminatory practices in international trade.

11. See Diebold, *op. cit.*, p. 230 and p. 304.

12. The origins of the ITO go back to a set of *Proposals for Expansion of World Trade and Employment*, formulated by a group of experts within the U.S. government and published in late November 1945. The *Proposals* called for an International Conference on Trade and Employment, under United Nations sponsorship, to consider specific measures for trade liberalization. A Preparatory Committee, consisting of nineteen U.N. members (six of whom later became CEEC countries), was appointed in February 1946. Its first session was held in London in the fall of 1946, during which time a draft charter for an International Trade Organization was prepared (hereafter referred to as the London Draft). The second session of the Preparatory Committee met in Geneva from April 10 to August 22, 1947, and drew up the draft that was presented to the U.N. Conference on Trade and Employment held in Havana, Cuba, from November 21, 1947, to March 24, 1948. As can be seen, the second session of the Preparatory Committee overlapped the CEEC conference in Paris.

13. See Article 14 of the London Draft; also Article 16 of the Havana Charter (the final draft).

14. Article 38 of the London draft.

15. See for Secretary and Lovett from Clayton, July 24, 1947, in *FRUS 1947*, Vol. III, pp. 340–41.

16. Article 42(b) of the draft charter prepared in Geneva (italics added).

17. Turkey was the only CEEC country that did not sign the Havana Charter. For an interesting commentary on the demise of the International Trade Organization, see William Diebold, *The End of ITO*, Essays in International Finance No. 16 (Princeton: Princeton University Press, October 1952).

18. General Agreement on Tariffs and Trade, Article XXIV, para. 5. Actually, the exception applied to the formation of free-trade areas was also contained in the Havana Charter, Article 44.

19. CEEC, *General Report*, p. 33.

20. Such declarations were made by the Scandinavian countries, by France and Italy, and by Greece and Turkey. See *Ibid.*, pp. 34–35, and p. 37.

21. *Ibid.*, p. 34.

22. *Ibid.*

23. *Ibid.*, p. 35.

24. European Customs Union Study Group, *First Report* (Brussels, March 1948), p. 91.

25. Such matters, of course, are quite related to the formation of customs unions.

26. See Diebold, *Trade and Patments in Western Europe, op. cit.*, pp. 317–18.

27. See *Ibid.*, p. 378.

28. See Gardner Patterson, *Survey of United States International Finance 1949* (Princeton: Princeton University Press, 1950), pp. 145–46. It may be recalled that around the same time, the OEEC called for removal of quantitative restrictions on 50 percent of private intra-OEEC trade.

29. A fairly detailed account of the early difficulties of Benelux may be found in Diebold, *Trade and Payments in Western Europe, op. cit.*, Chapter 18. See also A. Valentine, "Benelux: A Pilot Plant of European Union," *Yale Review*, Autumn 1954; J. E. Meade, "Benelux: The Formulation of the Common Customs," *Economica*, XXIII (1956); and J. E. Meade, "The Building of Benelux," *The Banker*, CVI (1956).

30. It has been suggested that even the Benelux customs union might not have materialized, had not the countries involved decided much earlier to commit themselves irrevocably to its pursuit. See Hans Schmitt, *The Path to European Union* (Baton Rouge: Louisiana State University Press, 1962), p. 29.

31. See Chapters 10 and 11 for these provisions.

32. The proposal was presented to the OEEC during the second week of June 1950. Its text is contained in OEEC, "Plan d'Action pour l'Integration Economique de l'Europe, Memorandum de la Delegation des Pays-Bas," OEEC Document C(50) 1950 (Paris, 1950). The text of the proposal was distributed in the United States by the Netherlands Information Bureau, under the title "The Netherlands Governments' Plan of Action for European Integration," dated June 14, 1950.

33. The rationale behind this proposal rested on the French argument that smaller percentage reductions in quotas on the same products, for all countries, would be preferable to larger percentage reductions on different products, for each country. See Brown and Opie, *op. cit.*, p. 296.

34. See ECA, *Tenth Report to Congress*, p. 27. Nevertheless, the reference to an "unrestricted" European market suggests that the bank was undoubtedly intended to assist industries whose products were included in the common list.

35. The Pella Plan did indeed recognize this fact and suggested that such consent be sought.

36. The sentence is: "The Italian plan places emphasis upon the preferential reduction of tariff among the member countries of the OEEC." See ECA, *Tenth Report to Congress*, p. 27.

37. See *Ibid.*; also ECA, *Ninth Report to Congress*, p. 33.

38. ECA, *Tenth Report to Congress*, p. 26.

39. ECA, *Eleventh Report to Congress*, p. 31.

40. The United Kingdom had been invited—in fact, strongly urged—to participate in the negotiations and to join the proposed coal-steel organization, but it refused. For a revealing account of French efforts to enlist Britain, and British refusal, see Mayne, *op. cit.*, pp. 180–89.

41. From London, Secretary of State Acheson called the proposal "bold and imaginative." In Washington, Paul Hoffman referred to it as "daring." And in New York, Thoams Dewey, the titular head of the Republican party, declared that the United States had a "solemn duty" to use its influence to hasten the plan's adoption.

42. In his memoires, *Present at the Creation* (New York: W. W. Norton, 1969), pp. 382–83, Acheson is naturally more restrained in recounting this meeting. The quotations here come from "Princeton Seminars," October 10–11, 1953, meeting (Box 69, Reel 3, Track 2, p. 10), Acheson Papers, HST Library.

43. *Ibid.*, p. 12.

44. For an early analysis of the economic prospects of the plan, see K. K. F. Zawadzki, "The Economics of the Schuman Plan," *Oxford Economic Papers*, Vol. 5, No. 2 (June 1953), pp. 157–89.

45. William Parker, "The Schuman Plan—A Preliminary Prediction," *International Organiation*, Vol. 6, (August 1952), p. 381.

46. Michael Shenstone, "The Schuman Plan—A Leap into the Unknown," *International Journal*, Vol. 7, No. 2 (Spring 1952), p. 116.

47. See remarks of Edward S. Mason during a February 20, 1951, meeting of a council on Foreign Relations group, Council on Foreign Relations Files, Records of Meetings, Vol. XI.

48. ECA, *Ninth Report to Congress*, p. 34.

49. ECA, *Thirteenth Report to Congress*, p. 38.

50. And so, supposedly, did American diplomatic representatives in other European capitals, in accordance with joint State-ECA instructions contained in Secretary of State to Certain Diplomatic Offices, June 2, 1950, in *FRUS 1950*, Vol. III, pp. 714–15.

51. See Beloff, *op. cit.*, p. 82.

52. William Diebold, *The Schuman Plan* (New York: Praeger, 1959), p. 557. For official documentation on U.S. activities related to the Schuman Plan negotiations during that period, see *FRUS 1950*, Vol. III, pp. 691–767.

53. In particular, limitations on steel production and on sales of coal and steel.

54. Specifically, during a September 12, 1950, meeting with Ernest Bevin and Robert Schuman in Washington, Acheson formally proposed the creation of German divisions, to be included among the NATO forces. See Mayne, *op. cit.*, p. 194.

55. These comments are attributed by C. L. Sulzberger to French Prime Minister Rene Pleven, during an interview on November 28, 1950. See Sulzberger, *A Long Row of Candles, op. cit.*, pp. 592–93.

56. A case in point was a speech made on October 1, 1950, by Dr. Robert Lehr at a Bavarian foreign trade day, in Munich. Dr. Lehr had been connected with a large German steel concern. But by the time the text of the speech was published, he had become the newly appointed Minister of the Interior for the German Federal Republic and, consequently, the speech began to attract wide attention. For more details, see Schmitt, *op. cit.*, p. 70; and Diebold, *The Schuman Plan, op. cit.*, pp. 70–71.

57. It should be pointed out, in this connection, that the decartelization of German industry had also been a goal of U.S. policy since the beginning of the occupation. With the passage of time, however, this policy had become inactive. In any event, the French insistence on decartelization and deconcentration was based not so much on U.S. attitudes as on a fear of German dominance of the coal-steel pool.

58. See *Survey of United States International Finance 1950, op. cit.*, pp. 263–64; also Diebold, *The Schuman Plan, op. cit.*, pp. 73–74.

59. The classic study of the ECSC in English is, of course, Diebold, *The Schuman Plan, op. cit.* Another excellent account, though with an institutional focus, is contained in Schmitt, *The Path to European Union, op. cit.* The interested reader may also wish to consult the *Treaty Constituting the European Coal and Steel Community*.

60. He was David Bruce, former U.S. Ambassador to France, who was succeeded in 1955 by W. Walton Butterworth.

61. Mutual Security Act of 1952, Section 2(b).

62. As well as with the principle of equal treatment of imports, embodied in the OEEC Code of Trade Liberalization.

63. See Diebold, *The Schuman Plan, op. cit.*, p. 559. It might be noted that a two-thirds majority was required for granting the waiver. And although, in the end, only one country, Czechoslovakia, voted against the waiver, the final vote could not have been taken for granted during the discussion.

64. Thus, it permitted the Benelux countries to withdraw certain concessions previously granted under GATT, by raising certain of their duties on steel products and imposing tariff quotas on steel imports. It also allowed Belgium to use quotas to protect its coal industry during the ECSC transitional period.

65. A similar agreement was concluded with Austria. See Diebold, *The Schuman Plan, op. cit.*, pp. 475–76, for details.

66. See *Ibid.*, p. 326 and p. 559. As it turned out, it was not until two years later, in July 1956, that the High Authority floated its second foreign loan, this time in Switzerland. Borrowings in the American money market took place in 1957 and 1958.

67. U.S. House of Representatives, Committee on Foreign Affairs, 83rd Cong., 2nd Sess., *Hearings on the Mutual Security Act of 1954*, 1954, p. 683.

68. Memorandum, "Reorganization of Western Europe," dated May 14, 1952, by Horst Mendershausen, Foreign Research Division, Federal Reserve Bank of New York (mimeographed), p. 29.

69. See Schmitt, *op. cit.*, pp. 232–33. Once again, Britain was invited to participate in the Spaak Committee work; but although the British government initially responded by sending a representative to attend the committee's meeting, it soon withdrew its participation. See Mayne, *op. cit.*, pp. 247–49.

70. It should be noted that while the EURATOM, like the ECSC, typified the "sector" approach to integration, the EEC treaty provided for the formation of a common market covering all goods and services traded among the participants. Agriculture, however, was to be treated separately.

71. For an early view of these institutions, the reader may wish to consult Emile Benoit, *Europe at Sixes and Sevens: The Common Market, the Free Trade Association, and the United States* (New York: Columbia University Press, 1961).

72. According to Richard Bissell, ". . . There was a clear intention [during the Marshall Plan] to try to bring about some structural changes in Europe." However: "The only structural change which received much attention was related to European unification." See Interview with Richard Bissell, Jr., 1952, Harry B. Price Oral History Interviews, HST Library.

73. Interview with Raymond Aron, 1952, Harry B. Price Oral History Interviews, HST Library.

74. See Interview with Robert Marjolin, 1964, Philip Brooks' ERP Oral History Interviews, HST Library.

CHAPTER 14

1. Charles P. Kindleberger, *Power and Money* (New York: Basic Books, 1970), p. 99.

2. For an account and analysis of the defense assistance programs during the Marshall Plan itself, the reader may wish to consult Lawrence Kaplan, *A Community of Interests: NATO and the Military Assistance Program, 1948–51* (Washington, D.C.: Office of the Secretary of Defense, Historical Office, U.S. Government Printing Office, 1980).

3. See *First Report to Congress on the Mutual Security Program, op. cit.*, p. 56.

4. Computed from data in OEEC, *Europe—The Way Ahead, op. cit.*, p. 112.

5. Thus, for example, it might be noted that in 1948 and 1949, ERP allotments constituted 19.7 percent and 13.2 percent, respectively, of Europe's gross domestic capital formation.

6. Including West Germany, the index of Western Europe's industrial production in 1951 registered an average increase of 35 percent above the prewar level—still in excess of the projected target.

Bibliography

PUBLIC DOCUMENTS

Bank for International Settlements. *Annual Reports*. 18th–29th. Basel: 1948–1959.

Committee of European Economic Cooperation. Vol. I, *General Report*. Paris: September 1947.

———. Vol. II, *Technical Reports*. Paris: September 1947. Export-Import Bank of Washington. *Semiannual Reports to Congress*. 2d, 7th, and 13th. Washington: Government Printing Office, 1946, 1949, 1952.

International Bank for Reconstruction and Development. *Annual Reports*. 2d, 3rd, and 4th. Washington, 1947–1949.

International Monetary Fund. *Annual Reports*. Washington, 1948, 1949, and 1951–1954.

Organization for European Economic Cooperation. *Report to the Economic Cooperation Administration on the First Annual Programme*. Paris: October 1948.

———. *Interim Report on the European Recovery Programme*. Vols. I and II. Paris: December 1948.

———. *Plan of Action for 1949–50*. Paris: March 1949.

———. *European Recovery Program: Second Report of the O.E.E.C.* Paris: February 1950.

———. *Economic Progress and Problems of Western Europe: Third Report of the OEEC*. Paris: June 1951.

———. *Europe—The Way Ahead: Fourth Annual Report of the OEEC*. Paris: December 1952.

———. *Liberalization of Europe's Dollar Trade*. Paris: March 1956.

———. European Payments Union. *Annual Reports of the Managing Board*. 8 Reports. Paris: 1951–1958.

———. *Report of the Managing Board of the European Payments Union on the Operations of the Union after 30th June 1952*. Paris, 1952.

———. *Final Report of the Managing Board of the European Payments Union*. Paris, 1959.

United Nations, Department of Economic and Social Affairs. *Patterns of Industrial Growth 1938–1958*. New York, 1960. U.S. Department of State. *Bulletin*. Vol. 16.

——. *Outline of European Recovery Program*. Washington: Government Printing Office, December 1947.

——. *Foreign Relations of the United States. 1947* (Vol. III), *1948* (Vol. III), *1949* (Vol. IV), *1950* (Vol. III). Washington: Government Printing Office, 1972, 1974, 1975, 1977.

U.S. Economic Cooperation Administration. *A Report on Recovery Progress and United States Aid*. Washington: Government Printing Office, February 1949.

——. *Country Data Book: All Participating Countries*. Washington: March 1950.

——. *Local Currency Counterpart Funds: Midpoint Review*. Washington: April 1950.

——. *Quarterly Reports to Congress*. 13 Reports. Washington: Government Printing Office, 1948–1951.

——. *Recovery Guides*. No. 14. Washington: June 1950.

——. *Report of the ECA-Commerce Mission*. Washington: October 1949.

U.S. House of Representatives, Committee on Foreign Affairs. *Hearings on European Recovery Program*. 80th Cong., 2d Sess., 1948.

——. *Hearings on Extension of European Recovery*. 81st Cong., 1st Sess., 1949.

——. *Hearings on Extension of European Recovery*. 81st Cong., 2d Sess., 1950.

——. *Hearings on Mutual Security Act of 1954*. 83rd Cong., 2d Sess., 1954.

U.S. House of Representatives, Select Committee on Foreign Aid. *Final Report on Foreign Aid*. Report No. 1845. 80th Cong., 2d Sess., 1948.

U.S. House of Representatives, Subcommittee on Appropriations. *Hearings on Foreign Aid Appropriations for 1951*. 81st Cong., 2d Sess., 1950.

U.S. President. *First Report to Congress on the Mutual Security Program*. Washington: Government Printing Office, 1952.

——. *Public Papers of the Presidents: Harry S. Truman, 1947*. Washington: Government Printing Office, 1963.

U.S. President's Committee on Foreign Aid. *Report. European Recovery and American Aid*. Washington: Government Printing Office, November 7, 1947.

U.S. Senate, Committee on Foreign Relations. *Foreign Relief Aid: 1947. Hearings Held in Executive Session*. 80th Congress, 1st Session, 1947.

——. *Hearings on European Recovery Program*. 80th Cong., 2d Sess., 1948.

——. *Hearings Held in Executive Session on European Recovery*. 80th Cong., 2d Sess., 1948.

——. *Report. European Recovery Program*. Report No. 935. 80th Cong., 2d Sess., 1948.

——. *Hearings on Extension of European Recovery*. 81st Cong., 1st Sess., 1949.

——. *Hearings on Extension of European Recovery*. 81st Cong., 2d Sess., 1950.

——. *Hearings on Mutual Security Act*. 82nd Cong., 1st Sess., 1951.

——. *Hearings on a Bill to Amend the Mutual Security Act of 1951*. 82d Cong., 2d Sess., 1952.

U.S. *Statutes at Large*. 80th–82d Cong., Vols. 62–66. *Treaty Constituting the European Coal and Steel Community*.

BOOKS AND PAMPHLETS

Acheson, Dean. *Present at the Creation*. New York: W. W. Norton, 1969.

Arkes, Hadley. *Bureaucracy, the Marshall Plan and the National Interest*. Princeton: Princeton University Press, 1972.

Barabash, J. *The Practice of Unionism*. New York: Harper and Row, 1965.

Beloff, Max. *The United States and the Unity of Europe*. New York: Vintage Books, 1963.

Beugel, Ernst Hans van der. *From Marshall Aid to Atlantic Partnership: European Integration as a Concern of American Foreign Policy*. Amsterdam: Elsevier, 1966.

Brookings Institution. *Administration of United States Aid for a European Recovery Program*. Report to the Committee on Foreign Relations, U.S. Senate. Washington: January 1948.

Brown, William A., and Opie, Redvers. *American Foreign Assistance*. Washington: The Brookings Institution, 1953.

Committee for Economic Development. *An American Program of European Economic Cooperation*. New York: February 1948.

Diebold, William, Jr. *The End of ITO*. Princeton: Princeton University Press, 1952.

———. *The Schuman Plan*. New York: Praeger, 1959.

———. *Trade and Payments in Western Europe*. New York: Harper & Bros., 1952.

Ellis, Howard S. *The Economics of Freedom: The Progress and Future of Aid to Europe*. New York: Harper & Bros., 1950.

Garwood, Ellen C. *Will Clayton: A Short Biography*. Austin: University of Texas Press, 1958.

Gimbel, John. *The Origins of the Marshall Plan*. Stanford: Stanford University Press, 1976.

Harris, Seymour E. *Foreign Aid and Our Economy*. Washington: Public Affairs Institute, 1950.

———. (ed.). *The European Recovery Program*. Cambridge, Mass: Harvard University Press, 1948.

———. *Foreign Economic Policy for the United States*. Cambridge, Mass.: Harvard University Press, 1948.

Hinshaw, Randall. *Toward European Convertibility*. Princeton: Princeton University Press, 1958.

Horsefield, J. Keith. *The International Monetary Fund 1945–1965*. Volume I, *Chronicle*. Washington: International Monetary Fund, 1969.

Jones, Joseph. *The Fifteen Weeks*. New York: The Viking Press, 1955.

Kaplan, Lawrence. *A Community of Interests: NATO and the Military Assistance Program, 1948–1951*. Washington, D.C.: Office of the Secretary of Defense, Historical Office, U.S. Government Printing Office, 1980.

Kennan, George F. *Memoires, 1925–50*. Boston: Little, Brown, and Company, 1967.

Kindleberger, Charles P. *Power and Money*. New York: Basic Books, 1970.

Kolko, Joyce, and Kolko, Gabriel. *The Limits of Power*. New York: Harper and Row, 1972.

Lutz, Frederick A. *The Marshall Plan and European Economic Policy*. Princeton: Princeton University Press, 1948.

Mayer, Herbert C. *German Recovery and the Marshall Plan*. New York: Edition Atlantic Form, 1969.

Mayne, Richard. *The Recovery of Europe*. New York: Harper and Row, 1970.

Meier, Gerald M. (ed.). *International Economic Reform; Collected Papers of Emile Despres*. New York: Oxford University Press, 1973.

Organization for Economic Cooperation and Development. *From the Marshall Plan to Global Interdependence*. Paris, 1978.

Patterson, Gardner. *Survey of United States International Finance, 1949*. Princeton: Princeton University Press, 1950.

Patterson, Gardner, and Behrman, Jack. *Survey of United States International Finance, 1950*. Princeton: Princeton University Press, 1951.

————. *Survey of United States International Finance, 1951*. Princeton: Princeton University Press, 1952.

Patterson, Gardner, and Gunn, John, Jr. *Survey of United States International Finance, 1952*. Princeton: Princeton University Press, 1953.

Perroux, François. *L'Europe sans Rivages*. Paris: Presses Universitaires de France, 1954.

Price, Harry B. *The Marshall Plan and Its Meaning*. Ithaca: Cornell University Press, 1955.

Scammel, W. M. *International Monetary Policy*. 2d ed. London: Macmillan & Co., 1961.

Schmitt, Hans A. *The Path to European Union, from the Marshall Plan to the Common Market*. Baton Rouge: Louisiana State University Press, 1962.

Sulzberger, C. L. *A Long Row of Candles*. New York: The Macmillan Company, 1969.

Triffin, Robert. *Europe and the Money Muddle*. New Haven: Yale University Press, 1957.

Vandenberg, Arthur, Jr. (ed.). *The Private Papers of Senator Vandenberg*. Boston: Houghton Mifflin, 1952.

Wightman, David. *Economic Co-Operation in Europe*. New York: Praeger, 1956.

Windmuller, J. P. *American Labor and the International Labor Movement 1940 to 1953*. Ithaca: Cornell University Press, 1954.

ARTICLES AND PERIODICALS

American Federationist. 1947–1951.

Bean, R. W. "European Multilateral Clearing." *Journal of Political Economy*, Vol. 56, No. 5 (October 1948), pp. 403–15.

Bennett, Jack F. "Europe's Money Game." *Journal of Finance*, Vol. 7, No. 3 (September 1952), pp. 434–46.

Bissell, Richard M. "European Recovery and the Problems Ahead." *American Economic Association, Papers and Proceedings*, Vol. 42 (May 1952), pp. 306–26.

————. "Foreign Aid: What Sort? How Much? How Long?" *Foreign Affairs*, Vol. 31, No. 1 (October 1952), pp. 15–38.

———. "The Impact of Rearmament on the Free World Economy." *Foreign Affairs*, Vol. 29, No. 3 (April 1951), pp. 385–405.

Blaisdell, Thomas, Jr. "The European Recovery Program—Phase Two." *International Organization*, Vol. 2, No. 3 (1948), pp. 443–54.

Clayton, William. "GATT, the Marshall Plan, and OECD." *Political Science Quarterly*, Vol. 78, No. 4 (December 1963), pp. 493–503.

Cromwell, William C. "The Marshall Non-Plan, Congress and the Soviet Union." *Western Political Quarterly*. Vol. 32, No. 4 (December 1979), pp. 422–43.

Diebold, William. "East-West Trade and the Marshall Plan." *Foreign Affairs*, Vol. 26, No. 4 (July 1948), pp. 709–22.

———. "Imponderables of the Schuman Plan." *Foreign Affairs*, Vol. 29, No. 1 (October 1950), pp. 115–29.

Fleming, Marcus J. "Regional Organization of Trade and Payments." *American Economic Association, Papers and Proceedings*, Vol. 42 (May 1952), pp. 345–58.

Galbraith, J. K. "European Recovery: The Longer View." *Review of Politics*, Vol. 12, No. 2 (April 1950), pp. 165–74.

Gomberg, William. "Labor's Participation in the European Productivity Program: A Study in Frustration." *Political Science Quarterly*, Vol. 74, No. 2 (June 1959), pp. 240–55.

Gordon, Lincoln. "ERP in Operation." *Harvard Business Review*, Vol. 27, No. 2 (March 1949), pp. 129–50.

Gurley, John G. "Excess Liquidity and European Monetary Reforms, 1944–1952." *American Economic Review*. Vol. 43, No. 1 (March 1953), pp. 76–100.

Haberler, Gottfried. "Some Economic Problems of the European Recovery Program." *American Economic Review*, Vol. 38, No. 4 (September 1948), pp. 495–525.

Heller, Walter. "The Role of Fiscal-Monetary Policy in German Economic Recovery." *American Economic Association, Papers and Proceedings*, Vol. 40 (May 1950), pp. 531–47.

Hirschman, A. O. "The European Payments Union: Negotiations and Issues." *Review of Economics and Statistics*, Vol. 33, No. 1 (February 1951), pp. 49–55.

Hitchens, Harold L. "Influences on the Congressional Decision to Pass the Marshall Plan." *Western Political Quarterly*, Vol. 21, No. 1 (March 1968), pp. 51–68.

Hoffman, Michael. "European Payments—An American View." *Lloyds Bank Review*, New Series, No. 25 (July 1952), pp. 13–27.

Hogan, Michael. "The Search for a 'Creative Peace': The United States, European Unity, and the Origins of the Marshall Plan." *Diplomatic History*, Vol. 6, No. 3 (Summer 1982), pp. 267–85.

Hoselitz, Bert. "Four Reports on Economic Aid to Europe." *Journal of Political Economy*, Vol. 56, No. 5 (October 1948), pp. 109–23.

Jackson, Scott. "Prologue to the Marshall Plan: The Origins of the American Commitment for a European Recovery Program." *Journal of American History*, Vol. 65, No. 4 (March 1979), pp. 1043–68.

Kahn, R. F. "The European Payments Union." *Economica*, New Series, Vol. 17 (August 1950), pp. 306–16.

———. "A Possible Intra-European Payments Scheme." *Economica*, New Series, Vol. 16 (November 1949), pp. 293–304.

Kindleberger, C. P. "The Marshall Plan and the Cold War." *International Journal*, Vol. 23, No. 3 (1968), pp. 369–82.

Klopstock, Fred H. "Western Europe's Attack on Inflation." *Harvard Business Review*, Vol. 26, No. 5 (September 1948), pp. 597–612.

Maier, Charles S. "The Politics of Productivity: Foundation of American International Economic Policy after World War II." *International Organization*, Vol. 31, No. 4 (Autumn 1977), pp. 607–33.

Mallalieu, William C. "Origins of the Marshall Plan: A Study in Policy Formulation and National Leadership." *Political Science Quarterly*, Vol. 73, No. 4 (December 1958), pp. 481–504.

Marjolin, Robert. "The European Trade and Payment System." *Lloyds Bank Review*, New Series, No. 31 (January 1954) pp. 1–15.

McKesson, John A. "The Schuman Plan." *Political Science Quarterly*, Vol. 67, No. 1 (March 1952), pp. 18–35.

Menderhausen, Horst. "First Tests of the Schuman Plan." *Review of Economics and Statistics*, Vol. 35, No. 4 (November 1953), pp. 269–88.

Mikesell, Raymond. "Regional Multilateral Payments Agreements." *Quarterly Journal of Economics*, Vol. 62, No. 4 (August 1948), pp. 500–518.

Parker, William N. "The Schuman Plan—A Preliminary Prediction." *International Organization*, Vol. 6 (August 1952), pp. 381–95.

Polk, J., and Patterson, G. "The Emerging Pattern of Bilateralism." *Quarterly Journal of Economics*, Vol. 62 (November 1947), pp. 118–42.

Rappaport, Armin. "The United States and European Integration: The First Phase." *Diplomatic History*, Vol. 5, No. 2 (Spring 1981), pp. 121–49.

Shenstone, Michael. "The Schuman Plan—A Leap into the Unknown." *International Journal*, Vol. 7, No. 2 (Spring 1952), pp. 116–26.

Weiler, Peter. "The United States, International Labor, and the Cold War: The Breakup of the World Federation of Trade Unions." *Diplomatic History*, Vol. 5, No. 1 (Winter 1981), pp. 1–22.

Williams, John H. "The Revision of the Intra-European Payments Plan." *Foreign Affairs*, Vol. 28, No. 1 (October 1949), pp. 153–55.

Young, Kimball. "Content Analysis of the Treatment of the Marshall Plan in Certain Representative American Newspapers." *Journal of Social Psychology*, Vol. 33 (May 1951), pp. 163–85.

Zawadzki, K.K.F. "The Economics of the Schuman Plan." *Oxford Economic Papers*, Vol. 5, No. 2 (June 1953), pp. 157–89.

ARCHIVAL MATERIAL AND LIBRARY COLLECTIONS

American Federation of Labor-Congress of Industrial Organization Library. Vertical File—The Marshall Plan.

British Library of Political and Economic Science. London School of Economics and Political Science. Diaries and Papers of Hugh Dalton, 1945–1948 (Folders 32–36).

Catholic University of America. The Mullen Library. Archives and Manuscripts Department, Labor History Collection. Phillip Murray Papers.

Columbia University. Oral History Research Office. Marshall Plan Interview Project. Oral History Collection of Columbia University.

————. Reminiscences of William Clayton. Oral History Collection of Columbia University.

————. Reminiscences of Ernest Gross, Vols. 2 and 3. Oral History Collection of Columbia University.

Columbia University. School of International Affairs. Rare book and Manuscript Library. Herbert H. Lehman Papers.

Council on Foreign Relations Files. Records of Groups, Vols. 14, 16, and 18 (1947–1950).

————. Records of Meetings, Vols. 8-ll (1947–1950). George C. Marshall Library. Cecilia Martin Collection, Book 10.

————. Secretary of State File.

Harry S. Truman Library.

Dean Acheson Papers ("Princeton Seminars," Boxes 67–69).

William Clayton Papers (Alphabetical File, 1948–1949).

Clark Clifford Files and Papers.

George Elsey Papers.

Joseph Jones Papers.

Frederick J. Lawton Papers.

J. Howard McGrath Papers.

Charles Murphy Files.

John Snyder Papers.

Harry S. Truman Papers (President's Secretary's Files).

Official Files (OF) Nos. 246 and 246 I-M.

Office Files of the Assistant Secretary of State for Economic Affairs and Under-Secretary of State for Economic Affairs.

Records of the Committee for the Marshall Plan.

Records of the President's Committee on Foreign Aid.

Phillip Brook's European Recovery Program Oral History Interviews.

Harry B. Price's Oral History Interviews.

U.S. National Archives (Suitland, Md.). Record Group 56. General Records of the Department of Treasury. (Minutes of Meetings of the National Advisory Council on International Monetary and Financial Problems, 1947–1950.)

————. Record Group 286. Records of the Agency for International Development. (Economic Cooperation Administration Files, 1948–1951).

MISCELLANEOUS UNPUBLISHED MATERIALS

Bernstein, Joel. "The Integration of the Sterling Payments System and the Intra-European Payments Arrangements, Embodied in the European Payments Union." Unpublished Ph.D. dissertation (University of Chicago, 1956).

Johnson, James H. "The Marshall Plan: A Case Study in American Foreign

Policy Formulation and Implementation." Unpublished Ph.D. dissertation (University of Oklahoma, 1966).

National Association of Manufacturers. "Statistical and Economic Background to the Marshall Plan." Prepared by the Research Department, National Association of Manufacturers (mimeographed, n.d.).

Private Papers of Harold Seidman. Storrs, Conn.

Index

Acheson, Dean, 4, 27, 32, 34, 170, 218, 219, 220–21, 222, 225, 239, 257 n.7, 291 n.57, 302 n.58, 307 nn.41, 42, 54

Agreements for Intra-European Payments and Compensations (1948–1949 and 1949–1950), 133, 137–53, 156, 157, 195–96. *See also* Conditional aid; Drawing rights

Agricultural production in Europe. *See* European production

Agriculture, U.S. Department of, 259 n.38

Aid, American: Administration's requests for, 25, 51, 64, 66–67; allotments by ECA, 62–63, 64, 68, 249; "conditional," 137–39, 143, 145, 146, 147, 149, 178, 179, 215; congressional authorizations and appropriations of, 51–52, 64, 66, 68, 177; estimated requirements of, 17–18, 62, 66; European country requests for, 62, 66–67; OEEC's division of, 59, 62, 66–68, 210–17

Aldrich, Winthrop W., 30, 32, 262 n.30

All Union Central Council of Trade Unions, Russian, 36

American Committee on United Europe, 304 n.106

American Farm Bureau Federation, 39

American Federation of Labor (AFL), 36, 37, 38, 39

American organized labor: involvement with Marshall Plan, 35–39, 92, 276 n.87; post-World War II international objectives, 36, 39. *See also* American Federation of Labor (AFL); Congress of Industrial Organizations (CIO)

Americans for Democratic Action, 39

Anderson, Clinton, 32, 46, 263 n.36, 267 n.32

Anglo-American Council on Productivity (AACP), 90–91, 276 n.85

Ansiaux, Hubert, 283 n.29, 284 n.54

Aron, Raymond, 248

Austria, 64, 95, 108, 109–10, 116, 140, 146, 178, 188, 247, 258 n.17, 278 n.14, 293 n.7

Balance of payments: and aid allocations, 69; estimated deficits of, 14–17, 138; and expansion of exports, 73; problems of, 76, 123, 144, 194, 254

Bank for International Settlements (BIS), 137, 140, 142, 180–82, 261 n.16, 282 n.17, 294 n.25, 297 n.99

Barkley, Alben, 44, 206
Bean, Robert W., 282 n.21
Belgium, 124, 125, 128, 129, 140, 143, 145, 146, 147, 148, 149, 151, 168, 171, 186, 188, 189, 218, 230, 235, 258 n.17, 277 n.95, 282 nn.8, 9, 287 n.57, 293 nn.95, 5, 294 nn.10, 25, 297 nn.82, 83, 97
Benelux customs union, 230, 232, 235–36, 306 n.30
Benton amendment, 276 n.83
Bevin, Ernest, 11, 12, 170, 171, 219, 220–21, 258 n.14, 291 n.57, 307 n.54
Bidault, Georges, 11, 12
Big Three Conference, Paris (1947), 11–12, 19, 36
Bilateral payments system in Europe, 121–24, 152, 198
Bilateral trade and payments agreements in Europe, 79, 138, 215
Bissell, Richard M., 28, 59–61, 111–13, 114, 145, 163, 169, 172, 173, 180, 270 n.28, 286 n.36, 309 n.72
Blaisdell, Thomas, 164, 173
Boggs, Hale, 299 n.3
Bonesteel, Charles, 20, 260 n.41
Brewster amendment, 45
Bridges, Styles, 53
Britain. See United Kingdom
Brookings Institution, 31
Brown, Irving, 38
Bruce, David K., 104, 105–6, 107, 241, 279 n.42, 308 n.60
Bruce, Howard, 213
Brussels Plan, 128–29, 132
Bullis, Harry, 263 n.35
Bureau of the Budget, 30, 73, 259 n.38
Burgess, W. Randolph, 28, 266 n.1
Burnett, Leo, 263 nn.35, 36
Butterworth, W. Alton, 308 n.60

Caffery, Jefferson, 13, 19, 20–21, 85, 104, 128, 211
Canada, 153, 254, 274 n.61
Carey, James B., 37, 263 n.39, 265 n.68, 266 n.16

Clayton, William, 4, 10, 11, 13, 14, 19, 21, 229, 230, 231, 257 n.7
Cleveland, H. van Buren, 299 n.4
Code of Trade Liberalization, 197, 198, 199, 201, 237
Commerce, U.S. Department of, 42, 77, 259 n.38
Committee for Economic Development (CED), 31, 261 n.13
Committee for the Marshall Plan to Aid European Recovery (CMP): activities of, 33; effectiveness and impact of, 35, 40; objectives of, 33; special relationship with State Department, 33–34
Committee of European Economic Cooperation (CEEC); formation of, 12; participating countries, 258 n.17; report of, 15, 20–22, 23, 47, 54, 57, 70, 71, 78, 99, 125, 207–8, 232, 236, 273 n.40
Conditional aid, 137–39, 143, 145, 146, 147, 149, 178, 179, 215. See also Drawing rights
Congress, U.S.: accommodation of special-interest groups in ERP, 45–47, 82–83, 85–86; appropriation of ERP aid, 51–52, 68, 177; authorization of the ERP, 53, 64, 66, 217; encouragement of European unification, 177, 205, 217, 224–25, 244, 299 n.6; hearings and debates on the ERP, 44–53, 66–68, 206. See also Economic Cooperation Acts; European Recovery Program; Foreign Relations Committee; Herter Committee; Mutual Security Acts
Congress of Industrial Organizations (CIO), 36, 37, 38, 39
Connally, Tom, 53
Convention for European Economic Cooperation, 99, 106, 208–9. See also Organization for European Economic Cooperation (OEEC)
Council of Economic Advisors, 26
Council on Foreign Relations, 100, 223, 266 n.1, 288 n.75, 290 n.44, 299 n.2

Counterpart funds: legislative provisions for, 49–50; utilization of, 86–87, 107–10, 112, 113, 281 n.73

Cripps, Stafford, 148, 219, 222, 276 n.84, 300 n.27

Curran, Joseph, 266 n.16

Currency devaluations of 1949, 152–53

Customs unions in Europe: consideration of, 232–35; proposals for formation of, 229–30, 233–35. *See also* European integration

Czechoslovakia, 79

Dalton, Hugh, 259 n.39

Debt retirement, as means to control inflation and promote internal financial stability, 108–12

Defense-oriented assistance, 68–69, 112, 114, 249

Denmark, 108, 110, 146, 165, 213, 247, 258 n.17, 280 n.50, 281 n.73

DeSelliers, Ernest, 163

Development Assistance Committee (DAC), 254

Development of European economic cooperation. *See* European integration; Organization for European Economic Cooperation (OEEC)

Dewey, Thomas, 307 n.41

Division of aid. *See* Aid, American; Organization for European Economic Cooperation (OEEC)

Douglas, Lewis, 10, 19, 21, 44–45, 50, 219, 220, 221

Drawing rights: bilateral and multilateral, 146, 149; convertibility into dollars, 144–46, 153; distribution of, 140–41, 150; establishment of, 139, 140–41, 148–49, 150–51; system of, 137–38; transferability of, 143–45, 147, 153, 157; utilization of, 140, 151, 196. *See also* Agreements for Intra-European Payments and Compensations; Conditional aid

Dubinsky, David, 37, 265 n.68

Dulles, John Foster, 299 n.2

Eastern Europe, 78–79, 82

East Germany, 79

East-West trade: American official attitudes and policies toward, 77–78, 79; European views on, 78–79; magnitudes of during ERP period, 81–82

Economic Cooperation Act of 1948, 3, 5, 31, 50, 52, 53, 54, 57, 78, 84, 88, 99, 206–7, 208, 250, 253, 288 n.1, 301 n.48

Economic Cooperation Act of 1950, 177, 217, 288 n.1

Economic Cooperation Administration (ECA): allotments of aid by, 62–63, 64, 68, 249; counterpart-funds policies, 86–87, 101, 107–10, 113; debate over form and nature of, 30–31; enforcement of shipping regulations, 82–84; interpretation of congressional mandate for European unification, 155, 217–18; investment policies, 86–88, 113; productivity and technical assistance programs, 90–93; promotion of European economic cooperation, 158, 209–10, 213, 214; promotion of internal financial stability, 100–101; promotion of trade and payments liberalization, 135–36, 144–45, 157, 159, 160–61, 169, 201, 218; screening of aid requests and OEEC's aid recommendations, 61, 65; views on East-West trade, 79

Economic integration, methods and forms of, 227–29. *See also* European integration

Eichelberger, Clark M., 263 n.39

Eisenhower, Dwight, 224

Elsey, George, 29

Emerson, William, 263 n.39

European Atomic Energy Community (EURATOM), 247, 309 n.70

European Coal and Steel Community (ECSC): aims and purposes of, 240; establishment of, 239; negotiations for, 241–43; official U.S. support for, 239, 244–46; organizational

European Coal and Steel (*cont.*)
structure of, 243; significance of, 239–40, 244. *See also* European integration

European Defense Community (EDC), 244, 305 n.2

European Economic Community (EEC), 247, 248, 254

European Free Trade Association (EFTA), 247

European integration: American attitudes and policies toward, 4, 5, 205–6, 217, 223–24, 225–26, 248; approaches to, 229–30, 237–38, 239, 246–47; instruments of, 155–56, 209, 229–30, 244, 248; obstacles to, 219–20, 236–37, 253; progress toward, 235, 246–47. *See also* European Coal and Steel Community (ECSC); European Economic Community (EEC); European Free Trade Association (EFTA); European Payments Union (EPU); Organization for European Economic Cooperation (OEEC)

European Interim Aid Act of 1947, 260 n.1, 278 n.14, 299 n.7

European Monetary Agreement (EMA), 193–94, 195, 297 n.99

European Movement, 225, 304 n.106

European payments arrangements. *See* Agreements for Intra-European Payments and Compensations (1948–1949 and 1949–1950); European Payments Union (EPU); First Agreement on Multilateral Monetary Compensation. *See also* Bilateral payments system in Europe

European Payments Union (EPU), 135, 153, 218, 235, 241, 252; accomplishments of, 195–99; conception and principles of, 155, 159–60; establishment of, 173–75; and European integration, 155–56; initial balances under, 178–79; members' quotas in, 171, 174, 189, 192–93; negotiations for, 166–72; opera-

tions of, 179–81, 196, 298 n.106; problems of, 182–83, 187–89, 190–91; renewals of, 187, 191, 192, 194; settlement terms, 168–71, 174–75, 190, 192; special repayment arrangements, 191; termination of, 194–95; and trade and payments liberalization, 173, 197–98; U.S. financial contributions to, 178–79; views of NAC regarding, 161–65, 172–73

European production: constraints on, 71, 72, 75–90; European-projected targets for, 58, 60, 72, 75, 89, 93, 94, 251; expansion of, 74–75, 93–96, 251–52; indices of, 94, 95. *See also* Productivity, European; Productivity and Technical Assistance Programs

European Recovery Program (ERP): aims of, 5, 54, 250; American public's attitude toward, 26, 40; announcement of by George C. Marshall, 3; bilateral undertakings by aid recipients, 47–48, 49; conceptual origins of, 3–5; congressional authorizations of, 53, 66, 217; declared economic objectives of, 5, 54, 205, 207, 250; "essential elements" of, 19–20, 22, 28; formulation of, 9, 18–19, 26, 27–31; impact of defense considerations on, 68–69, 112, 114, 116; involvement of American labor in, 35–39, 91, 276 n.87; President's special message to Congress, 25, 30; promotion of ERP in the United States, 31–35, 39–40; special-interest-group provisions, 45–47, 82–83, 85–86; successes and failures of, 250–54; termination of, 249

European trade: expansion of, 142, 198, 201, 252; hindrances to expansion of, 121–22, 200; liberalization of, 153, 155, 173, 197–98, 199, 201, 254; proposals for use of ERP aid to finance, 124–25, 128–29, 135–36;

restrictions on, 122, 168, 236, 252; stagnation of, 124

European unification. *See* European integration

Export Control Act of 1949, 78

Export controls, U.S. system of, 77–78

Export-Import Bank, 80, 213, 246

Federal Council of Churches, 40

Federal Reserve Bank of New York, 180, 181, 182

Federal Reserve Board, 77, 164, 172, 290 n.42

Feis, Herbert, 263 n.39

Financial stability. *See* Internal financial stability

Finebel, 234–35

Finland, 297 n.100

Finletter, Thomas, 212, 300 n.27

First Agreement on Multilateral Monetary Compensation, 125–27, 137, 284 n.12

"First category" compensations, 125–26, 127, 137, 140, 151, 160

Foreign Aid Appropriation Act of 1949, 47, 50, 52, 274 n.53

Foreign Aid Appropriation Act of 1951, 155

Foreign Assistance Act of 1948, 53

Foreign Economic Cooperation Trust Fund, 53

Foreign Ministers' Conference, Moscow (1947), 4

Foreign Relations Committee, U.S. Senate, 42, 43, 44, 46, 48, 50, 51, 52, 53, 97, 206, 225, 299 nn.2, 7

Foster, William, 111, 113, 169, 172, 173, 180–81, 184, 293 n.90

France, 10, 64, 84–85, 100, 101–7, 108, 109, 125, 140, 146, 147, 149, 150, 151, 158, 188, 189, 214, 218, 229, 230, 234, 235, 237, 239, 240, 242, 258 n.17, 270 n.18, 275 n.78, 278 nn.14, 17, 280 n.60, 282 n.8, 287 n.58, 294 n.18, 297 n.97, 298 n.116, 306 n.20

Franks, Oliver, 14–15, 22, 231

Fritalux. *See* Finebel

Fulbright, William, 206, 302 n.57

Gannett, Frank, 261 n.6

General Agreement on Tariffs and Trade (GATT), 161, 232, 238, 244–45

General Appropriation Act of 1951, 177

General Most-Favored-Nation (MFN) Treatment principle, 230, 231, 232

George, Walter, 48, 49

Germany. *See* West Germany

Gordon, Lincoln, 270 n.28

Gormley, J. R., 266 n.16

Greece, 4, 64, 93, 95, 108, 139, 140, 146, 148, 149, 150, 151, 178, 188, 258 n.17, 277 n.95, 287 n.55, 293 n.7, 306 n.20

Green, William, 36

Gross, Ernest, 14, 259 n.37

Guaranties for American private investment abroad, 88–89

Guindey, Guillaume, 283 n.29

Gurley, John, 280 n.50

Gutt, Camille, 130

Haberler, Gottfried, 100

Hall-Patch, Edmund, 83, 145, 211, 286 n.35, 288 n.75

Harriman, W. Averell, 22, 27, 32, 85, 100, 104, 148, 171, 211, 212, 218, 220, 221, 222, 272 n.17, 274 n.58, 300 n.27, 303 n.93

Harriman Committee, 16, 17, 22, 27, 30, 33, 259 nn.31, 38

Harris, Seymour E., 262 n.25

Hatch, Carl A., 44, 48, 49

Herter, Christian, 49–50, 263 n.4, 266 n.1

Herter Committee, 30, 299 n.6

Hiss, Alger, 263 n.39

Hoffman, Paul G., 57, 80, 111, 114, 155, 158, 161, 163, 169–70, 213, 218, 220, 221, 229, 276 n.84, 288 n.6, 289 n.14, 307 n.41

Holland. *See* Netherlands
Hoover, Herbert, 29, 34, 261 n.7
Hoselitz, Bert, 262 n.25
House Select Committee on Foreign Aid. *See* Herter Committee
Hungary, 79

Iceland, 65, 188, 258 n.17, 291 n.56
Industrial production in Europe. *See* European production
Industrial Projects Program, 87
Inflation, European: concern about implications of, 99, 114; contributing causes to, 97, 109; efforts to control, 97–98, 114; impact of rearmament programs on, 114, 116, 252; measurements of, 98, 111, 115, 116; persistence of, 107, 111, 114, 116–17, 252–53. *See also* Internal financial stability; Price indices for OEEC countries
Integration. *See* Economic integration, methods and forms of; European Integration
Interior, U.S. Department of, 259 n.38
Internal financial stability: European commitment to create and maintain, 22, 54, 99; investment expenditures versus, 113–14; promotion of through debt retirement, 108–12; as requisite to sound European recovery, 97; use of counterpart funds to promote, 101, 107–10, 112. *See also* Inflation, European
International Bank for Reconstruction and Development (IBRD). *See* World Bank
International Chamber of Commerce, 29
International Confederation of Free Trade Unions (ICFTU), 38
International Monetary Fund (IMF), 102, 125, 128, 129, 130–32, 152, 161, 162–63, 164, 172, 183–87
International Trade Organization (ITO), 230–31, 305 n.12, 306 n.17
International Trade Union Conference on ERP (ERP/ITUC), 38–39

Intra-European Commerce Commission, proposal for, 157–58
Ireland, 64, 65, 68, 211, 258 n.17, 291 n.56, 300 n.25
Italy, 10, 89, 92, 108, 114, 125, 140, 146, 148, 149, 189, 214, 229, 230, 234, 235, 237, 239, 258 n.7, 270 n.18, 275 n.78, 277 n.95, 278 n.14, 297 nn.82, 83, 97, 306 n.20

Jacobsson, Per, 28–29, 261 n.16
Japan, 254
Jones, Joseph, 257 n.5
Joyce, William H., 276 n.84

Katz, Milton, 175, 222, 286 n.36
Kem amendment, 78
Kennan, George F., 20, 260 n.41
Kindleberger, Charles, 249, 299 n.4
Korean War, 68, 112, 114, 116, 252, 253
Krug, Julius, 26, 27
Krug Committee, 26

Labor Advisors in ECA, 276 n.87
LaFollette, Robert, 30
Lehman, Herbert H., 263 n.39
Lehr, Robert, 308 n.56
Local currency counterpart funds. *See* Counterpart funds
Lodge, Henry Cabot, 48, 206, 299 n.7
Loveland, Albert, 164
Lovestone, Jay, 264 n.61, 265 n.68
Lovett, Robert, 20, 21, 22, 23, 69, 260 n.4
Lundenberg, Harry, 266 n.16
Lutz, Friedrich, 29
Luxembourg, 125, 230, 244, 258 n.17, 297 n.97

McCloy, John, 32, 80–81, 212–13, 239, 243, 263 n.37, 264 n.65
McKee, Frederick, 263 n.39
Maritime Commission, 42, 43, 44
Marjolin, Robert, 85, 175, 274 n.58, 288 n.75, 293 n.96
Marshall, George C., 3, 4, 5, 13, 20, 21, 23, 32, 35, 43, 128, 229, 257 n.7, 260 nn.41, 4, 263 n.37

Marshall Plan. *See* European Recovery Program (ERP)

Martin, William McC., 164, 172

Mason, Edward, 100, 307 n.47

Merchant, Livingston, 246

Millikin, Eugene, 52–53

Molotov, V. M., 11, 12

Monnet, Jean, 239, 241, 280 n.45

Monnet Plan, 109

Moore, Ben T., 299 n.4

Moore, Hugh, 263 n.39

Mullen, Robert, 92–93, 277 n.96

Murphy, Robert, 19, 221, 303 n.92

Murray, Phillip, 37, 266 n.16

Mutual Defense Assistance Act of 1949, 68

Mutual Defense Assistance Control Act of 1951, 78

Mutual Defense Assistance Program (MDAP), 68

Mutual Security Act of 1951, 224, 276 n.83

Mutual Security Act of 1952, 225, 244, 276 n.83

Mutual Security Agency (MSA), 185, 224–25, 304 n.106

Mutual Security Program (MSP), 90, 91, 185, 224, 225, 248

National Advisory Council on International Financial and Monetary Problems (NAC), 50, 80, 86, 87, 102, 112, 132, 135, 136, 153, 161–65, 172–73, 183, 184, 185, 199, 268 n.59, 269 n.15, 283 n.35

National Association of Manufacturers (NAM), 28

National Grange, 39–40

National Lawyers Guild, 261 n.13

National League of Women Voters, 40

National Planning Association (NPA), 30, 261 n.13

Navy, U.S. Department of, 42, 259 n.38

Netherlands, 125, 140, 146, 147, 149, 151, 158, 187–89, 214, 230, 234, 235, 237, 258 n.17, 270 n.18, 275 n.78, 287 n.58, 291 n.56, 297 n.97

Nitze, Paul, 14, 19

North Atlantic Treaty Organization (NATO), 68, 242, 244

Norway, 108–9, 111, 140, 146, 149, 165, 178, 247, 258 n.17, 280 n.50, 281 n.73, 291 n.56, 293 n.6

Nourse, Edwin, 26, 27

Office of Special U.S. Representative in Europe (OSR), 69, 113, 114, 152, 161, 170, 171, 173–74, 180–81, 183, 184–85, 212, 213–14, 225

Offshore procurements: authorization of, 127; consideration of, 136

Organization for Economic Cooperation and Development (OECD), 254

Organization for European Economic Cooperation (OEEC): convention of, 99, 106, 208–9; division of American aid by, 59, 62, 66–68, 210–17; establishment of, 208–9; membership in, 208; nature and structure, 208–9; organization and designated functions, 208–9; programming activities of, 59, 71–72, 210–17; role in promoting European economic cooperation, 165, 208, 216; role in trade and payments liberalization, 158, 171, 200–201; transformation into OECD, 254; U.S. attempts to strengthen authority of, 218–23

Overby, Andrew, 131, 132

Page, Arthur, 263 n.39

Patterson, Robert, 32, 37, 263 n.39, 299 n.2

Pella, Giuseppe, 238

Pella Plan, 238, 307 n.35

Perkins, George, 290 n.44

Perroux, François, 227, 229

Petsche, Maurice, 105, 148

Petsche Plan, 237–38, 239

Playfair, Edward, 283 n.29

Pleven, René, 308 n.55

Poland, 79, 80, 273 nn.37, 40

Policy Planning Staff (PPS), 4, 229, 258 n.20

Porter, Paul, 224

Portugal, 114, 137, 146, 188, 189, 222, 247, 258 n.17, 287 n.55, 294 n.18, 297 nn. 82, 83, 303 n.93
President's Commission on Foreign Aid. *See* Harriman Committee
Price, Harry B., 257 n.6
Price indices for OEEC countries, 98, 111, 115, 116
Procurement of surplus agricultural commodities, 46–47, 84–85
Productivity, European: levels of, 89–90; need for increase in, 89, 90; rise of, 93, 277 n.102
Productivity and Technical Assistance Programs, 90–93. *See also* Economic Cooperation Administration (ECA); Productivity, European
Public Advisory Board, 50, 51

Quantitative restrictions on trade. *See* European trade
Queuille, Henri, 105, 279 n.42
Quinn, John T., 92

Railway Labor Executives Association (RLEA), 38
Rasminsky, Louis, 131
Read, Harry, 265 n.68
Rearmament. *See* Defense-oriented assistance
Reconstruction Finance Corporation (RFC), 64
Reed, Philip, 263 n.39
Roll, Eric, 288 n.75
Rooth, Ivar, 186
Russia. *See* Soviet Union

Saillant, Louis, 37
Schuman, Robert, 218, 219, 220, 222, 239, 240, 303 n.93, 307 n.54
Schuman Plan. *See* European Coal and Steel Community (ECSC)
"Second category" compensations, 126–27, 137, 140, 151, 160
Second Decontrol Act of 1947, 78, 272 n.25
Sforza, Carlo, 230

Shipping provisions and regulations, ERP, 45–46, 82–83
Snyder, John, 161, 162, 164, 173
Southard, Frank, 162, 163–64, 172, 186
Soviet Union, 19, 77, 78, 82, 258 n.16
Spaak, Paul-Henri, 148, 218, 219, 222, 223, 247, 303 n.93, 304 n.95
Spain, 258 n.16
Stassen, Harold, 29
State, U.S. Department of, 10, 15, 17, 18, 19, 20, 21, 22, 25, 30, 31, 32, 33, 34, 42, 44, 112, 127, 164, 206, 212, 218, 220, 222, 223, 224, 229, 290 n.44, 302 n.58, 304 n.98
Steelman, John, 32
Stein, Harold, 33
Sterling area, 152, 290 n.42
Sterling Payments System (SPS), 166, 167, 168, 291 n.55
Stikker, Dirk, 222–23, 237, 303 n.92
Stikker Plan, 237–38, 239
Stoppani, Pietro, 283 n.29
Strategic materials: legislative provisions for, 49; purchases of, 87
Sulzberger, C. L., 304 n.99, 308 n.55
Sweden, 68, 140, 146, 148, 149, 189, 247, 258 n.17, 276 n.82, 282 n.9, 291 n.56, 294 nn.10, 25
Switzerland, 137, 143, 146, 152, 168, 188, 189, 247, 258 n.17, 282 n.8, 287 n.55, 293 n.95, 297 n.82
Swope, Herbert, 263 n.39
Szymczak, S. M., 172

Tasca, Henry, 172
Thorp, Willard, 68, 112, 164
Tomlinson, William, 241, 280 n.45
Trade Union Advisory Committee (ERP/TUAC), 39, 266 n.81
Trade Union Congress, British, 36, 38, 265 n.73
Treasury, U.S. Deparment of, 16, 30, 52, 53, 153, 163, 180, 181, 182, 283 n.28
Triffin, Robert, 184–85, 294 n.19, 295 n.48, 297 n.101

Truman, Harry S., 25, 127, 239, 243, 259 n.31, 304 n.98
Turkey, 114, 149, 152, 178, 258 n.17, 285 n.16, 293 n.6, 306 nn.17, 20

United Kingdom, 10, 64, 83–84, 91, 96, 108, 111–12, 116, 129, 140, 143, 145, 146–48, 149, 151, 153, 166–68, 170–71, 188, 189, 211, 214, 219–20, 229, 247, 258 n.17, 270 n.18, 275 n.78, 276 n.82, 280 n.50, 281 n.73, 282 n.9, 285 n.16, 287 n.55, 298 n.116, 303 n.92, 305 n.2
United Nations Relief and Rehabilitation Administration (UNRRA), 9
United States Associates of the International Chamber of Commerce, 261 n.13

Vandenberg, Arthur H., 27, 31, 44, 45, 48, 50, 51, 52, 53, 206, 260 n.4, 267 n.32
Van Zeeland, Paul, 221, 222
Veterans of Foreign Wars, 40
Vorys, John, 302 n.58

Wallace, Henry, 261 n.7
War, U.S. Department of, 42, 259 n.38
Webb, James, 42, 302 n.58
Western Europe: American concern over economic conditions in, 3–4, 253; continued dependence on U.S. assistance, 254; expansion of production and foreign trade, 251–52; financial crisis of 1947, 121; gross domestic capital formation, 251; increases in Gross National Poduct, 250–52; postwar economic conditions in, 3–4, 97–98, 122, 253. *See also individual "European" entries*
West Germany, 93, 115, 140, 143, 148, 151, 187–89, 234, 235, 239, 240, 241, 242, 251, 258 n.17, 275 n.78, 277 n.95, 297 n.97, 298 n.116
Williams, John H., 153, 288 n.75, 301 n.52
Wood, C. Tyler, 18
World Bank, 32, 80, 212
World Federation of Trade Unions (WFTU), 36, 37, 38, 265 n.73

Yugoslavia, 79

About the Author

Imanuel Wexler is Professor of Economics at the University of Connecticut. He is the author of *Fundamentals of International Economics* and articles published in *World Politics, Foreign Policy, Southern Economic Journal, Journal of Economic Studies, Challenge,* and *Monthly Labor Review.*